D0222971

STORM
CENTER

TWELFTH EDITION

Other Books by David M. O'Brien

CONSTITUTIONAL LAW AND POLITICS:
STRUGGLES FOR POWER AND GOVERNMENTAL ACCOUNTABILITY
Eleventh Edition

CONSTITUTIONAL LAW AND POLITICS:
CIVIL RIGHTS AND CIVIL LIBERTIES
Eleventh Edition

SUPREME COURT WATCH
(Annual, 1991–2015)

JUDGES ON JUDGING
Fifth Edition
(editor)

JUSTICE ROBERT H. JACKSON'S UNPUBLISHED OPINION IN *BROWN V. BOARD*:
CONFLICT, COMPROMISE, AND CONSTITUTIONAL INTERPRETATION

THE JUDICIAL PROCESS: LAW, COURTS, AND JUDICIAL POLITICS
Second Edition
(co-author)

TO DREAM OF DREAMS: RELIGIOUS FREEDOM AND
CONSTITUTIONAL POLITICS IN POSTWAR JAPAN

ANIMAL SACRIFICE AND RELIGIOUS FREEDOM:
CHURCH OF LUKUMI BABALU AYE V. CITY OF HIALEAH

CONGRESS SHALL MAKE NO LAW: THE FIRST AMENDMENT,
UNPROTECTED EXPRESSION, AND THE U.S. SUPREME COURT

PRIVACY, LAW, AND PUBLIC POLICY

THE PUBLIC'S RIGHT TO KNOW:
THE SUPREME COURT AND THE FIRST AMENDMENT

WHAT PROCESS IS DUE?

COURTS AND SCIENCE-POLICY DISPUTES

JUDICIAL ROULETTE

THE POLITICS OF TECHNOLOGY ASSESSMENT:
INSTITUTIONS, PROCESSES AND POLICY DISPUTES
(co-editor)

VIEWS FROM THE BENCH:
THE JUDICIARY AND CONSTITUTIONAL POLITICS
(co-editor)

ABORTION AND AMERICAN POLITICS
(co-author)

THE POLITICS OF AMERICAN GOVERNMENT
Third Edition
(co-author)

THE LANAHAN READINGS ON CIVIL RIGHTS AND CIVIL LIBERTIES
Third Edition
(editor)

GOVERNMENT BY THE PEOPLE
Twenty-second Edition
(co-author)

JUDICIAL INDEPENDENCE IN THE AGE OF DEMOCRACY:
CRITICAL PERSPECTIVES FROM AROUND THE WORLD
(co-editor)

COURTS AND JUDICIAL POLICYMAKING
(co-author)

STORM CENTER

The Supreme Court in American Politics

TWELFTH EDITION

DAVID M. O'BRIEN

LATE OF UNIVERSITY OF VIRGINIA

W. W. NORTON & COMPANY

Independent Publishers Since 1923

Copyright © 2020 by the Estate of David M. O'Brien

Copyright © 2017, 2014, 2011, 2008, 2005, 2003, 2000, 1996, 1993, 1990, 1986 by David M. O'Brien

All rights reserved
Printed in the United States of America

Editor: Peter Lesser
Associate Editor: Anna Olcott
Project Editor: Layne Broadwater
Production Manager: Elizabeth Marotta
Manufacturing by Maple Press
Composition by Westchester Publishing Services

Library of Congress Cataloging-in-Publication Data

Names: O'Brien, David M., author.
Title: Storm center : the Supreme Court in American politics /
David M. O'Brien, late of University of Virginia.
Description: Twelfth edition. | New York : W. W. Norton and
Company, [2020] | Includes bibliographical references and index.
Identifiers: LCCN 2019055283 | ISBN 9780393696738 (paperback)
Subjects: LCSH: United States. Supreme Court. | Political questions
and judicial power—United States. | Judicial process—United States.
Classification: LCC KF8742 .O27 2020 | DDC 347.73/26—dc23
LC record available at https://lccn.loc.gov/2019055283

ISBN: 978-0-393-69673-8 (pbk.)

W. W. Norton & Company, Inc., 500 Fifth Avenue, New York, N.Y. 10110
www.wwnorton.com

W. W. Norton & Company Ltd., Castle House, 75/76 Wells Street,
London W1T 3QT

2   3   4   5   6   7   8   9   0

For Benjamin, Sara, and Talia

Contents

Photos and Illustrations

Tables, Charts, and Graphs

xi

Preface

THE SUPREME COURT, Justice Oliver Wendell Holmes observed, is a "storm centre" of political controversy. The Court stands as a temple of law—an arbitrator of political disputes and an authoritative organ of law. But it remains a fundamentally political institution. Behind the marble facade, the justices compete for influence; the Court itself is locked in a larger struggle for power in society. This book is about the legal and political struggles among the justices and between the Court and rival political forces in the country.

Within a week of the publication of the first edition of this book, Chief Justice Warren E. Burger resigned. Less than a year later, Justice Lewis F. Powell stepped down. With the elevation of William H. Rehnquist from associate to chief justice and the addition of Justices Antonin Scalia and Anthony Kennedy, the Supreme Court moved in conservative directions. The second edition dealt with the changes in the life of the Court that occurred during the first few years of Rehnquist's chief justiceship. Shortly after that edition appeared, the Court's leading liberal and one of its most influential members, Justice William J. Brennan Jr., retired. One year later, his ideological ally, Justice Thurgood

Marshall, announced that he would step down. Their replacement on the bench by Justices David H. Souter and Clarence Thomas reinforced the conservative shift in direction of the Rehnquist Court. The third edition took account of how those further changes affected life within the marble temple. The fourth, fifth, sixth, and seventh editions dealt with President Clinton's two appointees to the high bench as well as incorporated new material made available in the papers of Justices Harry A. Blackmun, Thurgood Marshall, and Lewis F. Powell Jr., along with those of President Richard M. Nixon and at the Ronald Reagan Presidential Library. The eighth edition included new material on President George W. Bush's appointment of Chief Justice John G. Roberts Jr. and Justice Samuel Alito Jr. and how changes in the Court's composition affect its internal operations. The ninth edition incorporated material on the Democratic President Barack Obama's appointment of Justices Sonia Sotomayor and Elena Kagan. The tenth and eleventh included new material from recently released papers of Chief Justice Rehnquist and Justices Potter Stewart and Byron White, as well as papers from the Ronald Reagan Presidential Library.

This twelfth edition updates discussions of the appointment process, the Court's growing docket and workload, conferences, oral argument sessions, agenda setting, and decision-making processes as well as opinion-writing practices. In particular, this edition highlights the changes made during the first decade and a half of Chief Justice Roberts's tenure, and incorporates new material found in the justices' private papers and presidential libraries. Moreover, readers will find treatments of the Court's relation to public opinion, critical elections, and more emphasis on the institutional constraints and restraints on achieving implementation and compliance with its rulings.

The underlying themes and arguments appearing in the first edition, however, remain. As a political institution, the Court wields an antidemocratic power and is rarely held directly accountable for its decisions. Presidents invariably try to pack the Court and, as Chapter 2 shows, thereby influence public policy beyond their limited time in the Oval Office. Through their appointments, especially when filling a crucial seat or a number of vacancies in short order, presidents may indeed leave their mark on the Court's policy making. On the bench, however, justices are independent and may disappoint their presidential benefactors as well as find it difficult to refrain from off-the-bench activities. Instead of leaving the world of politics behind, the justices form a small political elite that may wield potentially enormous legal and political power.

Life in the marble temple constrains judicial behavior and the politics of making law. Chapter 3 examines, in historical perspective, the institutional development and dynamics of the Court and the changing working relations among the justices. It argues that the Court has become increasingly bureaucratic in response to growing caseloads. In addition, unlike any other federal court, the Court has virtually complete discretion over its selection of cases and, hence, sets its own agenda for policy making. The justices' control over deciding what to decide and the processes by which they select cases are examined in Chapter 4. In explaining how justices decide cases and the process of opinion writing, Chapter 5 shows why there is less collective deliberation than there used to be and how the Court has come to function more like a legislative body. Critics, on the left and the right, of unpopular rulings have often castigated the Court for being a "super legislature." However, I aim to show that the Court has instead come to function more like a legislative body because it possesses the power not only to manage its docket but to set its substantive agenda. The justices in turn now place less of a premium on collegial deliberations leading to institutional decisions and delegate more responsibilities to law clerks and larger staffs within the Court.

Although the Court has come to function like a roving commission monitoring the governmental process, its rulings are not self-executing. The Court depends on lower federal and state courts, other political institutions, and public opinion to carry out its decisions. But those forces may also curb the Court. The limitations of Supreme Court policy making are considered in the final chapter, but the basic conclusion may be stated at the outset: the Court by itself holds less power to change the country than either liberals or conservatives often claim. Major confrontations in constitutional politics, such as those over school desegregation, government support for religion, abortion, affirmative action, and same-sex marriages may carry over for generations and are determined as much by what is possible in a system of free government and in a pluralistic society as by what the Court says. The Court's policy making, as with its rulings on abortion and school desegregation, also evolves with changes in its composition and in the country. In sum, the Court's influence on American life rests on a paradox. Its political power is at once antidemocratic and countermajoritarian. Yet that power, which flows from giving meaning to the Constitution, truly rests, in Chief Justice Edward White's words, "solely upon the approval of a free people."

Acknowledgments

I N RESEARCHING and writing the first edition of this book, a large number of debts were incurred. It is fair to say that I might never have embarked on the project had it not been for Chief Justice Warren Burger and his administrative assistant, Mark Cannon. The opportunities they afforded me as a judicial fellow and then as a research associate in the Office of the Administrative Assistant to the Chief Justice were invaluable. Both later spent time talking with me and clarifying various matters. Although they did not agree with all my views, I remain grateful for their insights and kindness.

The experience at the Court provided a perspective, but only began my inquiry. The inquiry has led over the last three decades to the examination of the private papers of some sixty-three justices (over half of all the justices who have sat on the high bench, virtually all the collections available), as well as the papers of nine presidents. Although most of the collections are open to the public, access to some required special permission. For their permission to use certain collections, I am grateful to Justice William J. Brennan Jr., Paul Freund, Eugene Gressman, William E.

Jackson, Mrs. Carolyn Agger Fortas, Elizabeth Hugo Black, Hugo Black Jr., and Justice Lewis F. Powell Jr.

Assistance at various libraries was crucial. The splendid staff in the Manuscripts Division of the Library of Congress has been always helpful. Paul Freund, Erika Chadbourn, and Judith Mellins made my stays at the Harvard Law School Library fruitful. More recently at Harvard Law School, Lesley Schoenfeld was exceptionally helpful. Others who deserve mention for their assistance are Bill Cooper of the University of Kentucky Library; Nancy Bressler and Jean Holiday of the Seeley G. Mudd Manuscripts Library at Princeton University; Patricia Bodak Stark and Kristen McDonald of the Yale University Library; Dale Mayer of the Herbert Hoover Presidential Library; Carole Knobil of Special Collections at the University of Texas School of Law Library; Cynthia Fox of the National Archives and Records Service; Marjorie Barritt of the Bentley Historical Library at the University of Michigan; Michael Kohl of Special Collections at Clemson University; Karen Rohrer at the Dwight D. Eisenhower Library; Nancy Smith of the Lyndon Baines Johnson Library; Charles Warren Ohrvall of the Harry S. Truman Library; Dallas R. Lindgren of the Minnesota Historical Society; Gail Galloway and Diane Williams of the Curator's Office of the Supreme Court of the United States; David Pride of the Supreme Court Historical Society; and Carol A. Leadenham at the Hoover Institution Archives, Stanford University. No less helpful were the staffs of the Manuscripts Division of Alderman Library and the Arthur J. Morris Law Library at the University of Virginia; the John Marshall Papers Project at the College of William and Mary; the John Fitzgerald Kennedy Library; the Gerald R. Ford Library; the Hoover Institution on War, Revolution, and Peace; the Franklin D. Roosevelt Library; the Columbia Oral History Project and the Rare Books and Manuscripts Division in Butler Library at Columbia University; the library of the Cardozo School of Law at Yeshiva University; the National Archives at College Park, Maryland, which housed the papers of President Richard M.

Nixon; the Washington and Lee School of Law's collection of Justice Lewis F. Powell's papers; the Ronald Reagan Presidential Library in Simi Valley, California; the George H. W. Bush Presidential Library in College Station, Texas; and the William J. Clinton Presidential Library in Little Rock, Arkansas.

The justices' papers did not end my inquiry but instead raised further questions. Interviews and discussions of my tentative conclusions saved me from some (though possibly not all) mistakes. For their time and insights, I am indebted to Chief Justices Warren Burger and William H. Rehnquist and Justices William J. Brennan Jr., Arthur Goldberg, Sandra Day O'Connor, Ruth Bader Ginsburg, Lewis F. Powell Jr., Antonin Scalia, David H. Souter, Potter Stewart, John Paul Stevens, and President Gerald Ford. I am also grateful to Mark Cannon, William T. Gossett Jr., Fred Graham, Sidney Fine, Alpheus T. Mason, Walter Murphy, and Benno Schmidt. Justices Harry Blackmun, Thurgood Marshall, Antonin Scalia, David H. Souter, Ruth Bader Ginsburg, and Byron White also graciously corresponded or met with my students and me.

Without the support of a number of individuals and organizations, the research could not have been undertaken. Two grants from the American Philosophical Society got the project underway. The Gerald R. Ford Foundation, the Hoover Presidential Library Association, the Lyndon Baines Johnson Foundation, and the Harry S. Truman Institute made possible the examination of presidential papers. The National Endowment for the Humanities provided a small travel grant. Henry J. Abraham, Gordon E. Baker, Alpheus T. Mason, Jack Peltason, and C. Herman Pritchett wrote the necessary letters of recommendation.

The first edition benefited from the comments of John Schmidhauser and Martin Shapiro. There are no words to repay my teacher C. Herman Pritchett for reading two drafts and (as always) offering encouragement. I am no less indebted to my former and favorite colleague Henry J. Abraham for his support.

Subsequent editions incurred even more debt. I am especially grateful to Erwin N. Griswold for sharing his intimate knowledge of the Court. Steve York, producer of PBS's *This Honorable Court*, was also particularly kind in sharing portions of interviews with members of the Rehnquist Court that, alas, failed to make the final cut for the film but that were immensely helpful in updating this book. I also benefited from members of a Twentieth Century Fund Task Force on Judicial Selection, for which I served as rapporteur. Walter Berns, Lloyd N. Cutler, Philip Kurland, Jack W. Peltason, and Michael M. Uhlmann were very helpful, even when we disagreed. Others deserving special acknowledgment include the late Toni House, the Court's public information officer, and Tony Mauro, Ronald Collins, David Adamany, A. E. Dick Howard, Saul Brenner, William Coleman, Philip Cooper, Louis Fisher, Paul Freund, Herbert Kaufman, Milton Handler, Chief Judge Howard T. Markey, J. Mitchell Pickerill, E. Barrett Prettyman, and William R. Wilkerson. Christopher Banks, Stephen Bragaw, and Steve Brown, three of my much-valued students and research assistants, cheerfully lent their labor on different editions. This twelfth edition also incorporates new material from the sources already mentioned, and useful comments made by Professor Hu Xiaojin of the Chinese University of Political Science and Law in Beijing, who translated earlier editions. I also benefited from the time and opportunities afforded by a Fudan University Senior Fellowship, particularly discussions about the Court and comparative law with Professor Tu Yunxin, in the summers of 2017 and 2018 at the Fudan University School of Law, Shanghai, China.

At W. W. Norton, Donald Fusting, Hilary Hinzmann, and Amanda Adams were immensely helpful on the first edition, and Don was a faithful editor on the second and third editions. Steve Dunn served as the editor of the fourth, Sarah Caldwell was the editor of the fifth, Ann Shin worked on the sixth edition, Aaron Javsicas on the seventh and ninth, Brian Baker and Matt Arnold on the eighth edition, Jake Schindel and Sarah Wolf on the tenth,

Samantha Held on the eleventh edition, and Pete Lesser and Anna Olcott on this edition.

Claudine, my wife, continues to make life a joy. With the addition of our daughter, Sara, the second edition was affectionately dedicated to her and her big brother, Benjamin. The fourth edition was rededicated to them, along with our further addition and their sister, Talia. This twelfth edition is affectionately rededicated to our children.

December 2018   D. M. O.
Charlottesville, Virginia

A Note on Authorship

IN LATE 2018, we received the very sad news of David O'Brien's passing. Perhaps not surprisingly, given his dedication to this book and his passion for the subject, we soon learned that David had nearly completed revisions for this edition of *Storm Center*. We thank the O'Brien family for passing his work on to us for publication. We thank Gordon Silverstein of Yale University, who, with expertise and kindness, quickly signed on to help put the final polish on this edition. And we thank David O'Brien for his tremendous contributions to Norton and to the study of the Supreme Court, constitutional law, and the politics that shape them.

W. W. Norton & Co.

STORM
CENTER

TWELFTH EDITION

ONE

A Struggle for Power

ON A HOT NIGHT ON A SIDE ROAD OUTSIDE OF AUGUSTA, GEORGIA, in August 1969, Norma McCorvey, a twenty-one-year-old carnival worker nicknamed Pixie, was returning to her motel when she was allegedly gang-raped. The carnival and Pixie moved on to Texas, where, several weeks later, Pixie found herself pregnant. A high school dropout, divorced, with a five-year-old daughter and little money, Norma McCorvey unsuccessfully sought an abortion. Texas, like most other states at the time, prohibited abortions unless necessary to save a woman's life. "No legitimate doctor in Texas would touch me," she claimed. "I found one doctor who offered to abort me for $500. Only he didn't have a license, and I was scared to turn my body over to him. So there I was—pregnant, unmarried, unemployed, alone and stuck."[1]

That was how McCorvey originally told her story, yet it was only partially true. She was poor and pregnant—but not raped. Nearly twenty years later, McCorvey revealed making up the story about being raped, after a doctor told her she could not get an abortion in Texas. "That was a lie—I said it because I was desperate and wanted an abortion very, very bad and thought that would help the situation. It didn't."[2] McCorvey carried her pregnancy to term and gave up the child for adoption. A Dallas lawyer found someone to adopt the baby. Two recent graduates of the University of Texas Law School, Sarah Weddington and Linda Coffee approached McCorvey about abortion counseling for students. And the three women decided to challenge the constitutionality of the Texas law forbidding all abortions not necessary "for the purpose of saving the life of the mother." They aimed to establish a woman's constitutional right "to control of her own body" and became part of a larger historical movement and political struggle.[3]

What began as one woman's story of personal struggle unfolded into a half century of political controversy. "Pixie" became "Jane Roe" in a test case against Henry Wade, the district attorney, criminal division, for Dallas County, Texas. Her case led to the Supreme Court's landmark ruling in *Roe v. Wade* (1973). In recognizing a woman's "fundamental right" to control her body, the Court raised abortion to the national political agenda and became a storm center of political controversy. Almost five decades later, the country remains sharply divided over the issue of abortion. In that time, though, much changed. The Court's composition was altered dramatically, and in turn *Roe*'s original mandate failed to stand the test of time, as the Court returned more authority to states and localities to limit the availability of abortions. Further, McCorvey herself renounced the abortion-rights movement.[4]

In both the tortuous way the justices reached their decision in *Roe* and the ensuing controversy, the Court's rulings—from *Roe* and *Planned Parenthood of Southeastern Pennsylvania v. Casey* (1992) to *Stenberg v. Carhart* (2000), and *Gonzales v. Carhart* (2007) and to *Whole Woman's Health v. Hellerstedt* (2016)—illustrate the political struggles that occur within the Court's institutional development and over its role in American politics. This issue and these cases illustrate how we will examine, throughout this book, the Court, its decision-making processes, and its historic role in American politics.

Abortion, the Court, and American Politics

Little public attention was paid on May 4, 1971, when *Roe v. Wade* appeared on the Court's order list. It was one of the few cases from over 4,500 cases on the docket granted oral argument. The *New York Times* simply reported that the Court "agreed to consider if state anti-abortion laws violate the constitutional rights of pregnant women by denying their right to decide whether or not to have children." In the end the Court's decision would affect the laws in virtually every state. At the time, though, there was no way of predicting whether or how the Court would decide the issue.

Just one month earlier, in *United States v. Vuitch* (1971), a bare majority upheld the District of Columbia's statute prohibiting abortions unless "necessary for the preservation of the mother's life or health." Justice Hugo Black's opinion for the Court ruled that the law was not unconstitutionally vague in allowing abortions for "health" reasons—including psychological considerations. The District of Columbia statute, unlike the Texas law adopted in 1854, was one of the most liberal in the country at the time. By upholding the statute, the Court actually increased the availability of abortions in Washington, D.C. However, it did not address the question of whether women have a constitutional right to obtain abortions.

The movement to liberalize abortion laws grew throughout the turbulent 1960s with the "sexual revolution" and feminists' demands for women's freedom and the right to control their own bodies. Abortion was not a crime at the time of the adoption of the Constitution, but by the late nineteenth century every state had some form of abortion regulation or criminalization.

Most states permitted abortions, except after "quickening"—the first movement of the fetus—and then an abortion was usually considered only a minor offense for doctors but not women. The overwhelming majority permitted abortions only to save a woman's life. By the mid-twentieth century, an estimated one in four pregnancies was terminated by abortion or miscarriage. Upper-class, but not poor, women (like Jane Roe) could obtain abortions. Still, approximately 10,000 women died annually from abortions. The American Medical Association in 1970 responded by authorizing doctors to perform therapeutic abortions in appropriate cases. By the late 1960s and early 1970s, fourteen states and the District of Columbia had liberalized laws to permit abortions when the woman's health was in danger, when there was a likelihood of fetal abnormality, and when the woman was a victim of rape or incest. Four states—Alaska, Hawaii, New York, and Washington—had repealed all criminal penalties for abortions performed in early pregnancy.

By the time oral arguments were heard in *Roe* in 1971, Black and Harlan had retired. Black had been a leading liberal and Harlan a conservative member of the Court. But neither looked kindly on claims to a constitutional right to an abortion. At the conference discussion of *Vuitch*, Black would not go along "with a woman's claim of [a] constitutional right to use her body as she pleases." Burger shared that view. He rejected any "argument that [a] woman has [an] absolute right to decide what happens to her own body."[5] Without Black and Harlan, the Court was diminished. President Richard Nixon's last two nominations, Lewis Powell Jr. and William Rehnquist, had not yet been confirmed by the Senate.

On December 13, 1971, Chief Justice Burger opened the Court's oral argument session with the simple announcement, "We will hear arguments in No. 18, *Roe* against *Wade*." Sarah Weddington was calm in her first appearance before the high bench. She made no mention of McCorvey's story about being raped. (Nor did Weddington mention the fact that as a twenty-two-year-old daughter of a Texas Methodist minister in the late 1960s she herself had to cross the border in order to obtain an abortion in Mexico.)[6] Instead, Weddington began by reviewing the lower court's holding that Texas's law violated a woman's right to continue or terminate a pregnancy. But Burger interrupted to ask whether the issues had already been decided by the ruling in *United States v. Vuitch*. Weddington explained that *Vuitch* upheld a law that permitted abortions when necessary to the health or the life of a woman. Texas's law was more restrictive; it allowed abortions only when necessary to save the life of the woman. Doctors were not free to consider the effects of pregnancy on the woman's mental or physical health. *Vuitch* was not considered binding in Texas, and doctors were being prosecuted for performing abortions other than those necessary to save the woman's life. Women who sought to terminate unwanted pregnancies had to go to New York, the District of Columbia, or some other state. Women like Jane Roe, who were poor and for whom abortions were not necessary to save their lives, had no real choice. The irony of the Texas law, moreover, was that women who performed self-abortions were not guilty of any crime; the law authorized the prosecution only of doctors who performed abortions.

"It's an old joke, but when a man argues against two beautiful ladies like this, they are going to have the last word." There was no laughter in the courtroom, however, at that opening remark by Jay Floyd, an assistant attorney general who defended Texas's law. This controversy is not one for the courts, he argued, and arguments about freedom of choice when it comes to abortion are misleading. Floyd pressed the point:

There are situations in which, of course as the Court knows, no remedy is provided. Now I think she makes her choice prior to the time she becomes pregnant. That is the time of the choice. It's like, more or less, the first three or four years of our life we don't remember anything. But, once a child is born, a woman no longer has a choice, and I think pregnancy then terminates that choice. That's when.

After Weddington's presentation of the realities of abortion, the argument sounded surreal, out of date, and out of place. One of the justices impatiently shot back, "Maybe she makes her choice when she decides to live in Texas." Laughter almost drowned out Floyd's feeble reply: "There is no restriction on moving."

"What is Texas's interest? What is Texas's interest in the statute?" demanded Justice Thurgood Marshall. The state has "recognized the humanness of the embryo, or the fetus," Floyd explained, and has "a compelling interest because of the protection of fetal life." Yet, interjected Justice Potter Stewart, "Texas does not attempt to punish a woman who herself performs an abortion on herself." Floyd replied, "That is correct," and continued:

And the matter has been brought to my attention: Why not punish for murder, since you are destroying what you—or what has been said to be a human being? I don't know, except that I will say this. As medical science progresses, maybe the law will progress along with it. Maybe at one time it could be possible, I suppose, statutes could be passed. Whether or not that would be constitutional or not, I don't know.

But, Stewart countered, "We're dealing with the statute as it is. There's no state, is there, that equates abortion with murder?" There was none, Floyd admitted, and hastened to emphasize that though courts did not recognize the unborn as having legal rights, states have a legitimate interest in protecting the unborn. As to a woman's choice on abortion, Floyd reiterated, "[W]e feel that this choice is left up to the woman prior to the time she becomes pregnant. This is the time of choice."[7]

When *Roe* was discussed in the justices' private conference, Burger said that the case had not been well argued. He also thought that because the case presented such a "sensitive issue," it should be set for reargument so that Powell and Rehnquist could participate and the full Court could reach a decision. As chief justice, he led the discussion, observing that the Texas law was "certainly arcane," though not unconstitutional. He was inclined to the view that the law should fall for vagueness. Senior Associate Justice Douglas spoke next. He disagreed and did not doubt that the statute was unconstitutional. Justices Brennan and Stewart agreed, as did Marshall. White came out on the other side. He could not go along with the argument that women have a constitutional right of privacy. Justice Blackmun, then the newest member of the Court, spoke last: "Don't think there's an absolute right to do what you will with [your] body." But this statute was poorly drawn, he observed. It's too restrictive—it "doesn't go as far as it should and impinges too far on [Roe's] Ninth Amendment rights."[8] Blackmun appeared in the middle but inclined toward the position of Douglas, Brennan, Stewart, and Marshall.

After conference the chief justice, if he is in the majority, by tradition assigns a justice to write the opinion justifying the Court's decision. Here, Burger appeared to be in the minority, but nonetheless gave the assignment to Blackmun. When Douglas complained, Burger responded that the issues were so complex "that there were, literally, not enough columns to mark up an accurate reflection of the voting" in his docket book. He "therefore marked down no vote and said this was a case that would have to stand or fall on the writing, when it was done."[9]

Assigned to write the Court's opinion in late December 1971, Blackmun did not circulate a first draft until May 18, 1972. The draft immediately troubled Douglas and Brennan. Though striking down Texas's law, Blackmun's opinion did so on Burger's view that the law was vague, rather than on the view that it violated a woman's constitutional right of privacy. Douglas and Brennan wanted to know why the opinion failed to address the core issue, "which would make reaching the vagueness issue unnecessary." Blackmun claimed that he was "flexible as to results." He was simply trying his "best to arrive at something which would command a court." With "hope, perhaps forlorn, that we might have a unanimous Court," he explained, "I took the vagueness route."[10]

A "freshman" in his second year on the Court and assigned to write a difficult opinion, Blackmun found himself in the middle of a growing dispute. On the one hand, Burger had been his long-time friend and had recommended his appointment to the Court; on the other, Blackmun was attracted to Douglas's position on a woman's right of privacy. He began thinking that it might be better to have the case reargued the next term, as Burger and White suggested. "Although it would prove costly to [him] personally, in the light of energy and hours expended," Blackmun concluded, he would move for reargument. He explained that "on an issue so sensitive and so emotional as this one, the country deserves the conclusion of a nine-man, not a seven-man, court, whatever the ultimate decision may be."[11]

Douglas was taken aback by the prospect of Nixon's last two appointees participating; the final decision might go the other way. If Blackmun withdrew his motion for reargument, it would fail. If he didn't, there would be trouble. The vote would be four to three against reargument, and that could lead to a heated confrontation. Douglas appealed to Blackmun not to vote for reargument. Instead of complaining about the initial draft opinion, Douglas commended Blackmun for his "yeoman service" and emphasized that he had "a firm 5 and the firm 5 will be behind you." Brennan followed with a similar note.[12]

By tradition, only those justices participating in a case may vote on its reargument, but then came a memorandum from Powell. He noted that during the first months when decisions were made on rearguments he had taken "the position then, as did Bill Rehnquist, that the other seven Justices were better qualified to make those decisions." However, Powell explained, "The present question arises in a different context. I have been on the Court for more than half a term. It may be that I now have a duty to participate in this decision." He and Rehnquist would vote for a rehearing.[13] That made a majority for carrying *Roe* over to the next term.

Douglas was shocked and threatened: "If the vote of the Conference is to reargue, then I will file a statement telling what is happening to us and the tragedy it entails."[14] That would only have intensified tensions. Douglas was finally persuaded not to publicize his outrage and instead simply to note that he dissented from the order for reargument. Burger subsequently sent Douglas a lengthy memo justifying the rearguments on the ground that there was no solid majority at conference and that he assigned the case because "the final disposition [had] to wait on writing and grounds" for the Court's decision.[15]

On October 11, 1972, the Court heard rearguments. For a second time, Weddington stood before the high bench, but her arguments were repeatedly interrupted by questions from the justices. Justice White put it bluntly: "[W]ould you lose your case if the fetus was a person?" That would require a balancing of interests, Weddington replied, but that was not at issue here, since it had not been asserted that a fetus has any constitutional rights. The issue was simply a conflict between the constitutional rights of women and the interests of the state. The state would have to establish (which it could not) that the fetus is a "person" under the Fourteenth Amendment, which guarantees people "born or naturalized" in the United States the due process and equal protection of the law, before it would have a compelling interest in prohibiting abortions.

Chief Justice Burger then called Robert C. Flowers, who replaced Floyd as Texas's representative. From the outset, Flowers faced a steady barrage of questions about whether a fetus is a "person" under the Constitution. He was driven to concede that no case had recognized the fetus as a "person" and that the Fourteenth Amendment extends protection only to those born or naturalized in the United States. At the prodding of White, he was forced to agree that the case would be lost if the fetus is not recognized as a "person." Whether a fetus is a "person," Flowers argued, is an issue that should be left to the state legislatures. But that argument underscored the Court's dilemma and aroused Stewart:

Well, if you're right that an unborn fetus is a person, then you can't leave it to the legislature to play fast and loose dealing with that person. In other words, if you're correct, in your basic submission that an unborn fetus is a person, then abortion laws such as that which New York has are grossly unconstitutional, isn't it?

Liberal abortion laws, Flowers contended, allow "the killing of people." But put this way, the matter could not be left to the states, for it ran against the logic of constitutional law to say that a fetus is a "person" in one state but not in another. It is the Court's responsibility to interpret the Constitution. If the Court struck down the Texas law, it would invite attacks by those who believe that the fetus is a "person" entitled to constitutional protection. But even though there may be good, moral arguments for recognizing the personhood of an unborn, there was no constitutional basis for ruling that way. Neither the text nor the history of the drafting of the Constitution and the Fourteenth Amendment revealed that the unborn are "persons" with constitutionally protected rights. If Texas's century-old law was upheld on the ground that the unborn are "persons" under the Constitution, then the Court would be making law that ran counter to the text, "original intent," and history of the Constitution. Finally, Flowers confessed that he knew of no way "that any court or any legislature or any doctor anywhere can say that here is the dividing line. Here is not a life; and here is a life, after conception."

Weddington had a few minutes to give a final rebuttal. Again, she reiterated, the issue of a woman's right to decide whether to terminate an unwanted pregnancy had not been decided in *Vuitch*. The issue was one that the Court could not avoid or leave to the lower courts or state legislatures. The issue was basically one of human dignity versus political geography, that of a woman's struggle for power and for the right to have control over her own life on such a fundamental matter. "We are not here to advocate abortion," Weddington concluded.

We do not ask this Court to rule that abortion is good, or desirable in any particular situation. We are here to advocate that the decision as to whether or not a particular woman will continue to carry or will terminate a pregnancy is a decision that should be made by that individual; that, in fact, she has a constitutional right to make that decision for herself. . . .

THE *ROE V. WADE* DECISION AND ITS AFTERMATH

About a month after the Court heard rearguments, Blackmun finished a new draft of the opinion for *Roe*. "It has been an interesting assignment," he observed when circulating the draft that became the Court's final opinion. The opinion struck down Texas's law, but now along the lines originally advanced by Douglas and Brennan. The opinion announced that the constitutional right of privacy is "broad enough to encompass a woman's decision whether or not to terminate her pregnancy." During the rest of November and most of December, Blackmun continued to rework portions of the opinion in light of other justices' comments. On December 21, he sent around a third draft. Douglas, Brennan, Marshall, and Stewart immediately agreed to join. Soon after the Christmas holidays, Powell also signed on, commending Blackmun for his "exceptional scholarship."[16] By mid-January, Burger also agreed, though he did not support "abortion on demand." On January 17, 1973, Blackmun circulated the fourth and final draft, a little later than he had hoped, because he had aimed at handing down the decision during the week of January 15 so as "to tie in with the convening of most state legislatures."[17] Only Rehnquist and White did not join the opinion.

States could no longer categorically proscribe abortions. The promotion of maternal care and the preservation of the life of a fetus were not sufficiently "compelling state interests" to justify restrictive abortion laws. During roughly the first trimester (three months) of a pregnancy, the decision on abortion was that of a woman and her doctor. During the second, states could regulate abortions, but only in ways reasonably related to safeguarding the health of women. In the third trimester, states' interests in preserving the life of the unborn were compelling, and they could limit, even ban, abortions, except when necessary to save a woman's life.

At conference, Blackmun warned that the opinion "will probably result in the Court's being severely criticized." He therefore took special care in preparing the statement announcing the decision that he read from the bench, and even made copies available for reporters in the hope that they would not go "all the way off the deep end."[18] Brennan opposed the distribution of the copies "in order to avoid the possibility that the announcement [would] be relied upon as the opinion or as interpreting the filed opinion," whereas Powell enthusiastically endorsed the idea for "contribut[ing] to the understanding of the Court's decision."[19]

But immediate press coverage was muted. President Lyndon Johnson died the day the ruling came down, and so the announcement of the landmark decision shared the headlines in the *New York Times*, *Los Angeles Times*, and other major newspapers.

Initial reactions to the decision were mixed. The president of the Planned Parenthood Federation of America, Dr. Alan Guttmacher, hailed the ruling as "a wise and courageous stroke for the right of privacy, and for the protection of a woman's physical and emotional health." Others took a different view. The justices "have made themselves a 'super legislature,'" New York's Terence Cardinal Cooke charged.[20] "Apparently the Court was trying to straddle the fence and give something to everybody," concluded Philadelphia's John Cardinal Krol, "abortion on demand before three months for those who want that, somewhat more restrictive abortion regulations after three months for those who want that."[21]

Underlying these reactions was the irony of the Court's ruling liberally even though it was packed with "strict constructionists." The final ruling was handed down by a Court that President Nixon had tried to remold in his own image. As a presidential candidate in 1968 Nixon had attacked the "liberal jurisprudence" of the Warren Court (1953–1969) for being unfaithful to the text of the Constitution. Nixon's four appointees—Burger, Blackmun, Powell, and Rehnquist—were all selected for their conservative strict constructionist judicial philosophy. Yet only Rehnquist and JFK-appointee White dissented. Even those who favored the ruling sharply criticized *Roe* for resting on a constitutional right of privacy. The Court had created the right of privacy out of whole constitutional cloth when striking down laws limiting the availability of contraceptives in *Griswold v. Connecticut* (1965). In *Griswold*, Douglas held that a constitutional right of privacy may be found in the "penumbras," "emanations," or "shadows" of various guarantees of the Bill of Rights. A right of associational privacy may be found in the penumbra of the First Amendment. The Third Amendment's prohibition against the quartering of soldiers "in any house" without the consent of the owner was deemed another facet of constitutionally protected privacy. The Fourth Amendment explicitly guarantees the right "of the people to be secure in their persons, houses, papers, and effects, against unreasonable searches and seizures." The Fifth Amendment's safeguard against self-incrimination also "enables the citizen to create a zone of privacy." Finally, Douglas noted, the Ninth Amendment provides that "[t]he enumeration in the Constitution, of certain rights, shall not be construed to deny or disparage others retained by the people." Douglas's penumbra theory for a right of privacy was, perhaps, too imaginative to persuade many court watchers. And *Roe* went even further. A woman's interests in abortion appeared to have little to do with those privacy interests identified in *Griswold* with various guarantees of the Bill of Rights. Rather than privacy per se, abortion basically involves a woman's *liberty* under the Constitution, as Justice Harlan suggested in his concurring opinion in *Griswold*.

Other court watchers critical of *Roe* took their cue from Rehnquist's dissenting opinion. They attacked the Court for its "judicial activism." In overturning most abortion laws, the Court held that states' interests become compelling only at the point of "viability"—the point at which the fetus is "potentially able to live outside the mother's womb, albeit with artificial aid." For states' rights advocates like Rehnquist, the Court impermissibly imposed its own view on state legislatures.

Even before *Roe*, the Catholic bishops mobilized against the reform of state abortion laws. Yet, Evangelicals and the Republican Party prior to 1972 did not oppose abortion, and a Gallup poll in 1972 found that 62 percent of the public thought the matter should be between a woman and her doctor. After *Roe*, Catholics and Evangelicals gradually built a coalition of pro-family and "pro-life Christians." By the 1980s, antiabortion forces also turned attention to elect and pressure state legislatures and Congress to pass new restrictions and constitutional amendments. In the 1980s, some antiabortion groups also took to the streets and even resorted to violence. According to the National Abortion Federation, in the decade after *Roe*, bombs destroyed thirty-two abortion clinics, others were victimized by arson, and hundreds were picketed by demonstrators. Several doctors who performed abortions were murdered or wounded.

Like most Supreme Court rulings on major controversies, *Roe* left numerous questions unanswered. The Burger Court basically stood its ground, striking down most new state and local attempts to limit the impact of *Roe*.[22] The Court, though, upheld a city's policy of refusing nontherapeutic abortions in public hospitals and state restrictions on the funding of nontherapeutic abortions.[23] Still, as the Court's composition changed throughout the 1980s, pressure mounted with speculation that *Roe* would be restricted further, if not overruled.

"Right to life" amendments that would have returned to pre-*Roe* policies of allowing states to regulate abortion or recognize the unborn as "persons" were introduced in Congress. While these measures failed, the decade following *Roe*, Congress enacted some thirty laws restricting the availability of abortions. Among these statutes, Congress barred the use of funds for programs in which abortion is included as a method of family planning; barred government officials from ordering recipients of federal funds to perform abortions; barred lawyers working in federally funded legal aid programs from giving assistance to those seeking "nontherapeutic" abortions; and provided that employers are not required to pay health insurance benefits for abortions except to save a woman's life.

The Court responded to Congress's message when hearing challenges to some of its legislation. In *Harris v. McRae* (1980), for instance, the justices divided 5–4 when upholding the so-called Hyde Amendment (named after the Republican representative Henry Hyde of Illinois), which forbids federal funding of nontherapeutic abortions under the Medicaid program.[24]

From the 1980s into the 2010s, the Court's ruling on abortion was an issue in presidential politics as well. The Republican platforms endorsed by Presidents Ronald Reagan, George H. W. Bush, and George W. Bush supported a constitutional amendment "to restore protection of the right to life for unborn children." It was during Reagan's era that forces opposed to *Roe* gathered momentum. Although Reagan repeatedly called on Congress "to restore legal protections for the unborn," his administration never really pushed for congressional adoption of its stand on abortion. Instead, the strategy of Reagan's administration (and that of later Republican presidents) was to appoint to the federal bench only those opposed to abortion and then initiate litigation that might ultimately lead to overturning *Roe*.

But even after the retirements of Douglas and Stewart—and the appointments of John Paul Stevens in 1975 and Sandra Day O'Connor in 1981—the Court reaffirmed *Roe*. In *City of Akron v. Akron Center for Reproductive Health* (1983), the Court struck down several restrictions imposed on women seeking abortions, including requirements that they sign "informed consent" forms and wait at least twenty-four hours before having an abortion, along with requiring doctors to perform abortions after the first trimester in a hospital and dispose of fetal remains "in a humane and sanitary way."[25]

Significantly in *Akron*, O'Connor, along with Rehnquist and White, called into question *Roe*'s trimester framework, asserting that it was "clearly on a collision course with itself" because developments in medical technology would move the point of viability backward in the first trimester to the point of conception, and states may regulate abortion for maternal health. As an alternative, she proposed an "undue burden" test for determining women's access to abortion services and whether states had a "compelling state interest" in restrictions.

Three years later, the Reagan administration renewed its attack on *Roe*. This time Reagan's solicitor general, Charles Fried, dared do what his predecessors had refused: he argued that *Roe* should be overturned. Fried filed an extraordinary *amicus curiae* ("friend of the court") brief, boldly proclaiming that "the textual, doctrinal and historical basis for *Roe v. Wade* is so far flawed . . . that this Court should reconsider that decision and on reconsideration abandon it."

The Court remained in no mood to reconsider *Roe*, however, and again rebuffed the Reagan administration in *Thornburgh v. American College of Obstetricians & Gynecologists* (1986).[26] Yet, Chief Justice Burger broke with *Roe*'s supporters in *Thornburgh*, joining Justices O'Connor, Rehnquist, and White in dissent, and indicated that *Roe* should be "reexamined."

The 5–4 split in *Thornburgh* further escalated speculation about how another Reagan appointee might affect the Court and *Roe*. As the Court's composition changed, support for *Roe* among the justices appeared to decline. Within a week of the ruling in *Thornburgh*, Chief Justice Burger announced that he would step down. Reagan immediately responded by shrewdly elevating Rehnquist, one of *Roe*'s sharpest critics, to the chief justiceship and naming Antonin Scalia to his seat.

As an institution the Court does not usually shift course without major changes in its composition. While Justice Powell remained on the Court, he appeared to hold the pivotal vote for upholding *Roe*. The announcement of his retirement in June 1987 and Reagan's nomination of Judge Robert H. Bork—another of *Roe*'s sharpest critics—set off a political firestorm. Following the mobilization of special-interest groups and weeks of deliberation (discussed in the next chapter), Bork's nomination was defeated by a 58 to 42 Senate vote. Reagan's second nominee, Judge Douglas Ginsburg, was forced to withdraw after revelations, that as a Harvard Law School professor he had smoked marijuana, turned conservative Republican senators against him. Reagan's third nominee, Judge Anthony Kennedy, won easy Senate confirmation.

In the final days of the Reagan administration the Court seemed poised to reconsider *Roe*. During the summer of 1988 Reagan's Department of Justice talked Missouri's attorney general, William Webster, into appealing an appellate court's invalidation of that state's restrictions on abortions. At issue in *Webster v. Reproductive Health Services* was the constitutionality of four provisions of the 1986 Missouri law: (1) decreeing that life begins at conception and that "unborn children have protectable interest in life, health, and well being"; (2) requiring physicians, before performing an abortion on a woman believed to be twenty or more weeks pregnant, to test the fetus's "gestational age, weight, and lung maturity"; (3) prohibiting public employees and facilities from being used to perform abortions not necessary to save a woman's life; and (4) making it unlawful to use public funds, employees, and facilities for the purpose of "encouraging or counseling" a woman to have an abortion except when her life is in danger.[27]

Pressure-group activities intensified amid speculation about how Reagan's justices would line up in *Webster*. The activities of pro-life groups had already gained prominence through the "March for Life," an annual rally picketing the Court on the anniversary of *Roe* in front of the Capitol. Unlike legislators, the justices are rarely touched by such pressure-group activities. But the marches and letter-writing campaigns reflected how the politics of the abortion controversy had been transformed in the years after *Roe*. Groups on both sides of the controversy were greater in number, better organized, and more attuned to the politically strategic uses of litigation.

When the decision in *Webster* was announced, on the last day of the Court's term, Chief Justice Rehnquist read aloud portions of his opinion upholding Missouri's regulations but reluctantly declined to jettison *Roe*. The justices were bitterly divided. Only Kennedy and White joined Rehnquist's opinion, and O'Connor and Scalia concurred in separate opinions. Visibly distressed, Blackmun, the author of *Roe*, took the unusual step of reading from the bench his dissenting opinion, which Brennan and Marshall joined. Stevens also read from his dissent.

Justice O'Connor had come to hold the balance and cast the crucial vote. Agreeing with Rehnquist that *Roe*'s trimester approach was "problematic," she was nevertheless unwilling to overrule *Roe*. O'Connor reiterated her view in *Akron* that states were free to regulate abortion so long as they do not "unduly burden the right to seek an abortion." Scalia was infuriated by O'Connor's refusal to overrule *Roe* and predicted years of litigation during which, as he put it, "the mansion of constitutionalized abortion law, constructed overnight in *Roe v. Wade*, must be disassembled doorjamb by doorjamb, and never entirely brought down, no matter how wrong it may be."

Rehnquist's plurality opinion thus appeared part of a holding pattern, a pause in the continuing dialogue between the Court and the country. Rehnquist claimed to "leave [*Roe*] undisturbed" but noted that "[t]o the extent indicated in our opinion, we would modify and narrow *Roe*." His opinion substituted the more lenient "rational basis" test for *Roe*'s "strict scrutiny" test, requiring a "compelling state interest" in the regulations and whether they permissibly advance "the State's interest in protecting potential human life."

THE COURT AND THE CONTINUING CONTROVERSY OVER ABORTION

Although not expressly overruling *Roe*, the Rehnquist Court shifted course in *Webster*, ensuring a continuing battle. Both sides of the controversy immediately turned state legislatures into battlegrounds. Some states, such as Pennsylvania, quickly passed tougher regulations but stopped short of prohibiting abortions.

By the time the first of several challenges to states' post-*Webster* abortion laws reached the Court, support for *Roe*'s original mandate had further ebbed on the high bench. The last two staunchly liberal justices, Brennan and Marshall, had retired and were succeeded by President George H. W. Bush's appointees, Justices David H. Souter and Clarence Thomas. Of the seven-member majority in *Roe* only Justice Blackmun remained on the bench. The abortion controversy had intensified but for once both sides agreed on something—that when reviewing the challenge to Pennsylvania's abortion law the Court should make a final decision on *Roe* in *Planned Parenthood of Southeastern Pennsylvania v. Casey*.[28]

Yet, when granting *Casey*, the Court appeared in no mood to further fuel the abortion controversy before the 1992 presidential election. Notably, the Court did not ask the parties to address the question of whether *Roe* should be overruled, as it had done in *Webster*, though both sides asked for an answer to precisely that question. At issue in *Casey* were provisions in Pennsylvania state law that (1) require doctors to inform women about fetal development, provide a list of medical providers offering "alternatives to abortion," and obtain a woman's "informed consent" before performing an abortion; (2) mandate a twenty-four-hour waiting period after a woman had given her consent before she may obtain an abortion; (3) require minors to obtain the informed consent of at least one parent or a judge; and (4) require a married woman to notify her husband, except when he cannot be located, when the father is not the husband, when a pregnancy is due to "spousal sexual assault" that has been reported to the police, or when a woman "has reason to believe" that notifying her husband might result in "bodily injury." The Court of Appeals for the Third Circuit upheld all the regulations with the exception of that for spousal consent, which it deemed to impose an undue burden on women.

Planned Parenthood's petition for review asked the Court to rule on whether *Roe's* "holding that a woman's right to choose abortion is a fundamental right" had been overruled by subsequent decisions.[29] But when voting to grant review at conference on January 12, 1992, Justice O'Connor remained in no mood to do so and Souter pushed for a reformation of the question presented. He followed up by proposing that attorneys direct arguments to whether "the 'undue burden' standard of review [is] the appropriate standard of review" and whether the appellate court correctly applied it. Although agreeing on a rephrasing of the questions, Stevens suggested instead that counsel be asked simply whether the lower court erred in upholding certain provisions and "what weight is due to *stare decisis* in evaluating the constitutional right to abortion."[30] Justice Souter agreed but others disagreed with the latter question, even though it was central to the continuing controversy. As a result, when granting review the Court limited the issues to whether the appellate court erred in upholding provisions of the law and in striking down its requirement for spousal consent.[31]

Two days after hearing oral arguments in *Casey*, Chief Justice Rehnquist voted to uphold all the requirements. Justice White agreed, whereas Stevens thought the requirement for a twenty-four-hour waiting period was "an insult" and the spousal consent requirement was "outrageous." Blackmun would have struck down all the provisions but "passed." O'Connor remained in no mood to overrule *Roe* but said that the appellate court "got most [of it] right." Kennedy agreed, while Scalia and Thomas were firmly with the chief justice and would overrule *Roe*. Rehnquist thus had a majority and a few days later assigned himself the job of writing the opinion for the Court, as he had done in *Webster*.[32]

Not quite a month later, on May 27, Rehnquist circulated a draft, upholding all of Pennsylvania's restrictions as having a rational basis. The only concession he made was in noting that women were exempt from the spousal notice and consent requirements when confronted with a "significant threat to [their] life or health."[33] That outcome, as in *Webster*, had been anticipated, and Souter and O'Connor had been privately talking with Kennedy about not following the chief in *Casey* as he had done in *Webster*. They urged him to reaffirm *Roe*'s central holding on a woman's right to choose, while upholding most of Pennsylvania's restrictions based on O'Connor's "undue burden" test. Souter had already been working on a draft dealing with *stare decisis* and why *Roe* should be upheld. Kennedy agreed, and two days after the chief justice circulated his first draft, Kennedy sent Blackmun a note telling him that he had some "welcome news."[34]

On June 3, Justices O'Connor, Kennedy, and Souter circulated their draft opinion, concurring and dissenting in part from the chief's draft opinion. Justice Stevens followed up by joining certain sections of their opinion and urging Blackmun to do the same. Rehnquist circulated a second draft on June 17, which now included a new section taking issue with the analysis of *stare decisis* in the opinion circulated by the "troika," as law clerks referred to O'Connor, Kennedy, and Souter. He dismissed their analysis as "*dicta*" and reaffirmed *Webster*'s rejection of a woman's "fundamental right" to abortion. But it proved too late. Stevens and Blackmun agreed to join portions of the O'Connor-Kennedy-Souter draft and thereby formed a new bare majority. Five days later, the second draft opinion by O'Connor, Kennedy, and Souter circulated, but now as the opinion for the Court. Subsequently, Rehnquist circulated a third draft but one now concurring and dissenting in part, rather than speaking for the Court. The next day, the final draft of the opinion for the Court that would come down on June 29 circulated, reaffirming *Roe*'s "central holding" while upholding all of Pennsylvania's restrictions except for that requiring spousal consent. On the first page of their sixty-page opinion, Justices O'Connor, Kennedy, and Souter observed:

It must be stated at the outset and with clarity that *Roe*'s essential holding, the holding we reaffirm, has three parts. First is a recognition of the right of the woman to choose to have an abortion before viability and to obtain it without undue interference from the State. Before viability, the State's interests are not strong enough to support a prohibition of abortion or the imposition of a substantial obstacle to the woman's effective right to elect the procedure. Second is a confirmation of the State's power to restrict abortions after fetal viability, if the law contains exceptions for pregnancies which endanger a woman's life or health. And third is the principle that the State has legitimate interests from the outset of the pregnancy in protecting the health of the woman and the life of the fetus that may become a child.

But the plurality proceeded to reject or significantly redefine much of what *Roe* stood for. *Roe*'s trimester analysis for balancing the interests of women and the states in protecting the unborn was rejected. The plurality overturned portions of earlier rulings in *Akron v. Akron Center for Reproductive Health, Inc.* (1983) and *Thornburgh v. American College of Obstetricians & Gynecologists* (1986), where, in the latter case, a bare majority had invalidated similar Pennsylvania restrictions like those that the Court now found acceptable. Even more significant, the plurality no longer recognized *Roe* as guaranteeing women a "fundamental right." Instead, the plurality redefined the "central principle" of *Roe* as guaranteeing a woman a liberty interest under the Fourteenth Amendment "to choose to terminate or continue her pregnancy before viability." And in replacing *Roe*'s trimester analysis with an "undue burden" analysis of women's substantive liberty interests, the plurality drew a line on overly restrictive regulations, but left open how far states could limit access to abortion clinics. In other words, while reaffirming the "essence of *Roe*"—namely, that women have a right to abortion prior to viability—the plurality indicated that states may enact legislation to promote the state's interests in potential life and women's health throughout a pregnancy, subject to the "rational basis" test, not the "strict scrutiny" test requiring a compelling governmental interest.

The balance on the Court had shifted to allowing states to impose more restrictions on the availability of abortions. But the balance had not shifted far enough for Chief Justice Rehnquist and Justices Scalia, Thomas, and White, who attacked the plurality's "undue burden" test as "standardless." They also ridiculed the plurality's invention of a novel theory of *stare decisis*—that is, when the Court should defer to precedents. Indeed, the heart of the plurality's opinion, written by Justice Souter, that defended upholding *Roe* on the grounds that the Court's institutional integrity would otherwise suffer. If the Court overruled *Roe*, he reasoned, it would be perceived as both bowing to political pressure and undercutting its legitimacy for those who relied on *Roe*. But the chief justice countered that the plurality's theory of *stare decisis* appeared disingenuous because much of what *Roe* laid down was discarded, while reaffirming its "central holding." "*Roe* continues to exist," added Rehnquist, "but only in the way a storefront on a western movie set exists: a mere facade to give the illusion of reality."

Casey divided the justices not only over *Roe* but over the Court's role in American politics. Justices O'Connor, Kennedy, and Souter feared that the Court's legitimacy and institutional integrity would suffer if *Roe* were expressly overturned and the Court thereby perceived as just a "naked-power organ"—a political institution whose decisions simply turn on personnel changes in its composition. Chief Justice Rehnquist and three others, however, maintained that neither the Court's legitimacy nor *stare decisis* was served by adhering to a ruling they deemed improperly decided in the first place.

Casey represented another political compromise within the Court that was destined to continue the struggle over abortion. The Court had struck a new balance that would not change until the composition of the bench further changed. President Bill Clinton's two appointees, Justices Ruth Bader Ginsburg and Stephen Breyer, reinforced the centrists on the Court in favor of upholding *Roe*. (Likewise, President Obama's two appointees, Justices Sotomayor and Kagan, did not alter the balance on the Court.) That new balance was underscored by the 5–4 ruling in

Proponents on both sides of the abortion issue demonstrate outside the Supreme Court building. (*Saul Loeb/AFP/Getty Images*)

Stenberg v. Carhart (2000),[35] striking down Nebraska's so-called partial-birth abortion law. "Partial-birth abortion" is a politically symbolic term, not a medical one, coined after *Casey* to mobilize support and promote new antiabortion legislation. Nebraska's law and those in eighteen other states enacted after *Casey* forbid a rare procedure known as "dilation and extraction" (D&X) or "intact dilation and evacuation" (D&E), performed in the second trimester. Writing for the Court and joined by Justices Stevens, O'Connor, Souter, and Ginsburg, Justice Breyer held that the law placed an "undue burden" on women and provided no exception for instances when the procedure was necessary to preserving a woman's health. Justice O'Connor cast the pivotal vote, and Chief Justice Rehnquist and Justices Scalia, Kennedy, and Thomas dissented.

The bare majority's ruling in *Stenberg v. Carhart* (*Carhart* I) did not lay the controversy to rest, however. Proponents of banning partial-birth abortions kept pressure on Congress to enact a federal law banning the procedure. In 2003, the Republican-controlled Congress passed and President George W. Bush signed into law the first federal restriction on an abortion procedure since *Roe*; Congress had twice before passed similar laws, but President Clinton vetoed them. The statute, the Partial-Birth Abortion Ban Act of 2003, was immediately challenged in federal courts. Critics charged that the law was even vaguer than Nebraska's law, and like the Nebraska law struck down in *Carhart* I, the statute failed to provide an exception for when the procedure is necessary to preserve a woman's health. Supporters nonetheless aimed to galvanize voters around the issue in the 2004 presidential election.

Following the death of Chief Justice Rehnquist and the retirement of Justice O'Connor in 2005, along with President George W. Bush's appointments of Chief Justice John G. Roberts Jr. and Justice Samuel Alito Jr., the Court upheld the Partial-Birth Abortion Ban Act in *Gonzales v. Carhart* (*Carhart* II) (2007).[36] Writing for a bare majority, Justice Kennedy upheld Congress's criminalization of second and third trimester "intact dilation and evacuation" (D&E) abortions, even though the statute did not provide an exception for when a woman's health is endangered. Notably, although not overruling *Carhart* I, Justice Kennedy ruled that laws restricting abortion were no longer subject to "facial" challenges under *Casey*'s "undue burden" test but only to "as applied" challenges in particular instances of women seeking late-term abortions.

Casey and *Carhart* I and II also sent a signal that a new majority on the Roberts Court would uphold further restrictions on abortion and invited state and local governments to enact new restrictions on abortion, which would result in more lawsuits aimed at chipping away at *Roe* and *Casey*.

After the Republican sweep of governorships and state legislatures in the 2010s, states enacted more restrictions on abortion than in the entire decade previous.[37] In lobbying for new restrictions, opponents of abortion also gradually made a strategic shift in framing the debate from barring or dissuading women from ending a pregnancy to focusing on regulations ostensibly safe-guarding the women's health (and the life of the unborn) by tar-geting abortion providers with more onerous restrictions, such as building and zoning standards, doctors' licensing and admitting privileges in hospitals, and telemedicine—telephone prescrip-tions, for instance, for mifepristone (Mifeprex) and misoprostol, taken two days later, to induce a miscarriage (30 percent of all abortions are no longer surgical). The aim was to raise the cost of providing abortion services, and ultimately putting clinics (where most abortions are performed) out of business. As a result, while a few states expanded the availability for abortion and contracep-tives, thirty-seven introduced new restrictions. Forty-two states require abortions to be performed by licensed physicians and/or have visiting privileges at hospitals; twenty-seven require manda-tory ultrasound of the unborn; seven (Arkansas, Kentucky, Mis-souri, North and South Dakota, West Virginia, and Wyoming) have only one clinic; and several (Iowa, Mississippi, and Ohio) have proposed or banned pre-viability abortions. Some of these laws have been enjoined in the lower courts, but antiabortion pro-ponents aim to create a basis for chipping away, if not overruling, *Roe* and *Casey.*

In the first major ruling on new state restrictions on abortion, in *Whole Woman's Health v. Hellerstedt* (2016),[38] a majority of the Court (dividing five to three, without Justice Scalia participating) struck down Texas's 2013 regulations requiring abortion clinics to (1) employ doctors with admitting privileges at a hospital within thirty miles of their location, and (2) to meet the facility stan-dards of surgical centers and hospitals. Proponents maintained that the regulations were in the interests of the health and safety of women; whereas opponents countered that they were medi-cally unnecessary, burdensome, costly, and simply aimed at lim-iting the availability of abortions. Almost half of the state's clinics were forced to close because they were not compliant with these laws. Writing for the majority, Justice Breyer held that Texas's restrictions imposed an "undue burden" on women seeking an abortion and that standard, established in *Casey*, "requires that courts consider the burdens a law imposes on abortion access together with the benefits those laws confer." Chief Justice Roberts and Justices Thomas and Alito dissented.

While opponents of a woman's right to choose pushed for new state restrictions like those challenged in *Whole Woman's Heath*, they also had their eyes on the prize of the next presidential election and possible changes in the Court's composition. In 2016, Justice Scalia—a conservative champion of "originalism" and outspoken critic of *Roe* and *Casey*—died. And the Republican-controlled Senate refused to even hold a hearing for almost a year on Obama's nominee to fill Scalia's seat, contending that "the people should decide" and the winner of the presidential election make the appointment. Abortion opponents were also optimistic (and promised) the winner might fill two or more seats on the Court; it was widely speculated that after thirty years on the bench Justice Kennedy might retire. Kennedy had proven a profound disappointment for Reaganites and others in the antiabortion movement. Not only the "swing" vote, siding with the four liberals on social controversies like same-sex marriage, he joined the plurality in *Casey* and the majority in *Whole Woman's Health*.

Donald Trump campaigned on naming pro-life justices and judges to the courts and pursuing an antiabortion agenda. For a running mate, Trump picked Indiana's governor, Mike Pence, in order to reassure and carry Republican voters. Pence had a long pro-life record: as a member of Congress in the 2000s, he led a fight to defund federal spending for abortions; as governor, he signed into law restrictions on abortion providers, like those struck down in *Whole Woman's Health,* and banned abortions in cases of fetal abnormality or disability; and as vice president in 2017, he cast the tie-breaking vote in the Senate for a bill allowing states to withhold federal family planning (for birth control and cancer screenings) to clinics providing abortion services. The

Trump administration also tried to stop a pregnant 17-year-old undocumented immigrant in detention from obtaining an abortion, but was blocked by the Court of Appeals for the D.C. Circuit (though Judge Brett Kavanaugh, who Trump subsequently named to the Court, dissented).

For his part, Trump made good on promises about federal judicial appointments. Within weeks of his inauguration in 2017, he nominated Judge Neil Gorsuch to Scalia's seat; Gorsuch described himself as a "Scalia look-alike." At the end of Gorsuch's first term on the bench, Justice Kennedy retired. And to replace him, Trump promptly nominated Judge Brett Kavanaugh. Both Gorsuch and Kavanaugh had clerked for Kennedy, but were more solidly and predictably conservative. Indeed, Kavanaugh would lock in a more reliably conservative majority, which Reaganites and those in the antiabortion movement had sought over the last thirty years, since the Senate's defeat of Judge Robert Bork's nomination to the Court in 1987. (The judicial selection process and backgrounds of the justices are further discussed in Chapter 2).

With the Roberts Court's changing composition, the balance shifted and was certain to move in new directions. That was clear even before Kavanaugh's arrival on the high bench. In *National Institute of Family and Life Advocates v. Becerra* (2018),[39] the Roberts Court split 5–4 when striking down a state law requiring "crisis pregnancy centers," operated by religious groups opposed to abortion, to post notices about the availability of contraception and low-cost abortion services, as government-compelled speech in violation of the First Amendment. The California Reproductive Freedom, Accountability, Comprehensive Care, and Transparency Act (FACT Act) of 2015 required "crisis pregnancy centers," pro-life centers offering prenatal-related services, to post notices notifying women that the state provided free or low-cost abortion services, and for unlicensed clinics to give notice that they did not provide those services. Writing for the majority, Justice Thomas invalidated both requirements because they failed to survive "strict scrutiny," since they compelled speech about abortion services that the clinics opposed on religious grounds. Thomas held that California had other means of informing women about the availability of abortion and may not "co-opt the licensed facilities to deliver its message." By contrast, writing for the dissenters—Justices Ginsburg, Sotomayor, and Kagan—Justice Breyer criticized the majority for inconsistency, since a bare majority upheld provisions of a Pennsylvania law requiring doctors who perform abortions to inform patients about adoption and alternatives in *Casey*, and in *Rust v. Sullivan* (1991),[40] upheld federal regulations banning counseling on abortion by organizations receiving federal funding. In Justice Breyer's words: "If a state can lawfully require a doctor to tell a woman seeking an abortion about adoption services, why should it not be able, as here, to require a medical counselor to tell a woman seeking prenatal care or other reproductive health care about childbirth and abortion services?"

The Roberts Court, nonetheless, appears unlikely to overrule *Roe* in the near future. For one thing, *Casey*, not *Roe*, is the precedent that matters. *Casey* abandoned much of that for which *Roe* stood—the trimester framework and "strict scrutiny" test. *Casey* substituted the "undue burden" test and "rational basis" standard for judicial review. Moreover, *Casey* upheld restrictions that were just like those struck down in the decade and a half following *Roe*. In other words, *Roe's* mandate was transformed in *Casey*. Similarly, over a half century the landmark school desegregation ruling in *Brown v. Board of Education* (1954) was transformed—from ending dual school systems to achieving racially integrated public schools—and then chipped away, and finally abandoned by the Rehnquist and Roberts Courts, without expressly overturning *Brown* (as further discussed in Chapter 6). So too, the Roberts Court appears poised to chip away at *Casey* in upholding on the "rational basis" test more restrictions on access to and the availability of abortion services.

No Longer the "Least Dangerous" Branch

Like other rulings—*Brown* and other controversial watershed decisions—on major issues of public policy, *Roe* invited criticism that the Court is no longer, in Alexander Hamilton's words, the "least dangerous" branch. Rather, critics (on both sides of the political aisle, at different times) charged that the Court has become a "super legislature." But the Court's responsibility has always been to interpret the Constitution. Political conflicts are raised to the level of constitutional intelligibility. And with its rulings, the Court engages the country in a dialogue over the meaning of the Constitution.

The role and power of the Court has changed with American politics. The Court first struck down an act of Congress in *Marbury v. Madison* (1803), when Chief Justice John Marshall interpreted the Judiciary Act of 1789 to have expanded impermissibly the Court's original jurisdiction under Article III of the Constitution. The Marshall Court also overturned a number of state laws and thereby legitimated the power of the national government and its own power of judicial review. But the Court did not challenge Congress again until the Taney Court's 1857 decision in *Dred Scott v. Sandford*.

Since the late nineteenth century, the Court increasingly has played a major role in monitoring the governmental process. The Court regularly overturns acts of Congress, of the states, and of local governments. The following table illustrates the trend toward overturning decisions of other political institutions, even though Chief Justice Roberts has tried to decide cases with the narrowest possible rulings and to distinguish without expressly overruling precedents, as well as to decide cases on statutory rather than constitutional grounds. The Court, regardless of its composition, increasingly asserts its power. The more ideologically conservative Burger, Rehnquist, and Roberts Courts, for example, were as "activist" as the liberal Warren Court. Their differences lie in the directions in which they have pushed constitutional law and politics.

DECISIONS OF THE SUPREME COURT OVERRULED, ACTS
OF CONGRESS HELD UNCONSTITUTIONAL, AND STATE LAWS
AND MUNICIPAL ORDINANCES OVERTURNED, 1789–2018

Years	Supreme Court Decisions Overruled	Acts of Congress Overturned	State Laws Overturned	Ordinances Overturned
1789–1800, Pre-Marshall				
1801–1835, Marshall Court	3	1	18	
1836–1864, Taney Court	4	1	21	
1865–1873, Chase Court	7	8	33	
1874–1888, Waite Court	11	7	7	
1889–1910, Fuller Court	4	14	73	15
1910–1921, White Court	5	9	107	18
1921–1930, Taft Court	5	12	131	12
1930–1940, Hughes Court	14	14	78	5
1941–1946, Stone Court	12	1	25	7
1947–1952, Vinson Court	12	1	38	7
1953–1969, Warren Court	56	23	150	16
1969–1986, Burger Court	55	30	192	15
1986–2005, Rehnquist Court	42	42	97	21
2005–, Roberts Court	16	15	50	11
TOTALS:	246	178	1,020	127

Note that in *Immigration and Naturalization Service v. Chadha* (1983) the Burger Court struck down a provision for a "one-house" legislative veto in the Immigration and Naturalization Act but effectively declared all one- and two-house legislative vetoes unconstitutional. Although 212 statutes containing provisions for legislative vetoes were implicated by the Court's decision, *Chadha* is here counted as a single declaration of the unconstitutionality of congressional legislation. Note also that the Court's ruling in *Texas v. Johnson* (1989), striking down a Texas law making it a crime to desecrate the American flag, invalidated laws in forty-eight states and a federal statute, as have other rulings striking down a state's law and thereby invalidating other states' similar laws. They are counted here, however, only once. The data here is based on Leon Friedman and Fred Israel, eds., *Justices of the United States Supreme Court*, Vol. 4, 4th ed. (New York: Facts on File, 2013), 573–600, and Library of Congress studies, as updated by the author's tabulations through the Court's 2018 term, as of July 1, 2019.

The Court is a human institution, and as its composition and the country change so do constitutional politics. The reasons this is so are the subject of this book. The controversial appointment of justices and their struggles for influence and power within the Court, as well as the political controversies sparked by important cases such as *Roe* and *Casey*, highlight the vexing yet central role played by the Supreme Court in American political life. Ultimately, though, the Court's power, as Chief Justice Edward White observed, "rest[s] solely upon the approval of a free people"[41] and their struggles for power.

TWO

The Cult of the Robe

B ECAUSE JUSTICES serve for life, they furnish a president with historic opportunities to influence the direction
of national policy well beyond his or her own term. Still,
the myth occasionally circulates that appointments should be
made strictly on merit. Attorney General Ramsey Clark, for
instance, confided to President Lyndon Johnson, "I think a most
significant contribution to American government would be the
non-political appointment of judges."[1] Yet LBJ's appointments of
Abe Fortas and Thurgood Marshall were political, as were those
of all other presidents.

Once on the bench, justices often forget their political history
and complain that presidents do not know enough about the Court
to make intelligent appointments. Justice Felix Frankfurter, for
one, felt that President John F. Kennedy and his attorney general,
Robert Kennedy, chose inferior judges. "What does Bobby understand about the Supreme Court? He understands about as much
about it as you understand about the undiscovered 76th star in
the galaxy. . . . He said Arthur Goldberg was a scholarly lawyer. I
wonder where he got that notion from."[2] What perturbed Frankfurter was that the Kennedy administration did "not adequately

appreciate the Supreme Court's role in the country's life and the functions that are entrusted to the Supreme Court and the qualities both intellectual and moral that are necessary to the discharge of its functions." Distinguished individuals were accordingly passed over, in Frankfurter's opinion, in favor of such "wholly inexperienced men as Goldberg and White, without familiarity with the jurisdiction or the jurisprudence of the Court either as practitioners or scholars or judges."[3]

The fact is that merit competes with other political considerations such as personal and ideological compatibility; the forces of support or opposition in Congress and the White House; and demands for representative appointments on the bases of geography, religion, race, gender, and ethnicity.

The Myth of Merit

The Supreme Court is not a meritocracy. This is so for essentially two reasons: the difficulties of defining merit and the politics of judicial selection.

Any definition of "judicial merit" is artificial. Henry Abraham, a leading scholar on the appointment of justices, proposed the following six criteria of judicial merit: demonstrated judicial temperament; professional expertise and competence; absolute personal and professional integrity; an able, agile, lucid mind; appropriate professional educational background or training; and the ability to communicate clearly, both orally and in writing.[4] Yet justices themselves have difficulty defining such qualities as "judicial temperament." Judicial merit is perhaps reducible only to the standard of "obscenity" offered by Justice Potter Stewart: "I know it when I see it."[5]

A disproportionate number of justices are appointed from the lower federal and state courts, especially in the last thirty years; the legal profession; and the executive branch. The prior positions of the 114 justices who served on the Court are as follows[6]:

Federal bench	31
Private legal practice	25
Executive branch	22
State bench	22
U.S. Senate	6
State governorship	3
House of Representatives	2
Law school professorship	2
State employee	1

But legal education and previous judicial experience have not been necessary for appointment to or achievement on the bench. In the first seventy-five years of the nineteenth century, law schools as we know them did not exist, and up until World War I the majority of the legal profession learned law through apprenticeship. Justice James Byrnes, appointed in 1941, was the last to have studied law through apprenticeship. But not until 1957, when Justice Charles Whittaker replaced Justice Stanley Reed, did all nine justices hold law degrees. Lack of prior judicial experience has not traditionally been a barrier either, though that may no longer be the case. No fewer than 85 of the 114 justices who have sat in the Court had fewer than ten years of previous federal or state court experience. Six chief justices had no prior experience—John Marshall, Roger Taney, Salmon Chase, Morrison Waite, Melville Fuller, and Earl Warren. Neither did some outstanding associate justices, including Joseph Story, Louis Brandeis, Harlan Stone, Charles Evans Hughes, Felix Frankfurter, and Robert Jackson. By contrast, Sandra Day O'Connor was the last justice who brought the experience of serving as an elected official before joining the Court—as a member of the Arizona state Senate.

Judicial selection, as Justice Stone put it, is like a "lottery" from a pool of more or less qualified individuals. One of Stone's close friends, Harvard law professor and political scientist Thomas Reed Powell, was even more blunt: "[T]he selection of Supreme Court Justices is pretty much a matter of chance."[7] Powell saw this illustrated in the fact that

[President] Taft met [his appointee Mahlon] Pitney at a dinner given to advance Swayze's prospects and preferred him to Swayze; . . . that [Justice Joseph] McKenna was a personal associate of [President William] McKinley; that [Justice William] Day also was and that his appointment by [President Theodore] Roosevelt was a legacy from McKinley; that [Justice Pierce] Butler was known to Taft in the Canadian Railways Valuation work and was a Catholic who could be substituted for Manton without having to turn down a Catholic; . . . that [Justice Stone] had been in college with [President Calvin] Coolidge; that [Justice] Brandeis had a closer relation with [President Woodrow] Wilson than with members of the Boston Bar, etc.[8]

"Luck," along with ability, agrees Justice Ruth Bader Ginsburg, "has a lot to do with who will get [appointed]."[9] Likewise, Justice Gorsuch observed about his 2017 appointment to the Court that he was "the luckiest man I know." Indeed, he would not have even been nominated if the Republican-controlled Senate had not refused to hold a single confirmation hearing on President Barack Obama's nominee—the highly respected D.C. Circuit appellate judge, Merrick Garland. Gorsuch also was not on President Trump's initial list of potential nominees to the deceased Justice Scalia's seat, and only later added to the list of potential nominees that was released to the public.

Meritorious individuals are thus often passed over, though a few may eventually find their way to a seat on the highest court in the land. Chief Justice Roberts, for example, was nominated to the Court of Appeals for the D.C. Circuit in 1992 by President George H. W. Bush but blocked by Senate Democrats. In 2001, almost a decade later, he was again nominated to the D.C. Circuit by President George W. Bush and once again blocked, only to be renominated and confirmed in 2003. Two years later, Bush nominated him to fill retiring Justice Sandra Day O'Connor's seat. Shortly afterward, however, Chief Justice Rehnquist died, and Roberts was renominated to serve as chief justice. Justice Elena Kagan, like Roberts and others, also faced setbacks; but unlike Roberts, Kagan's primary challenges came from within the administrations that sought to nominate her. President Clinton considered her for an appointment to the Court of Appeals for the D.C. Circuit in 1999, but she was passed over, even though she worked in the Clinton administration.[10] Subsequently, President Barack Obama named her as the first female solicitor general (SG)—a launching pad for elevation to the Court. In 2009, she was in the running to fill retiring Justice David Souter's seat, but was passed over with the appointment of Justice Sonia Sotomayor, the first Latina justice. A year later, though, Kagan replaced retiring Justice John Paul Stevens. In short, besides timing and compatibility with presidential priorities, there are obstacles external to an administration that nominees must overcome (as with Roberts) and internal within an administration's political calculations and vetting of potential nominees (as with Kagan).

Perhaps no appointment has been more widely acclaimed as meritorious than that of Benjamin Cardozo, yet even that appointment was primarily due to political expediency. When telling President Herbert Hoover of the numerous letters he received hailing the appointment, Justice Stone noted, "The interesting thing about Judge Cardozo's appointment is that, although there is nothing political in it, it will prove I believe, to be of immense political advantage to the President. No appointment he has made has been better received."[11]

A leading liberal judge on the New York Court of Appeals, Cardozo was indubitably distinguished. But he had been passed over several times before the Republican President Hoover nominated him in 1932. He had been mentioned for the seat vacated by William Day in 1922. Leaders of the New York Bar continued to push him for positions filled by Presidents Warren Harding and Calvin Coolidge. Cardozo was first considered by Hoover when Edward Sanford died in 1930. The president wanted to appoint someone from the West, because that region was not represented on the Court at the time. However, Hoover's adviser George Wickersham failed to find anyone from the West who merited serious consideration. Wickersham proposed naming Attorney

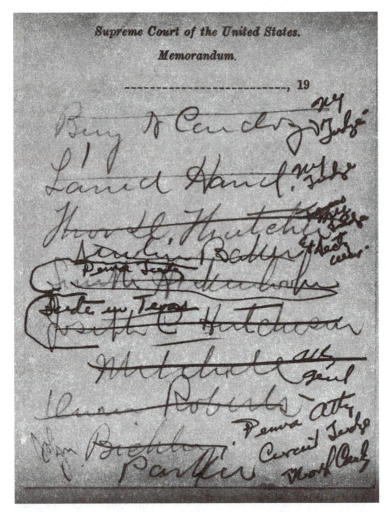

Memo from Justice Harlan Stone recommending individuals for appointment to the Supreme Court in 1930, with President Herbert Hoover's notes. (*Herbert Hoover Presidential Library*)

General William Mitchell, the Pennsylvania attorney Owen Roberts, or the prominent attorney and unsuccessful 1924 presidential candidate John W. Davis. Hoover's close friend Justice Stone also sent his list of candidates. At the top was Cardozo, and at the bottom was the conservative North Carolina circuit court of appeals judge John J. Parker.[12] The president went down the list, eliminating potential nominees on the basis of their geographical location and political leanings, and finally settled on Judge Parker.[13]

Hoover's nomination was immediately attacked by labor organizations, because one of Parker's decisions was interpreted as anti-union. The National Association for the Advancement of Colored People (NAACP) also lobbied against his confirmation, because he was deemed an enemy of black voting rights. After a six-week battle, the Senate for the first time in the twentieth century rejected a nomination to the Court, by the narrow margin of 41 to 39. Republican attorney Owen Roberts was subsequently nominated and confirmed. Hoover was badly embarrassed by the defeat of Parker. When the opportunity arose to make his next and last appointment, in 1932, he nominated Cardozo, for his reputation was unimpeachable, his nomination politically opportune, and his confirmation certain.

Politics conspired to ensure Cardozo's appointment, just as it may at other times defeat meritorious candidates. Politics in the Senate, after all, defeated Parker, yet he served with distinction for another twenty-eight years on the court of appeals and was again considered for an appointment during the Roosevelt and Truman administrations.[14] The Senate tends to vote for nominees who are well qualified and ideologically compatible with their constituents.[15] However, senators may turn against nominees viewed as too ideologically extreme. The Senate's rejection of a nominee may also be affected by whether the president's party is a minority in the Senate and whether the occupant of the Oval Office is a lame-duck president. In addition, the White House's management or mismanagement of the nominee during the confirmation process may contribute to success or failure in the Senate.[16] In any event, the ultimate verdict on candidates for the Court turns less on merit than on political visibility, support, and circumstance.

Process of Appointment

The appointment of justices is guided by the Constitution and the competitive politics of the nomination and confirmation process. Article II, Section 2, of the Constitution stipulates that the President "shall nominate, and by and with the Advice and Consent of the Senate, shall appoint" members of the federal judiciary.* The Senate's power to reject nominees is the crucial obstacle that a president must overcome. Thirty-one nominees to the Court have fallen prey to partisan politics, either because of opposition due to the mobilization of interest groups against a nominee or the Senate wanting to deny lame-duck presidents' appointments to the high court. Thanks to the tradition of "senatorial courtesy," which began in the 1840s, the Senate may also refuse to confirm an individual opposed by the senators of the president's party and the nominee's home state. Only five nominees—John C. Spenser in 1844, Reuben H. Walworth in 1845, George Williams in 1873, G. Harrold Carswell in 1970, and Harriet Miers in 2005—suffered defeat, arguably, due to mediocre professional qualifications.

---

*In contrast with the system of appointing federal judges, the methods of selecting state court judges are rather complex. They vary from state to state and among different courts within particular states. The methods of selection include popular—partisan and nonpartisan—election, appointment by governors or legislatures, and some combination of both or the so-called merit system. In the merit system, a nonpartisan commission provides lists of nominees from which the governor or legislature makes appointments; then, after one year of service, the judges' names are placed on ballots and voters decide whether they should be retained.

The influence of the Senate has eroded in the selection of judicial appointees. Traditionally, Senate rules required a supermajority of two-thirds to permit a confirmation vote for federal judicial appointments and provided the nominee's home-state senators with a veto over appointments in their state. The supermajority requirement for judges other than the Supreme Court were dropped in 2013 by the then Democrat–controlled Senate. The supermajority requirement for Supreme Court nominees was terminated by the Republican-controlled Senate in 2017 to permit a final vote for Neil Gorsuch. The Senate still retains significant influence in lower court appointments, and these life-tenure appointments can be used as bargaining chips for the president and the Senate to influence national policy and confer political patronage. The Senate retains greater influence over the district court–level, while the president now has greater autonomy at the Supreme Court–level and with appointments to appellate courts whose jurisdiction spans several states. The administration may play senators against each other by claiming the need for representation of different political parties, geographical regions, religions, races, and the like within a circuit. "In the case of the Supreme Court Justices," Hoover's attorney general William Mitchell observed, "with the whole country to choose from, the Senators from one state or another are in no position, even if they were so inclined, to attempt a controlling influence. Such an appointment is not a local matter, and the entire nation has an equal interest and responsibility."[17]

The Senate as a whole, nonetheless, still has the power to influence the selection of, and to defeat, a president's nominee. Notably, when Justice Scalia—a conservative icon and champion of "original textualism" on the bench for thirty years—died in January 2016, the leadership of the Republican-controlled Senate maintained that the winner of the 2016 presidential election should fill his seat; in effect, his replacement should be determined by the next president and the "voice of the people." Senate Majority Leader Mitch McConnell (R-Ky.) immediately

Supreme Court Nominations Rejected, Postponed, or Withdrawn because of Senate Opposition[*]

Nominee	Year Nominated	Nominated by	Actions[1]
Robert H. Harrison[7]	1789	Washington	Unsuccessful
William Paterson[2]	1793	Washington	Withdrawn (for technical reasons)
John Rutledge[3]	1795	Washington	Rejected
Alexander Wolcott	1811	Madison	Rejected
Levi Lincoln	1811	Madison	Unsuccessful
John J. Crittenden	1828	Adams, J. Q.	Postponed, 1829
Roger B. Taney[4]	1835	Jackson	Postponed
William Smith[7]	1837	Jackson	Rejected
John C. Spencer	1844	Tyler	Rejected
Reuben H. Walworth[6]	1844	Tyler	No action
Edward King[5]	1844	Tyler	Withdrawn, 1845
John M. Read	1845	Tyler	No action
George M. Woodward	1845	Polk	Rejected, 1846
Edward A. Bradford	1852	Fillmore	No action
George E. Badger	1853	Fillmore	Withdrawn
William C. Micou	1853	Fillmore	No action
Jeremiah S. Black	1861	Buchanan	Rejected
Henry Stanbery	1866	Johnson, A.	No action
Ebenezer R. Hoar	1869	Grant	Rejected, 1870
Edwin Stanton[7]	1869	Grant	Unsuccessful
George H. Williams[3]	1873	Grant	Withdrawn, 1874
Caleb Cushing[3]	1874	Grant	Withdrawn
Stanley Matthews[2]	1881	Hayes	No action
Roscoe Conkling[7]	1882	Arthur	Unsuccessful
William B. Hornblower[5]	1893	Cleveland	Rejected, 1894
Wheeler H. Peckham	1894	Cleveland	Rejected
John J. Parker	1930	Hoover	Rejected
John Marshall Harlan[2]	1954	Eisenhower	Postponed
Abe Fortas[3]	1968	Johnson, L. B.	Withdrawn
Homer Thornberry	1968	Johnson, L. B.	Withdrawn
Clement F. Haynsworth Jr.	1969	Nixon	Rejected
G. Harrold Carswell	1970	Nixon	Rejected
Robert H. Bork	1987	Reagan	Rejected
Douglas H. Ginsberg	1987	Reagan	Withdrawn
Harriet Miers	2005	Bush, G. W.	Withdrawn
John G. Roberts Jr.[4]	2005	Bush, G. W.	Withdrawn
Merrick Garland	2016	Obama	No action

[1] A year is given if different from the year of nomination.
[2] Renominated and confirmed.
[3] Nominated for chief justice.
[4] Renominated and confirmed as chief justice.
[5] Second nomination.
[6] Nominated three times.
[7] Unsuccessful or if confirmed did not serve.

[*] SOURCE: Lee Epstein et al., eds., *The Supreme Court Compendium* (Washington, D.C.: CQ Press, 5th ed., 2012), Table 14–12, pp. 374–381; and U.S. Senate, Supreme Court Nominations, Present–1789 (March 7, 2017).

announced that no vote would be taken on any nominee because, given the sharp ideological split on the Court, the next "justice could dramatically change the direction of the Court, and our country, for a generation." The chair of the Senate Judiciary Committee, Chuck Grassley (R-Iowa), likewise vowed that there would be no hearings on any Obama nominee. Obama shrewdly nominated sixty-three-year-old Judge Merrick B. Garland from the Court of Appeals for the District of Columbia Circuit (as we discuss in this chapter). A historical perspective helps to put Garland's nomination in context: of the 163 nominees prior to Garland, thirty-seven (some of whom were nominated two or three times) were withdrawn, rejected, or there was no action taken due to Senate opposition. Of those, nine were renominated and six of them ultimately confirmed, and several declined to serve. Prior presidents have made twenty-eight nominations during a presidential election year and twenty-one of them were confirmed. Moreover, the Senate confirmed seven of the eleven nominated during an election year in which the presidency and Senate were held by opposing parties. The Senate thus retains the power to delay and, of course, deny a nominee's confirmation, as with Obama's 2016 nomination of Garland. The Senate Republican majority stood firm on refusing to hold hearings and a vote on Garland until after the November presidential election. Even more dramatically, President Andrew Johnson's 1866 nomination of his attorney general, Henry Stanbery, was defeated by a Senate that went so far as to reduce the size of the Court from the then ten justices to seven, and thereby eliminate the seat for which Stanbery was nominated.

Most recent presidents have delegated responsibility to their attorneys general and close White House advisers for selecting nominees for federal judgeship. The assistant attorney general in charge of the Office of Legal Policy usually begins by compiling a list of candidates from recommendations by White House staff, members of Congress, governors, bar associations, and interest groups. A committee of the president's top advisers narrows the number down to two or three, on the basis of a political evaluation

James H. Wilson, Jr.   *most brilliant + Howard need*
Atlanta, Georgia   *first lawyer*
Born 1920

Harvard, ~~highly recommended~~

1 - Vincent Lee McKusick, Born 1921, Maine   *no Journam problem*
                                                     confirmation fight
X Dallin Oaks, B. 1932, President of Brigham Young

Philip Areeda, b. 1930

4 Robert Bork, b. 1927

Philip Kurland, b. 1921 (Illinois)

Bennett Boskey, b. 1916 (Washington, D.C.)

Antonin Scalia, 1936

7 - Robert P. Griffin

8 - Charles E. Wiggins

9 - Judge J. Clifford Wallace, Ninth Circuit, 46 (Cal.) *second category*

5 - Judge Alfred T. Goodwin, Ninth Circuit, 52 (Oregon)

X Judge Paul Roney, Fifth Circuit, 53 (Fla)

(1,2,8) - Judge Philip Tone, 7th Circuit, 52 (Ill.) ✓

6 - Judge William Webster, Eighth Circuit, 51 (Mo.)

3 - Judge Arlin M. Adams, Third Circuit, 54 (Pa.) ✓

1 - Judge John Paul Stevens, 7th Circuit, 55 (Illinois) ✓

(4,5,6) - Judge Malcolm R. Wilkey, D.C. Circuit, 56 (Texas)

(4,5,6) - *Judge Clarke* ✓ ( )

(7,8,9) - *Judge Kennedy*

(7,8,9) - *Carla Hills*

**President Gerald Ford's list of potential nominees for the Supreme Court in
1975, as prepared by his attorney general. Ford rank ordered the candidates
and penciled in other possible choices before nominating John Paul Stevens.**
(*Gerald Ford Presidential Library*)

and (until the Reagan administration) informal approval by
the American Bar Association (ABA). Once these reports are
reviewed, a recommendation is sent to the president. If he
approves, it is formally submitted to the Senate. The Senate Judiciary Committee sends a "blue slip" to the senators of the same
states as lower court nominees for their approval. If there is no
objection, a confirmation hearing is held before a subcommittee
of the Judiciary Committee, which then moves for confirmation
by the full Senate. But that one-hundred-year-old Senate tradition is not fixed in stone (three lower court nominees were
defeated by a home state senator's refusal to return a "blue slip"
printed on blue paper on which they indicate support for a
nominee from their home state); in 2016 the Senate Judiciary
Committee's chair, Chuck Grassley (R-Iowa), allowed several
lower court nominees to proceed with hearings over the strong
objections of Democratic senators. In recent decades, battles over
confirmations, with a few exceptions, have become more polarized, particularly when the new appointment would shift the
balance on the Court. The Senate Judiciary Committee also has
become much more aggressive in questioning nominees.[18]

Presidents are now generally less involved in the process of
selecting nominees. That was especially the case with President
Trump. As the Republican presidential candidate, he vowed to
appoint judges in the mold of Justice Scalia. He then turned to the
Federalist Society and the Heritage Foundation to provide him
with a list of top conservative candidates. Shortly before the 2016
election, he released two lists of potential nominees for the Court,
stressing that they were young, staunchly conservative, and all had
prior judicial experience. And after his election, he hired as his
chief judge picker Leo Leonard, the longtime executive director
of the Federalist Society (which was founded in the early 1980s in
order to counter liberal legalism on the federal bench).

But presidents' greater reliance on staff in the selection
process has brought the possibility of more fighting within the
White House. In other words, appointments to the Court have

become less a personal presidential decision than a hard choice among candidates promoted by various vested-interest groups. The appointment of John Paul Stevens in 1975 illustrates the diverse pressures within the contemporary presidency.

In an irony of history, the opportunity to fill the seat of the outspoken liberal Justice Douglas fell to the Republican President Gerald Ford. As a congressman, Ford had sought to impeach Douglas in 1970. Yet Ford had no electoral mandate. He was appointed vice president by President Nixon and had moved into the Oval Office when Nixon resigned rather than risk impeachment in 1974. With his own possible election and place in history in mind, Ford faced the forces of competing interests within the White House and the watchful eye of liberal senators. There was considerable pressure on him to appoint the first woman to the Court. Conservatives in the administration, however, urged the nomination of the Yale law professor and American Enterprise Institute associate Robert Bork. Bork, later appointed by Reagan to the Court of Appeals for the District of Columbia Circuit, served as Nixon's SG and acting attorney general during the Watergate episode. "He is young and is a strict Constructionist," wrote Arizona Senator Barry Goldwater, "and would give continuity to the kind of Court that you want for at least twenty-five years." But for precisely those reasons, the nomination of such a conservative, associated with the disgraced Nixon administration, would have been extremely controversial. It might have been defeated by Senate Democrats and hurt Ford's bid for the 1976 election. As a moderate Republican, Ford leaned toward the advice of Attorney General Edward Levi, who was on leave from the University of Chicago School of Law and who promoted the elevation of John Stevens, a Nixon appointee, to the federal court of appeals in Chicago. Ford made a pragmatic, rather than ideologically controversial, nomination based on Stevens's professional qualifications.[19]

The nomination and confirmation process thus involves political compromises and "horse trading." The role of the ABA in that process deserves special attention. Its evaluations certify the legal qualification of nominees and thus become political bargaining chips. The ABA's Standing Committee on the Federal Judiciary began screening prospective candidates for the Court with the nomination of Brennan in 1956, rating them as "qualified" or "unqualified." This system continued until the appointment of Blackmun in 1970. Criticism of the Senate's rejection of Nixon's nominees Clement Haynsworth and G. Harrold Carswell—whom the committee had ranked as "highly qualified" and "qualified," respectively—led to a change in the ABA system of rating. Nominees for the Court were then rated "highly qualified," "not opposed," or "not qualified." But after a controversy over the ABA's rating of Reagan's unsuccessful nominee, Judge Bork, in 1989, the ABA again changed its system of rating Supreme Court nominees to "well qualified," "qualified," and "not qualified." (Nominees for lower courts are also now rated the same way.)[20] After Blackmun's appointment, Nixon's attorney general John Mitchell refused to submit any further candidates to the ABA committee because of an unfavorable news story about possible nominees for the seats of retiring Justices Harlan and Black. The ABA committee nonetheless conducted its own investigation of Nixon's last two appointments to the Court. With Ford's nomination of Stevens in 1975, the ABA reestablished its formal role in the confirmation process. Twenty-five years later, in 2001 President George W. Bush stopped seeking the ABA's evaluation of potential judicial nominees. In 2009, however, President Obama renewed asking for the ABA's evaluations of potential candidates prior to their nomination. The Trump administration, however, refused to send the names of judicial nominees to the ABA prior to their nomination, reverting back to George W. Bush's stance.

Political Trade-Offs

Packing the Court has come to mean not merely filling the bench with political associates and ideological kin but accommodating the demands for other kinds of symbolic political representation. Some people maintain that merit rather than political favoritism should govern appointments; Justice Stone lamented that "the view has come to prevail that in addition to political considerations, considerations of race, religion and sectional interests should influence the appointment."[21] In fact, it is neither merit nor representative factors like geography, religion, race, and gender that prove controlling. Instead, they are competing political considerations in presidential attempts to pack the Court.

IDEOLOGICAL COMPATIBILITY AND GEOGRAPHY

President George Washington initiated the practice of appointing only ideological kin to the Court. When Thomas Jefferson won the election in 1800, President John Adams wanted to ensure the preservation of Federalist philosophy in the national government before Jefferson took office and appointed his secretary of state, John Marshall, as chief justice. It fell to Andrew Jackson in 1835 to appoint Marshall's successor, and he immediately turned to his longtime supporter and secretary of the treasury, Roger B. Taney. President Abraham Lincoln, in turn, appointed his secretary of the treasury, Salmon Chase, to fill Taney's seat in 1864.

The swing of presidential elections invariably controls judicial appointments. Presidents make little effort to balance the Court by crossing party lines. The party affiliations of those who have served on the Court largely reflect those of their presidential benefactors: thirteen Federalists, one Whig, eight Democratic-Republicans, forty-six Republicans, and forty-six Democrats.

Only two Democratic presidents crossed party lines to fill a vacancy on the Court. Harlan Stone, a Republican, was elevated to the post of chief justice by FDR in 1941. But FDR filled eight other seats with Democrats before he died in the spring of 1945. His successor, Harry Truman, faced considerable political pressure to name a Republican to the seat of retiring Justice Owen Roberts. Although this pressure inspired the selection of Harold

Burton, a Republican senator, Truman was perfectly comfortable with his appointment because they had been close friends.[22]

Republican presidents in the twentieth century named Democrats more often than Democrats nominated Republicans, but only when politically expedient or as a reward for ideological compatibility. President John Tyler, a nominal Whig, made the first crossover appointment. After several rejections of earlier nominees, he named the Democrat Samuel Nelson in 1845, just before the Democratic President James Polk took office. After he was elected by a minority of the popular vote, President Lincoln appointed California's Stephen Field as a gesture to northern and western Democrats. Benjamin Harrison was defeated for reelection in 1892, and he named Howell Jackson only days before the inauguration of the Democratic President Grover Cleveland. President William Taft elevated Justice Edward White to the post of chief justice and appointed his friend Horace Lurton. His other Democratic appointee, Joseph Lamar, was the only pure crossover to achieve political balance within the Court. Presidents Warren Harding and Dwight D. Eisenhower appointed Pierce Butler and William Brennan, respectively, because of their Catholic affiliation and reportedly conservative views. Nixon named Lewis Powell, a Democratic-Republican from Virginia, for his "strict constructionist" views.

Geography used to figure prominently in appointments. During the founding period, geographical representation was considered crucial to establishing the legitimacy of the Court. Congress encouraged geographical diversity by requiring the justices to ride circuit. Each justice would sit with federal district judges to hear cases in a geographical circuit assigned to the Supreme Court justice. From the appointment of John Rutledge from South Carolina in 1789 until the retirement of Hugo Black in 1971, with the exception of the Reconstruction decade of 1866–1876, there was always a southerner on the bench. Until Cardozo's appointment in 1932, the third seat was reserved for New Englanders.

As the country expanded westward, presidents were inclined to give representation to new states. Yet after the Civil War, the influx of immigrants and the gradual nationalization of the country diminished the importance of geographical regions. Congress's elimination of circuit riding in 1891 reinforced the declining influence of geography. A few appointments in the twentieth century turned on geography, but they were exceptional. President Taft selected Willis Van Devanter from Wyoming in 1910 because he was determined to have a westerner on the Court. After he became chief justice, Taft continued to lobby Presidents Harding and Coolidge on the need for geographical balance on the Court.[23]

The appointment of Wiley Rutledge in 1943 illustrates how little geography influences appointments to the modern Court. From FDR's first appointment in 1937, Rutledge, dean of Iowa's law school, was mentioned as a possible nominee because he was considered a "westerner." In 1936, before his own appointment to the high bench, Senator Hugo Black recommended him "as possible material for the Supreme Court." But in 1939, even Black supported the president's decision to pass over Rutledge: "[M]any circumstances," he wrote, "combine to make Felix Frankfurter the only possible nominee at this time, and the balancing of the Court geographically ought to be held back till the next vacancy occurs."[24] Rutledge and geography were repeatedly pushed aside until FDR's last appointment to the Court.[25] Even then, FDR had other reasons for the appointment. Frankfurter made a pest of himself by lobbying for the appointment of Judge Learned Hand, and FDR set his mind against him. During a dinner conversation, Justice Douglas recalled, FDR said, "Well, this time your Brother Frankfurter has overplayed his hand." Douglas then asked, "Well, in what respect?" And FDR responded, "Nineteen people have seen me or called me saying that I must appoint Learned Hand. By God, I am not going to do it." Later that evening, Irving Brant, a St. Louis newspaper editor and friend of the president, came by to urge Rutledge's nomination, as he had done many times before. This time FDR agreed, "That's my man."[26]

Geographical considerations had even less influence on subsequent appointments to the Court. When a justice from the Deep South, Hugo Black, was still on the bench, Nixon nominated Clement Haynsworth of South Carolina and G. Harrold Carswell of Florida. Both were defeated—an outcome Senator Roman Hruska (R-Neb.) insisted was because they were both southerners. Opponents insisted these defeats were the result of two profoundly underqualified candidates. Indeed, Senator Hruska defended Carswell's alleged mediocrity in the Senate in 1970, insisting about Carswell that "even if he were mediocre there are a lot of mediocre judges and people and lawyers." They are "entitled to a little representation, aren't they, and a little chance?" Hruska added that "we can't have all Brandeises, Frankfurters and Cardozos."[27] After the Senate refused to confirm either Haynsworth or Carswell, Nixon turned north and appointed Harry Blackmun from Minnesota, even though his earlier appointee, Chief Justice Burger, was from that state. Geography also did not dissuade Reagan from appointing Rehnquist's former Stanford law school classmate Sandra Day O'Connor, though both were from Arizona. Although geographical diversity remains important in the selection of lower federal appellate court judges,[28] it is no longer compelling on the Supreme Court: only thirty-one states have been represented by the 114 members of the Court. Over half came from seven states—seventeen from New York, ten from Ohio, nine from Massachusetts, eight from Virginia, seven from Pennsylvania, six from Tennessee, and five from Kentucky.

RELIGION, RACE, GENDER, AND BEYOND

Religion, race, and gender were historically barriers to, rather than bases for, appointments to the Court. The overwhelming majority (93) of the 114 justices have come from established Protestant religions: fifty-five from old-line faiths—Episcopalian, Unitarian, Congregationalist, and Quaker—and thirty-seven from others, such as Baptist, Methodist, Lutheran, and Disciples of

Christ. Of the remaining twenty-one, thirteen were Catholics and eight were Jews.

Religion has political symbolism, but played little role in judicial selection until the twentieth century. The "Catholic seat" and the "Jewish seat" were created accidentally, rather than by presidential efforts to achieve religious balance. Representation, of course, is purely symbolic. Catholics and Jews do not have well-defined positions, for example, on statutory interpretation. Nor does the appointment of a Catholic or a Jew guarantee that the views of either faith will be reflected in the justice's voting.

The first Catholic, Chief Justice Taney, was appointed in 1835, but religion had little to do with Jackson's selection of his friend. Thirty years after Taney's death, the next Catholic was named. Edward White was appointed in 1894, but again religion played a minor role (though in 1910 President William Howard Taft was urged to promote him to chief justice because he was "a democrat, a Catholic, and from the South.")[29] From White's appointment until 1949, the Court always included one, and usually two, Catholics: Joseph McKenna served from 1898 to 1925, Pierce Butler from 1923 to 1939, and Frank Murphy from 1940 to 1949. For almost thirty years (from 1898 to 1925), there were two Catholics on the Court, even though Catholics lacked the political influence they later acquired in the New Deal coalition. Roosevelt rewarded Catholic supporters with an unprecedented number of lower federal court judgeships, but he did not do the same with his appointments to the Court.[30] When Murphy died in 1949, Truman did not feel compelled to appoint another Catholic. None sat on the high bench until Eisenhower's appointment of Brennan in 1956. Devoted to bipartisanship, Eisenhower wanted "a very good Catholic, even a conservative Democrat," in order to "show that we mean our declaration that the Court should be non-partisan."[31] By contrast, Reagan appointed two Catholics, Antonin Scalia and Anthony Kennedy, even though he paid no attention to his nominees' religious affiliations in his quest to infuse a sharply conservative judicial philosophy into the Court. When nominated in 1991 by President George H. W. Bush, Justice Clarence Thomas belonged to a charismatic Episcopal church, but he was raised as a Catholic and attended a seminary. In 1996, a few years after his appointment, he again began attending a Catholic church. Like Reagan, President George W. Bush named two Catholics: Chief Justice John G. Roberts Jr. and Justice Samuel Alito Jr. And religion was no obstacle in President Barack Obama's selection of Justice Sonia Sotomayor, another Catholic, though representative factors weighed heavily in his appointing the first Latina and the third woman to serve on the Court.

In 1853, President Millard Fillmore offered a position to Judah Benjamin, but he wanted to stay in the Senate. Not until President Woodrow Wilson's appointment of Louis D. Brandeis in 1916 did the Court acquire its first Jewish justice. Opposition to Brandeis was not necessarily anti-Semitic but based on antagonism toward his progressive legal views. Seven prior ABA presidents, including William Howard Taft, proclaimed that Brandeis was "not a fit person to be a member of the Supreme Court of the United States."[32] After Brandeis's appointment, an expectation of a "Jewish seat" developed. With the confirmation of Cardozo in 1932 and his subsequent replacement by Frankfurter, two Jewish justices sat on the Court until Brandeis retired in 1939. When Frankfurter stepped down in 1962 the Jewish factor mattered, and Kennedy named Arthur Goldberg, his secretary of labor.[33] Three years later, Johnson persuaded Goldberg to become ambassador to the United Nations, and his vacancy was filled by the president's friend Abe Fortas. After Fortas's resignation in 1969, no other Jew sat on the high court until 1993, when Justice Ruth Bader Ginsburg was appointed. Less than a year later, President Clinton named a second Jewish justice, Stephen Breyer. With the confirmation of Obama's second appointee, Elena Kagan, the Court had six Catholic and three Jewish justices, and for the first time in the Court's history had no Protestant justice. When Scalia died in February 2016, again no consideration was given to religion when President Obama nominated to fill his seat appellate court judge Merrick B. Garland, who if confirmed would have been the ninth Jewish justice. Because the Senate refused to consider Garland's nomination, it was left to Trump to nominate Judge Neil Gorsuch, a Protestant who was raised as a Catholic. In 2018 Trump also named Brett Kavanaugh, another Catholic, to fill Justice Kennedy's seat.

Although politically symbolic, religious representation on the Court never amounted to a quota system. Catholics and Jews were more often selected because of personal and ideological compatibility with the president. "There is no such thing as a Jewish seat," Goldberg observed, though his religion was a factor when LBJ considered coaxing him to leave the Court. Johnson was intent on appointing Fortas, regardless of his religion. The two had known each other since the New Deal, and in 1964 LBJ had unsuccessfully urged Fortas to become attorney general. Fortas initially declined appointment to the Court because he wanted "a few more years of activity."[34] LBJ persisted, and in the end Fortas reluctantly agreed to enter the marble temple. In sum, although once symbolically important, religious representation is no longer deemed crucial. "In contrast to Frankfurter, Goldberg, and Fortas," as Justice Ginsburg observed, "no one regarded [her] and Breyer as filling a Jewish seat."[35]

In 1967, LBJ's advisers told him the time had come for the appointment of a black person to the Court.[36] And when announcing his nomination of Thurgood Marshall, LBJ told the nation that it was "the right thing to do, the right time to do it, the right man and the right place."[37] The symbolism of appointing an African American was never lost on the president, nor had LBJ's commitment to naming Thurgood Marshall ever waned. As director of the NAACP Legal Defense and Education Fund, Marshall gained national recognition while arguing a companion case to the landmark school desegregation case, *Brown v. Board of Education* (1954).[38] In 1961, Kennedy named him to the U.S. Court of Appeals for the Second Circuit. Subsequently, Johnson persuaded him to give up the judgeship and become his SG. LBJ wanted "that image, number one," of having a black SG, Marshall recalled. The president told him at the time, "You know this has nothing to do with any Supreme Court appointment. I want that distinctly understood. There's no quid pro here at all. You do your job. If you don't do it, you go out. If you do it, you stay here. And that's all there is to it."[39] That, of course, was not all there was to it. The solicitor generalship offers experience in representing the government before the Court and a springboard for elevation to the high bench. Always a wheeler dealer, LBJ named Ramsey Clark as attorney general in order to pressure his father, Justice Tom C. Clark, to resign so he could elevate Marshall from SG to a seat on the high bench,[40] just as he had earlier enticed Justice Goldberg to become ambassador to the United Nations so that he could appoint his old friend, Abe Fortas, to the Court.

When Justice Marshall announced his retirement at the end of the term in 1991, he was a larger-than-life metaphor for the civil rights movement and an era in American politics. Four days later, President George H. W. Bush nominated his successor, Judge Clarence Thomas. Despite the president's defending him as "the best man for the job on the merits," Thomas's appointment was politically symbolic and his qualifications were immediately questioned. At age forty-three, he was one of the youngest ever to join the Court. He also had little prior judicial experience. Just fifteen months earlier Bush had named him to fill Robert Bork's seat on the Court of Appeals for the District of Columbia Circuit. Before that Thomas spent eight years as head of the Equal Employment Opportunity Commission (EEOC). Still, he had a law degree from Yale Law School and had pulled himself up from an impoverished childhood in Pin Point, Georgia. More than his qualifications sparked controversy, however. During the 1980s he had established a reputation as a rising black conservative within the Republican Party. He had attacked affirmative action, the welfare state, and the judiciary's efforts to integrate public schools. His nomination was thus not unexpected yet bound to invite controversy: Marshall and Thomas, the first two African Americans to sit on the Court, stood for and symbolized very different legal policies and eras in American politics. Whereas Marshall fought against segregation and defended affirmative action, for example, Thomas staunchly opposes affirmative action because, in his view, it "stamp[s] minorities with a badge of inferiority and may cause them to develop dependencies or to adopt an attitude that they are 'entitled' to preferences."[41]

Political pressure for the appointment of a woman had been building for decades and intensified in the 1970s with the battle over the adoption of the Equal Rights Amendment to the Constitution. During the Truman administration, the respected federal court of appeals judge Florence Allen was considered for an appointment.[42] Later, LBJ was urged to consider Barbara Jordan or Sarah Hughes.[43] Nixon also considered nominating a woman, but he claimed "that in general the women judges and lawyers qualified to be nominated for the Supreme Court were too liberal to meet the strict constructionist criterion" he had set for his appointees.[44] In fact, Nixon submitted the name of Judge Mildred Lillie to the ABA judiciary committee in 1971, but she was unanimously ranked "not qualified."

In 1980, Reagan made a campaign promise to appoint a woman. Less than a year later, he fulfilled that pledge by naming Sandra Day O'Connor. In May 1981, Justice Potter Stewart privately told the president that he would retire at the end of the term. A two-month search concluded with O'Connor, who had risen through the ranks of Republican politics, advancing from assistant state attorney general and Arizona state senator to state appellate court judge. Her nomination was supported by both senators from Arizona, Chief Justice Burger and Justice Rehnquist. By contrast, when George W. Bush nominated his legal counsel and longtime friend Harriet Miers to fill O'Connor's seat, her nomination was attacked by conservatives who challenged her judicial philosophy and lack of judicial experience. Within ten days, her nomination was withdrawn.

The Court's first four female justices. From left to right: Retired Justice Sandra Day O'Connor with Justices Sonia Sotomayor, Ruth Bader Ginsburg, and Elena Kagan. (*Photo by Steve Petteway, Collection of the Supreme Court of the United States*)

Religion, race, ethnicity, and gender considerations are politically symbolic and largely reflect changes in the electorate. Such considerations, as earlier noted, led President Obama to nominate Justice Sotomayor as the first Latina (and third woman) to sit on the high bench, but did not bar his subsequent nomination of Elena Kagan as the Court's 112th (and fourth woman) justice. Still, as Justice Ginsburg put it after becoming the Court's second female justice, "I don't think we should ever have anything like proportional representation, so that there will be this seat or that for a particular constituency. But, of course, diversity is important."[45] Indeed, "representative appointments" are certain to remain less important than ideological compatibility in presidential attempts to pack the Court.

Packing the Court

The presidential impulse to pack the Court with politically compatible justices is irresistible. The "tendency to choose a known, rather than an unknown, evil," as Justice Stone put it, "can never be eliminated from the practical administration of government."[46] Yet Court packing depends on the politics of the possible—on presidential prestige and political expediency. The politics of packing the Court is well illustrated by the appointments of Roosevelt, Truman, Eisenhower, Nixon, Reagan, George H. W. Bush, Clinton, George W. Bush, Obama, and Trump.

Before turning to those appointments, however, it bears emphasizing that presidents tend to weigh five broad considerations in selecting nominees: (1) their professional competence; (2) personal patronage and rewarding party faithful; (3) "representative" factors, such as religion, race, ethnicity, and gender; (4) ideology and legal policy goals; and finally (5) confirmability by the Senate. Each of these factors has been given different priority during different presidencies.

As a result, there are three "models" of presidential appointments to the Court. First is the "classic Democratic model" of rewarding friends and party faithful. Roosevelt, Truman, Kennedy, and Johnson paid primary attention to personal patronage and rewarding party faithful, giving some (but not great) consideration to professional competence, and occasionally to symbolic representation. These presidents gave little consideration to pursuing their policy agendas through their appointments, and some of their appointees ended up opposing their policies.

By contrast, Eisenhower, Ford, Clinton, and Obama pursued the second model, a "Bipartisan Approach," for various reasons. They emphasized their nominees' competence, with some (but not overriding) attention to rewarding party faithful and achieving symbolic representation on the bench. But none of these presidents imposed rigorous ideological screening of potential nominees. Charges of cronyism leveled at FDR's and Truman's nominees contributed to Eisenhower's bipartisan approach, whereas Ford, Clinton, and Obama were institutionally constrained by opposition in the Senate and would have faced fierce confirmation battles over more ideological nominees. Obama pursued a generally non-confrontational approach: nominating Sotomayor and emphasizing her prior judicial experience (seventeen years)—more than other nominees in recent history at the time of their nominations—then elevating his SG, Elena Kagan, as his second appointee, followed by selecting Judge Merrick B. Garland to fill Scalia's seat in the face of Senate Republican obstructionism.

Finally, a third model—that of "Republican Ideological Judicial Selection"—was inspired by Nixon and championed by Reagan, Bush I and II, and Trump. Appointments were viewed as symbols and instruments of presidential power: ideology and policy goals had top priority, even over rewarding party faithful, and only occasionally did representative factors enter into their nominations. Perhaps no other president before Nixon and Reagan in the twentieth century had such great contempt for the Court. Nixon vehemently opposed the "liberal jurisprudence" of the Warren Court, and Reagan attacked many of the social-policy rulings of the more conservative Burger Court; both named only those perceived to agree with their conservative social-policy positions.

With the exception of George Washington, no president had more opportunities to pack the Court than FDR. He made eight appointments and elevated Justice Stone to the chief justiceship. Although Nixon and Reagan later achieved remarkable success in remolding the Court in their images, Roosevelt succeeded more than any other president in packing the Court. In contrast to Nixon and Reagan, Roosevelt attacked the conservative economic politics of the Court in the 1930s for impeding the country's recovery from the Great Depression.

During FDR's first term, the Court invalidated most of the early New Deal program. Yet the president had no opportunity to fill a seat on the bench. After his landslide reelection in 1936, Roosevelt proposed judicial reforms allowing him to expand the

The Hughes Court. From left to right, top row: Owen Roberts, Pierce Butler, Harlan Fiske Stone, Benjamin Cardozo; bottom row: Louis Brandeis, Willis Van Devanter, Charles Evan Hughes, James McReynolds, George Sutherland. (*MPI/ Getty Images*)

size of the Court to fifteen by appointing a new member for every justice over seventy years of age. In the spring of 1937, when the Senate Judiciary Committee was debating his "Court-packing plan," the Court abruptly upheld major pieces of New Deal legislation. The Court had previously been sharply divided 5–4 in striking down progressive New Deal legislation. Justices George Sutherland, James McReynolds, Pierce Butler, and Willis Van Devanter were known as the "Four Horsemen" because they voted together and regularly arrived at the Court in the same car; Stone and Cardozo, however, followed Brandeis in supporting progressive economic legislation. Hughes and Roberts were the swing votes, with the more conservative Roberts casting the crucial fifth vote to strike down FDR's programs. Yet, Roberts had already changed his mind, and in March he abandoned the Four Horsemen in *West Coast Hotel Co. v. Parrish* (1937) to uphold

Washington state's minimum-wage law.[47] Two weeks later, in *National Labor Relations Board v. Jones & Laughlin Steel Corporation* (1937), he again voted to affirm a major piece of New Deal legislation, the National Labor Relations Act.[48]

The Court's so-called "switch in time that saved nine" was speculated to have been due to FDR's Court-packing plan. But even though the rulings did not come down until the spring, Roberts switched his vote at conference in December 1936, two months before FDR announced his plan. The reversal of the Court's position nonetheless contributed to the Senate Judiciary Committee's rejection of FDR's proposal in May. Then Justice Van Devanter—one of the president's staunchest opponents— resigned. FDR had the first of eight appointments in the next six years to infuse his political philosophy into the Court. Although his plan to enlarge the size of the Court failed, FDR eventually succeeded in packing the Court.

When FDR made his first appointment, he was angry at the Senate for defeating his plan to enlarge the Court and angry at the Court for destroying his program for recovery. For the appointment, FDR chose Senator Hugo Black, who had led the unsuccessful fight for the Court-packing plan. Roosevelt, recalled Justice Jackson, wanted to "humiliate [the Senate and the Court] at a single stroke by naming Black." Only in extraordinary circumstances would the Senate refuse to confirm one of its own. "The Senate would have to swallow hard and approve," Jackson observed. "The Court would be humiliated by having to accept one of its most bitter and unfair critics and one completely alien to the judicial tradition."[49]

At Black's confirmation hearings, rumors circulated that he had been a member of the Ku Klux Klan in the mid-1920s, when Klan membership reached its peak of over 4 million and virtually ensured the election of Democrats in the Deep South. When evidence of Black's prior KKK membership materialized after his confirmation, the revelation confirmed for many that the appointment was an act of revenge. FDR claimed "that he had not known of any Klan link when he appointed Black to the Court." Black

Justice Hugo Black in his chambers. Black was President Roosevelt's first appointee and a leader of liberals on the Court. (*Collection of the Supreme Court of the United States*)

went on national radio to explain briefly, though not to apologize for, his membership in the Klan from 1922 to 1925. Although FDR denied having any knowledge of the KKK association, he must have known. Moreover, Black left a note in his private papers to "correct for posterity any idea about Pres. Roosevelt's having been fooled about my membership in the Klan." He recollected:

President Roosevelt, when I went up to lunch with him, told me that there was no reason for my worrying about having been a member of the Ku Klux Klan. He said that some of the best friends and supporters he had in the State of Georgia were strong members of the organization. He never in any way, by word or attitude, indicated any doubt about my having been in the Klan nor did he indicate any criticism of me for having been a member of that organization. The rumors and statements to the contrary are wrong.[50]

Roosevelt's subsequent appointments all turned on support for the New Deal and personal connections. When the conservative westerner George Sutherland retired in 1938, FDR momentarily considered nominating another senator—either South Carolina's James Byrnes, later appointed in 1941, or Indiana's Sherman Minton, who was forced to wait until Truman selected him in 1949. But he worried about taking too many supporters from the Senate. Attorney General Homer Cummings urged the elevation of Solicitor General Stanley Reed. Reed was from Kentucky, and FDR initially remarked, "Well, McReynolds is from Kentucky, and Stanley will have to wait until McReynolds is no longer with us." Cummings countered that McReynolds was "closely identified with New York City" because of his earlier law practice and that Reed's record justified his nomination. Roosevelt agreed: "Tell Stanley to make himself so disagreeable to McReynolds that the latter will retire right away."[51]

Reed joined the Court in 1938, but McReynolds did not retire until 1941, and the pressure for an appointee from the West steadily grew. In 1938 Cardozo died. The vacancy would be hard to fill, for "Cardozo was not only a great Justice, but a great character, a great person and a great soul," Cummings observed, "whoever followed him, no matter how good a man he might be would suffer by comparison."[52] Roosevelt had long contemplated appointing Frankfurter to Brandeis's seat. Anticipating "a terrible time getting Frankfurter confirmed," he had earlier unsuccessfully urged Frankfurter to become SG. "I want you on the Supreme Court, Felix," Roosevelt told him, "but I can't appoint you out of the Harvard Law School. What will people say? 'He's a Red. He's a professor. He's had no judicial experience.' But I could appoint you to the Court from the Solicitor General's office."[53] When Cardozo died, FDR at first told Frankfurter, "I've got to appoint a fellow west of the Mississippi—I promised the party leaders he'd be a Westerner the next time."[54] A number of westerners were considered, but FDR found lesser-known candidates unacceptable. Frankfurter was appointed despite criticism that it put two Jews and an excessive number of justices from the Atlantic seaboard on the Court.

Geography did not dissuade FDR from then filling Brandeis's seat in 1939 with his Securities and Exchange Commission (SEC) chairman, William O. Douglas. At first, Senator Lewis Schwellenbach was considered, but opposition emerged from his counterpart senator from the state of Washington. Frank Murphy had replaced Cummings as attorney general and urged FDR to disregard pressure for the selection of a westerner. "Members of the Supreme Court are not called upon nor expected to represent any single interest or group, area or class of persons," Murphy insisted. "They speak for the country as a whole. Considerations of residential area or class, interest, creed or racial extraction, ought therefore be subordinate if not entirely disregarded."[55] Brandeis had recommended Douglas. Born in Minnesota and raised in Yakima, Washington, Douglas claimed Connecticut as his legal residence because he had taught at Yale Law School before joining the SEC. There was accordingly opposition to naming another nonwesterner, but powerful Senate leaders like Idaho's William Borah endorsed the nomination. Douglas later recalled, "When Roosevelt named me he didn't name me from the State of Washington, but he stuck to the record, and named me from Connecticut."[56]

When the midwesterner Pierce Butler died in 1939, there was even greater pressure to appoint a westerner and a Catholic. Butler was a Catholic, and Catholics were a crucial part of the New Deal coalition. FDR settled on Attorney General Murphy—a Catholic, an affable "Irish mystic," and a former governor of Michigan. Murphy's midwestern Catholic background, however, was only a politically useful rationalization. No less important, morale within the Department of Justice (DoJ) was abysmally low. Murphy was not intellectually equipped to handle the position of attorney general. His appointment was another example of FDR's lack of concern for the Court.[57] Roosevelt was not unaware of Murphy's faults. Assistant Attorney General Robert Jackson told him, "Mr. President, I don't think that Mr. Murphy's temperament is that of a judge." His elevation to the Court was nevertheless politically opportune. And FDR explained to Jackson, "It's the only way I can appoint you Attorney General."[58]

Roosevelt promised to eventually make Jackson chief justice if he accepted the attorney generalship. Jackson reluctantly agreed. In 1941 McReynolds retired, and Chief Justice Hughes informed the president that he would step down at the end of the term. FDR had the opportunity to fill two more seats and to appoint Jackson. Hughes suggested that the chief justiceship go to Stone. He had long aspired to the position and had been disappointed because his friend, President Hoover, passed him over when appointing Hughes.[59] Frankfurter preferred Jackson but agreed that Stone was "senior and qualified professionally to be C.J." He also told FDR that the elevation of Stone, a Republican, would inspire confidence in him "as a national and not a partisan President."[60] In July, Senator Byrnes was named to McReynolds's seat, Stone was elevated to the post of chief justice, and Jackson was nominated associate justice. When trying to mollify Jackson, FDR noted that Stone was within a couple of years of retirement and explained, "I will have another chance at appointment of a

Chief Justice, at which time you'd already be over there [in the Court] and would be familiar with the job." At the time, the arrangement appeared politically advantageous: "one Republican for Chief Justice and two Democrats will not be too partisan."[61] FDR, however, made his last appointment little over a year later. Byrnes left the Court to become director of the Office of Economic Stabilization, and Rutledge, as described earlier, got his seat.

Chief Justice Stone's death in 1946 presented a ready-made controversy over a successor, but President Truman found a politically expedient solution. The Roosevelt Court had become badly divided. Black led the liberals—Reed, Douglas, Murphy, Rutledge, and Burton—against Jackson and Frankfurter, who tended to advance the basic conservatism of Roberts and Stone. The Black–Jackson disputes were deep-seated, ideological, and personal. When Stone died, senior Associate Justice Black temporarily assumed the responsibilities of chief justice. Having long labored under Roosevelt's promise to make him chief justice, Jackson immediately became vindictive, convincing himself that his rival would be named chief justice. Unpersuaded by the president's assurances that he had not talked with Black about the position, Jackson, who at the time was away serving as chief prosecutor at the Nuremburg trials, made public a telegram that he sent to the chairman of the House and Senate Judiciary Committees attacking Justice Black and airing the animosities within the Court.[62]

Outraged by the Black–Jackson controversy, Truman lamented, "The Supreme Court has really made a mess of itself."[63] He decided to appoint his friend Fred Vinson, who had been appointed to the Court of Appeals for the District of Columbia Circuit and made director of the Office of Economic Stabilization by FDR, and was quickly elevated within Truman's administration. In 1945, less than one year after Truman took office, he was named secretary of the treasury. Vinson was a friend and an experienced politician with "an uncanny knack of placating opposing minds."[64] That was precisely what Truman thought the

Court needed: an outsider and proven negotiator, rather than an insider and legal scholar. As William Rogers, Eisenhower's deputy attorney general, later observed, "Fred Vinson would not have been on the Court but for the fact that he was a successful politician."[65]

The appointments of Chief Justices Earl Warren in 1953 and Warren Burger in 1969 both sprang from the 1952 Republican Convention. Why did Eisenhower appoint Warren? Justice Douglas, among others, insisted that Vice President Nixon and Senator William Knowland of California viewed Warren—an extremely popular governor with bipartisan support in California—as "an unorthodox, off-beat kind of Republican." They "went to Eisenhower when Vinson died, and urged that Eisenhower name Warren as chief justice because Nixon and Knowland wanted to get Warren out of the State of California so they could take over the Republican machine."[66] But that story is too simple to be true.[67] Shortly after the election in November 1952, Eisenhower indicated to Warren that he could have the "first vacancy" on the Court. Later, in the summer of 1953, he persuaded Warren to become solicitor general so as to gain experience arguing cases before the Court. When Vinson died that summer, his job was immediately (though somewhat reluctantly) offered to Warren.[68]

Eisenhower was committed to appointing Warren because he "was firmly convinced the prestige of the Court had suffered severely in prior years, and that the only way it could be restored was by the appointment to it of men of nationwide reputation, of integrity, competence in the law, and in statesmanship." He also refused to appoint anyone over sixty-four years of age, which barred several prominent jurists. As California's favorite-son candidate for the presidency in 1952, Warren had "national stature" and, in Eisenhower's opinion, "unimpeachable integrity," "middle-of-the-road views," and "a splendid record during his years of active law work" as state attorney general.[69]

Warren's popularity and role in the 1952 Republican Convention impressed Eisenhower. But what happened at that convention also set the political stage for the eventual appointment of Warren

Burger as chief justice. Eisenhower and Senator Robert Taft (the son of Chief Justice William Taft) were leading contenders, though it remained uncertain right up to the convention who would win the nomination. Herbert Brownell, Eisenhower's campaign manager, was convinced that his candidate could not win without the support of the favorite-son candidates Earl Warren of California and Harold Stassen of Minnesota. Just before the convention opened, a dispute arose over whether contested delegates could vote on their seating at the convention. If they were allowed to vote, Brownell believed, Taft would have the nomination. If they were not, no candidate could expect a majority on the first ballot, but Eisenhower's chances of getting the nomination would be better. Brownell proposed and secured a "fair play" amendment to the rules of the convention; it forbade any contested delegate to vote, with the result that the Taft candidacy began to disintegrate before the convention opened. During negotiations over the "fair play" amendment, Brownell and Stassen's campaign manager, Warren Burger, came to know and admire one another. Burger worked to get the Minnesota delegation to agree on the amendment. No less helpful was the freshman Senator Richard Nixon, who made a moral appeal to the California delegation to vote for the "fair play" amendment. Although pledged as a delegate to support Warren, Nixon was committed to seeing that Eisenhower got the nomination. Warren reluctantly agreed to the amendment, even though it hurt his chances of winning the nomination if there were a deadlock at the convention. When it then looked as though Eisenhower could win the nomination on the first ballot if either the California or Minnesota delegation swung over to him, Burger and others pressed Stassen to turn his delegates over to Eisenhower. Stassen "objected strenuously to it," and his adviser Bernard Shanley later recalled telling him that "it was going to happen whether he liked it or not."[70] Toward the end of the first roll-call vote, Stassen released the Minnesota delegation to Eisenhower, giving him a first-ballot nomination, while members of the California delegation continued to support Warren.

Warren's "statesmanship" at the convention impressed Eisenhower. Warren had not opposed the "fair play" amendment, as
he might have done. Because he had not turned over any of his
delegates on the floor of the convention, Eisenhower felt "there
was no possibility of charging that his appointment was made as
payment for a political debt."[71] Stassen and his advisers went into
the Eisenhower-Nixon administration, Burger as assistant attorney
general under Attorney General Brownell. Burger further
developed his friendship with Brownell and in 1956 was appointed
to the prestigious Court of Appeals for the District of Columbia
Circuit.

In 1969, President Nixon's first choice to fill the seat of retiring Chief Justice Warren was Brownell. However, since Brownell
"had been Eisenhower's Attorney General in 1957 at the time of
the Little Rock school crisis," he concluded that confirmation
would be difficult, for "many Southerners were still deeply embittered by his role in the use of federal troops to enforce integration." Nixon's attorney general, Mitchell, told Brownell that
"confirmation would be messy," and the latter withdrew from consideration.[72] Nixon could not nominate Mitchell, since that would
open him to the charge of "cronyism"—a charge that Republicans
had just used in 1968 to defeat Johnson's effort to promote Fortas to the chief justiceship. Nixon wanted someone who had judicial experience but was young enough to serve at least ten years.
Most important, he wanted someone who shared his own "strict
constructionist" philosophy of constitutional interpretation;
Nixon's advisers urged him to remold the Court in a more conservative image.[73] Nixon knew Burger from the Eisenhower
administration and had read his speeches on law and order, which
Burger sent him. But Nixon was not close personally to Burger,
and so his nomination would not raise the charges of cronyism.
Just two weeks before receiving the presidential nod in May 1969,
Burger lobbied for the nomination in a letter to Nixon, advising
him how to deal with the Court and the controversy over Fortas's
extrajudicial activities (discussed later in the chapter), as well as

President Dwight D. Eisenhower and Chief Justice Earl Warren with Vice President Richard Nixon, who later appointed Warren Burger chief justice. (*Dwight D. Eisenhower Presidential Library*)

lamenting that Nixon's first nominee would probably become the media's "whipping boy."[74]

Burger came to the Court determined to reverse the "liberal jurisprudence" of the Warren Court and restore "law and order." Warren's Court had revolutionized constitutional law and American society with the unanimous 1954 school desegregation ruling, *Brown v. Board of Education*, the 1962 ruling in *Baker v. Carr* that announced the "reapportionment revolution" guaranteeing equal voting rights, and a series of rulings on criminal procedure that extended the rights of the accused. Eisenhower later called his appointment of Warren "the biggest damnfooled mistake" he had ever made. Nixon sought to rectify that mistake.

Nixon's appointments of Burger, Blackmun, Powell, and Rehnquist, however, failed to forge a "constitutional counter-revolution." This was because the Burger Court was increasingly fragmented and polarized, dividing 6–3 or 5–4, and pulled in different directions by either its most liberal or most conservative members. There were only modest "adjustments," as Burger put it when announcing his retirement, in the jurisprudential house built by the Warren Court. But the Burger Court also made a few new additions. It upheld abortion, affirmative action, and busing, and gave greater scope to the Fourteenth Amendment's equal protection clause. Those rulings, even more than those of the Warren Court, embittered New Right "movement conservatives," who set the stage for the Reagan era and his attempt to pack the Court anew.

Reagan campaigned in 1980 and 1984 on a promise to appoint only those opposed to abortion and "judicial activism." No other president had as great an impact on the federal judiciary since FDR. Before leaving the Oval Office, Reagan appointed almost half of all lower-court judges and elevated Rehnquist to chief justice, as well as appointed three other justices to the Court.[75] Numbers are only part of the story. Reagan put into place the most rigorous process ever for judicial selection. Judges were viewed as symbols and instruments of presidential power and a way to ensure Reagan's legacy. Through judicial appointments, as Attorney General Edwin Meese III claimed, the administration aimed "to institutionalize the Reagan revolution so it can't be set aside no matter what happens in future presidential elections."[76]

Reagan's first opportunity to name a justice came with the appointment of Sandra Day O'Connor. Unlike Reagan's other appointees, O'Connor was chosen more for symbolic rather than ideological reasons: Reagan had promised to name the first woman to the Court,[77] and her confirmation hearings (the first to be televised) generated little controversy.

Reagan's next opportunity to pack the Court came on May 27, 1986, when Chief Justice Burger told the president that he would step down to head full time the Commission on the Bicentennial of the Constitution. He also provided a memo recommending Justices Rehnquist and White, and federal appellate court judges Robert H. Bork, Antonin Scalia, and J. Clifford Wallace for consideration as his replacement.[78] Two days later, Chief of Staff Donald Regan, Attorney General Meese, and White House counsel Peter Wallison met and decided to have files previously prepared by the DoJ on potential Court nominees sent to the White House for review. Those files focused on seven candidates: Justices O'Connor and Rehnquist; Judges Bork, Scalia, and Wallace; and two other federal appellate court judges. The DoJ also had considered, among others, Ninth Circuit Court of Appeals Judge Anthony Kennedy, who was deemed "bright and conservative" but, unlike Bork and Scalia, an "intellectual rather than practical [conservative], leading to an occasional anomalous result."[79] Subsequently, the list was narrowed to Justices O'Connor and Rehnquist and Judges Bork and Scalia. On June 9, Reagan met with Regan, Meese, and Wallison and indicated that he wanted to begin by meeting Rehnquist, but also said he was intrigued by Scalia, who would be the first Italian American to sit on the high bench. Three days later, Reagan met with Rehnquist and offered him the position, which Rehnquist immediately accepted. They then discussed the possibility of naming to his seat either Bork or Scalia; both were acceptable to Rehnquist. Although both were considered predictable conservatives, Scalia was ten years younger and deemed more energetic.

The decision to elevate Rehnquist from associate to chief justice and to appoint Scalia to his seat was politically strategic. Both could claim to be intellectual architects of Reagan's legal-policy agenda. Through their writings and judicial opinions, they had largely defined the administration's positions on abortion, affirmative action, federalism, and the role of the courts in American society. Their law clerks regularly came from or went to top positions within Reagan's Justice Department and presidency.

Reagan's advisers knew Rehnquist would prove controversial because of his long-standing, often extremely conservative views. But naming him chief justice symbolized Reagan's judicial legacy, and Rehnquist's elevation while he was an incumbent justice made it virtually impossible for the Senate to deny confirmation. Rehnquist had gone to the Court in 1972 from Nixon's DoJ, where he had served as an assistant attorney general. His conservative credentials were established years earlier, initially when he was a law clerk for Justice Robert Jackson and later an Arizona attorney and supporter of Arizona Senator Barry Goldwater's presidential candidacy. On the Burger Court, Rehnquist staked out a conservative philosophy, which earned him the nickname "Lone Dissenter" for writing more solo dissents (fifty-four) than any of his colleagues in his fifteen years as an associate justice (although Justice Douglas [1939–1975] holds the record [208] for solo dissents).[80]

The attack on Rehnquist's nomination was spearheaded by Massachusetts's Democratic Senator Edward M. Kennedy, who had also challenged him when he was first named to the Court. Kennedy called Rehnquist "too extreme on race, too extreme on women's rights, too extreme on freedom of speech, too extreme on separation of church and state, too extreme to be Chief Justice." Utah's Republican Senator Orrin Hatch countered that the confirmation hearings threatened to become a "Rehnquisition."

But the Senate Judiciary Committee's televised hearings were less enlightening than an occasion for speeches by supporters and attackers. Rehnquist was repeatedly asked about his judicial opinions, despite his refusal to discuss them. He also confronted charges, aimed at tarnishing his integrity, that as a law clerk in 1953 he had supported segregated schools and in the 1960s had harassed minority voters at polling places.

About all that the committee accomplished was a reassertion of its power to consider the judicial philosophy of nominees, no less than the president does when picking them. Subsequently, the Senate confirmed Rehnquist by a vote of 65 to 33 with southern Democrats voting with Republicans and two Republicans siding with thirty-one Democrats in opposition.

In contrast with its scrutiny of Rehnquist, the Senate Judiciary Committee spent little time on Scalia; his confirmation hearings were quick and amicable. The differences are reflected in the committee's final reports: Rehnquist's runs 114 pages, while Scalia's, only 76 words. On the committee's unanimous recommendation, the Senate voted (98 to 0) for confirmation.

Less than a year later, Justice Powell announced his resignation. The respected "Virginia gentleman" privately told his colleagues that his decision was "motivated by (i) the imminence of my 80th birthday, (ii) by having served 15-1/2 years when I contemplated no more than ten years of service, and (iii) by concern—based on past experience [with three major operations for cancer]—that I could handicap the Court in the event of reoccurrences of serious health problems."[81] Powell's resignation, however, gave way to an extraordinary confirmation battle over Judge Bork's nomination.

The controversy over Bork underscores the Reagan administration's effort to make the Court a symbol and instrument of his presidency, as well as the power of the Senate to defeat a nominee.[82] Reagan chose, over more moderate Republicans and conservative jurists, one of the most outspoken critics of the Warren and Burger Courts. He did so despite the Democrats' regaining control of the Senate after the 1986 elections, which meant a fight over any nominee closely aligned with New Right Republicans. Reagan also underestimated the extent of the opposition. Yet Powell's seat was considered pivotal, because he had often cast

the crucial fifth vote in cases upholding a woman's right to choose
an abortion, among other divisive issues. In addition, Bork had
been passed over three times before, by Ford in 1975 and by
Reagan in 1981 (the result of his promise to appoint a woman)
and 1986 (because Reagan's advisers rated Scalia higher than
Bork, owing to his age and reputation as a "team player"). Shortly
after Scalia's appointment, the White House leaked a rumor that
the next vacancy would go to Bork. Liberal interest groups thus
were prepared to fight his confirmation.

During five days of televised testimony before the Judiciary
Committee, Bork sought to clarify and amend his twenty-five-year
record as a Yale Law School law professor, SG, and judge. That
broke with tradition and gave the appearance of a public relations
campaign. Bork also seemed to refashion himself into a "centrist"
jurist. Besides the desertion of much of his past record, Bork's
lengthy explanations were unprecedented in other ways. Since
1925, when Harlan F. Stone first appeared as a witness during his
confirmation hearings, down to Reagan's previous appointees, all
nominees had refused to talk about their views on specific cases,
let alone discuss how they might vote on issues likely to come
before the Court. But Bork gave unusual assurances on how he
might vote if confirmed. By the time Bork finished thirty hours of
testimony, he had contradicted much of what he had stood for
and for which he had been nominated. As a result, the vote of the
committee went 9 to 5 against Bork. Other conservative southern
Democrats and six moderate Republicans came out against him
in the final 58 to 42 vote on the Senate floor.

Bork's defeat was a major setback. Meese and others in the
DoJ bitterly blamed White House staff for not pushing hard
enough. They vindictively persuaded Reagan to nominate Judge
Douglas Ginsburg, rather than Ninth Circuit Court of Appeals
Judge Anthony M. Kennedy, a less controversial conservative.

Why Ginsburg? Because he was Bork's protégé, sharing more
than a nomination and a seat on the same appellate court. Twenty
years younger, Ginsburg tracked Bork's path back to law school

days at the University of Chicago. After graduating, he followed Bork into the field of antitrust law and an academic career. In 1983 Ginsburg joined the DoJ as an assistant attorney general in the antitrust division. There he quickly moved the division in the direction long advocated by Bork.

In its haste to find a suitable successor to Bork, the DoJ failed to investigate Ginsburg's background fully. Within ten days of his nomination, Ginsburg was forced to withdraw, amid disclosures that he had smoked marijuana when a Harvard Law School professor. A few days later Reagan nominated Anthony Kennedy, whom the president had met only briefly once before and had passed over in favor of Ginsburg because Kennedy was considered too traditional, not a "movement conservative."[83]

Kennedy's nomination met with immediate and generally bipartisan praise. After graduating from Harvard Law School, he practiced law for more than a decade before Ford appointed him to the Ninth Circuit in 1975. Kennedy's record was solidly conservative, but more that of a legal technician than an outspoken legal philosopher like Bork. His confirmation hearings were reminiscent of most in the past. Few reporters showed up; none of the commercial television networks broadcast them; his testimony was subdued and his answers to questions were reserved, straightforward, and largely descriptive discourses on developing constitutional law. When pressed on issues such as abortion, he claimed "no fixed view." Kennedy also distanced himself from some of the Reagan administration's and Bork's controversial positions. He expressly rejected, for instance, that "a jurisprudence of original intention" provides a sure guide for constitutional interpretation. The latter, in Kennedy's words, is a "necessary starting point," rather than a "methodology," and "doesn't tell us how to decide a case." Although such responses troubled some conservatives, the Judiciary Committee unanimously approved him, and he was confirmed in 1988.

The conservatism of the Reagan/Rehnquist Court was further (partially) reinforced by President George H. W. Bush's appointments. In Reagan's shadow, Bush picked his nominees from a list of potential candidates originally compiled during Reagan's administration. Three days after Justice Brennan, one of the most liberal justices in the twentieth century, retired in July 1990, Bush nominated Judge David Hackett Souter. Just over a year earlier the fifty-year-old, soft-spoken bachelor had been nominated by Bush to the Court of Appeals for the First Circuit. Prior to that, he had served as New Hampshire's attorney general before being elevated to that state's supreme court by then governor, and later Bush's White House chief of staff, John Sununu. At his confirmation hearing, Souter endeavored, as had Justice Kennedy, to reassure senators that he had no agenda or rigid jurisprudence. By a vote of 13 to 1 (with only Senator Kennedy dissenting), the Senate Judiciary Committee recommended confirmation. Souter was then confirmed as the 105th justice by a vote of 90 to 9, with only liberal Democratic senators voting against him.

Major controversy erupted over Bush's second appointee to the Court to fill the seat of Justice Marshall. When announcing the nomination of Clarence Thomas, Bush proclaimed him "the best person for this position" and stated, "The fact that he is black and a minority has nothing to do with this in the sense that he is the best qualified at this time."[84] Yet Thomas was a well-known black conservative judge whom Bush had named a year earlier to the Court of Appeals for the District of Columbia Circuit in anticipation of Marshall's eventual retirement. Indeed, Thomas was groomed for a judgeship while serving in the 1980s as the head of the Equal Employment Opportunity Commission (EEOC). Women's groups, including the National Organization for Women and the National Abortion Rights League, as well as the NAACP, immediately voiced opposition. The ABA rated Thomas "qualified," though two members of the committee dissented and one abstained; this was the lowest the commission had rated a nominee for the high court since the ABA began reviewing nominees in 1956.

During his testimony before the Senate Judiciary Committee, Thomas sought to deflect criticism by repeatedly emphasizing his "up-by-the-bootstraps" philosophy and personal struggle

Clarence Thomas responding to charges that he had sexually harassed Anita Hill. (*AP Photo/Dennis Cook*)

in overcoming the poverty of his youth. When asked about his prior writings, however, he gave only guarded answers. In response to more than seventy questions about the constitutionality of *Roe v. Wade*, Thomas steadfastly, though surprisingly, maintained that he had never seriously thought about the legitimacy of that controversial ruling.

After almost two weeks of hearings, the judicial committee was deadlocked, split 7 to 7 on whether to recommend him. It finally voted 13 to 1 to send Thomas's nomination to the full Senate without a recommendation. Several new allegations then surfaced, including one that Thomas had sexually harassed a female assistant a decade earlier when he chaired the EEOC. An FBI report on the allegations was subsequently leaked to the press, and the law school professor Anita F. Hill, who had been Thomas's assistant at the EEOC, was forced to come forth to explain her charges.

Amid rising public anger over the accusations and counter-charges that Hill was part of a conspiracy to derail Thomas's con-

Law school professor Anita Hill testifying before the Senate Judiciary Committee. (*AP Photo/Greg Gibson*)

firmation, the Judiciary Committee rushed to hold hearings that pitted Hill against Thomas on nationwide television. Hill coolly and confidently charged that in the early 1980s Thomas sexually harassed her, repeatedly asked for dates, frequently talked about pornographic movies, and created a hostile work environment. Thomas in turn angrily protested that the confirmation process had become "a high-tech lynching for uppity blacks." The nasty drama of "she said, he said" raised larger issues of racism and sexism, but failed to resolve the immediate questions about the veracity of either Hill or Thomas. At the end of another week of bitter fighting, the Senate voted 52 to 48 to confirm Thomas as the 106th justice to serve on the Court.

After almost a quarter of a century in which Republican presidents made ten consecutive appointments to the Court, the Democratic President Bill Clinton named Justice Ruth Bader Ginsburg in 1993. Drawing on a list of fifty possible candidates, Clinton first offered the position to New York Governor Mario Cuomo, but he turned it down.[85] Clinton's final choice came down to two incumbent appellate court judges, Stephen Breyer and Ginsburg, the leader of the women's law movement in the 1970s.[86] Both had the support of the ranking Republican on the Senate Judiciary Committee, Orrin Hatch. Both had won seats on the federal bench as appointees of Jimmy Carter in 1980. Breyer had served as chief counsel to the Senate Judiciary Committee and had the support of both Republicans and Democrats on the committee. Hatch was also instrumental in pushing Ginsburg's appointment through in 1980, when Republicans threatened to block all of Carter's further nominees. Hatch agreed to meet her at the request of H. Ross Perot, who was asked to arrange the meeting by his Washington tax attorney and Ginsburg's husband, Martin. Ginsburg had impressed Hatch then and later with thirteen years of service on the Court of Appeals for the District of Columbia Circuit, during which time she served with the future justices Scalia and Thomas, as well as Judge Bork. In 1993, though, Ginsburg's husband and New York Senator Daniel Patrick Moynihan, along with leaders of prominent women's groups, were her strongest supporters.

After meeting Judge Breyer for a luncheon amid speculation that he would get the nod, Clinton met with Ginsburg the next day and was touched by her charm. In fact, vetting of Judges Ginsburg and Breyer within Clinton's DoJ and White House Counsel's office favored Ginsburg over Breyer. "Judge Ginsburg's work has more of the humanity that the President highly values and fewer of the negative aspects," wrote Joel Klein to White House counsel Bernard Nussbaum; whereas another viewed Breyer as a "rather cold fish" and concluded that "Nothing in Judge Breyer's opinions suggests that he would be a great Supreme Court justice."[87] When Clinton subsequently announced his selection, he called Ginsburg the Thurgood Marshall of the women's movement, a comparison drawn earlier by the former SG Erwin Griswold in 1985, when he observed that "in modern times two appellate advocates altered the nation's course . . . Thurgood

Marshall and Ruth Ginsburg." Ginsburg's nomination as the 107th justice sailed through the Senate with a final vote of 96 to 3.

Less than a year later, Justice Blackmun announced that he would retire and Clinton had his second opportunity to fill a vacancy. He settled on Stephen Breyer, whom he had passed over a year earlier. Clinton picked Breyer because his other top two candidates, Bruce Babbitt and Judge Richard Arnold, might have set off a confirmation fight in the Senate. As expected, Breyer won easy confirmation in the Senate by a vote of 87 to 9. After graduating from Harvard Law School, he had served as a law clerk to Justice Arthur Goldberg and later taught at Harvard Law School, as well as once served as counsel to the Senate Judiciary Committee. Unlike that former very liberal justice, however, Justice Breyer is much more of a legal technician and pragmatist.[88] And for that reason Clinton's advisers correctly anticipated relatively low-key confirmation hearings.

President George W. Bush campaigned in 2000 and 2004 with the promise to appoint judges like Justices Scalia and Thomas, who would not "legislate from the bench." In the summer of 2005 Justice O'Connor informed him of her retirement upon the confirmation of a successor. A little over two weeks later Bush nominated Judge John G. Roberts Jr. of the Court of Appeals for the District of Columbia Circuit to fill her seat.

In fact, in anticipation that the chief justice might retire, Bush delegated responsibility for screening potential nominees to White House officials led by Vice President Dick Cheney, not to his attorney general as recent presidents had done. From an initial list of eleven, Cheney's group narrowed the list down to five federal appellate court judges: John G. Roberts Jr., Samuel A. Alito Jr., James Harvie Wilkinson Jr., Michael Luttig, and Edith Brown Clement. Cheney's group interviewed each and probed their legal philosophies and personalities before Bush met briefly with each nominee. On July 19, Bush nominated Roberts to fill O'Connor's seat.[89]

In naming Roberts, Bush satisfied his conservative base. A graduate of Harvard College and Law School, the fifty-year-old Roberts had served on the appellate bench for just two years and had written few opinions. After law school, he clerked for Justice Rehnquist before moving into the Reagan administration, first as special assistant to the attorney general and later as associate counsel to the president. After a few years in private practice, he became a deputy SG in the administration of George H. W. Bush, who nominated him in 1992 to the federal bench, but a Senate vote was never taken. Following another eight years in private practice, he was nominated by President George W. Bush in 2001 to the appellate bench. After his confirmation was blocked by Senate Democrats, Bush renominated him in 2003; he was then confirmed in 2006 by the Senate without a roll call vote. Throughout his legal career, Roberts earned a reputation as a solid conservative and a skillful litigator, arguing thirty-nine cases before the Court and winning twenty-five of them.

Before confirmation hearings could be held, however, Chief Justice Rehnquist died, and Bush renominated Roberts to fill his seat. During his confirmation hearings, he presented himself as a "modest judge," and famously claimed that "courts have a limited role in general, and they only interpret the law. . . . Judges are like umpires. Umpires don't make the rules; they apply them. . . . Nobody ever went to a ball game to see the umpire. Judges have to have humility to recognize that they operate within a system of precedent . . . . [T]he worst thing you can say about a judge," he concluded, is that he or she is "result-oriented."[90] Although his analogy of judges to umpires was appealing, it was also misleading and unrealistic.[91] Still, during his first decade as chief, Roberts clearly tried to live up to his philosophy of minimalism and institutionalism, as exemplified by his dissent from the majority opinion striking down states' constitutional bans on same-sex marriage in *Obergefell v. Hodges* (2015).[92] More concerned with the Court's institutional prestige and limited role, Roberts has eschewed strict textualism and, as championed by Justices Scalia, Thomas, and Gorsuch, adherence to the "original public understanding" of the Constitution. He was confirmed by a Senate vote of 78 to 22. Three hours later Roberts was sworn in as the 109th justice and seventeenth chief justice.

President Bush then faced competing pressures in selecting another nominee for Justice O'Connor's seat. Hispanic groups renewed pressure to name Attorney General Gonzales, but conservatives opposed him. Women's groups pushed for the appointment of a woman, while liberal Democratic senators urged the appointment of a moderate in the mold of Justice O'Connor. Shortly before the Court opened its 2005 term with Chief Justice Roberts presiding, Bush departed from Cheney's recommendations and nominated his friend and legal counselor, Harriet Miers. Within hours conservatives turned against her, contending that she was not a proven conservative and had no prior judicial experience. Criticisms quickly grew and finally Miers was pushed to withdraw. Even before she submitted her letter withdrawing, the White House discussed nominating Judge Samuel Alito Jr. of the U.S. Court of Appeals for the Third Circuit.[93]

Bush sought to satisfy his conservative base by nominating the fifty-five-year-old Judge Alito, who had been named to the federal bench in 1990 by President George H. W. Bush. Like Chief Justice Roberts, Alito had spent much of his early legal career working in the Reagan administration. As an attorney in the DoJ's Office of Legal Counsel and as an assistant to the solicitor general, he staked out positions opposing a woman's right to choose and affirmative action, as well as supporting limits on congressional power. As an appellate judge, he had a mixed record, though more conservative than that of Justice O'Connor. Indeed, in 2001 he was interviewed by the DoJ of George W. Bush's administration as a possible nominee for a future vacancy on the Court.[94]

During four days of testimony before the Senate Judiciary Committee, Alito appeared humble, while refusing to explain positions he held as an attorney in the Reagan administration and as an appellate court judge. The committee split along party lines, with all ten Republicans voting for him and the eight Democrats in opposition. The full Senate confirmed Alito as the 110th justice by a vote of 58 to 42.

At the end of April 2009, Justice Souter announced his retirement. President Barack Obama anticipated filling one or more vacancies on the high bench even before his election, and in December directed a small group of White House staff to begin the process of narrowing the pool of about forty potential nominees. The list was narrowed to nine, then to a final four—Second Circuit Court of Appeals Judge Sonia Sotomayor, Seventh Circuit Court of Appeals Judge Diane P. Wood, Solicitor General Elena Kagan, and Homeland Security Secretary Janet Napolitano. Although he knew Judge Wood from teaching at the University of Chicago and had appointed Kagan and Napolitano to positions in his administration, Obama had not met Judge Sotomayor until an interview on May 21, 2009. Five days later he announced her nomination, observing that she would bring diversity to the Court and had a compelling personal background and an impressive legal record. The fifty-five-year-old Judge Sotomayor grew up in the Bronx, the daughter of parents from Puerto Rico, and then went to Princeton University and Yale Law School. After spending five years as a prosecutor in Manhattan and then working in corporate practice, she was appointed in 1992 to the federal district court by the Republican President George H. W. Bush on the recommendation of the Democratic Senator Daniel Patrick Moynihan. She was then elevated to the Court of Appeals for the Second Circuit by President Clinton in 1998. In announcing her nomination, President Obama aimed to have the Democratically controlled Senate's confirmation by the beginning of the Court's term. After four days before the Senate Judiciary Committee, Sotomayor was confirmed by the Senate by a vote of 68 to 31 as the 111th justice, the first Latina, and the third woman to serve on the Court.

President Obama with his Supreme Court nominee, Judge Sonia Sotomayor.
(*AP Photo/Alex Brandon*)

Almost a year later, Justice Stevens announced that he would retire at the end of the 2009–2010 term. Appointed by President Ford in 1975, Justice Stevens had become the leader of liberals on the Court, following the retirements of Justices Brennan in 1990 and Marshall in 1991. Prior to announcing his nominee, Obama met again with Judge Wood and Solicitor General Kagan, along with appellate court judges Merrick Garland and Sidney Thomas. But, in fact, Obama's selection team contacted Kagan about serving on the Court more than a month before Stevens announced that he would retire. Kagan was born on the Lower East Side of Manhattan in 1960. She received her B.A. from Princeton in 1981, an M. Phil. from Oxford University in 1983, and her J.D. from Harvard Law School in 1986. Subsequently, Kagan clerked for Justice Thurgood Marshall, practiced law for three years, and taught at the University of Chicago Law School before serving in the Clinton administration from 1995–1999. Afterward, she taught at Harvard Law School and became a dean. President Obama appointed her SG in 2009. There was a fight with Republicans over her confirmation, but Obama planned on her confirmability. Ultimately, at age fifty, Kagan became the 112th justice, fourth woman, and eighth Jewish justice to serve on the Court.

When Obama had a third opportunity to fill a seat on the Court upon Justice Scalia's death in 2016, he confronted and was constrained even more by the obstructionism of the Republican-controlled Senate—bent on denying any nominee to fill Scalia's seat until after the 2016 presidential election. Obama responded by promising that a nominee would be (first) "eminently qualified," with "an independent mind, rigorous intellect, impeccable credentials, and a record of excellence and integrity"; (second) one who "recognizes the limits of the judiciary's role" and approaches "decisions without any particular ideology or agenda"; and (third) a judge with "a keen understanding that justice is not about abstract legal theory, nor some footnote in a dusty casebook. It's the kind of life experience earned outside the classroom and courtroom." Republicans and Obama's supporters alike expected him to name someone young, left of center, and, perhaps, the first Asian-American or African-American woman. But, instead, Obama called Senate Republicans' bluff by selecting Chief Judge Merrick B. Garland, a sixty-three-year-old Jewish judge, who had served almost two decades on the D.C. Circuit. Republican senators nevertheless opposed his elevation based on "principle"— that is, they wanted to let the people decide who should fill Scalia's seat after the outcome of the 2016 presidential election.

As the 2016 Republican presidential candidate, Donald Trump promised to nominate someone in the mold of Justice Scalia, who would overturn *Roe v. Wade* and defend the Second Amendment right to bear arms. He initially released a list of eleven possible candidates and later a second, expanded list of twenty-one (on which Gorsuch was included), and then a third (on which Kavanaugh was added). The list was complied by White House counsel Donald McGahn based on the recommendations of the Federalist Society and the Heritage Foundation, and Leo Leonard, executive vice president of the Federalist Society, who was hired to serve as an adviser. The list was subsequently narrowed to six and then three—all federal appellate court judges: Thomas Handiman, Richard Pryor, and Neil Gorsuch. Opposition developed against Pryor from conservatives because of some votes in LGBTQ cases, and from the left due in part to his characterizing *Roe v. Wade* as "the worst abomination of constitutional law in our history." Handiman faced less opposition but was passed over in favor of Gorsuch, who appeared slightly more "mainstream" though still a judge with a strong conservative judicial philosophy akin to Scalia's "originalism." He also had Ivy League credentials, graduating from Columbia University, Harvard Law School, and earning a D. Phil at Oxford University, as well as a decade serving on the federal appellate bench. Moreover, he was young (at age forty-nine, he could possibly sit on the bench for at least three decades), from the Midwest, and a Protestant (an Episcopalian, though raised as a Catholic). In addition, he clerked for Justice Kennedy and, on the bench, might move him in more conservative directions—perhaps even leading him to retire, thereby giving Trump a second opportunity to shift the balance on the bench farther to the right.

With the Republican-controlled Senate and Democrats embittered by the majority's refusal to give Chief Judge Garland a hearing, a confirmation battle was certain. Trump urged the Senate to invoke the so-called "nuclear option" of abolishing the rule permitting filibustering of Supreme Court nominees, requiring 60 votes for confirmation, instead of a simple majority. The Senate majority leader, Mitch McConnell, initially opposed that, but after Democrats marshalled enough votes (52) to filibuster, the Senate voted along party lines (52 to 48) to no longer allow filibusters of nominees to the Court. McConnell later rationalized the matter as "political"; in his words, "advice and consent" means "whatever a majority at a given moment think it means."

Gorsuch's three-day confirmation hearing proved low-key. He refused to answer basic questions about precedent and doctrine, portraying himself as a "Scalia look-alike" and preferring to discuss fly fishing in Colorado.[95] In the end, Gorsuch was confirmed by a vote of 54 to 45, becoming the 113th justice and the only justice to sit with a justice for whom he clerked. (Five earlier clerks were named to the Court but after the justice for whom they clerked was no longer sitting; White, Rehnquist, Stevens, Breyer, Roberts, and Kagan clerked, respectively, for Vinson, Jackson, Rutledge, Goldberg, Rehnquist, and Marshall.)

On the last day of the 2017–2018 term, Justice Kennedy announced his retirement. Trump moved quickly to nominate a successor, briefly interviewing seven potential nominees—all judges drawn from the Federalist Society's list—before settling on Court of Appeals for the D.C. Circuit Judge Brett M. Kavanaugh. Like Gorsuch, Kavanaugh clerked with Kennedy, was young enough (at age fifty-three) to serve for three decades, and (like Roberts, Thomas, Alito, and Gorsuch) closely linked to the Federalist Society. Moreover, he held the promise of locking in a strong conservative majority, since Kennedy turned out to be a pragmatic, not ideological, conservative who in his thirty years on the bench became a "swing voter," casting the pivotal vote on controversial social issues like abortion and same-sex marriages; hence, he had proven a profound disappointment for Reaganites and those in the Federalist Society.

Kavanaugh was expected to be controversial for a number of reasons: he would lock in a solid conservative majority on the Court, was an outspoken critic of many of the Court's rulings, and had a sharply partisan background. Indeed, McConnell advised Trump against his nomination. After graduating from Yale Law School, he clerked for two federal appellate judges and held a fellowship in the Office of Independent Counsel, headed by

Kenneth Starr, before clerking for Kennedy, and then returned to work for Starr's investigation of President Clinton's affair with Monica Lewinsky. After George W. Bush became president in 2001, he worked as an associate to the White House counsel and later as an assistant in the Office of the President and as White House Staff Secretary. In 2003, Bush nominated him to the Court of Appeals for the D.C. Circuit, but opposition and contentious Senate hearings delayed his appointment until 2006. Kavanaugh's hearings raised more concerns than they answered, and inconsistencies in his testimony raised questions about his veracity. The ABA had rated him "well qualified" but downgraded its rating to "qualified," because he appeared to lack "open mindedness." In the end, he was confirmed for a seat on the D.C. Circuit by a 51-to-49 vote.

Kavanaugh's 2018 Senate hearings were even more contentious. He testified for two days during the four-day hearing. His veracity was again questioned when it came to working in the Bush White House; he was also evasive and less than forthcoming about his view of presidential power, the ongoing investigations of President Trump, and his dissent in a D.C. Circuit ruling permitting a young, illegal immigrant held in detention to terminate her pregnancy, though he said *Roe v. Wade* was "settled law" but declined further explanation. In addition, the Republican majority and the White House declined to release to the Judiciary Committee 90 percent of his records from working in the Bush administration. Then, after the committee concluded its hearings, the unexpected happened. A confidential letter from a California professor alleging she was sexually assaulted by Kavanaugh when they were attending prep schools thirty years earlier was leaked to the media. The letter, from Christine Blasey Ford, had been sent to Senator Dianne Feinstein (D-Calif.) prior to Kavanaugh's nomination. Immediately, there were demands for a second round of hearings, amid other accusations of Kavanaugh's drunkenness and sexual misconduct in high school and college. The Republican majority on the committee finally agreed to a one-day hearing on

Ford's allegations and Kavanaugh's responses, and then to send the nomination to the full Senate for a vote. For his part, Kavanaugh spent most of the following week in the White House with lawyers participating in "murder boards"—practicing answering potential questions about his personal and professional life.

At the Judiciary Committee's hearing, Ford appeared sincere and credible, testifying that she had a polygraph test and was "absolutely" certain Kavanaugh assaulted her, while one of his classmates watched. Yet, there were gaps in her memory and, except for what she had told her husband and therapist years earlier, no corroboration. By contrast, Kavanaugh was angry and passionate in his denials and, conceding Ford had been sexually assaulted, claimed it was a case of mistaken identity. He also criticized the hearings for becoming a "circus," a "calculated and orchestrated hit" by Democrats and "revenge on behalf of the Clintons" for his role in the Starr investigation. In an unprecedented fashion, he singled out Democratic senators to ask whether they had ever been drunk or had blackouts. In his words, the committee's "advice and consent" role had become a "search and destroy" mission.

The committee voted along party lines (11 to 10) to advance the nomination to the full Senate for a vote. But, at the urging of Senator Jeff Flake (R-Ariz.) and Democrats, only if the FBI conducted a one-week, limited background investigation of the allegations. In the week that followed, protests grew over not allowing other witnesses to testify, other allegations of sexual misconduct and drunkenness arose, and demands increased for the FBI to interview Ford and Kavanaugh and other witnesses. Still, the Republican majority stood firm in limiting the FBI's investigation and promised a vote at the end of the week.

Kavanaugh's confirmation hearings were unprecedented in a number of ways. No nominee in recent decades (if ever) gave as starkly aggressive and partisan testimony. Moreover, before the Senate's vote, Kavanaugh defended himself in an extraordinary television interview on Fox News, and the next day published in

The Roberts Court, 2019. From left to right, top row: Neil Gorsuch, Sonia Sotomayor, Elena Kagan, Brett M. Kavanaugh; bottom row: Stephen Breyer, Clarence Thomas, John G. Roberts, Ruth Bader Ginsburg, Samuel Alito Jr. (*Kevin Dietsch/picture-alliance/dpa/AP Images*)

the *Wall Street Journal* an op-ed piece, "I Am an Independent, Impartial Judge."[96] No less unusual, retired Justice John Paul Stevens publicly said that Kavanaugh was not qualified to sit on the high bench. Ultimately, the Senate voted 50 to 48, with Senator Joe Manchin (D-W.Va.) joining Republicans, the closest vote since 1881.[97]

Betrayed by Justice

"Whenever you put a man on the Supreme Court he ceases to be your friend. I'm sure of that." Lamenting that "packing the Supreme Court simply can't be done," Truman confessed, "I've tried and it won't work."[98] Like other disappointed presidents, Truman felt he had misjudged his appointee. "Tom Clark was my biggest mistake. No question about it." With characteristic blunt-ness, he expressed his disillusionment:

That damn fool from Texas that I first made Attorney General and then put on the Supreme Court. I don't know what got into me. He was no damn good as Attorney General, and on the Supreme Court . . . it doesn't seem possible, but he's been even worse. He hasn't made one right decision that I can think of. . . . It's just that he's such a dumb son of a bitch.[99]

In a letter to Justice Douglas, Truman further explained that he could not "see how a Court made up of so-called 'Liberals' could do what that Court did to" him in *Youngstown Sheet & Tube Co. v. Sawyer* (1952).[100] Six members—including two of his appointees, Tom Clark and Harold Burton—held that Truman had exceeded his power by seizing steel mills in order to avert a nationwide strike that, he claimed, threatened the country's war effort in Korea. Chief Justice Vinson and Justice Minton, his other two appointees, dissented along with Stanley Reed. The ruling was Truman's "*Dred Scott* decision." He felt that it "seriously ham-strung" the modern presidency.[101]

Clark's desertion was especially troubling because earlier, as attorney general, Clark advised Truman that he had the power to deal with such emergencies. That was not the first time, however, that an appointee changed his mind on an important constitutional question after coming to the Court. Lincoln's sec-retary of the treasury Salmon Chase wrote the Legal Tender Acts, allowing the use of paper money to repay the Union's debts incurred in the Civil War. But after his confirmation as chief jus-tice, he struck them down in *Hepburn v. Griswold* (1870) and then dissented when a new majority overturned that decision a year later in the *Legal Tender* cases (1871). Justice Jackson like-wise reversed himself on a position he had taken as attorney gen-eral, explaining simply, "The matter does not appear to me now as it appears to have appeared to me then."[102]

Like most presidents, Truman expected loyalty. Yet justices frequently disappoint their presidential benefactors. Two years after joining the Court, Justice Holmes disappointed President Theodore Roosevelt by voting against his administration's anti-trust policies. The president was prompted to observe that he "could carve out of a banana a Judge with more backbone than that!"[103] FDR "thought that Judge Frankfurter was going to be a flaming liberal, but he turned out in many areas to be a rank conservative." Tom Clark also recalled how Eisenhower was "very much disturbed over Chief Justice Warren and Justice Brennan."[104] Byron White disappointed the Kennedys.[105] Nixon was surprised when Burger voted in *United States v. Nixon* (1974) to deny his claim of executive privilege as a shield against having to turn over the Watergate tapes. Blackmun also proved a disappointment because of his authorship of the ruling on abortion in *Roe v. Wade*. Likewise, Justices Kennedy, O'Connor, and Souter disappointed supporters of Presidents Reagan and George H. W. Bush when voting to uphold *Roe* in *Planned Parenthood of Southeastern Pennsylvania v. Casey* (1992). Justice Kennedy was especially disappointing for conservatives when he cast the crucial vote and authored the majority opinion of *Obergefell v. Hodges* (2015), extending constitutional protection to same-sex marriages, among other decisions. Likewise Chief Justice Roberts disappointed when he delivered the Court's opinions upholding the Affordable Care Act (Obamacare).[106]

Presidential efforts to pack the Court are only partially successful, for a number of reasons. "Neither the President nor his appointee can foresee what issues will come before the Court during the tenure of the appointees," Chief Justice Rehnquist once pointed out. "Even though they agree as to the proper resolution of [past or] current cases, they may well disagree as to future cases involving other questions when, as judges, they study briefs and hear arguments. Longevity of the appointees, or untimely deaths such as those of Justices Murphy and Rutledge, may also frustrate a President's expectations; so also may the personal antagonism developed between strong-willed appointees of the same President." Fundamentally, presidents are disappointed because they fail to understand "that the Supreme Court is an institution far more dominated by centrifugal forces, pushing towards individuality and independence, than it is by centripetal forces pulling for hierarchical ordering and institutional unity."[107]

There is no denying that presidents influence Supreme Court decision making through their appointments. One or two appointments can make a crucial difference in the direction of Supreme Court policy making.[108] But life in the marble temple also frustrates presidential attempts to influence that direction. "The Court functions in a way," Justice Jackson concluded, "that is pleasing to an individualist." Each justice gets to the Court "under his own steam" and, Douglas observed, becomes "a sovereign in his own right."[109] Unlike the presidency, the Court does not have a "mission." Phrases like "the Court as an institution" and "the Court as a team," Frankfurter concluded, amount to question-begging clichés.[110] Each member serves justice in his or her own way. Justices also change and react differently to life in the marble temple.

Off-the-Bench Activities

The myth of the cult of the robe—that justices are "legal monks" removed from political life—has been perpetuated by justices such as Frankfurter, who hypocritically proclaimed, "When a priest enters a monastery, he must leave—or ought to leave—all sorts of worldly desires behind him. And this Court has no excuse for being unless it's a monastery."[111]

The reality is that justices are political actors and have found it more or less hard to refrain from outside political activities. More than seventy of those who have sat on the Court advised presidents and members of Congress about matters of domestic and foreign policy, patronage appointments, judgeships, and legislation affecting the judiciary.[112] Even more justices have made their views on public policy known through speeches and publications.[113] Justice Gorsuch, for one, shortly after joining the Court, drew sharp criticism for addressing the Federalist Society's gala and then a conservative group's luncheon at the Trump International Hotel in Washington, D.C. The ethics code of the U.S. Judicial Conference prohibits judges from being "a speaker or the guest of honor at an organization's fund-raising events" and making partisan endorsements. But the code does not apply to members of the Court, and occasionally justices invite criticism for appearing to engage in ideological activities. However, in the 1990 term the Court adopted its own ethics guidelines. Under them, if justices are offered honoraria or compensation for teaching short courses or seminars, the details of the arrangement are disclosed and approved by all the justices at a conference. Still, in 2012, Chief Justice Roberts told the Senate Judiciary Committee that the Court would not adopt a binding ethical code and that the rules governing lower federal court judges do not apply to them.[114]

POLITICAL CAMPAIGNING AND CONSULTING

Justice Ginsburg—known as the "Notorious RBG"—created a stir in a 2016 CNN interview by calling the Republican Party's presidential nominee, Donald Trump, a "faker"; she later admitted: "In the future, I will be more circumspect." Most justices, nonetheless, now frequently offer their extrajudicial observations in lectures, interviews, and books.

Moreover, for much of the Court's early history, justices used their positions for political influence. Chief Justice Marshall served for brief periods as secretary of state, and Oliver Ellsworth accepted the post of minister to France. Chief Justice Salmon Chase sought the presidency in 1868, and throughout the rest of the nineteenth century numerous justices worked actively for presidential candidates. With the growing institutional prestige of the Court in the twentieth century, fewer justices sought greener political pastures. Hughes resigned as associate justice after he was nominated Republican presidential candidate in 1916, whereas Douglas, Vinson, and Warren declined opportunities to run as national political candidates.

A far more prevalent activity has been consulting on public policy. Justices on the pre-Marshall Court frequently offered advice. Yet when President Washington formally requested the Court's views on a treaty in 1793, it responded that there were "considerations which afford strong arguments against the propriety of our extra-judicially deciding such questions."[115] The letter of 1793 remains a precedent for the Court's not rendering advisory opinions. But justices have not felt precluded from giving their individual views off the bench on issues of public policy.

In the twentieth century, virtually all chief justices served as presidential consultants. Taft pursued the broadest range of activities. He helped shape the 1924 Republican Party platform and regularly advised Presidents Harding and Coolidge on everything from patronage appointments and judicial reform to legislation.[116] Stone was an intimate adviser of Hoover, joining his "Medicine Ball Cabinet," at which policy questions as well as an exercise ball were thrown around. When Roosevelt came into office, Stone thought that his advisory role would end, but he cultivated a relationship with FDR and continued to offer advice on problems with the Court and even on the DoJ's conduct of criminal prosecutions.[117]

Vinson was an intimate adviser of Truman, frequently conferring with him by telephone or on fishing trips to Key West.[118] Eisenhower met with Warren and asked his attorney general to seek the chief justice's advice on pending cases before the Court.[119] Both the Kennedy and the Johnson administrations went to Warren for advice on judicial appointments and other matters. According to Nixon's White House aide John Ehrlichman, Burger "sent a steady stream of notes and letters to Nixon" in his campaign to reform judicial administration. Ehrlichman also claimed, though both Nixon and Burger denied it, that the president and the attorney general "openly discussed with the Chief Justice the pros and cons of issues before the Court."[120] Moreover, Nixon's presidential papers contain numerous letters from Burger, including some advice and historical support for Nixon's claims to White House confidentiality, on which the Court eventually ruled and rejected in *United States v. Nixon* (1974).[121]

Just as justices seek to influence presidents, the latter have tried to influence the former. Warren recalled two such instances. The first occurred at the White House when *Brown v. Board of Education* was being considered. At a dinner, the newly appointed chief justice sat next to President Eisenhower and within speaking range of John W. Davis, who was representing South Carolina's segregated schools in a companion case before the Court with *Brown*. During dinner conversation, Eisenhower stressed "what a great man Mr. Davis was." Afterward he took Warren by the arm, and as they walked to another room and spoke of the southern states in the segregation cases, he observed, "These are not bad people. All they are concerned about is that their sweet little girls are not required to sit in school alongside some big overgrown Negroes."[122] The second incident occurred in the first months of the Nixon administration, shortly after the Court ruled against the government in some wiretapping cases. Attorney General Mitchell worried about other pending cases and sent the DoJ's public information officer Jack C. Landau to talk with Brennan and Warren. If the Court disapproved of the government's wiretapping practices, Landau told them, the electronic surveillance of over forty-eight foreign embassies might be jeopardized. Warren was appalled at "this surreptitious attempt to influence the Court."[123]

Isn't it wrong for justices and presidents to consult with each other? The traditional view was well expressed by Senator Sam Ervin during the confirmation hearing on the nomination of Fortas as chief justice in 1968:

I just think it is the height of impropriety for a Supreme Court justice, no matter how close he may have been to the President, to advise him or consult with him on matters, public matters, that properly belong within the realm of the executive branch of Government, and which may wind up in the form of litigation before the Court.[124]

History, nevertheless, is replete with instances of justices advising presidents, and standards of judicial propriety evolve. Ultimately, the crucial point is whether off-the-bench activities bring the Court into a political controversy. Fortas's relationship with LBJ and the battle over his confirmation as chief justice illustrate, perhaps, the extreme consequences of off-the-bench activities.

Fortas's relationship with LBJ was by no means unprecedented. FDR, for example, had relied on advice from Brandeis, who had been an adviser to President Wilson. "I need Brandeis everywhere," Wilson observed, "but I must leave him somewhere."[125] A respected "prophet of reform," Brandeis stood as a "judicial idol" for New Deal lawyers. During the early years of the New Deal, Brandeis used Frankfurter, who was then a professor at Harvard Law School, as his "scribe," his intermediary for promoting his ideas in the Roosevelt administration.[126] But the "Brandeis/Frankfurter connection" was neither deemed newsworthy nor improper in Washington political circles.[127]

When Roosevelt filled vacancies on the Court, he continued to turn to his appointees for advice. Shortly after leaving the post of SG, Justice Reed sent a note requesting a meeting with FDR and revealed the attitude of the Roosevelt Court toward its president. "If it is not too much of an intrusion," he wrote, "[our meeting] will help me to maintain, in some degree, my understanding of your objectives."[128] After Frankfurter joined the Court, he continued his advisory relationship, though his constant meddling sometimes backfired. Frankfurter competed for influence with others on the Court; Stone, Black, and Douglas also advised the president on judicial appointments and other matters of public policy. Murphy frequently met with FDR to discuss the war in the

Justice Abe Fortas with National Security Adviser Clark Clifford, advising President Lyndon Johnson in the Oval Office of the White House. (*Lyndon B. Johnson Presidential Library*)

Pacific, and Byrnes, during his brief one-year stay on the bench, continued to offer advice on the constitutionality of legislation.[129] Unlike Frankfurter, after FDR's death Douglas continued to offer advice to Truman, Kennedy, and Johnson on concerns ranging from saving the redwoods in the West and protecting the environment to Soviet influence in the Middle East and the wisdom of diplomatic recognition of China.[130] When a president like FDR and justices find commonality of purpose and personal and ideological compatibility, consultations are, perhaps, inevitable and questions of propriety are overlooked.

Johnson's relationship with Abe Fortas was more intimate and extensive than that of FDR with his Court, however. It stemmed from the days of the New Deal and was shaped by the experience of those associated with the inner circle of Democratic politics dating back to the Roosevelt administration. LBJ considered

Fortas to be in his elite group of foreign policy advisers. Regularly joining White House meetings on the Vietnam War, Fortas attended more cabinet meetings than the man he replaced on the bench, UN Ambassador Arthur Goldberg, who was one of the few "doves" in the administration.[131] "Should we get out of Vietnam?" was the central question at the November 2, 1967 meeting of the foreign policy advisers (and a question continually debated throughout LBJ's term). "The public would be outraged if we got out," Fortas observed. "What about our course in North Vietnam?" The president asked, "Should we continue as is; go further, moderate it; eliminate the bombing?" Both "hawks" on the war, "Fortas and Clark Clifford recommended continued bombing as we are doing."[132]

Fortas was no less active in the formulation of domestic policy. He attended meetings on fiscal policy, labor legislation, election reform, and campaign financing, often offering his views on matters that would eventually come before the courts.[133] Senator Thruston Morton remembered making a telephone call to learn LBJ's position on pending legislation and being told, "Well, the President is away, but Mr. Justice Fortas is here and he's managing the bill for the White House."[134] Fortas also helped write LBJ's speeches and messages to Congress on civil rights and criminal justice reform, and recommended individuals for federal judgeships.[135]

Fortas's nomination for the chief justiceship was defeated, but not primarily because of his advising LBJ. Even after it was revealed that he accepted $15,000 for teaching a seminar at American University, the public supported confirmation by a 2-to-1 margin.[136] Several factors contributed to his defeat. LBJ overestimated his influence after announcing that he would not seek reelection. Anticipating Nixon's victory in the 1968 election, Republican senators wanted to deny him any appointments to the Court. White House advisers also told LBJ that it was a mistake to name another close personal friend, Homer Thornberry, to fill the vacancy that would be created by Fortas's promotion.[137]

Senate opposition focused on Fortas's support of the Warren Court's "liberal jurisprudence." Defeat, Fortas told Warren, ultimately came from the "bitter, corrosive opposition to all that has been happening in the Court and the country: the racial progress and the insistence upon increased regard for human rights and dignity in the field of criminal law. Other elements," he added, "contribute to the mix, but it's my guess that they are minor."[138] Shortly before he asked LBJ to withdraw his nomination, Fortas explained to Justice Harlan that he had "not been a governmental 'busybody'" and "never 'volunteered' suggestions or participation in the affairs of State. On the other hand," he went on, "I felt that I had no alternative to complying with the President's request for participation in the matters where he sought my help—or more precisely, sought the comfort of hearing my summation before his decision—That's about what it amounted to in the case of President Johnson." He had no regrets about his off-the-bench activities and did not believe that he "injured the Court as an institution."[139]

Less than a year later, however, Fortas resigned from the Court. He did so because of further publicity that he accepted $20,000 as an adviser to the Wolfson Family Foundation, which was devoted to racial and religious cooperation. Fortas had terminated his relationship with the foundation during his first year on the Court and returned the $20,000. He conceded "no wrong doing." But, Fortas told Warren, "the public controversy relating to my association with the foundation is likely to continue and adversely affect the work and position of the Court." The Court's prestige, he concluded, "prompts my resignation which, I hope, by terminating the public controversy, will permit the Court to proceed with its work without harassment of debate concerning one of its members."[140]

Off-the-bench consultations and honoraria for justices' lectures and teaching of seminars remain matters of some controversy. Justices often recuse themselves from participating in cases, but they generally do not explain why. There are no fixed rules for recusal. Some of the justices also disagree with and do not feel personally bound by the Court's rulings on when lower federal-court judges should recuse themselves. In *Liljeberg v. Health Services Acquisition Corporation* (1988), for instance, Justice Stevens held that judges should recuse themselves when "a reasonable person" knowing the relevant facts would expect them to know of a conflict requiring their disqualification. But Chief Justice Rehnquist and Justices Scalia and White dissented.[141]

Justices never strictly observed what Frankfurter termed "judicial lockjaw." While Justices Thomas and Alito tend to avoid the limelight and remain guarded about making off-the-bench remarks (except before small groups and law schools), they are exceptions. Justices Thomas, Ginsburg, Breyer, Sotomayor, Kagan, and Gorsuch often lecture at law schools and other forums. Overall, in the last thirty years most of the justices have been more high-profile, and increasingly give lectures and interviews as well as make off-the-bench comments.[142] Indeed, some lower court judges and Court watchers refer to them as "celebrity justices."[143]

Special Assignments

Justices have either volunteered or given in to presidential pressure to assume the duties of quasi-diplomats, arbitrators of foreign and domestic controversies, and heads of commissions, particularly in the nineteenth and early twentieth centuries. The practice began when Jay and Ellsworth served as special envoys to Great Britain and France. During the Civil War era, Samuel Nelson was an intermediary for peace proposals to southern states. In 1876, however, a controversy over off-the-bench public service seriously threatened the Court's prestige. Congress had established a commission to resolve the disputed presidential election of 1876 between the Republican Rutherford Hayes and the Democrat Samuel Tilden. The commission included three Republican and two Democratic senators, two Republican and three Democratic representatives, and five justices—two from each party and the fifth, the Republican Joseph Bradley, designated by the Court. When Bradley cast the deciding vote giving the election to Hayes, attacks on the partisanship of the Court were inevitable. In his dissenting opinion in *Bush v. Gore* (2000), Justice Breyer cited the 1876 controversy in charging that the Court should have stayed out of the dispute over the 2000 presidential election. The fact that there were five justices on the commission, including Justice Bradley, "did not lend that process legitimacy." "Nor," he said, "did it assure the public that the process had worked fairly, guided by the law. Rather it simply embroiled members of the Court in partisan conflict." Chief Justice Rehnquist agreed that the Hayes-Tilden controversy hurt the Court but contended that the commission helped avert violence over the election.[144]

Justices became more reluctant to assume special assignments after the controversy over the Hayes-Tilden commission. A number, though, nevertheless served on nonpartisan commissions and investigatory bodies. But the potential for controversy and the burden of work at the Court during the twentieth century persuaded many to resist taking on additional duties. Stone was prevailed on by his brethren not to accept Hoover's offer of chairmanship of the Law Enforcement Commission. He declined FDR's plan to make him the "rubber czar" during World War II, when rubber products were in short supply, and turned down Truman's proposal that he head the National Traffic Safety Commission.[145] The patriotic spirit sparked by World War II nonetheless led several justices to accept off-the-bench assignments. Owen Roberts chaired the Commission to Investigate the Pearl Harbor Disaster. When Frank Murphy was denied a military commission because of his age, he joined the army reserves. He went to boot camp during summer recess; begged FDR for special military assignments; and much to the ire of Chief Justice Stone, drew a salary both as a justice and as a commissioned army officer.[146]

Justice Jackson's absence from the bench while serving as chief prosecutor at the Nuremberg trials of Nazi war crimes created serious problems. Within the Court his acceptance of the post was opposed, his absence was resented, and his failure to vote on cases when the others were evenly divided was extremely aggravating. Antagonism toward Jackson ran deep and, in Justice Burton's words, "the failure of any member to bear his full share of the work immediately results in increasing the burdens of the other members of the Court."[147]

Justices have since been reluctant to assume additional time-consuming duties. Chief Justice Warren, though, finally gave in to LBJ's request that he head the commission to investigate the assassination of JFK. Yet, Chief Justice Burger took great pleasure in serving as chancellor of the Smithsonian Institution, but that was not the case with his successors, who had less interest in these kinds of extrajudicial activities.

The Constitution, however, assigns chief justices the special role of presiding over Senate trials of presidents who have been impeached by the House of Representatives. In 1868, Chief Justice Salmon Chase presided over the trial of the Democratic President Andrew Johnson for firing his secretary of war in violation of the Tenure in Office Act of 1867. In 1999, Chief Justice Rehnquist presided over the trial of President Clinton, who was impeached and tried for allegedly committing perjury before a grand jury and obstructing justice in covering up evidence pertaining to his sexual relationship with White House intern Monica Lewinsky. In 2020, Chief Justice John Roberts presided over the trial of Donald Trump for his alleged attempt to pressure the Ukrainian government to investigate a political opponent and an obstruction of justice. Presidents Clinton and Trump were both narrowly acquitted.

Congressional Lobbying

Judicial lobbying for legislation has a long history. On legislation affecting the administration of justice in particular, Chief Justice Burger insisted, "the separation of powers concept was never remotely intended to preclude cooperation, coordination, communication and joint efforts."[148]

Virtually all major legislation affecting the Court's jurisdiction was drafted by justices and came about as the result of their lobbying. John Jay, James Iredell, and Thomas Johnson lobbied for modifications in the Judiciary Act of 1789 and for the elimination of circuit riding. Joseph Story advised his friend in the House of Representatives, Daniel Webster, on judicial reform and drafted legislation on criminal punishment, bankruptcy, and the jurisdiction of federal courts. In the 1840s John Catron actively lobbied for judicial improvements.[149] Chief Justice Salmon Chase and Justice Samuel Miller later pushed bills giving the Court some relief from its growing caseload. The latter wrote in 1872, "I have prepared and carried through the House a bill curtailing our jurisdiction and facilitating its exercise. I can do no more, and shall leave the responsibility where it belongs."[150] Miller's proposals achieved some success in 1875 and 1879, but Chief Justices Morrison Waite and Melville Fuller and others continued to press for the elimination of circuit-riding duties and for the expansion of the Court's discretionary power to decide which cases should be granted review. Their lobbying finally succeeded in 1891, when Congress passed the Circuit Court of Appeals Act, eliminating circuit riding and creating federal courts of appeal.

Notably, Chief Justice William Taft championed major reforms in judicial administration. "If you go pussyfooting," the former president and unblushing judicial lobbyist observed, "my experience convinces me that you will fail."[151] Relying on Justices Van Devanter, Day, and McReynolds to draft proposed legislation, Taft successfully lobbied Congress to enact the Judges' Bill, or Judiciary Act of 1925, which established the basic jurisdiction of the modern Court.[152] Chief Justice Hughes was more reserved but no less shrewd. When Roosevelt sent his Court-packing plan to Congress, Hughes responded with a letter to the Senate Judiciary Committee implying that all the justices opposed the plan. As he hoped, Senator Burton Wheeler proclaimed that the justices were "unanimous with reference to the letter of the Chief Justice." The letter was skillfully written to give that impression, but Hughes had in fact talked only with Van Devanter and Brandeis. Cardozo and Stone strongly disapproved of Hughes's action and would have refused to sign the letter but were not consulted.[153]

Since Taft, chief justices have used a number of organizations in lobbying Congress. The Judicial Conference, established in 1922 and chaired by the chief justice, is the principal policy-making body of the federal judiciary. It develops rules of procedure for federal courts and recommends or responds to proposed legislation affecting the courts.[154] The Administrative Office of the United States Courts, created in 1939, studies federal caseloads and helps implement recommendations of the chief justice and the Judicial Conference. The Federal Judicial Center, established in 1969, undertakes research projects aimed at improving the administration of justice.

Chief justices have a number of other ways of coopting members of Congress and mobilizing support. After Taft, Burger was the most active in lobbying Congress and getting the assistance of the ABA in promoting his proposals. Rehnquist did not share his predecessor's preoccupation with judicial administration, but as head of the federal judiciary he publicly called on Congress not to expand federal courts' jurisdiction "into areas of the law that have traditionally been reserved to state courts." In his annual reports on the state of the federal judiciary, Chief Justice Roberts has been even more circumspect—primarily urging Congress to address the problems of salary and workload of federal judges, although once lamenting how the confirmation process has become too partisan and politicized. However, in November 2018 Roberts issued an extraordinary rebuke of President Trump's criticisms of a federal district court judge in California who blocked a new asylum ban on those seeking asylum except at an official border entry point. Trump criticized him for being an "Obama judge" and further attacked the Court of Appeals for the Ninth Circuit—the largest circuit, covering nine western states with 20 percent of the nation's population, and known for left-of-center rulings.

Throughout his presidential campaign and first two years in the Oval Office, Trump periodically blasted the Ninth Circuit for decisions blocking his initial travel ban on those from predominately Muslim countries, among other decisions, as "a terrible, costly, and dangerous disgrace," along with proclaiming Roberts "an absolute disaster" for his pivotal vote upholding portions of the Affordable Care Act (Obamacare) of 2012, in *National Federation of Independent Business* (2012). Roberts, defending the independence and integrity of the federal courts, countered, "We do not have Obama judges or Trump judges, Bush judges or Clinton judges. . . . What we have [are] dedicated judges doing their level best. . . ." Trump in turn responded via Twitter: "Sorry Chief Justice John Roberts, but you do indeed have 'Obama judges,' and they have a much different point of view than the people who are charged with the safety of our country."

Independence and Accountability

Justices enjoy a remarkable degree of independence. Article III of the Constitution prohibits Congress from diminishing their salary and provides for lifetime tenure, subject to "good behavior." Article II contains the threat of removal by impeachment in the House of Representatives and a trial and conviction by the Senate for "high crimes and misdemeanors."

Salaries have historically ranged somewhat below that of leading members of the legal profession. Associate justices make $255,300 and the chief justice, $267,000. Moreover, they may still earn book royalties and speaking and teaching fees, as well as reimbursement of travel expenses abroad to give lectures or attend conferences. Justices Thomas and Sotomayor, for instance, received million-dollar advances for their autobiographies.

Removal from office has never been a serious threat. Impeachment is a "mere scarecrow," concluded Thomas Jefferson, after the unsuccessful 1805 effort to convict Samuel Chase for expounding

Federalist philosophy while riding circuit. Forty-seven federal judges have been subject to impeachment proceedings, but only fifteen faced trials and only eight were convicted. Chase and William Douglas were the only two Supreme Court justices to confront the possibility of impeachment. Chase was acquitted, and two impeachment resolutions against Douglas failed to pass the House. Douglas was attacked in 1953 for his temporary stay of executions of the convicted spies Julius and Ethel Rosenberg, and then again in 1970.

The drive to remove Douglas in 1970 illustrates the political difficulties of impeachment. After Fortas resigned in 1969 and Nixon's first two nominees to fill his seat were defeated, House Republicans sought to impeach Douglas in retaliation. A 1966 *Los Angeles Times* story had disclosed that Douglas was receiving $12,000 a year as a consultant to the Parvin Foundation, which funded seminars on Latin America and on combating the forces of international communism. In light of Fortas's resignation and his association with the Wolfson Foundation, Douglas's activity became newsworthy again. Shortly after Fortas resigned from the Court, Douglas resigned from the Parvin Foundation.

To the House Republican leader, Gerald Ford, the activities of Douglas stretched the ABA's canon of judicial ethics that a "judge's official conduct should be free from impropriety and *the appearance of impropriety*." Although Douglas's relationship with the Parvin Foundation had been known, the allegation of impropriety was politically opportune for Republicans.

What really disturbed Ford and others was Douglas's lifestyle and judicial philosophy. Ford, as his legislative assistant Robert Hartmann recalled, "disapproved of Douglas the way a Grand Rapids housewife would deplore the behavior of certain movie stars. The old man [Douglas] took too many wives and he seemed to encourage any new fad in youthful rebellion."[155] Antagonism grew, and House Republicans pressed Ford to do something when an excerpt of Douglas's book *Points of Rebellion* appeared in *Evergreen*, a left-wing magazine.

When Ford finally went to the floor of the House to call for a special committee to investigate Douglas, Representative Andrew Jacobs, a Democrat, beat him to the punch by introducing a resolution for impeachment. Under the rules of the House, the matter immediately went to the Judiciary Committee, which at the time was controlled by Democrats. After the committee found no grounds for impeachment, Ford called it a "travesty." He continued to maintain that "over the past decade Justice Douglas' extensive extra-judicial earnings and activities have impaired his usefulness and clouded his contribution to the United States Supreme Court."[156] Yet the momentum for impeachment had declined by the time of the committee's report. The Senate had confirmed Blackmun, Nixon's third nominee for Fortas's seat. Douglas's association with the Parvin Foundation also no longer appeared extraordinary in view of the revelation during Blackmun's confirmation hearing that as a federal appellate court judge, he was associated with the Mayo Clinic.

The drive to remove Douglas also was made difficult by disagreement on the standard for removing justices. Some members of Congress contend that judges may be removed for failure to maintain "good behavior" or for "willful misconduct in office, willful and persistent failure to perform duties in the office, habitual intemperance, or other conduct prejudicial to the administration of justice that brings the judicial office into disrepute." By contrast, others claim that impeachment requires conviction for an indictable criminal offense. During his attempt to remove Douglas, Ford claimed that the two standards are essentially the same and depend on "historical context and political climate." A justice may be removed, Ford contended, for "whatever a majority of the House of Representatives [decides] at a given moment in history."[157] That position would severely limit judicial independence and make members of the Court sensitive to political opposition in Congress. But the Founders sought to ensure judicial independence by making removal possible only by impeachment, and no federal judge has been impeached except for a criminal offense.

Although impeachment is rare, neither the Court nor the justices are totally unaccountable. The Court is institutionally accountable for its decisions (discussed further in Chapter 6). Other political institutions and public opinion may thwart and openly defy particular rulings. Justices are subject to the norms of life in the marble temple. A kind of internal institutional accountability is imposed by the processes of decision making. Lower-court judges and leading members of the legal profession impose an additional measure of professional accountability through personal communications and legal publications. Justices also look to their place in history. Like all political actors, they desire, in the words of Adam Smith, "not only to be loved, but to be lovely."

THREE

Life in the Marble Temple

"THE 'VILLANEOUS' sea-sickness which generally afflicts me in a Stage [coach] has yielded, in some degree, to my suffering from the extreme cold," Justice Levi Woodbury wrote his wife in the 1840s. "I think I never again, at this season of the year, will attempt this mode of journeying. Besides the evils before mentioned I have been elbowed by old women—jammed by young ones—suffocated by cigar smoke—sickened by the vapours of bitters and w[h]iskey—my head knocked through the carriage top by careless drivers and my toes trodden to a jelly by unheeding passengers." In the early nineteenth century, a justice earned much of his pay on rough roads. Justices had to ride circuit and twice a year travel to Washington for the Court's sessions. Travel on horseback or by carriage was a hardship, "amid clouds of dust and torrents of rain," and involved long stays in taverns away from family and friends. Woodbury's wife constantly complained about his long absences, and once on his return he found that his wife had gone on vacation without him. "Why do you talk of regret at my necessary absence on the Circuit to support my family and object to my going to

Washington," the devoted justice pleaded, "and are still so unwilling to stay with me when at home?"[1]

The Court is a human institution that has adapted to changing conditions. "The great tides and currents which engulf the rest of men," as Justice Cardozo observed, "do not turn aside in their course, and pass judges by."[2] Justices no longer ride circuit, and the caseload now keeps them in Washington for much of the year. These changes have been shaped by American society and politics. But they have also been shaped by the institutionalization of the Court.

Institutionalization is a process by which the Court establishes and maintains its internal procedures and norms and defines and differentiates its role from that of other political branches. Institutionalization reflects justices' interactions and responses to the Court's distinctive history and changing political environment. It remains a central force, conditioning judicial behavior. Whereas the early Court struggled to create procedural norms and an institutional identity, the structure and processes of the contemporary Court have become more bureaucratic.

Before the Marble Temple

In its first decade (1790–1800), the Court had little business, frequent turnovers in personnel, no chambers or staff of its own, and no clear institutional identity. It indeed appeared, in Alexander Hamilton's words, to be the "least dangerous" branch. When the Court initially convened, on February 1, 1790, only Chief Justice John Jay and two other justices arrived at the Exchange Building in New York City, where they were to meet. The Court adjourned until the following day, when Justice John Blair and Attorney General Edmund Randolph arrived from Virginia. The other two appointed justices of the first Court never arrived. Its business largely limited to the admission of attorneys who would practice before its bar, the Court concluded its first session in ten days and its second in two. Later that year, the capital of the United States moved from New York City to Philadelphia. Thereafter the Court met in Independence Hall and in Old City Hall, where it shared the courtroom of the Mayor's Court until the capital again moved to Washington, D.C. in 1800.

In these first years, the justices wore British-style wigs and colored robes. The wigs soon became controversial and were abandoned; Thomas Jefferson pleaded, "For Heaven's sake, discard the monstrous wig which makes the English Judges look like rats peeping through bunches of oakum!"[3] The justices also adopted, but gradually abandoned, the British practice of rendering *seriatim* (individual) opinions. Chief Justice Jay initially wore a red robe and the associate justices wore black robes. Since the chief justiceship of John Marshall, however, all members of the Court have dressed in black robes. However, in January 1995, Chief Justice Rehnquist broke with that long-standing tradition by wearing a black robe with four golden stripes on each sleeve. Rehnquist modeled the robe after one worn by the British Lord Chancellor in a production of Gilbert and Sullivan's *Iolanthe*. Chief Justice Roberts returned to wearing a solid black robe.

With few cases, the Court initially held two sessions a year, one in February and one in August, neither lasting more than two or three weeks. As the workload increased, sessions became somewhat longer, and an annual session, or term, as it is called, was established. By 1840 the Court was convening in January and sitting until March. Yet sessions remained rather short and by the end of the 1860s lasted only about seventeen weeks a year.[4] Because of an increasing workload throughout the late nineteenth century, Congress moved the beginning of each term back in stages to, finally in 1917, its present opening day on the first Monday in October. The term now runs through the following June.

The problems presented by frequent changes in personnel, few customs, and short sessions were exacerbated by the requirement, under the Judiciary Act of 1789, that the justices ride circuit. Circuit riding was the principal means by which the people of the new country became acquainted with the Court. Twice a year each justice would hold court, in the company of district judges, throughout their circuit of the country in order to hear appeals from the trial courts, travelling long distances on horseback or by coach. Justice James Iredell's southern circuit not only carried him through North and South Carolina and Georgia, but twice a year also took him back north to attend the Court's sessions. He likened himself to a "travelling postboy." In 1792, the justices urgently requested the president and Congress to find an alternative to circuit riding, insisting that it was "too burdensome" and unfair for them "to pass the greater part of their days on the road, and at inns, and at a distance from their families."[5] Chief Justice Jay complained that serving on the Court "was in a degree intolerable and therefore almost any other office of a suitable rank and emolument was preferable." Chief Justice John Marshall suffered a fractured collarbone while riding circuit, after the wheels of the coach in which he was traveling broke, causing the coach to turn over. Rather than ride circuit, Justice Thomas Johnson resigned.

Circuit riding was not merely burdensome, it also diminished the Court's prestige, for a decision by a justice on circuit could afterward be reversed by the whole Court. As Chief Justice John Jay observed, "The natural tendency of such fluctuations is obvious; nor can they otherwise be avoided than by confining the Judges to their proper place, *viz.* the Supreme Court."[6] Jay resigned his chief justiceship after winning the governorship of New York and later declined reappointment as chief justice because he "was not perfectly convinced that under a system so defective [the Court] would obtain the energy, weight and dignity which were essential to its affording due support for the National Government, nor acquire the public confidence and respect which, as the last resort of justice of the nation, it should possess."[7]

The development of the Court's institutional identity was necessarily difficult because the justices resided primarily in their circuits rather than in Washington, D.C. and often felt a greater allegiance to their circuits than to the Court.[8] Justices not only faced the problem of divided loyalties but also had opportunities for teaching, practicing law, and consulting in their circuits, thereby supplementing (if not surpassing) their judicial salaries.[9] Accordingly, the distinction between official status and personal interests was far from clearly drawn. Though Congress periodically altered circuit-riding duties, the responsibilities and burdens continued to plague the justices throughout the nineteenth century; they even grew worse for those who had to travel west of the Mississippi.[10]

When the capital moved to Washington, D.C. in 1800, no courtroom was provided for the Court. Between 1801 and 1809, the justices convened in various rooms in the basement of the Capitol until remodeling took place, and the Court met for a year in Long's Tavern. In 1810, the justices returned to the Capitol but now met in a room designed for their use. At the time, the room was also shared by the circuit court and the Orphan's Court of the District of Columbia. The courtroom, however, was rendered unusable in the War of 1812 when the British burned the Capitol on August 24, 1814. For two years the Court met in a rented house, the Bell Tavern. In 1817, the Court moved back into the Capitol, where it held its sessions in a small room, "little better than a dunjeon," until its courtroom was restored in 1819. A newspaper reporter in 1824 described the courtroom as being

not in a style which comports with the dignity of [the Court], or which bears a comparison with the other Halls of the Capitol. In the first place, it is like going down a cellar to reach it. The room is on the basement story in an obscure part of the north wing. In arriving at it, you pass a labyrinth, and almost need the clue of Ariadne to guide you to the sanctuary of the blind goddess. A stranger might traverse the dark avenues of the Capitol for a week, without finding the remote corner in which Justice is administered to the American Republic.[11]

Nevertheless, the Court met in this room until 1860, when it moved upstairs to the room previously occupied by the Senate.

In the "old Senate Chamber," preserved on the ground floor of the Capitol today, the Court met for three-quarters of a century, until the completion of its own building in 1935.

Coincident with the move into the Capitol, John Marshall assumed the position of chief justice, presiding over the Court for the next thirty-four years, until 1835. The Court's internal norms were as uncertain as its institutional identity, but Marshall managed to establish regularized procedures and enhance the Court's prestige. In contrast to the first decade, the entire first half of the nineteenth century saw a remarkable degree of continuity in the Court: seventeen of the twenty-two justices who served were on the bench for fifteen years or more. During this period, with decisions like *Marbury v. Madison* (1803), the Court established, more or less delineated, and maintained its own institutional boundaries. To be sure, the public had little interest in the judicial process, other than attending an occasional session of the Court. Still, after 1811 the *Niles' Register* and a few other Washington, New York, and Philadelphia newspapers began covering the Court's decisions. No less important, after 1821 the Court for the first time provided for the filing of written briefs by attorneys, though not until 1833 did it require the printing of records. Briefs and records were rarely preserved until after 1854. Only after 1870 do the yearly sets in the Supreme Court Library become complete.[12] (Since 2007 the Court has required the filing of briefs both electronically and in printed form.)

For most of the nineteenth century, life remained transitory in the Court, as in the Washington community; in the early part of the century, Washington, D.C. was the capital of the country in search of a city. The justices continued to reside in their circuits and to stay in boardinghouses while attending sessions of the Court. Chief Justice Roger B. Taney (1836–1864) was the first to reside permanently in the city, and as late as the 1880s most justices did not bring their families or maintain homes there. The justices had no offices and shared the law library of Congress in the Capitol. They relied on a single clerk of the Court to answer correspondence, manage the docket, collect fees, and locate boarding rooms for them on their annual visits. The marshal of the Court also worked for other courts in the District of Columbia. On days when the Court heard oral arguments, which ran from eleven in the morning to three or four in the afternoon and often carried over for several days, the marshal would (and still does) announce the sitting of the justices with the now traditional introduction:

Oyez! Oyez! Oyez! All persons having business before the Honorable, the Supreme Court of the United States, are admonished to draw near and give their attention, for the Court is now sitting. God save the United States, and this Honorable Court.

From across the hall, where they put on their robes in the presence of spectators, the justices proceeded into the courtroom, following the chief justice in order of their seniority. There they would sit at a long straight bench, the chief justice in the center and the others on both sides in alternating order of their seniority. The reporter of decisions recorded arguments and compiled and published the final decisions at his own expense and for his own profit. The Court had no other employees or assistants until the 1860s, when each justice acquired a messenger or servant. Not until the 1880s did the justices gain a secretary or law clerk.[13]

The development of the Court's institutional identity, regularized procedures, and norms of decision making flowed largely from the creative skills of "the Great Chief Justice," John Marshall. Few fixed customs bound Marshall, and his associates shared his Federalist philosophy. Being chief justice gave him special prerogatives: presiding at public sessions, leading discussion and directing the order of business in private conferences, either writing or assigning to another the Court's opinion, and serving as the executive officer of the Court and the titular head of the federal judiciary. But although the office of chief justice entitled Marshall to lead, his personality—inventive, shrewd, exacting, yet amiable and unassuming—enabled him to mass the Court. For

Justice Stephen J. Field in his home office and library, 1896. Like other justices in the late nineteenth and early twentieth centuries, he worked in his home office; justices acquired chambers in the Court only after its building was completed in 1935. (*C. M. Bell, Collection of the Supreme Court of the United States*)

other justices, it was "both easy and agreeable to follow his lead" as well as "both hard and unpleasant to differ with him."[14]

One of John Marshall's great legacies has been the Court's ongoing collegiality. Although he once thought that the Court had "external & political enemies enough to preserve internal peace," Marshall sought to maintain "harmony of the bench" by ensuring that all justices roomed in the same boardinghouse.[15] He thus turned the disadvantage of transiency into strategic opportunity. After a day of hearing oral arguments, the justices would dine together and around seven o'clock begin discussing cases. Marshall used the talks to achieve his overriding institutional goal—unanimity. He perceived that unanimous decisions would build the Court's prestige. He discouraged *seriatim*, especially dissenting opinions, sought to accommodate opposing views, and wrote the overwhelming number of the Court's opinions, even when he disagreed with a ruling.[16] Defending his practice, Marshall observed:

> The course of every tribunal must necessarily be, that the opinion which is to be delivered as the opinion of the court, is previously submitted to the consideration of all the judges; and, if any part of the reasoning be disapproved, it must be so modified as to receive the approbation of all, before it can be delivered as the opinion of all.[17]

Justice William Johnson of South Carolina, one of President Jefferson's appointees, took a different view. When Jefferson urged him to press for a return to the practice of individual opinions, Johnson's lengthy reply explained how difficult Marshall made it to disagree:

> While I was on our State-bench I was accustomed to delivering *seriatim* Opinions in our Appellate Court, and was not a little surprised to find our Chief Justice in the Supreme Court delivering all the opinions in Cases in which he sat, even in some Instances when contrary to his own Judgement and Vote. But I remonstrated in vain; the Answer was he is willing to take the trouble and it is a Mark of Respect to him. I soon however found out the real Cause. Cushing was incompetent. Chase could not be got to think or write—Paterson was a slow man and willingly declined the Trouble, and the other two [Chief Justice Marshall and Justice Bushrod Washington] are commonly estimated as one Judge. Some Case soon occurred in which I differed from my Brethren, and I felt it a thing of Course to deliver my Opinion. But, during the rest of the Session I heard nothing but Lectures on the Indecency of Judges cutting at each other, and the Loss of Reputation which the Virginia Appellate Court has sustained by pursuing such a Course. At length I found that I must either submit to Circumstances or become such a Cypher in our Consultations as to effect no good at all. I therefore bent to the Current, and persevered until I got them to adopt the Course they now pursue, which is to appoint someone to deliver the Opinion of the Majority, but to leave it to the rest of the Judges to record their Opinions or not ad Libitum.[18]

The Taney Court largely emulated the Marshall Court's decision-making practices. Justice John McLean provided the following view of the Court's conferences in that period:

Before any opinion is formed by the Court, the case after being argued at the Bar is thoroughly discussed in consultation. Night after night, this is done, in a case of difficulty, until the mind of every judge is satisfied, and then each judge gives his views of the whole case, embracing every point of it. In this way the opinion of the judges is expressed, and then the Chief Justice requests a particular judge to write, not his opinion, but the opinion of the Court. And after the opinion is read, it is read to all of the judges, and if it does not embrace the views of the judges, it is modified and corrected.[19]

The justice assigned to write the Court's opinion would read his draft at conference but not circulate a printed version. Thus the justices would typically agree only on the main points of the decision and not on the precise wording of the Court's opinion. The decision would be announced and the opinion read the next day. This practice discouraged dissenting and concurring opinions. Occasionally, other justices complained, most notoriously about Taney's opinion in *Dred Scott*, that the opinion read from the bench and the final printed version differed from that agreed to in conference.[20] In the latter part of the nineteenth century, this complaint helped lead to the practice of circulating draft opinions for comments and changes before a final vote and announcement. Not until the chief justiceship of Melville Fuller (1888–1910) were draft opinions circulated among the justices before their delivery—a practice, as we shall see, that is now central to the Court's decision making.[21]

Dred Scott and the Civil War changed the Court as well as the country. During Reconstruction the capital became a city, the Court's workload steadily increased, and its terms lengthened. The justices deserted boardinghouses for fashionable hotels along Pennsylvania Avenue. Instead of dining together and discussing cases after dinner, they held conferences on Saturdays and announced decisions on Mondays. (In 1955, the Warren

Court abolished the Saturday conferences and moved them to Fridays, and started delivering opinions on any day of open session at ten o'clock.) Justices still dined in company, but more frequently they were joined by members of the Court's bar—attorneys admitted to argue cases before the justices—with whom they frequently discussed pending cases.[22]

After 1860 the Court met upstairs in the old Senate Chamber in the Capitol between the new chambers of the Senate and those of the House of Representatives. The justices still had no offices of their own. In the 1920s, Justices Sutherland and Sanford and a few others managed to secure small rooms on the gallery floor of the Capitol. During the chief justiceships of Salmon Chase (1864–1873) and Morrison Waite (1874–1888), conferences were held downstairs in a "consultation" room that also served as a library. Chief Justice Melville Fuller (1888–1910) proudly held conferences at his own red-brick home, which had earlier boarded the Marshall Court in 1831 and 1833.[23] Fuller also inaugurated the customary handshake among the justices before they ascend the bench or begin conference deliberations. These marks of conviviality aside, Fuller, unlike his predecessor Waite, spurned Washington social life. His successor, Chief Justice Edward White (1910–1921), was similarly austere.

By the turn of the twentieth century, the justices resided in the capital and for the most part worked at home. Congress provided funds for each justice to maintain a working library and employ a messenger and a secretary or law clerk. In his library, for instance, Justice Holmes wrote his opinions with a sputtering ink pen at a "stand-up" desk inherited from his grandfather. "There is nothing so conclusive to brevity," he often remarked, "as a feeling of weakness in the knees."[24] He had no typewriter. "How I loathe conveniences," Holmes cherished saying.[25] Former Secretary of State Dean Acheson, who clerked for Justice Brandeis, recalled, "Poindexter, the messenger, and I constituted the whole office staff; and Poindexter, half the household staff as well."[26] Law clerks worked in a variety of capacities, from assisting in legal work to serving

The Supreme Court in session in the "Old Senate Chamber" of the U.S. Capitol, where the Court held its sessions from 1860 until 1935, when it moved into the building it now occupies. (*Engraving by Carl Becker for* Harper's Weekly, *Collection of the Supreme Court of the United States*)

cocktails at weekly social gatherings. Relations among the justices varied widely, for each worked principally alone at home. Brandeis and Holmes, for example, had a warm, lifelong friendship. Justice McReynolds, on the other hand, was abrasive and worked poorly with others; he even had trouble keeping law clerks.[27]

Since the early part of the twentieth century, the Court's procedures have depended less on sociability than on institutional norms and majority rule. The Court now functions on the basis of a shared or pooled interdependence. The chief justice has a special role in maintaining certain rules and routines, scheduling and coordinating conferences, and assigning opinions. But the deliberative process—the conference discussions, the voting, and

The Supreme Court in 1892. Seated in the front row, left to right: Justices Horace Gray and Stephen Field, Chief Justice Melville Fuller, and Justices John M. Harlan and Samuel Blatchford. Standing in the second row, left to right: Justices Henry Brown, Lucius Lamar, David Brewer, and George Shiras Jr. (*Photograph by C. M. Bell, Collection of the Supreme Court of the United States*)

the circulation of draft opinions—entails a mutual adjustment among equals. The Court, Frankfurter once noted, "is an institution in which every man is his own sovereign."[28] The justices' independence, as well as the need for mutual adjustment, was reinforced by the fact that each justice now resided in Washington, D.C. and worked primarily and independently at home, with little or no assistance. The justices had come to function like "nine little law firms," as Justice Jackson later observed. This was a matter of great pride for justices such as Brandeis, who said, "The reason the public thinks so much of the Justices of the Supreme Court is that they are almost the only people in Washington who do their own work."[29]

When William Howard Taft became chief justice in 1921, he set out to construct the Court's own building. His associates balked.[30] In 1896 the justices had unanimously rejected a congressional proposal to move them from the Capitol to the more spacious Congressional Library Building across the street.[31] On Taft's Court, Brandeis thought that there was more than symbolic importance to the Court's sitting at the center of the Capitol, midway between House and Senate. And he abhorred the opulence of Taft's design. By contrast, Taft envisioned a building that would symbolize the Court's prestige and independence.

Taft tirelessly lobbied Congress and in 1925 persuaded the Senate to fund his marble temple. He died before the completion of the building in 1935. Built in the Greek Corinthian style, at a cost of slightly less than $10 million, the four stories above the ground featured Vermont marble outside and Alabama marble in the interior corridors and in the Great Hall at the entrance; Georgian marble was used for four inner courtyards surrounding the main-floor courtroom, constructed of marble from Italy, Spain, and Africa. Handcrafted American white oak was used throughout the building with particularly impressive carvings on the arches and ceiling of the library.

The main floor holds two large conference rooms, offices for the marshal and the solicitor general, and a lawyers' lounge. Circling the four courtyards and the courtroom at the center are the justices' chambers—each a suite of three to four rooms—with the chambers of the chief justice, the justices' robing room, and a private conference room directly behind the courtroom. One floor up are the Office of the Reporter of Decisions, the Legal Office, and the justices' dining room, with smaller private dining rooms on each side. The remaining rooms on the floor house law clerks and records. On the third floor is the library. Half a floor above the library, there is now a basketball court, commonly referred to as the "highest court in the land," where law clerks play basketball and work out on exercise equipment. In the 1980s Justice O'Connor instituted aerobic exercise classes. Subsequently, additional exer-

Justices Oliver Wendell Holmes (left) and Louis D. Brandeis, two of the Court's "great dissenters." (*Bettmann/Corbis via Getty Images*)

cise equipment was added, as was a separate exercise room for the justices—where Justices Ginsburg and Kagan have a weekly exercise trainer work out with them. In 2017, however, the Court decided that exercise classes for employees and nonemployees would no longer be held, and the exercise room would be solely for the use of the justices. On the ground floor, the curator displays historical exhibits, and the Supreme Court Historical Society has a kiosk. The offices of the clerk, the public information officer, the director of personnel and organizational development, and the curator; the police; and a barbershop, seamstress, nurse, and cafeteria are also on the ground floor. In 1987, a makeshift theater began showing a short film on the history of the Court, but was replaced by a new theater in 2010. Created as part of the Court's modernization project, this new venue presents visitors with a short film about the Court produced by C-SPAN. Below the ground floor, there is a parking garage for the justices, the Court's printing shop, a carpentry shop, and a laundry.

Though Chief Justice Taft managed to persuade four other justices—a bare majority—to support his lobbying for the building, he would find it difficult to get them to move into the marble temple; only Justices George Sutherland and Owen Roberts moved in, followed by FDR's subsequent appointees.[32] Chief Justice Hughes later referred to the building as simply "a place to hang my hat," and Justice Sutherland reportedly commented snidely that the justices would look like "nine black beetles in the temple of Karnak."[33] When a guest at one of Brandeis's Sunday teas remarked that Stone was complaining about the building and the acoustics and lighting in the courtroom, Brandeis, recalled his former law clerk Paul Freund, replied hotly, "Well, he voted for it!" Although the Hughes Court (1930–1941) held its sessions and conferences there, Brandeis and the others worked in their home offices. In 1937 Justice Black became the first to move in, leading the way for FDR's seven other appointees. Still, even when Stone was elevated from associate to chief justice, he continued to work primarily at home (1941–1946).[34] The Vinson Court (1946–1953) was the first to see all nine justices regularly working in the building.

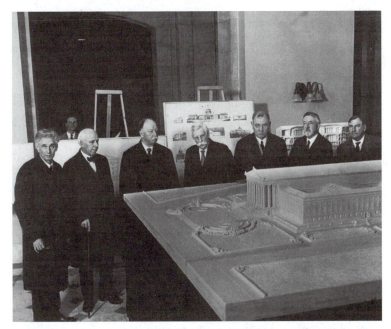

Members of the Taft Court in 1929 examining a model of the building that now houses the Supreme Court. From left to right: Justices Brandeis and Van Devanter, Chief Justice Taft, and Justices Holmes, Butler, Sanford, and Stone. (*George Rinhart/Corbis via Getty Images*)

In the Marble Temple

Completion of the marble temple preceded by two years FDR's attack on the Court as a "super legislature" for its invalidation of early New Deal legislation. The building, as Taft envisioned, nonetheless symbolizes the Court's changed role in American politics—its move from being the "least dangerous" to being a coequal branch of government. "The function of the Supreme Court," Taft and later chief justices affirmed, had become "not the remedy of a particular litigant's wrong, but the consideration of cases whose decision involves principles, the application of which are of wide public or governmental interest, and which should be authoritatively declared by the final court."[35] The modern Court is not, as it once was, a tribunal for correcting errors in the lower courts. Instead, it is an institution devoted to public policy making through constitutional and statutory interpretation.

The marble temple, however, is more than a symbol of the modern Court. Once again, the institutional life of the Court changed. The building further removed the justices from political life in the Capitol. Within the building, basic institutional norms—in particular, along with the justices' independence from each other and outside political accountability, the norms of secrecy, tradition, and collegiality—were reinforced. The building also signified the modern Court's becoming more insular and bureaucratic with the gradual increase in the number of law clerks and greater delegation of responsibilities for screening cases and opinion writing, as well the incorporation of contemporary computer and office technologies.

Isolation from the Capitol and the close proximity of the justices' chambers within the Court promote secrecy to a degree that is remarkable, considering the rather frequent disclosures in the nineteenth century by justices to presidents, congressmen, and attorneys. The decision in *Dred Scott*, for instance, was leaked well before its announcement from the bench, and Chief Justice Salmon Chase later informed the secretary of the treasury "about two weeks in advance of the delivery of the opinions" in the *Legal Tender* cases (1870 and 1871). These were not the only breaches of secrecy by justices in the nineteenth century.[36] Once justices spent most of their time in the same building, they became more careful about their revelations and certainly more conscious of the consequences of rumors that they had revealed votes or the outcome of cases, though that did not stop some justices from making off-the-bench comments or giving interviews about the Court's operations, conferences, and deliberations.[37] The norm of secrecy conditions the employment of the justices' staff, and it has become more important as the number of employees increased. Messengers were excluded from the justices' conferences because of a leak about the *Carbonic Gas* case (1911), and in 1919 Justice Joseph McKenna's clerk was indicted for disclosing the vote in a pending case to speculators on the New York Stock Exchange.[38]

A problem, some justices have felt, has been that law clerks have discussed cases with reporters and scholars, thus breaking occasionally with the tradition of secrecy. Although leaks happened before the Court's move into the marble temple, the problem appears to have grown. A former clerk to Justice Brandeis attributed that to the fact that after the Court moved into the marble temple, law clerks (who had previously worked at their justices' homes and rarely saw each other) socialized more, regularly met for lunch, and increasingly discussed pending cases with clerks from other chambers, as well as "sophisticated newspaper commentators or reporters."[39] Indeed, during the 1954 term the press published stories about the justices' deliberations that were attributable to overhearing law clerks talking about pending cases in the Court's public cafeteria. As a result, a separate room on the ground floor was designated as the law clerks' luncheon room. Still, some justices—like Frankfurter—encouraged law clerks to gossip with clerks in other chambers and report back. No one today follows his practice of sending clerks—"Felix's happy hotdogs"—scurrying around the building.

Chief Justice Roberts and other justices continue to stress the importance of confidentiality when clerks first arrive at the Court. Still, there is ample evidence that clerks continue to gossip and report their "news" from other chambers, particularly since the creation of the "*cert.* pool," the use of emails and the law clerks' Thursday evenings "happy hour" and dinner.[40]

Since 1987, law clerks have been given a memorandum, "The Code of Conduct for Supreme Court Law Clerks," instructing them not to discuss the work of the Court with anyone other than the justices or their fellow clerks, even after their clerkship year has ended! When the code of conduct was revised in 1989, law clerks were also admonished that "discussions with law clerks from other chambers should be circumspect" and to "avoid any hint about the Justice's likely action in a pending case." Those injunctions, however, as one of Justice Marshall's clerks observed, do "not match the way clerks work," "may impede discussions among clerks," and interfere with their First Amendment rights.[41] More recently, Justice Alito admitted, contradictory to the code, that "the law clerks are very free to talk to the law clerks of other chambers."[42]

Indeed, the unreliability of the clerks' "code of silence" was underscored when former clerk for Justice Blackmun and Harvard Law School professor Edward Lazarus published *Closed Chambers: The First Eyewitness Account of the Epic Struggles inside the Supreme Court.*[43] Having clerked during the 1988 term, shortly after the battle over Judge Bork's ill-fated nomination, and drawing on clerks' emails and private conversations, Lazarus portrayed the justices as "clerk driven" and the justices and their clerks as politically embattled. Nor was Lazarus the last former clerk to publish details and reflections on their clerkship year.[44]

The controversy over such disclosures underscores the importance with which the Court regards its tradition of secrecy. Yet justices, no less than their clerks, have broken with that tradition—with impunity. Perhaps the most notable breach of the rule of secrecy by the justices themselves was the 1979 publication of *The Brethren: Inside the Supreme Court,*[45] by the *Washington Post's* Bob Woodward and Scott Armstrong, which revealed details of the Court's decision making during seven terms in the 1970s, sharply criticizing Chief Justice Burger's leadership. They claimed to have interviewed 170 former clerks.[46] Indeed, years later Woodward revealed that the idea for the book came from Justice Potter Stewart, who offered his assistance. At least four other justices—Blackmun, Powell, Rehnquist, and White—also gave interviews and perhaps drafts of opinions and other documents.[47] Nor was this the last time that the Court's code of silence was broken by clerks and justices alike. Information was also leaked related to the highly controversial decisions in *Bush v. Gore*,[48] which effectively decided the 2000 presidential election, and the Roberts Court's bare majority decision upholding (due to Chief Justice Roberts's switch in votes) the Affordable Care Act (Obamacare) of 2010,[49] in *National Federation of Independent Business v. Sebelius* (2012).[50]

Another controversy over the Court's secrecy has involved public access to the justices' private papers. When Justice Thurgood Marshall's working papers became available to the public in 1993, a majority of the Rehnquist Court stirred a minor controversy over what it deemed a breach of confidentiality and pushed to curtail access to the papers. Following his retirement in 1991, Marshall donated his papers to the Library of Congress with the stipulation that the collection, upon his death, be opened to "researchers or scholars engaged in serious research." Less than two years later, he died and his papers became available. Subsequently, the *Washington Post* ran a series of articles based on his papers that portrayed the conservative shift on the Court and described how close it came to overruling *Roe v. Wade* in *Webster v. Reproductive Health Services* (1989). Chief Justice Rehnquist protested the "release [of] Justice Marshall's papers dealing with deliberations which occurred as recently as two terms ago" and asked that the papers be closed. The library, nonetheless, refused to yield.

The release of Justice Marshall's papers, though, was unique only in providing access to the justices' deliberations in cases decided just two years earlier. Even more unprecedented was Justice Brennan's release of some of his papers while he was still sitting on the bench. In the 1980s Brennan made available papers from his initial years on the Warren Court (1956–1969) and later, the basis of installments that covered cases decided five years earlier. Brennan partially bowed to pressure and changed his policy to allowing only "selective access" for limited periods of time. But when doing so he also justified his practice, explaining that "[w]orks published by scholars who have used my papers among other collections have been uniformly substantive and, on the whole, worthwhile."[51]

Justices, of course, differ on whether, when, and to whom their papers should be made available. Indeed, when Rehnquist pressed to end the public's access to Marshall's papers, Justice White sent the Library of Congress a letter disagreeing with the chief justice's view. Retired Justice Blackmun donated his papers to the Library, whereas Chief Justice Warren Burger gave his to the College of William & Mary School of Law with a twenty-five year bar on access. No rules govern, nor has there been a common practice with respect to what justices do with their papers. Approximately 40 percent of those who served on the Court (most of them in the nineteenth century) destroyed their papers. In the twentieth century, justices tended to give their papers to the Library of Congress, though usually on the condition that they become available only after their death or until all the justices with whom they served had left the bench.

A related controversy brewed for a while over access to the Court's deliberations by journalists, scholars, and visitors. For instance, the Court began recording oral arguments in 1955. They were initially made available from the National Archives but solely for educational purposes and without identifying the justices asking questions. In 1971, however, Chief Justice Burger imposed the additional restriction that tapes would not be available until three years after oral arguments. In 1977 CBS aired portions of the oral arguments in *New York Times Co. v. United States* (1971), in which a bitterly divided Court ruled that the government's attempt to enjoin the publication of the *Pentagon Papers* (a top-secret history of America's involvement in the Vietnam War) was a prior restraint in violation of the First Amendment.[52] Subsequently, Burger no longer permitted the transfer of recordings to the National Archives. But when several of the justices learned about Burger's actions in 1985, they agreed that the recordings should once again be sent to the National Archives.

The justices have also periodically discussed television coverage of oral arguments. Although a few justices favored television coverage, a majority worried that only selected segments of oral arguments would be shown on the evening news, and that might denigrate the Court. As a result, the Court has repeatedly rebuffed requests from radio and television companies to broadcast oral arguments in important cases.[53] After a consortium of broadcasters demonstrated how cameras might be introduced into the Court, Chief Justice Rehnquist again rejected the possibility of television coverage, explaining that "[a] majority of the Court remains of the view that we should adhere to our past practice and not allow camera coverage of our proceedings."[54]

Members of Congress and the American Bar Association have pressed for legislation to require cameras in the courtroom,[55] and according to Justice Breyer, it is "almost inevitable," much as audio recordings and transcripts of oral arguments were gradually made available to the public, as well as allowing members of the public in the courtroom to take notes on oral arguments.[56] Unlike Justice Souter, who once said that cameras would cover oral arguments "over his dead body," Justice Sotomayor testified at her Senate confirmation hearing that she was not opposed to television coverage. However, Sotomayor later recanted, saying that cameras in the courtroom would "be more misleading than helpful." "It's like reading tea leaves," she explained. "It is true that in almost every argument you can find a hint of what every judge would rule. But most justices are actually probing all of the arguments. . . . Oral argument is the forum in which the judge plays devil's advocate with lawyers." Justice Kagan has likewise said that cameras in the courtroom will not happen soon and that she worries about only sound bites of oral arguments being aired, and "that may upset the dynamic of the institution." Breyer agrees that there is a "risk," while Gorsuch during his confirmation hearings said he was "open" to cameras but declined to take a position on televised proceedings.

Still, the Court's ban on cameras in the courtroom may be outpaced by technology. In 2014, 99Rises, an activist group opposed to the Roberts Court's campaign-finance ruling striking down limitations on corporate and union political contributions in *Citizens United v. Federal Election Commission* (2010),[57] managed to secretly video segments of an oral argument and, later, recorded their staged protests in the courtroom during another oral argument. Both clips were then uploaded to YouTube. Afterward, the Court further tightened security and admission into the courtroom. But enhanced metal detectors may not be enough in the digital age to detect pen and eyeglass cameras.[58]

In any event, since April 2000 transcripts of oral arguments, along with opinions and orders, have been available on the Court's website at www.supremecourt.gov and subsequently deposited at the National Archives at the end of each term. In 2003 the Court also began digitally recording oral arguments, making it easier to put them on the Internet. Since 2006, the Roberts Court has posted transcripts on its website on the same day as oral arguments. In addition, the transcripts now identify the justices asking questions and responding to attorneys. In 2012 the Court revamped its website to allow access by mobile devices. The Court has also expedited posting on its website the audio recordings and transcripts of oral arguments in highly controversial cases like *Obergefell v. Hodges* (2015), in which a bare majority extended constitutional protection to same-sex marriages; and *Trump v. Hawaii* (2018), on the controversial travel ban.

As the controversy over televising oral arguments indicates, the Court has a profound sense of tradition. Brass spittoons still flank chairs on the bench, and goose-quill pens and pewter inkwells grace the tables for participating counsel. There have been, of course, other changes in the justices' chambers and in other aspects and practices of the Court. From 1790 to 1972, the justices sat in a straight line. Chief Justice Burger modified the straight bench to a half-hexagonal shape, so that the justices seated on the two wings could better hear and see both the attorneys and each other.

Previously, the Warren Court had amplifying equipment installed because of poor acoustics in the courtroom. Notably, the Burger Court's changes in the high bench led to fewer interruptions during oral arguments of justices by other justices, especially those of the most junior justices on either side of the bench.[59]

Still other traditions have been abandoned or modified. Pages abandoned knickers for gray trousers and dark blue blazers in 1963. The tailcoat required of attorneys was abandoned around the turn of the twentieth century, though the solicitor general and his staff continue to wear tailcoats when appearing before the Court. Shortly before Justice O'Connor's appointment in 1981, the practice of addressing a member of the Court as "Mr. Justice" was dropped; with the exception of the chief justice, each member of the Court is now referred to simply as "Justice." In 1982, after a complaint, the Court started using the term "Esquire" when addressing female and male attorneys. Down through Chief Justice Warren's time, almost all the justices' messengers were black—virtually the only black employees in the Court until the first black page was appointed in 1954.[60] The first black law clerk, William Coleman, was chosen by Frankfurter in 1948. The first woman, Lucile Loman, was picked by Douglas in 1944. But no others were chosen until Black selected the daughter of his New Deal friend and Washington lawyer-lobbyist Thomas ("Tommy the Cork") Corcoran in 1966. The racial, ethnic, and religious character of Court employees, however, is now more diverse, and employment more professional with the creation of an officer of personnel and organizational development.[61]

While altering working relations among the justices, the building to some extent also reinforces collegiality. Justices collectively decide (by majority vote) not only cases but also changes in procedures and other organizational matters. In Chief Justice Waite's time (1874–1887), for instance, the justices agreed (over two dissents) that the reporter of decisions should live in Washington, D.C. during the term and not participate in pending cases while the Court is in session.[62]

The Supreme Court in session, February 8, 1935, in the "Old Senate Chamber." (*bpk Bildagentur/Erich Salomon/Art Resource, NY*) **Another photograph was taken in 1937 in the Court's new courtroom by a woman who concealed a small camera in a handbag with a hole through which a camera's lens peeped.**

Most matters come to a vote.[63] Typically a committee of three justices studies proposed changes affecting life in the marble temple and then makes a recommendation on which the justices vote at conference. In recent years, the Court has adopted regulations and policies on such matters as the number of group photographs the justices will sign each year, guidelines for tours of the Court, and the code of conduct for law clerks.[64] If a majority fails to agree on proposed changes, then past practice prevails.

Majority rule on organizational matters occasionally proves unsatisfactory. In a letter to Chief Justice Vinson, who pushed a change in 1947 to admit attorneys to the bar before, rather than after, oral arguments in order to accommodate the schedules of politicians and other supporters of the lawyers (to which Justice Jackson proposed to publish a dissent from that break with tradition), Justice Frankfurter observed:

Of course votes—a majority vote—must decide judicial business, and such votes must be acted upon. But very different considerations apply to the family life of the Court—the way it should carry on in its corporate life, its relations to the other branches of Government, to the Bar, and the public. In such matters, the controlling considerations are those that relate to the best way of assuring inner harmony, whatever intellectual differences there may be. And that means not votes but accommodation— the give-and-take of comradeship, accommodation to the purpose and not mere counting of heads.[65]

After his retirement, Chief Justice Warren recollected, "When you are going to serve on a court of that kind for the rest of your productive days, you accustom yourself to the institution like you do to the institution of marriage, and you realize that you can't be in a brawl every day and still get any satisfaction out of life."[66]

Over eighty years after the construction of the marble temple, the Court undertook a major modernization project to upgrade its operations and improve security. The project cost about $122 million and includes a two-story underground annex on the Maryland Avenue side of the building to provide space for the Court's police, new mechanical equipment, and exhibits for the more than 1 million tourists who annually visit. As part of the modernization project, visitors are no longer allowed to enter through the bronze doors at the top of the stairs, but must enter through doors on the ground floor with security checks. Justices Breyer and Ginsburg objected, issuing a statement that security concerns did not justify closing the front doors and lamenting the symbolism of closing of the main entrance to the Court.

The internal dynamics and institutional life of the Court reflect the norms, vested interests, and interplay of personalities among the justices and their staffs. The modern Court still functions more or less like nine little law firms, but life in the marble temple also has become more bureaucratic. As caseloads have increased dramatically over the last fifty years, the number of law clerks has more than tripled and the number of other employees has also increased.[67]

Justice and Company—Nine Little Law Firms

Justice Robert H. Jackson (1941–1954), who moved into the marble temple just seven years after its completion, rather famously observed that the modern Court functions like "nine little law firms." "The fact is that the Court functions less as one deliberative body than as nine, each Justice working largely in isolation except as he chooses to seek consultation with others. These working methods tend to cultivate a highly individualistic rather than a group viewpoint."[68] Subsequent justices embraced that view. Justice Harlan (1955–1971), who succeeded Jackson on the bench, likewise observed, "decisions of the Court are not the product of an institutional approach, as with a professional decision of a law firm . . . . They are the result merely of a tally of individual votes cast after the illuminating influences of collective debate."[69] When Potter Stewart (1958–1981) joined the Court, he expected to find "one law firm with nine partners, if you will, the law clerks being the associates." But Harlan told him, "No, you will find here it is like nine firms, sometimes practicing law against one another." "As much as 90 percent of our total time," Justice Lewis F. Powell (1972–1987) underscored, "we function as nine small, independent law firms."

I emphasize the words *small* and *independent*. There is the equivalent of one partner in each chamber, three or four law clerks, two secretaries, and a messenger. The informal interchange between chambers is minimal, with most exchanges of views being by correspondence or memoranda. Indeed, a justice may go through an entire term without being once in the chambers of all the other eight members of the Court.[70]

Indeed, Justice Brennan often referred to his opinions as the product of the "Brennan chambers"—the work of "judge and company."[71]

A number of factors isolate the justices. The Court's members decide together, but each justice deliberates alone. Their interaction and decision making depend on how each and all of the nine justices view their roles and common institutional goals. Intellectual and personal compatibility and leadership may determine whether justices embrace an institutional, consensual approach to their work or stress their own policy objectives. As Chief Justice Rehnquist once put it, "When one puts on the robe, one enters a world . . . which sets great store by individual performance, and much less store upon the virtue of being a 'team player.'" At worst, as Blackmun observed, the justices are "all prima donnas."[72]

The growing caseload affected the Court in several ways. Notably, the number of law clerks increased. Likewise, the number of secretaries increased, at first in place of additional clerks and later to help the growing number of clerks.[73] The legal office was created in 1975 to assist the justices; subsequently, the staff of research librarians was increased.

Computer technology also affected the operation of the chambers. In the late 1970s each chamber acquired a photocopying machine and computers. The Court now has two computer networks, and each justice and law clerk has a laptop. Justices once circulated eight carbon copies—called "flimsies"—of their draft opinions for comments by other justices. And they still send printed memos and draft opinions to other chambers and receive other justices' comments. Typically, justices respond with a one-page, one-line reply such as "Please join me" or "I am still with you."[74] Law clerks, however, now communicate and exchange drafts by email.[75] Yet the justices continue to primarily communicate via printed memos. As Justice Kagan put it, "The justices are not necessarily the most technologically sophisticated people" and "the Court (except for law clerks) hasn't really 'gotten to' email." In addition, she emphasized, there have been "emails that

I've sent—I don't know about you—where I click the send button and then think, 'Eh, what did I just do?'" Likewise, Justice Alito confirms, "[t]he communications about cases are almost all written except when we're in conference."[76]

The justices' chambers tend to resemble, in Chief Justice Rehnquist's words, "opinion writing bureaus."[77] Each chamber now averages about eight people: the justice, four law clerks, two secretaries, and a messenger. The managing of chambers and supervising of paperwork consume more of the justices' time than in the past and also keep them apart.

Law Clerks in the Chambers

Law clerks have been in the Court for over a century. In that time their roles have evolved and become institutionalized to the point that some refer to them as "junior justices."[78] As the Court's caseload increased, the justices acquired more clerks and delegated more work to them. In addition to relieving some of the justices' workload pressures, clerks bring fresh perspectives to the Court. For young lawyers one or two years out of law school, the opportunity of clerking is invaluable for their careers. After their year at the Court, during which they make over $87,000, clerks go on to teach at leading law schools or to work for prestigious law firms. They may command hiring bonuses of over $400,000 after their clerkships on top of their starting salaries of over $200,000, which perhaps explains why an increasing number go into corporate legal practice afterward, with some specializing in Supreme Court litigation.[79]

Congress first appropriated funds for the justices to hire a stenographic clerk in 1886. Upon his appointment in 1882, Horace Gray initiated (at his own expense) the practice of hiring each year a graduate of Harvard Law School as "secretary" or law clerk.[80] When Holmes succeeded Gray, he continued the practice and other justices gradually followed him. In 1920 Congress authorized the hiring of one law clerk, along with a secretary, for each justice. But many justices—Chief Justice White and

Justices Holmes, Brandeis, and Sutherland—simply elevated their secretaries so they could earn more as clerks, and continued to hire just one assistant. By the 1948 term the number of clerks per justice doubled, and with the chief justice allocated an additional clerk. After 1970 the number of clerks rose to three and then to four in 1974, with one additional clerk for the chief justice, though Roberts, unlike Burger and Rehnquist, relies on only four. Retired justices retain one law clerk, who may be assigned to work for other justices.

Most clerks serve for only one year. But there have been some notable exceptions. In the nineteenth century, Chief Justice Fuller and Justice Brewer each kept clerks for seventeen years, and Owen Roberts had a husband-and-wife team as his clerk and secretary for fifteen years. Chief Justice Taft had a clerk for ten years, and Justice Murphy kept Eugene Gressman for five, while Chief Justice Burger had a senior clerk sign on for four to five years. More recently, Justices Stevens, Scalia, and Kennedy each had clerks stay on for two terms.

The selection of clerks is entirely a personal matter and may be one of the most important decisions a justice makes. About 1,000 people annually apply for clerkships, often to more than one justice. The selection process varies from justice to justice, but four considerations appear crucial: the justice's preference for (1) certain law schools, (2) specific geographic regions, (3) prior clerking experience on certain courts or with particular judges, and (4) ideological and personal compatibility. In addition, since the 1970s justices have primarily drawn clerks from lower federal courts. Consequently, clerking for a respected federal judge is now just as important as attending a top law school. There is also evidence that in the last couple of decades the trend has been for conservative justices to hire clerks with prior experience clerking for conservative lower-court judges, and likewise for liberal justices to pick clerks from leading liberal lower-court judges.[81]

The typical clerk is twenty-five years old, white, male, and a year out of Harvard, Yale, Stanford or the University of Virginia law school. During the last thirty years, fewer than 8 percent were Asian Americans, 4 percent African Americans, and only a little over 1 percent Hispanic. The number of female clerks has increased in recent years to about one-fourth of the clerks annually selected. In short, they are less diverse than recent law school graduates. Among the lower federal-court "feeder" judges, whose clerks tend to go on to the Court, are Second Circuit Judge Robert A. Katzmann, Fourth Circuit Judge J. Harvie Wilkinson, and Sixth Circuit Judge Jeffrey Sutton; and an even larger number of clerks previously worked for D.C. Circuit Judges Merrick Garland, David S. Tatel, and (then judge and now justice) Brett Kavanaugh.[82]

The position and duties of clerks vary with the justice and have varied over the Court's institutional development. Holmes initially had little casual contact with his clerks, but when his eyesight began to fade in his later years, they served as companions and often read to him. According to Walter Gellhorn, Stone "made one feel a co-worker—a very junior and subordinate co-worker, to be sure, but nevertheless one whose opinions counted and whose assistance was valued."[83] Likewise, Harold Burton told his law clerks that he wanted each "to feel a keen personal interest in our joint product," and he encouraged "the most complete possible exchange of views and the utmost freedom of expression of opinion on all matters to the end that the best possible product may result."[84] However, Earl Warren's law clerks communicated with him almost always by memorandum.[85] By contrast, Scalia and Ginsburg, among others, have had warm working relationships with their clerks.

The level of work and responsibility depends on the capabilities and the number of the clerks, but still varies from justice to justice and over the course of the clerkship year. At one extreme, perhaps, is Dean Acheson, who said of working with Brandeis in the 1930s, "He wrote the opinion; I wrote the footnotes."[86] Acheson recalled Brandeis's admonition: "Please remember that your function is to correct my errors, not to introduce errors of your own."[87] Justice Scalia, unlike Brandeis, had his clerks do first drafts of opinions but had a similar view. For him, "what clerks are for [is] to make sure I don't make mistakes."[88] Justices like Black, Jackson, and Souter did virtually all of their first drafts, except at the end of the term when they relied on their clerks.[89] At the other extreme—though now much more common—are clerks who drafted almost all of their justices' written work.

In the last forty years justices have increasingly relied on their clerks to write first drafts of their opinions. A study based on interviews with former clerks found that about 30 percent of the clerks reported that their first drafts of opinions were issued without modification at least some of the time. Recent clerks have exerted substantial influence on opinion writing and there is a strong relationship between the ideology of the justices and the clerks they hire.[90] As a result, some scholars lament the political polarization of law clerkships.[91]

In historical perspective, most clerks' roles typically fall somewhere between these two extremes, but have nonetheless grown and become central to the conduct of the Court's business of screening cases for review and the opinion-writing process. Justice Stone let his clerks craft footnotes that often announced novel principles of law.[92] Stone's technique, in the view of his clerk Herbert Wechsler, was like that of "a squirrel storing nuts to be pulled out at some later time."[93] Frankfurter had his clerks prepare lengthy memoranda such as the ninety-one-page examination of segregation and the "original" intent of the Fourteenth Amendment, prepared by Alexander Bickel in 1954, as well as some of his better-known opinions such as his dissent in the landmark reapportionment case *Baker v. Carr* (1962).[94]

From the perspective of other justices, Frankfurter "used his law clerks as flying squadrons against the law clerks of other Justices and even against the Justices themselves. Frankfurter, a proselytizer, never missed a chance to line up a vote."[95] Similarly, "F. F.'s" former student at Harvard Law School Justice Brennan used the informal communications network among the law clerks to find out other justices' views. Unlike Frankfurter, however, Brennan rarely tried to lobby his colleagues directly. Instead, as one of his law clerks recalled, Brennan used his clerks "to talk to other clerks and find out what their Justices [were] thinking." Brennan then would pitch his points at conference or in draft opinions at particular justices in order to mass or hold onto a majority. Blackmun's papers indicate that he did much the same. By contrast, some justices don't believe in "lobbying" others. As one former clerk to Stevens revealed, when he urged Stevens to lobby Justice O'Connor for her vote in an abortion case, Stevens replied, "The opinion . . . ought to stand or fall on the force of its reasons. He would feel uncomfortable talking to O'Connor about the opinion because she might feel pressured by the conversation."[96]

A justice's background, facility in writing, dedication, and age may affect his or her reliance on law clerks. Few are academic lawyers such as Stone, "a New England wood carver" devoted to craftsmanship. Exceptional are justices who have the ability of Justice Douglas or Jackson to write quickly and with flair. Stanley Reed, for one, struggled to write what he wanted to say. "Wouldn't it be nice if we could write the way we think," he once lamented.[97] Like most of his successors, Reed for the most part relied on clerks for first drafts—"the clerk had the first word and he had the last word."[98]

By all accounts, most justices now delegate the preliminary writing of opinions to their clerks. Chief Justice Rehnquist, for instance, had one of his clerks do a first draft within ten days after conference, without bothering about style. Before having a clerk begin work, Rehnquist would go over the conference discussion and vote with the clerk and explain how he thought "an opinion can be written supporting the result reached by the majority." It was not "a very sweeping original type of assignment," he emphasized. "It is not telling the clerk just figure out how you'd like to decide this case and write something about [it]. It's not that at all." Once the clerk finished a preliminary draft, Rehnquist reworked the opinion—using some, none, or all of the draft—to get his own style down. The draft then typically circulated three or four times among his clerks before it was sent to the other justices. As a result, Chief Justice Rehnquist conceded that his "original contributions to [some opinions] are definitely a minor part of them; other opinions, my original contributions are a major part of them."[99]

Chief Justice Roberts follows Rehnquist's practice of giving clerks ten days to draft opinions (that do not need to be in final, publishable form), which he then revises. Justices Thomas and Alito (like most others now) likewise have clerks do the first draft, which then undergoes two or three edits by other clerks, before doing the final edit.[100] So, too, Justice Scalia admitted, "I almost never do the first draft." As he further explained: "I'll tell them [a clerk] what's supposed to be in it, but he'll write it out. Then I'll put it up on my screen and take it apart and put it back together."[101]

Even though they now delegate much of the opinion writing, justices differ in their approach to revising drafts. If a clerk's draft is "in the ball park," they often just edit rather than rewrite. But some virtually rewrite their clerks' drafts, whereas others, like Reed, tend to insert paragraphs. As one former clerk recalled, Reed simply "didn't like to start from the beginning and go to the ending." Consequently, his opinions tend to read like a dialogue with "a change of voice from paragraph to paragraph."[102] Reed's patchwork opinions did not stem from excessive delegation of responsibility or lack of dedication. At least in his early years on the Court, he took opinion writing seriously but found that words did not flow easily for him. "The problem with Stanley," Frankfurter once said, "is that he doesn't let his law clerks do enough of the work. The trouble with Murphy is that he lets them do too much of the work."[103]

Though there are differences in the duties and manner in which clerks function, certain responsibilities are now commonly assigned in all chambers. Clerks came to play an indispensable role in the justices' deciding what to decide. As the number of filings each year rose, justices delegated the responsibility of initially reading all filings: appeals, which required mandatory review, and petitions for *certiorari*—"pets for *cert.*," as Holmes referred to them—which seek review but may be denied or granted at the Court's own discretion. Clerks then wrote a one- to two-page summary of the facts, the questions presented, and the recommended course of action—that is, whether the case should be denied, dismissed, or granted full briefing and plenary consideration.

This practice originated with the handling of indigents' petitions—*in forma pauperis* (Ifp) petitions and the creation of the "Dead List" (cases not discussed at conference and simply denied)—by Chief Justice Hughes and his clerks. Unlike paid petitions and appeals, which are filed in multiple copies, petitions of indigents are typically filed without the assistance of an attorney in a single, handwritten copy. Until 1935 every *cert.* petition was considered by all the justices at conference. From the time of Hughes through Warren, these petitions were solely the responsibility of the chief justice and his law clerks. (This partially explains why the chief justice had an additional clerk.) Except when an Ifp petition raised important legal issues or involved a capital case, Chief Justice Hughes as a matter of course neither circulated the petition to the other justices nor placed it on the conference list for discussion. Stone, Vinson, and Warren had their clerks' one- to two-page *certiorari* memos routinely circulate to the other chambers. Chief justices, of course, differ in how carefully they study Ifps. Hughes and Warren were especially conscientious about Ifps; the latter told his clerks, "[I]t is necessary for you to be their counsel, in a sense."[104] As the number of Ifps grew, they became too much for the chief's chambers to handle alone. They were thus distributed along with paid petitions to all chambers. Accordingly, almost all filings, with the exception of those handled by the Legal Office, circulate to the chambers.

With the mounting workload, the role of clerks in the screening process grew again. In 1972, at the suggestion of Justice Powell, a majority of the justices began to pool their clerks, dividing up all filings and having a single clerk's *certiorari* memo circulate to all those participating in the *"cert.* pool" (see the further discussion in Chapter 4). Seven justices—Roberts, Thomas, Ginsburg, Breyer, Sotomayor, Kagan, and Kavanaugh—share the memos prepared by their pool of clerks. When Justice Alito was appointed he joined the *cert.* pool, but after a term opted out; Justice Gorsuch also opted out. Former clerks estimate that the preparation of a *cert.* memo may take from fifteen minutes to, in a rare case, a full day. Since 2013 *cert.* memos are due in the chambers of the other justices within eight days after the Clerk of the Court distributes the briefs (14 days after receiving briefs in opposition to an appeal or *cert.* petition, and usually in batches of cases on Wednesdays). When the memos from the *cert.* pool are circulated, each justice typically has a clerk go over each memo and make a recommendation on whether the case should be granted or denied. Each clerk in the pool writes roughly 250 *cert.* memos per term.[105]

Those justices who objected to the establishment of the *cert.* pool and refused to join nevertheless had their clerks prepare memos on the most important of those hundred or more filings that come in each week. Brennan once described his use of clerks this way: although "I try not to delegate any of the screening function to my law clerks and to do the complete task myself," he reported, "I make exceptions during the summer recess when their initial screening of petitions is invaluable training for next Term's new law clerks. And I also must make some few exceptions during the Term on occasions when opinion work must take precedence."[106]

By contrast, Justice Stevens had a somewhat different practice, as he explained: "I have found it necessary to delegate a great deal of responsibility in the review of *certiorari* petitions to my clerks . . . They examine them all and select a small minority that they believe I should read myself. As a result, I do not even look at the papers in over 80 percent of the cases that are filed."[107] Stevens's clerks wrote memos on only those petitions they deemed important. He reviewed them and read the lower-court opinions on all cases to be discussed at conference. For Stevens, the preliminary screening of cases consumed about a day and a half per week. Newly appointed justices may also find it impossible to read all the *certiorari* petitions that accumulate over the summer and stay abreast of the Court's workload. Justice Scalia, for instance, at the beginning of his service found it necessary to limit himself to reading only those memos in cases on which at least three justices had voted to grant *certiorari* and set for discussion at another conference.[108]

After the justices vote in conference to hear a case, each usually assigns that case to a clerk. The clerk then researches the background of the case and prepares a "bench memo" for the justice. Bench memos outline pertinent facts and issues, propose possible questions for attorneys during oral arguments, and address the merits of the cases.[109] The clerk stays with the case as long as the justice does, helping with research and drafting opinions. The nature of the work at this stage varies with the justice and the case, but now includes usually writing the first draft of an opinion and commenting on other justices' responses, as well as subsequently checking citations and proofreading the final version. As each term draws to a close and the justices feel the pressure of completing their opinions by the end of June, clerks inevitably assume an even greater role in the opinion-writing process.[110]

Has too much responsibility been delegated to law clerks? Do they substantively influence the justices' votes and the final disposition of cases? After thirty-six years on the bench, Douglas claimed that circumstances were such that "many law clerks did much of the work of the justices."[111] Rehnquist provided one perspective on the function of law clerks: "I don't think people are shocked any longer to learn that an appellate judge receives a draft of a proposed opinion from a law clerk." He added, however,

I think they would be shocked, and properly shocked, to learn that an appellate judge simply "signed off" on such a draft without fully understanding its import and in all probability making some changes in it. The line between having law clerks help one with one's work, and supervising subordinates in the performance of *their* work, may be a hazy one, but it is at the heart . . . [of] the fundamental concept of "judging."[112]

Over seventy years ago, though, Rehnquist, who clerked for Justice Jackson, charged that clerks—who he also claimed tended to be more "liberal" than the justices for whom they worked—had a substantive influence on the justices when preparing both *certiorari* memos and first drafts of opinions.[113] The degree to which law clerks substantively influence justices' voting and opinion writing is nonetheless difficult to gauge, and certainly varies from justice to justice. Yet even when Rehnquist served as a clerk and the caseload was much less than its present size, justices no doubt voted overwhelmingly along the lines recommended by their clerks. Vinson, for one, tallied the number of times he differed with his clerks. There were differences in less than 5 percent of the cases.[114]

Clerks would look very powerful indeed if they were not transients in the Court. Clerks, as Alexander Bickel once noted, "are in no respect any kind of a powerful kitchen cabinet."[115] As a clerk, Rehnquist, for instance, was unable to dissuade Justice Jackson from going along with the decision in the landmark school desegregation ruling in *Brown v. Board of Education* (1954). In a memorandum titled "A Random Thought on the Segregation Cases," Rehnquist charged that if the Court struck down segregated schools, it would do so by reading "its own sociological views into the Constitution," just as a majority of the Court had read its own economic philosophy into the Constitution when it struck down most of the early New Deal legislation. Later, at his own confirmation hearing in 1971, Rehnquist claimed that the memo was written at Jackson's request and reflected the justice's views rather than his own. And he maintained that position during his 1986 confirmation hearings on being elevated to chief justice. But the content and the style of the memo (as well as the fact that there are several other similar memos written by Rehnquist in Justice Jackson's private papers) indicate that it was Rehnquist's own handiwork. Rehnquist wrote in the conclusion of the memo, "I realize that it is an unpopular and unhumanitarian position, but I think *Plessy v. Ferguson* [1896] was right and should be reaffirmed. If the Fourteenth Amendment did not enact Spencer's *Social Statics*, it just as surely did not enact Myrdal's *American Dilemma*."*116

As part of the institutionalization of the Court, law clerks now undeniably play a major role in the justices' screening process. The following chart, listing Chief Justice Vinson's votes on granting review diverging from his law clerks' recommendations (prior to the creation of the *cert.* pool) demonstrates, and recent research

CASE SELECTION: CHIEF JUSTICE VINSON AND HIS CLERKS' RECOMMENDATIONS

Term	Number of Cases Disposed	Number of Times Chief Justice Vinson's Vote Diverged from Law Clerks' Recommendation
1947	1,331	38 (2.8%)
1948	1,434	53 (3.6%)
1949	1,308	52 (3.9%)
1950	1,216	51 (4.1%)
1951	1,286	46 (3.5%)

* *Social Statics* (1866), by the English philosopher Herbert Spencer, profoundly influenced late nineteenth-century American legal, political, and economic thought by popularizing Charles Darwin's evolutionary theory of the "survival of the fittest" and by inspiring the movement of Social Darwinism. The Court was not immune to the intellectual currents of its times. A majority legitimated laissez-faire capitalism by striking down economic regulation under the guise of a "liberty of contract," which it invented and inserted into the Fourteenth Amendment's prohibition against any state depriving a person of "life, liberty, or property, without due process of law." When *Lochner v. New York* (1905) overturned a New York statute regulating the number of hours that bakers could work, the dissenting Justice Holmes charged that the Court had become a "super legislature" by impermissibly reading into the Constitution a "liberty of contract" in order to enforce its own conservative social-economic theory. As Holmes put it, "The Fourteenth Amendment does not enact Mr. Herbert Spencer's *Social Statics*." Later, when enforcing the Fourteenth Amendment in the landmark school segregation ruling in *Brown v. Board of Education*

confirms, a strong correlation between *cert.* pool law clerks' recommendations and whether the Court grants or denies a case. A study, based on Justice Blackmun's papers, found that in 75 percent of approximately 9,500 *cert.* votes justices followed their clerks' recommendation, and were most likely to agree with the recommendation of his or her own clerk, as well as that of another justice closest to their own ideological positions.[117]

In short, law clerks today play a far greater role in screening cases and recommending which should be placed on the conference "Discuss List,"[118] writing "bench memos" for justices' use during oral arguments[119] and in the opinion-writing process, advising justices of their conversations with clerks in other chambers and about their concerns with drafts of circulated opinions.[120] Some former clerks and observers even claim that the Court is "clerk driven" and that the justices are now too dependent on them.[121] The clerk network connections among the chambers also have been reinforced by the use of emails. As a result, clerks play a larger role in communicating to their justices how draft opinions are shaping up in other chambers and how their justices might respond and possibly forge a new coalition when circulating a draft opinion. No less important, the growing number of law clerks and of delegated responsibilities have contributed to an increase in the volume of concurring and dissenting opinions, as well as longer, more heavily footnoted

(1954), the Warren Court cited seven social science studies in support of overturning the racial doctrine of "separate but equal facilities." Among those studies showing the adverse social and psychological effects of racial segregation was the Swedish economist and sociologist Gunnar Myrdal's book, *An American Dilemma* (1944), the premier work on race relations in America. The Court's mention of *An American Dilemma* intensified the antagonism of powerful southerners, such as the South Carolina governor, former Supreme Court Justice James F. Byrnes, and the Mississippi Senator James O. Eastland. They and others attacked the Court for citing the work of "foreign sociologists"; for bad social science research; and, most of all, for drawing on social science in the first place, rather than simply sticking to the text and historical context of the Constitution.

opinions, as well as criticisms that the justices often do not take sufficient time to edit their opinions.

The Legal Office—A Tenth Little Law Firm

Justice Brandeis, who spoke proudly of the justices' doing their own work, would have abhorred the Legal Office. In 1975 the Court hired two legal officers, or staff counsel—a legal assistant and a legal intern. A growing caseload was only one reason for creating this tenth little law firm. Several of the justices also thought they needed more permanent and specialized help because their clerks are transients.

Staff counsel generally serve two or more years. They advise the justices on procedure and jurisdiction. They recommend action on special motions, such as requests for expedited proceedings and petitions for rehearings. For example, in *United States v. Nixon* (1974), in the heat of the Watergate crisis, the Legal Office advised the Court to expedite the case, ordering the president to turn over secret White House tapes before the court of appeals had ruled on his claim of executive privilege. At the time, Congress had not finished investigating the Watergate break-in and the possibility of impeaching Nixon for conspiracy and obstruction of justice.[122]

The Legal Office also handles cases that come on original jurisdiction under Article III of the Constitution. These cases tend to carry over from one year to the next and involve, for example, complex land and water disputes. In addition, the Legal Office may advise the justices on personal legal matters pertaining to taxes, ethics, and receiving honoraria.[123] And it is a liaison to the Department of Justice when disgruntled individuals file nuisance suits against individual justices.[124] Finally, the Legal Office, along with the counselor to the chief justice, prepares memoranda on such matters as proposed changes in the Federal Rules of Evidence and Criminal Procedure, along with how new legislation may affect the Court.

As the business of the Court has steadily increased, so has the work of the Legal Office. The office now handles applications for the Supreme Court's bar, original cases, petitions for rehearings, and miscellaneous motions.[125] The Legal Office annually handles more than a thousand such matters.[126]

Administrative Staff

The days of unassisted justices are long past. The court as an institution now includes five officers outside the chambers: the clerk, the reporter of decisions, the marshal, the librarian, and the counselor to the chief justice. Each office has grown in number of staff and contributed to the further bureaucratization of the Court.

THE CLERK OF THE COURT

The Office of the Clerk is central to the Court's administration. It has also traditionally served as the primary liaison with attorneys practicing before the Court.

For most of the Court's history, the clerk earned no salary. Instead, he pocketed filing fees and attorneys' bar admission fees. Thus, even at the turn of the twentieth century, the clerk's income often exceeded that of the justices. In 1883, the Court limited the clerk's access to filing fees to $6,000 a year. The clerk still took in all admission fees until 1921, when Taft became chief justice. The incumbent clerk died the same year, and with the change in the office, Taft lobbied for legislation that put the office in his hands. The clerk became a salaried employee, paid out of fees but receiving a salary set by the justices.[127]

The clerks' early financial independence often made them players in the Court's internal politics. From the very first, justices were lobbied by those seeking the position.[128] After their appointment, clerks often rendered personal favors to the justices. In the nineteenth century, for example, they secured lodgings for the justices—occasionally with considerable diplomacy, as when the aging and feeble Justice Grier proposed living in the Capitol itself. At other times, the clerk became involved in rather bitter conflicts with the justices and other officers. One of the more astonishing incidents arose when the clerk, at Chief Justice Taney's request, refused to give Justice Benjamin Curtis a copy of the final written opinion in *Dred Scott* so that he could prepare his dissent. Curtis was furious, but the clerk and Taney stood firm.[129]

Over the years, the responsibilities and size of the clerk's office became greater and more crucial. The office continues to collect filing and admission fees; receive and record all motions, petitions, jurisdictional statements, briefs, and other documents; and circulate them to each chamber. The clerk establishes the oral argument calendar; approximately seventy-five cases are now heard each term at the rate of one hour each, two or three days a week, for two weeks out of every month, from the first of October through April. In addition, the office prepares and maintains the order list of cases granted or denied review and formal judgments, as well as the *Supreme Court Journal*, containing the minutes of its sessions. It has also become the practice for the clerk to go over with attorneys prior to oral arguments the Court's procedures for argument sessions. Due to the rising number of death row inmates and the Court's rulings expediting executions the number of death penalty appeals and motions increased dramatically and, as a result, the clerk's office now has a so-called "death penalty clerk" to oversee the processing of these cases. The clerk's office has a staff of over thirty, including four attorneys and interns.

The clerk's office maintains the computer system, which automatically notifies counsel of the disposition of filings, produces conference and order lists, and prints out the majority of simple Court orders and opinions. The clerk may also conduct case searches and statistical computations within the system. Attorneys now file briefs electronically, along with printed filings. Since 2000 the Court's website (www.supremecourt.gov) provides public access to cases on the docket, the Court's calendar, orders, and recent opinions, as well as other information. In 2013 Chief Justice Roberts appointed Scott Harris, a longtime head of the Legal Office, as the twentieth Clerk of the Court.

THE REPORTER OF DECISIONS

During the first quarter century of the Court there was no official reporter of decisions, and not until 1835 were the justices' opinions given to the clerk. In 1816 the Court officially appointed a reporter, Henry Wheaton, an action that preceded congressional authorization by almost a year. Early reporters, following the British custom, worked at their own expense as well as for their own profit. For most of the nineteenth century the reporter could practice law before the Court or serve as a judge in a lower court. In publishing the Court's decisions, the reporter could advertise his legal services as well. Until the chief justiceship of Taft, the reporter continued to engage in this semiprivate enterprise and supplement his salary by selling to the public the *United States Reports*, containing the final opinions of the Court. In 1922 Congress established that the reporter's salary be fixed by the justices and paid by the government, and for the Government Printing Office to oversee the printing and binding of the *United States Reports*.[130] Printing of the opinions subsequently changed and the Court took over the responsibility of publishing final opinions.[131]

The practices of early reporters engendered numerous controversies. When Richard Peters succeeded Henry Wheaton in 1827, for instance, he updated and revised the entire series of prior Court decisions, omitting a good deal of Wheaton's headnotes, which summarized the opinions and other matters. Wheaton was furious and sued Peters. The latter countered with the argument, rather novel at the time, that "the opinions of the Court are public property." The Court eventually held in *Wheaton v. Peters* (1834) that its opinions were indeed in the public domain but that Wheaton's notations were private property subject to copyright.[132] Though Peters won, he had other problems. In 1831 he published the decision in *Cherokee Nation*—denying Indians the right to sue under the Court's original jurisdiction—as a separate pamphlet along with, in his words,

"Mr. Wirt's great argument in behalf of the Cherokees, which had been taken down by stenographers employed for that purpose."[133] This displeased Jacksonian populists—and Justice Henry Baldwin, in particular. A decade later he had his revenge. In the absence of Justice Joseph Story, a close friend of the reporter, the Court voted 4 to 3 to fire Peters and hire Benjamin Howard, a Jacksonian.[134] Considering the status of the reporter in the nineteenth century, not surprisingly there were other such instances of patronage and ideological divisions over the selection and tenure of the Court's reporter.

The responsibilities of writing headnotes or syllabi (or "syllabuses," according to the reporter of decisions), making editorial suggestions, and supervising the publication of opinions invite controversy. Though at the turn of the twentieth century Justice Horace Gray wrote headnotes for his opinions, most justices did not bother. Headnotes are now considered the work of the reporter and not part of the Court's decision.[135] Since 1970 the reporter has included a "lineup" of the justices, indicating how each voted in a case.[136]

Besides being useful for attorneys and the press, headnotes have tangible and symbolic importance. There is perhaps no better illustration of the consequence of a headnote than in *Santa Clara County v. Southern Pacific Railroad Company* (1886).[137] There, after consulting Chief Justice Waite, the reporter at his own discretion decided to note in an otherwise uninteresting tax case that the Court considered corporations "legal persons" entitled to protection under the Fourteenth Amendment.[138] Corporations, like individual citizens, could thereafter challenge the constitutionality of congressional and state legislation impinging on their interests.

Editing was especially difficult when justices wrote their opinions by hand. When asked to decipher one of his opinions, Justice Stephen Field replied, "How the Hell should I know!"[139] The Court's word-processing system is now integrated with the publishing of decisions, and the reporter has a staff of ten. Nevertheless, editing approximately 200 opinions each term takes time. As each term closes, the work becomes relentless and mistakes happen. In 1983 one opinion referred to a second opinion that had not yet been announced.[140] Following that mistake, the reporter instituted a cite- and quote-checking service, which allows the checking of the more than 16,000 citations for each case signed or *per curiam* opinion.[141] Without careful attention, even to the statement of facts in a case, mistakes may become part of a permanent record and distort the Court's decision.[142] For this reason the final bound volumes of the Court's decisions sometimes include corrections, and additions to the opinions initially issued.[143] Still, some factual errors may remain. In *United States v. Windsor* (2013), striking down a section of the Defense of Marriage Act and holding that same-sex couples may not be denied federal benefits, Justice Kennedy's opinion for the Court observed that "most states permit first cousins to marry, but a handful—such as Iowa and Washington . . . prohibit the practice." In fact, half of the states, including Iowa and Washington, prohibit the practice.[144]

Sometimes errors and disagreements are inescapable even for the Court's reporter, once described as a "double-revolving peripatetic nitpicker." For example, not until 1986 did the Court spell the word *marijuana* consistently. According to Henry C. Lind, a former reporter, it had six acceptable spellings. Some justices would spell it "marihuana," while others spelled it "marijuana." In one opinion, it was spelled both ways in the same footnote! After a memo was circulated to all the justices, it was finally agreed henceforth to use "marijuana."[145]

Ironically, given contemporary computer technology, over the last decade it has taken longer and longer for the Court's final, authoritative opinions to be published. There are now actually four versions of the Court's opinions: (1) so-called "bench opinions," which are delivered and available on the day a decision is handed down; (2) "slip opinions," now posted on the Court's website soon after they are announced; (3) followed by preliminary softcover prints (later published privately by the *Supreme Court Reporter*); and (4) the final official version in the *United States Reports*. In historical perspective, in 1825 the Reporter published the Court's opinions the same year they were delivered, in 1875 within a year later, in 1925 within a year, and in 1975 in fewer than two years. More recently, it has typically taken four or more years. In the last decade, for example, opinions handed down in 2008 did not appear in the official authoritative version until 2013. Moreover, the revisions were not merely corrections of typos but also occasionally substantive corrections, though that is not unprecedented—Chief Justice Taney added 18 pages to his 1857 opinion in *Dred Scott*.[146] Notably, in 2015 the Roberts Court began posting on its website edits of slip opinions and the date of their correction.

Still, most changes are minor, though sometimes significant and amusing. In a 2015 decision,[147] holding that a Department of Agriculture's marketing order for raisin growers was a Fifth Amendment "takings" requiring just compensation, Justice Sotomayor's dissent, put up immediately on the Court's website after the decision was announced, stated that, under the Court's precedents, the order "should easily escape our approbation" (approval), but she meant "opprobrium" (disgrace at shameful conduct). The next day a new PDF file was uploaded to the Court's website, as are numerous other corrections each term.

In 2011 Christine Luchok Fallon became the sixteenth and first female reporter of decisions; she had previously served as deputy reporter for twenty-two years.

THE MARSHAL

For most of the nineteenth century order in the courtroom was overseen by U.S. marshals. At the request of Chief Justice Salmon P. Chase, Congress created the Office of the Marshal in 1867. Like other employees, the marshal tended to get his job either through personal friendship with the justices or through previous employment in some other capacity at the Court. The first marshal, Richard Parsons, was an intimate friend of Chief Justice Chase. Others, such as Thomas Waggaman, the marshal from 1938 to 1952, first came to the Court as a page. More professional criteria have now replaced personal patronage.

The marshal maintains order in the courtroom and times oral arguments. The marshal is authorized to set regulations, subject to the chief justice's approval, for ensuring the decorum of the courtroom. But there are few fixed standards other than those of tradition. For example, women (but not men) may wear hats in the courtroom, although Orthodox Jewish men may wear yarmulkes; and no visitor wearing a swimsuit is allowed to enter.[148] Rarely do incidents breaching protocol occur when the Court is in session, though Larry Flynt, the owner of *Hustler* magazine, was forcibly removed from the courtroom after making a profane outburst during the oral arguments of *Keeton v. Hustler Magazine, Inc.*[149] In 2015 on several occasions individuals from a group known as 99Rises, which opposes the ruling on unlimited corporate and union spending in federal elections, in *Citizens United v. Federal Election Commission* (2010),[150] were removed from the courtroom when they shouted, "We rise to reclaim our democracy! One person, one vote! Overturn *Citizens United.*" Unlike past protesters the government took a harder line, prosecuting them for making a "harangue" or "oration" and being "loud," as well as seeking jail time. In 2017, four were sentenced to a weekend in jail and a fifth to two weekends.

In addition to overseeing building maintenance and security (there are about a hundred Supreme Court police), the marshal serves as business and payroll manager. The Office of the Marshal now manages about 500 employees—messengers, carpenters, police, workmen, a nurse, a physiotherapist, a barber, a seamstress, and cafeteria workers—along with fifty building and groundskeepers. In 2001 Pamela Talkin became the tenth marshal and the first woman to hold the position.

THE LIBRARIAN

In the Court's early years, justices relied on their own personal libraries as well as those of friends and local libraries. In 1832, thirty years after the establishment of the Library of Congress, Congress directed the Librarian of Congress to create a separate collection of law books for the Court. A decade later this collection was moved closer to where the Court heard oral arguments, in the old Senate chamber, and became known as the Conference Room collection. In 1887 the Court appointed its first librarian but it was not until 1948 that the librarian was designated a statutory officer. By 1901 the Court's collection had grown to 11,000 volumes and provided the foundation for the modern Court's library, which it acquired with the move into the Supreme Court building in 1935. Located on the third floor, the library is a breathtaking room with hand-carved American white oak walls, medallions, and arches, representing various disciplines of study and learning. It is, however, not open to the public and remains for the exclusive use of the justices, their clerks, members of the Supreme Court bar, and Congress.

The library now has a staff of over twenty-five, including many who have both law and library degrees. It houses over half a million volumes in paper, microform, and digital formats. There is access to the Internet; national bibliographic databases; and online resources, such as Lexis, Westlaw, and library catalogs from around the world. Although the justices and their clerks now do most of their work on their own computers in their chambers, and thus few people actually work in the library, the librarians remain busy. The library annually responds to approximately 9,000 questions, circulates about 10,000 books, and receives over 3,500 requests a year for use of the bound Records and Briefs of Supreme Court cases.[151] In 2012 Linda Maslow, a longtime research librarian, became the eleventh Librarian of the Court.

THE CHIEF JUSTICE, THE COUNSELOR TO THE CHIEF JUSTICE,
AND THE PUBLIC INFORMATION OFFICER

The chief justice is more than *primus inter pares*—first among equals—in terms of administrative responsibilities within the Court and for the federal judiciary. Since the chief justiceship of Taft, the responsibilities of the office have grown enormously. By statute and custom, the chief justice is the executive officer of the Court. Over eighty statutes confer additional administrative duties, ranging from serving as chairman of the Judicial Conference and of the Board of the Federal Judicial Center to supervising the Administrative Office of the U.S. Courts and serving as chancellor of the Smithsonian Institution.[152]

Unlike Taft and Hughes, Chief Justice Stone felt overwhelmed by the duties. He wrote President Truman just two months before he died:

Few are aware that neither my predecessor, nor I in more than twenty years since I have been a Justice of the Supreme Court, have been able to meet the daily demands upon us without working nights and holidays and Sunday. The administrative duties of the Chief Justice have increased, and many other duties have been imposed on him by acts of Congress which my predecessors were not called on to perform.[153]

Stone told Truman that the duties of a chief justice, unlike those of executive branch officials, could not be delegated. His successor, Fred Vinson, however, immediately increased the number of his law clerks and appointed an administrative assistant to deal with internal administrative matters and to work with the Administrative Office of the U.S. Courts. This prompted a number of the justices to refer to his chamber as "Vinson, Ltd." But Vinson's staff, like that of Earl Warren later, remained rather small, at least by comparison with later chief justices.

Whereas Chief Justice Taft envisioned a marble temple symbolizing the Court's importance as a coequal branch, Burger brought the marble temple into the world of modern computer technology and managerial practices. He also asked Congress to create an Office of Administrative Assistant to the Chief Justice, which Congress did in 1972. Burger wanted someone to handle day-to-day administration and act as a liaison with judicial and legal committees, organizations, and interest groups outside the Court. The office grew to include a special assistant or research associate, four secretaries, a judicial fellows program—in which lawyers and academics work for one year at the Court—and an internship program for undergraduates and law students.

Although less interested in judicial administration, Chief Justices Rehnquist and Roberts continued a number of the programs created by Burger, including the judicial fellows and intern programs. Unlike Burger, though, Rehnquist appointed his administrative assistants to serve only two- to three-year terms. Rehnquist, nonetheless, estimated spending "on average 20 to 25 percent of his time on administrative matters."[154] By contrast, Chief Justice Roberts named Jeffrey P. Minear, an old friend and former associate in the solicitor general's office, as his administrative assistant in 2006. In 2008 the title of administrative assistant was changed to Counselor to the Chief Justice.[155] Unlike Rehnquist, who rotated his administrative assistant every three years or so, Roberts has kept Minear on a permanent basis, which under the statute establishing the office entitles him to retire with the full salary of a federal district court judge after fifteen years of service.

Since 1973 the Court has had a full-time public information officer. Before that, beginning in 1935 there was a "press clerk," later called "the press officer." The Public Information Office has grown to include a staff of six, plus interns. It is with the press, however, not the public, that the office primarily works. It furnishes reporters with copies of the justices' opinions and speeches, as well as maintains a room with copies of all the filings for the use of the Court's press corps. The office also issues full-time reporter credentials ("hard passes"), which provide guaranteed seats on opinion days and use of its office facilities, including carrels for the media's use. The hard passes must be annually renewed and have been limited to twenty-six journalists, though the office also issues about 1,000 day passes each term for reporters covering widely watched cases. Unlike other government public relations offices, though, the public information officer does not explain or comment on the Court's decisions. As the late Toni House, who first headed the office, put it, "We do not do spin."[156]

Managing the Caseload

Throughout the Court's history, justices have complained of "relentless schedules" and "unremitting toil." The growth of the caseload has stimulated institutional reform, procedural change, and the evolution of internal norms and practices.

AN INCREASING CASELOAD

The Court's docket has grown phenomenally. The following graph illustrates the increase in the total docket, which includes cases carried over from the previous term and cases decided by the Supreme Court.[157] Sometimes a ruling of the Court swells the docket. For example, decisions on the constitutional rights of indigents significantly contributed to an increase in filings. But by and large, the docket reflects the course of legislation and broader socioeconomic and political changes.

During the first half of the nineteenth century the caseload grew largely because of population growth, territorial expansion, and the incremental expansion of federal regulation. The Civil War and Reconstruction, both great sources of legal conflict, and the late nineteenth-century business boom dramatically swelled the docket. No less important, Congress greatly expanded the jurisdiction of all federal courts. In particular, federal jurisdiction reached out to include civil rights, *habeas corpus* appeals, questions

DOCKET AND DECISIONS, 1800–2018

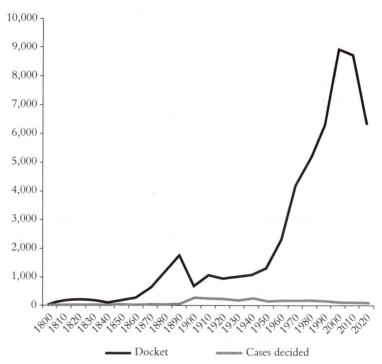

Docket   Cases decided

Data through the 2017–2018 term.

of federal law decided by state courts, and all suits over $500 aris-
ing under the Constitution or federal legislation.[158]

By the 1870s the Court was confronting a growing backlog of
cases. In response, Congress first raised the jurisdictional amount
in diversity cases—cases between citizens of different states—to
$2,000 (now over $50,000). With the 1891 Evarts Act, Congress
provided immediate, if not long-lasting, relief by creating and
staffing circuit courts of appeals. These courts were given final
jurisdiction over most appeals, with the exception of certain civil

cases and cases involving capital or otherwise infamous crimes. The courts of appeals had final say in admiralty and diversity suits, criminal prosecutions, and violations of revenue and patent law. The act preserved access to the Court by providing, instead of mandatory rights of appeal, petitions for writs of *certiorari*, which the Court could refuse to grant. The act thus for the first time gave the Court some power of discretionary review.

In the early twentieth century the docket grew again, in part because of population increase. Economic changes and World War I also brought a rash of disputes over war contracts and suits against the government. A large measure of the congested docket was due nonetheless to expanding congressional legislation and regulation. Congress inflated the docket by enlarging the opportunities both for government and special-interest groups to appeal directly to the Court. Mandatory review was extended, for instance, to government appeals from dismissals of criminal prosecutions. Individuals and businesses challenging administrative decisions under antitrust and interstate commerce laws, the Federal Employer's Liability Act (FELA), and injunctions issued by three-judge courts were also given the right of appeal to the Court.

The Court once again could not stay abreast of its caseload. Congress initially responded piecemeal. It slightly enlarged the Court's discretionary jurisdiction by eliminating mandatory rights of appeal in narrow, though important, areas, such as under the FELA. Then, as a result of a campaign waged by Chief Justice Taft for further relief, Congress passed the "Judges' Bill" or the Judiciary Act of February 13, 1925, which basically established the jurisdiction of the modern Court.[159] That act replaced mandatory review of appeals with discretionary review of petitions for writs of *certiorari*. The act enabled the Court largely to manage its docket, set its own agenda, and decide only cases of national importance.[160]

After World War II, the Court's business increased yet again. In the 1970s Congress provided further incremental relief by eliminating many provisions for mandatory review of appeals.

Major Legislation Affecting the Jurisdiction and
Business of the Court

Legislation	*Commentary*
Judiciary Act of 1789	Provided basic appellate jurisdiction; a three-tier judiciary system staffed by justices and district court judges; required circuit riding
Acts of 1793, 1801, 1802, and 1803	Provided rotation system for circuit riding, then eliminated the responsibilities, only to have Jeffersonians reinstate circuit-riding duties
Act of 1807	Added seventh circuit and justice
Act of 1837	Divided country into nine circuits and brought number of justices to nine (Court's jurisdiction was also expanded to include appeals from new states and territories in 1825, 1828, and 1848)
Acts of 1855 and 1863	Added California as tenth circuit with tenth justice
Acts of 1866, 1867, 1869, and 1871	Expanded federal jurisdiction over civil rights; reorganized country into nine circuits and reduced number of justices to seven, and later fixed the number at nine; expanded jurisdiction over *habeas corpus* and state court decisions
Act of 1875	Greatly expanded jurisdiction over civil disputes; gave review of writs of error; granted full federal question review from state courts
Act of 1887	Curbed access by raising amount of dispute in diversity cases; provided writ of error in all capital cases
Circuit Court of Appeals Act of 1891	Established nine circuit courts and judgeships; broadened review of criminal cases and provided for limited discretionary review via writs of *certiorari*
Act of 1892	Provided for *in forma pauperis* filings

Legislation	Commentary
Act of 1893	Created District of Columbia Circuit
Acts of 1903 and 1907	Provided direct appeal under antitrust and interstate commerce acts; granted government right of direct appeal in dismissals of criminal prosecutions
Acts of 1910, 1911, and 1913	Altered federal injunctive power; established three-judge courts because of abuses by single judges in enjoining state economic regulation; later extended the jurisdiction of three-judge courts and direct appeals to Court
Acts of 1914, 1915, and 1916	Made jurisdiction over some state cases discretionary and eliminated right to review in bankruptcy, trademark, and FELA
Judiciary Act of 1925	Greatly extended the Court's discretionary jurisdiction by replacing mandatory appeals with petitions for *certiorari*
Act of 1928	Made appeals the sole method of mandatory appellate review
Act of 1939	Expanded review of decisions by Court of Claims over both law and fact
Act of 1948	Revised, codified, and enacted into law the judicial code
Act of 1950 (Hobbes Act)	Eliminated three-judge court requirement in certain areas
Voting Rights Act of 1965	Provided direct appeal over decisions of three-judge courts in area of voting rights
Acts of 1970, 1971, 1974, 1975, and 1976	Reorganized District of Columbia courts; expanded Court's discretionary review; repealed direct government appeals under Act of 1907; eliminated direct appeals in antitrust and ICC cases; further cut back jurisdiction and direct appeals from three-judge courts, with the exception of areas of voting rights and reapportionment

(*Continues*)

MAJOR LEGISLATION AFFECTING THE JURISDICTION AND
BUSINESS OF THE COURT (*continued*)

Legislation	Commentary
Federal Courts Improvement Act of 1982	Created Court of Appeals for the Federal Circuit by joining the Court of Claims with the Court of Customs and Patent Appeals
1988 Act to Improve the Administration of Justice	Eliminated virtually all the Court's nondiscretionary appellate jurisdiction, except for appeals in reapportionment cases, suits under the Civil Rights and Voting Rights acts, antitrust laws, and the Presidential Election Campaign Fund Act

Excluded, necessarily, is the vast amount of legislation expanding the administrative state and providing opportunities for challenging law and policy in federal courts.

In 1988 Congress finally eliminated virtually all of the Court's nondiscretionary appellate jurisdiction. The only mandatory appeals that the Court must now review are those involving reapportionment, some antitrust matters, and cases under the Civil Rights and Voting Rights acts and the Presidential Election Campaign Fund Act. The table above summarizes the principal legislation altering the Court's jurisdiction and extending its power of discretionary review, enabling further control of the docket.

ALTERNATIVE INSTITUTIONAL RESPONSES

In historical perspective, the process of institutionalization paralleled the growth of the caseload. There are basically three ways in which the Court responded to the rising caseload and workload.

First, a *bureaucratic response*: the Court may make managerial and technological changes. In the late nineteenth century, for example, the Court's terms were lengthened, the time allowed for oral arguments was shortened, and the justices gradually acquired staff. In the latter half of the twentieth century and especially during the Burger Court years (1969–1986), the justices hired larger and more professional staffs and incorporated modern office equipment.

The bureaucratic response, however, may prove counterproductive in some ways. One problem is that caseload is not equivalent to workload. Filings and cases are not fungible; some take a great deal more time than others. Another problem is that larger staffs and the delegation of work force justices to spend more time supervising their chambers. Consequently, the nature of the justices' workload may change but does not necessarily diminish. The justices, moreover, have less opportunity or inclination to talk and try to reach accommodations with each other. The present pattern of formal written communications among the chambers, in turn, encourages even greater reliance on law clerks for screening cases and draft opinions.

Some justices concede that adding more law clerks and secretaries does not necessarily help in managing the increasing docket and might even prove counterproductive. "You reach a point of diminishing returns with law clerks," Justice Scalia observed during a hearing on funding for the federal judiciary. "It's not healthy," he added, "It's not necessarily the case that the more clerks you have, the more cases you can pump out."

A second response to the burgeoning docket has been *jurisdictional* changes. Such changes include a further enlarging of the Court's power of discretionary review and creating new lower appellate courts so that the justices may decide only those cases of national importance. The Court must decide cases arising under its original jurisdiction, as is specified in Article III of the Constitution. But over 99 percent of all filings now come under its appellate jurisdiction. Since the Judiciary Act of 1925, as noted, Congress has incrementally enlarged the Court's discretionary jurisdiction, allowing the justices to deny review to more cases. In Justice White's words, "the power to deny cases helps to keep us current."[161] With the 1988 Act to Improve the Administration of Justice, Congress eliminated most of the remaining provisions for mandatory appellate review.[162] The Court now enjoys virtually complete discretionary jurisdiction, with the exception of those few cases coming under its original jurisdiction. Such jurisdictional changes, however, do not reduce the Court's caseload; they only affect the justices' workload and process of deciding what to decide.

The modern Court's docket grew so large that Chief Justices Burger and Rehnquist endorsed the idea of Congress's establishing a national intermediate appellate court, located between the thirteen courts of appeals and the Supreme Court.[163] Such a national intermediate appellate court would either screen and decide cases or have cases referred to it by the Court. But the idea never commanded political support and certainly such a major institutional change is unlikely in the future. That is because, as discussed in the next chapter, in spite of a rising caseload, the Rehnquist and Roberts Courts cut back sharply on the number of cases granted review, thereby undercutting arguments that the justices have a workload problem that they cannot resolve themselves. In addition, as a young attorney in the Reagan administration, Roberts staunchly opposed the creation of an intermediate court of appeals, which he deemed an expansion of the "judicial bureaucracy." He argued that the Court was not overworked because "only the Court and school children are expected and do take the entire summer off." In his view, the proposal was a "terrible idea" and "[t]he fault lies with the Justices themselves, who unnecessarily take too many cases and issue opinions so confusing [and] that often do not even resolve the question presented." Indeed, he concluded, when Court ends its annual term "the Constitution is safe for the summer."[164] Moreover, since becoming chief justice, the number of cases granted review by the Roberts Court has shrunken by well over 50 percent of that previously decided by the Warren, Burger, and Rehnquist Courts.

A third and final institutional response relates to the Court's internal *procedures and processes*: formal jurisdictional and procedural rules, along with informal processes and practices in the screening and disposing of cases may be modified by the justices. The Court has often changed formal requirements for accepting cases, raising filing fees, and imposing penalties for filing "frivolous" cases, for example. It has also altered internal processes and practices of judicial review. Such changes in procedure and process are examined in the next chapter, on how the Court decides what to decide.

FOUR

Deciding What to Decide

"I'LL TAKE my case all the way to the Supreme Court," people say when they feel they have been treated unjustly and want a fair hearing. But few actually do take their cases all the way to the Court, and even fewer are granted a hearing. Clarence Earl Gideon was one who succeeded. Gideon, a fifty-one-year-old rambler, in and out of jail for most of his life, was convicted in a state court of breaking into the Bay Harbor Poolroom in Panama City, Florida. At his trial, he claimed he was too poor to afford an attorney and requested that one be provided. The judge refused, but Gideon persisted. While serving a five-year sentence for petty larceny, he mailed a petition, printed childishly on lined paper obtained from a prison guard. His petition led to the landmark ruling in *Gideon v. Wainwright* (1963) that indigents have a right to counsel in all felony cases.[1]

Gideon was exceptional, for the overwhelming number of all petitions are now denied. Fewer than 1 percent of the cases on the Court's docket are granted and decided by written opinion. Out of over 9,000 cases that now arrive each term, only about seventy to eighty get the Court's full attention. Unlike other federal judges, the justices have virtually complete discretion to screen out the few they will decide. By deciding what to decide, the Court stays abreast of its caseload. The cornerstone of the modern Court's operation, as Justice Harlan remarked, "is the control it possesses over the amount and character of its business."[2]

The power to decide what to decide also enables the Court to set its own substantive agenda—the kinds of cases granted review. Like other courts, the Court must await issues brought by lawsuits. One hundred fifty years ago, the Court's docket did not include issues of personal privacy raised by the use of thermal imaging and GPS searches, for instance, or controversies over abortion and same-sex marriage. As technology develops and society changes, courts respond. Law evolves (more or less quickly) in response to social, economic, and technological changes. Unlike any other court, however, the Supreme Court has the power to pick which issues it will decide and when. The Court now functions like a roving commission, or legislative body, in responding to social forces, as underscored by its ruling on same-sex marriages in *Obergefell v. Hodges* (2015).

Gideon's petition provided a vehicle for the Warren Court to change the course of American law. Gideon was wrong in claiming that the Court had said that the poor had a right to a court-appointed attorney—he was in fact asking the Court to reverse itself. The Sixth Amendment provides simply that in criminal cases the accused has the right "to have the Assistance of Counsel for his defense." The guarantee applied only in federal, not in state, courts; and it did not require the government to provide attorneys for indigent defendants. The Court first addressed the issue of a right to counsel in *Powell v. Alabama* (1932).[3] Nine black youths—the "Scottsboro boys," as they were called—were convicted of raping two white women by an all-white jury in a small southern town. Under these circumstances, the Court ruled, without the benefit of counsel "the defendants, young, ignorant, illiterate [and] surrounded by hostile sentiment," were denied a fair hearing. Six years later, in *Johnson v. Zerbst* (1938), Justice Black

(*Mike Luckovich Editorial Cartoon, used with the permission of Mike Luckovich and Creators Syndicate. All rights reserved.*)

wrote for a bare majority that the Sixth Amendment requires counsel for indigents in all federal criminal cases.[4] A majority of the Court nonetheless refused to apply that ruling to indigents in state courts. In *Betts v. Brady* (1942), the Court held that only in "special circumstances" like those in the Scottsboro case was counsel required.[5] Justices Black, Douglas, and Murphy dissented. Anticipating his eventual opinion for the Court in *Gideon* that overturned *Betts*, Black insisted that no one should be "deprived of counsel merely because of his poverty," and that "any other practice seems to me to defeat the promise of our democratic society to provide equal justice under the law."

Gideon was not part of a special-interest group seeking legal reform. Yet he "was part of a current history." Constitutional law is a constantly changing dialogue between the Court and the country. *Betts*'s special-circumstances rule stood for two decades, but it was increasingly criticized by Black. Only three justices who decided *Betts* remained on the bench when Gideon's petition was granted: two of the dissenters (Black and Douglas) and Frankfurter, who was eighty years old, ill, and in his last year on the bench. They had been joined by Tom Clark and Eisenhower's appointees—Earl Warren, John Harlan, William Brennan, Charles Whittaker, and Potter Stewart. By the time *Gideon* was decided, Frankfurter had retired and Whittaker was disabled. They had been replaced by Kennedy's appointees—Arthur Goldberg and Byron White.

Gideon fitted the agenda of a majority of the Warren Court. In cases such as Gideon's, their "liberal jurisprudence" revolutionized criminal law by extending the guarantees of the Bill of Rights to the poor and others in state as well as in federal courts. By contrast, the Burger, Rehnquist, and Roberts Courts largely selected cases in order to cut back, if not reverse, the direction of the Warren Court's rulings.

The Court under Chief Justices Rehnquist and Roberts became more conservative than the Warren and Burger Courts and took steps to discourage indigents from filing what it deemed frivolous appeals. Indeed, the Clerk's office's *Guide to Prospective Indigent Petitioners for Writs of* Certiorari emphasizes, "The primary concern of the Supreme Court is not to correct errors in lower court decisions, but to decide cases presenting issues of importance beyond the particular facts and parties involved."

Although the Court now grants less than 1 percent of all cases on the docket, petitions from indigents and "jailhouse" lawyers, like Gideon, still on occasion command the Court's attention.[6] Most litigants before the Court are either government attorneys or hired and experienced members of the Supreme Court's bar (as further discussed in this chapter). For indigents, like Gideon, the Court appoints a lawyer to argue their cases; in Gideon's case, the Warren Court appointed Abe Fortas, a well-known appellate attorney and future justice. On very rare occasions do litigants argue their own cases. Michael Newdow—an atheist, doctor, and nonpracticing lawyer—argued that the phrase "under God" did not belong in the Pledge of Allegiance, which his daughter was required to recite in school, in *Elk Grove Unified School District v. Newdow* (2004),[7] for instance. He lost on technical grounds, but his passionate argument drew applause in the courtroom. In *Snyder v. Phelps* (2010),[8] Margie Phelps, a member of the small Westboro Baptist Church in Kansas, calmly and successfully argued that the First Amendment protects its hateful protests against the LGBTQ at military funerals. Recently, Theodore Frank argued his case against abusive class-action settlements, in which class members are not afforded the opportunity to protest the settlement, in *Frank v. Gaos* (2018).[9] The case involved a class-action lawsuit against Google over users' privacy rights that resulted in a settlement in which members of the class received nothing, but more than $2 million went to leading law schools and centers concerned with privacy on the Internet with which the class-action lawyers were associated.

In sum, each Court, with its unique combination of justices, sets its own agenda. Justices, of course, differ on what cases should be decided. "There is an ideological division on the Court," as Chief Justice Rehnquist once observed, "and each of us has some cases we would like to see granted, and on the contrary some of the other members would not like to see them granted."[10] Justices compete for influence in setting the Court's agenda. That competition flows from the jurisdictional rules and doctrines governing access to the Court's power.

Access to Justice

Jurisdiction is power over access to justice and the exercise of judicial review. The Court's jurisdiction derives from: (1) Article III of the Constitution, which defines the Court's original jurisdiction; (2) congressional legislation, providing appellate jurisdiction;

and (3) the Court's own interpretation of (1) and (2), together with its own rules for accepting cases.

Article III of the Constitution provides that the judicial power extends to all federal questions—that is, "all Cases, in Law and Equity, arising under this Constitution, the Laws of the United States, and Treaties." The Court also has original jurisdiction over specific kinds of "cases or controversies": those affecting ambassadors, other public ministers, and consuls involving disputes to which the United States is a party; between two or more states; between a state and a citizen of another state; and between a state (or its citizens) and foreign countries. The Court today has only a handful of such cases. Most involve states suing each other over land or water rights, and they tend to be carried over for several terms before finally being decided. For instance, the Court held in *New Jersey v. New York* (1998) that 90 percent of Ellis Island's 27.5 acres, created by silt and landfill long after an 1834 agreement dividing the island, belongs to New Jersey, thereby ending a 164-year dispute between those two states.

Congress establishes (and may change) the appellate jurisdiction of the federal judiciary, including the Supreme Court. Most cases used to come as direct appeals, requiring obligatory review. But as the caseload increased, as noted in the last chapter, Congress expanded the Court's discretionary jurisdiction by replacing appeals with petitions for *certiorari*, which the Court may grant or deny. Before the Judiciary Act of 1925, which broadened the Court's discretionary jurisdiction, appeals amounted to 80 percent of the docket and petitions for *certiorari* fewer than 20 percent. Today 99 percent of the docket comes on *certiorari*.

Although most cases now come as *certiorari* petitions, Congress provides that appellate courts may also submit a writ of certification to the Court, requesting that justices clarify or "make more certain" a point of federal law; only a handful of such cases arrive each term. Congress also gave the Court the power to issue certain extraordinary writs, or orders. In a few cases, the Court may issue writs of mandamus and prohibition, ordering lower

**AVENUES OF APPEAL: THE TWO MAIN ROUTES
TO THE SUPREME COURT**

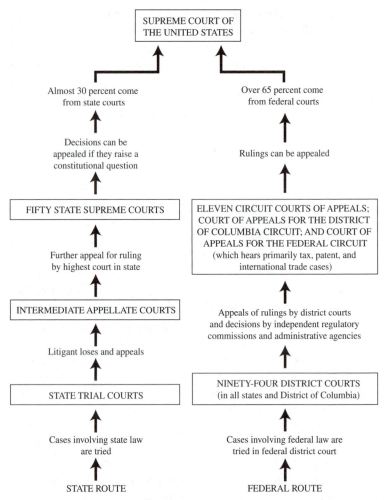

Note: In addition, some cases come directly to the Supreme Court from trial courts
when they involve reapportionment or civil rights disputes. Appeals from the Court of
Military Appeals also go directly to the Supreme Court. Few cases come on "original
jurisdiction" and involve disputes between state governments.

courts or public officials either to do something or refrain from some action. In addition, the Court has the power to grant writs of *habeas corpus* ("produce the body"), enabling it to review cases by prisoners who claim that they are unlawfully imprisoned.

Congress also established the practice of giving indigents, like Gideon, the right to file without the payment of fees. When filing a petition for *certiorari*, indigents must also file an affidavit requesting that they be allowed to proceed *in forma pauperis* ("in the manner of a pauper"), without the usual filing fees and forms. Gideon's first petition, for example, was returned because he failed to include a statement that he was an indigent.

The Court sets both the rules governing filing fees and the form that appeals, *certiorari* petitions, and other documents must take. Except for indigents, the Court requires $300 for filing any case and $200 for filing a petition for a rehearing. Indigents are exempt also from the Court's rule specifying particular colors and lengths of paper for various kinds of filings. All *certiorari* petitions, for instance, must have a white cover, whereas opposing briefs are orange, and the reply to the response, tan. If the Court grants review, the petitioner's brief on merits must have a light blue cover and a red cover for the respondent. Any document filed by the federal government has a gray cover. Historically, no petition or appeal could exceed thirty pages; and for those few cases granted oral argument, briefs on the merits of cases were limited to fifty pages. The Court changed its rules to require pauper petitioners to file ten copies (instead of one) of their petitions, unless they are incarcerated and without counsel; otherwise, lawyers must file forty copies of each brief and submit them electronically. More recently, the Roberts Court, in response to the increasing length of briefs, stipulated that briefs should be set in New Century Schoolbook; printed on paper that is "opaque, unglazed, and not less than 60 pounds in weight"; in 12-point type, and reduced their length to 15,000 words (unless an exception is granted). Briefs on the merits of cases must be filed forty-five days after a case is granted, respondent's reply briefs filed within thirty days afterward, with thirty days more for the reply brief by the petitioner. The number of words in reply briefs is limited to between 6,000 and 7,500 words. In 2010 revisions to the rules, the Court also limited the filing of an *amicus curiae* brief to attorneys admitted to practice before the Court. Moreover, the Court's online system now makes all petitions, responses, briefs, and other public documents in cases available on its website, www.supremecourt.gov.

The Constitution and Congress thus stipulate the kinds of cases and controversies the Court may consider. Yet, as Chief Justice Hughes candidly remarked, "We are under the Constitution, but the Constitution is what the judges say it is."[11] The Court has developed its own doctrines for denying review to a large number of cases and for setting its own agenda. These doctrines depend, in one justice's words, on "our sense of self-restraint."[12]

Jurisdictional Doctrines and Policies

Each "case or controversy" has, as Chief Justice Warren observed,

an iceberg quality, containing beneath [the] surface simplicity, submerged complexities which go to the very heart of our constitutional form of government. Embodied in the words "cases" and "controversies" are two complementary but somewhat different limitations. In part those words limit the business of federal courts to questions presented in an adversary context and in a form historically viewed as capable of resolution through the judicial process. And in part those words define the role assigned to the judiciary in a tripartite allocation of power to assure that the federal courts will not intrude into areas committed to the other branches of government. Justiciability is a term of art employed to give expression to this dual limitation placed upon federal courts by the case and controversy doctrine.[13]

In other words, the Court considers first whether it has jurisdiction over a "case or controversy" and then whether that dispute is justiciable—capable of judicial resolution. Justices thus may (or may not) deny a case if it (1) lacks adverseness; (2) is brought by parties who lack "standing to sue"; poses issues that either (3) are not "ripe" or (4) have become "moot"; or (5) involves a "political question."

Adverseness and Advisory Opinions • The Court generally maintains that litigants must be real and adverse in seeking a decision that will resolve their dispute and not a hypothetical issue. This means the Court will not decide "friendly suits" in which the parties do not have adverse interests, nor will the Court give "advisory opinions" on issues not raised in an actual lawsuit. The Jay Court denied two requests for advisory opinions from President Washington's administration: one in 1790 by Secretary of the Treasury Alexander Hamilton for advice on the national government's power to assume state Revolutionary War debts, and another in 1793 by Secretary of State Thomas Jefferson for an interpretation of certain treaties. Chief Justice Jay held that it would be improper to judge such matters because the president might call on Cabinet heads for advice. In doing so, the Jay Court broke with the British practice of advisory opinions and set a precedent which the Court continues to honor.[14]

Historically, justices have nevertheless extrajudicially advised attorneys, members of Congress, and presidents (see Chapter 2). They occasionally even accuse each other of including opinions *dicta*—statements of personal philosophy not necessary to the decision handed down—that amount to "giving legal advice."[15] The Court, furthermore, upheld the constitutionality of the Declaratory Judgment Act, authorizing federal courts to make clear legal relationships even before a law has taken effect, though only in "cases of actual controversy."[16]

The requirement of adverseness, nevertheless, from time to time admits exceptions. When both parties in a suit agree on how an issue should be decided but need a judicial ruling, the Court may approve a special counsel or *amicus curiae* ("friend of the court") to argue the other side and ensure opposition. That occurred in the 1983 one-house veto case, *Immigration and*

Naturalization Service v. Chadha (1983).[17] Jagdish Rai Chadha came to the U. S. on a student visa but remained after it expired. The Immigration and Naturalization Service (INS) moved to deport him, but the attorney general suspended deportation and, as required, reported his decision to Congress. One house of Congress then passed a resolution vetoing the suspension of Chadha's deportation. The INS, the Department of Justice, and Chadha all agreed that the INS's action was unconstitutional. The appellate court, which initially heard the case, requested Congress to submit *amicus* briefs arguing the opposite. Ultimately, the Supreme Court held that one-house vetoes of executive branch agencies' decisions are unconstitutional.

Standing to Sue • Standing, like adverseness, is a threshold requirement for getting into court. "Generalizations about standing to sue," Justice Douglas discouragingly but candidly said, "are largely worthless as such."[18] Nonetheless, the basic requirement is that an individual show injury to a legally protected interest or right and demonstrate that other opportunities for defending that claim before an administrative tribunal or a lower court have been exhausted. The claim of an injury "must be of a personal and not official nature" and of "some specialized interest of [the individual's] own to vindicate, apart from political concerns which belong to it."[19]

The injuries and legal interests that were claimed traditionally turned on showing proprietary damage. Typically, plaintiffs had suffered some "pocketbook" or monetary injury. Since the 1980s, however, individuals have sought standing in order to represent nonmonetary injuries and the "public interest."

The law of standing is a combination of judge-made law and congressional legislation, as interpreted by the Court. In *Frothingham v. Mellon* (1923), the Taft Court denied individual taxpayers standing to challenge the constitutionality of federal legislation. Mrs. Frothingham, a taxpayer, attacked a congressional appropriation to the states for a maternal and infant care program. She claimed that Congress exceeded its power and intruded on "the reserved rights of the states" under the Tenth Amendment. The Taft Court avoided confronting the merits of the claim by denying standing on the ground that an individual taxpayer's interest in the financing of federal programs is "comparatively minute and indeterminable," when viewed in light of the interest of all taxpayers. Frothingham's injury was neither direct nor immediate, and the issue raised was basically "political, not judicial."[20] The government relied on *Frothingham* to provide an absolute barrier to subsequent taxpayer suits.

The Warren Court, however, substantially lowered the threshold for standing and permitted more litigation of some public policy issues by making an exception to the *Frothingham* doctrine in *Flast v. Cohen* (1968).[21] *Flast* involved a taxpayer's challenge, under the First Amendment (dis)establishment clause, to the appropriation of funds for private religious schools in the Elementary and Secondary Education Act of 1965. Here the Court found that Mrs. Florance Flast, unlike Mrs. Frothingham, had standing. The Court ruled that she had a "personal stake in the outcome," which ensured concrete adverseness and litigation that would illuminate the constitutional issues presented. In so doing, the Warren Court created standing where there is a logical relationship between a taxpayer's status and the challenged legislative statute, as well as a connection between that status and the "precise nature of the constitutional infringement alleged." The Warren Court's two-pronged test invited more taxpayer lawsuits.

The Burger Court tightened the requirements for standing in some cases, but relaxed them in others. In two closely divided decisions, the Court denied standing to a group challenging military surveillance of lawful political protests in public places and to the Sierra Club, when challenging the construction of a ski resort in Sequoia National Park. In both cases, a bare majority found that the groups failed to show a "personal stake in the outcome" of the litigation.[22] In *Sierra Club v. Morton* (1972),[23] a bare majority held that the group failed to show a "personal stake in the outcome," over Justice Douglas's powerful dissent. Douglas argued:

Inanimate objects are sometimes parties in litigation. . . .
    The ordinary corporation is a "person" for purposes of the adjudicatory process, whether it represents proprietary, spiritual, aesthetic, or charitable causes.
    So it should be as respects valleys, alpine meadows, rivers, lakes, estuaries, beaches, ridges, groves of trees, swampland, or even air that feels the destructive pressures of modern technology and modern life. The river, for example, is the living symbol of all the life it sustains or nourishes—fish, aquatic insects, water ouzels, otter, fisher, deer, elk, bear, and all other animals, including man, who are dependent on it or its life. . . .
    Those people who have a meaningful relation to that body of water—whether it be a fisherman, a canoeist, a zoologist, or a logger—must be able to speak for the values which the river represents and which are threatened with destruction.

A year later, a majority of the Court embraced Justice Douglas's dissent in *Sierra Club* when it granted standing to a group of law students attacking a surcharge on railroad freight containing recycled materials. The students contended that the surcharge would discourage the recycling of bottles and cans by making recycling more expensive, and thus contribute to environmental pollution. In *United States v. Students Challenging Regulatory Agency Procedures (SCRAP)* (1973), the Court granted standing, observing,[24]

Aesthetic and environmental well-being, like economic well-being, are important ingredients of the quality of life in our society, and the fact that particular environmental interests are shared by the many rather than the few does not make them less deserving of legal protection through the judicial process.

Plaintiffs must still claim personal injury, but they may now act as surrogates for special-interest groups. The personal injuries claimed thus may embrace public injury. Congress at the same time expanded the principle even more by providing that any individual "adversely affected or aggrieved" may challenge administrative decisions. Even when legislation does not provide for such "citizen suits," individuals may claim personal injuries, or a "private cause of action," to gain access to the courts and force agency compliance with the law.

The Court, however restricted standing requirements in several other ways. First, it refused to recognize certain types of new interests and injuries in granting standing. In *Paul v. Davis* (1976), for example, a majority of the Court rejected a claim of injury to personal reputation by an individual who objected to the circulation of a flier to local merchants that carried his photograph along with that of other alleged "Active Shoplifters."[25] Second, the Court limited *Flast* by holding that standing is not a right but a set of prudential rules. In *Valley Forge Christian College v. Americans United for Separation of Church and State* (1982), the Court denied standing to an organization challenging the Department of Health, Education, and Welfare (now the Department of Health and Human Services) for giving a former military hospital to a religious college. Writing for a bare majority, Rehnquist held that standing under *Flast* was limited to challenging congressional acts and did not extend to decisions of administrative agencies.[26]

A bare majority of the Roberts Court further limited taxpayers' standing to challenge federal policies under *Flast* in *Hein v. Freedom from Religion Foundation, Inc.* (2007).[27] Although declining to overrule *Flast*, writing for the majority, Justice Alito limited *Flast*, which permits taxpayer suits under the First Amendment (dis)establishment clause, to challenges to congressional appropriations, but not to general expenditures of the executive branch. Notably, concurring Justices Scalia and Thomas would have overturned *Flast*. By contrast, dissenting Justice Souter, joined by Justices Stevens, Ginsburg, and Breyer, would have granted standing to challenge President George W. Bush's faith-based initiatives, which established centers to help faith-based organizations compete for federal grants without congressional authorization.

The Court also tightened the law of standing in the area of environmental litigation in *Lujan v. Defenders of Wildlife* (1992). There, the Court denied two environmentalists standing to sue the Department of Interior under the Endangered Species Act (ESA) for reinterpreting the ESA as no longer applying to federally funded projects abroad and failing to consult with other agencies about a federally funded irrigation project in Sri Lanka and a redevelopment project on the Nile River in Egypt. The president of Defenders of Wildlife and another member claimed those projects threatened endangered elephants and leopards in Sri Lanka and crocodiles in Egypt. They testified that they were environmentalists who had traveled to each of the sites and would again visit, though not specifying when. Writing for the majority, Justice Scalia denied standing because of the failure to show "imminent injury."[28] "That the two women 'had visited' the areas of the projects," as Scalia put it, "proves nothing." Dissenting Justices Blackmun and O'Connor, however, charged the majority with "what amounts to a slash-and-burn expedition through the law of environmental standing."

The law of standing and personal injuries thus permits the justices to avoid and delay addressing controversies. The Court, by denying standing in *Elk Grove Unified School District v. Newdow* (2004),[29] for instance, avoided the controversy over whether requiring school children to recite "under God" in the Pledge of Allegiance violates the First Amendment (dis)establishment clause. Writing for the Court, Justice Stevens held that Michael A. Newdow, who challenged the policy on behalf of his daughter, even though he was not her legal guardian, lacked "prudential standing." In other words, when legal claims are made on behalf of another person on the basis of domestic relations law, a field largely left to states, "the prudent course is for a federal court to stay its hand rather than reach out to resolve a weighty question of federal constitutional law." But in concurring opinions, Chief Justice Rehnquist and Justices O'Connor and Thomas dismissed the majority's theory as "novel" and "like the proverbial excursion ticket—good for this day only." They would have granted standing and rejected Newdow's claims.

The Roberts Court, even more than the Rehnquist Court, invokes standing doctrines and demands for concrete personal injuries in order to avoid or delay deciding major controversies. For example, prior to the ruling in *Obergefell v. Hodges* (2015), two same-sex couples sued state officials claiming that California's Proposition 8, a ballot initiative banning same-sex marriages, violated their due process and equal protection rights. Yet the state officials, including the governor, attorney general, and others, refused to enforce Proposition 8. And the original proponents of Proposition 8 sought to intervene and defend the law on behalf of the state. In *Hollingsworth v. Perry*, 133 S. Ct. 2652 (2015), however, the Court denied standing because they merely asserted a "generalized grievance" rather than a "direct stake" in Proposition 8's enforcement. As Chief Justice Roberts explained, "Without a judicially cognizable interest of their own, [the original proponents of Proposition 8] attempt to invoke that of someone else," namely state officials. Hence, they do not have a "sufficiently concrete interest" in the dispute and thus not an "injury in fact."

Likewise, the Roberts Court avoided ruling on extreme partisan gerrymandering by denying standing in *Gill v. Whitford* (2018).[30] The Wisconsin Republican legislature and governor in 2011 redrew voting district lines in order to favor Republicans. As a result, in the next election Republican candidates won 48.8 percent of the statewide vote but captured a 60-to-39 seat advantage in the state legislature. They did so through a process of "packing" and "cracking" districts—that is, by cramming Democratic voters into a few districts and thinly spreading them across other districts, giving Republicans an advantage. Writing for the Court, Chief Justice Roberts held that the challengers, claiming an unconstitutional vote dilution, did not have standing to sue, because they claimed only a statewide injury and not a personal injury based on their individual voting districts. Quoting *Baker v. Carr* (1962), the chief justice ruled that they failed to demonstrate a "personal stake in the outcome," as distinct from a "generally available grievance about government."

Ripeness and Mootness • With these doctrines the Court wields a double-edged sword. A case may be dismissed as not yet "ripe" because it was brought too early or the issues are "moot" because the case was brought too late or the underlying facts have changed. A case is usually rejected as not ripe if the injury claimed has not yet occurred or if other avenues of appeal have not been exhausted. Petitioners raising a federal claim when appealing a state court ruling, for example, must exhaust all appeals in the state courts, and the Court will not exercise jurisdiction until a "final judgment" has been rendered by the highest court in the state.

Alternatively, a case may be dismissed if pertinent facts or laws change so that there is no longer real adverseness or an actual case or controversy. The issue becomes moot since "there is no subject matter on which the judgment of the court can operate," and hence a ruling would not prove "conclusive."[31]

In practice, both doctrines bend to the Court's will. The requirement of ripeness, for instance, permits the Court to avoid or delay deciding certain issues. Between 1943 and 1965, the Court refused standing to individuals attacking the constitutionality of a late nineteenth-century Connecticut statute, prohibiting virtually all single and married individuals from using contraceptives and physicians from giving advice about their use. In *Tileston v. Ullman* (1943), a doctor sued, charging that the statute prevented him from giving information to patients.[32] But the Court ruled that he had no real interest or personal injury, since he had not been arrested. Over a decade later in *Poe v. Ullman* (1961), a doctor and a patient were likewise denied standing on the ground that the law had not been enforced for eighty years, even though the state had begun to close birth control clinics.[33]

Finally, after two individuals were found guilty of prescribing contraceptives to a married couple, the Court in *Griswold v. Connecticut* (1965) struck down what Justice Stewart called an "uncommonly silly law."[34] The ruling was limited to the privacy and marital decisions of couples. Consequently, in *Eisenstadt v. Baird* (1972), in order to gain standing to claim that single individuals also have a right to acquire contraceptives, a doctor arranged to be arrested after delivering a public lecture on contraceptives and handing out samples to single women in the audience.[35] The Court accepted the case and ruled that single women also have the right to acquire contraceptives.

A finding of mootness likewise enables the Court to avoid, if not escape, deciding controversial political issues. *DeFunis v. Odegaard* (1974), for example, involved a white student who was denied admission to the University of Washington Law School.[36] The student claimed that the school's affirmative action program discriminated against him and allowed the entrance of minorities with lower Law School Admission Test scores. After the trial judge ruled in his favor, he was admitted into the law school. But by the time his case reached the Court, he was completing his final year and assured of graduation. Over four dissenters, the majority held that the case was moot. Yet, as the dissenters predicted, the issue would not go away. Within four years, the Court reconsidered the issue of "reverse discrimination" in university affirmative action programs in *Regents of the University of California v. Bakke* (1978).[37] In *Bakke*, Justice Powell held that quota systems in college admissions are unconstitutional but affirmative action programs are permissible to achieve diverse student bodies.

The issue of mootness presented no serious problem, however, when the Court tackled abortion in *Roe v. Wade* (1973). Here, as we saw in Chapter 1, a Texas criminal statute prohibiting abortions was attacked as infringing on a woman's right of privacy as recognized in *Griswold*. In defending the law, the state attorney general argued that the plaintiff was a single woman whose pregnancy had come to term by the time the case reached the Court and that hence her claim was moot. Writing for the Court, Justice Blackmun rejected that view:

> [W]hen, as here, pregnancy is a significant fact in the litigation, the normal 266-day human gestation period is so short that the pregnancy will come to term before the usual appellate process is complete. If that termination makes a case moot, pregnancy litigation seldom will survive much beyond the trial stage, and appellate review will be effectively denied. Our law should not be that rigid. Pregnancy often comes more than once to the same woman, and in the general population, if man is to survive, it will always be with us. Pregnancy provides a classic justification for a conclusion of nonmootness. It truly could be "capable of repetition, yet evading review."

More recently, in *United States v. Microsoft* (2018),[38] the Roberts Court in a *per curiam* opinion declared a case against Microsoft moot, because of a newly enacted law, Clarifying Lawful Overseas Use of Data Act (CLOUD Act) of 2018. The government had obtained a warrant directing Microsoft to turn over all emails and other records of an account believed to be associated with drug trafficking. Microsoft refused because the account's emails were stored in a data center in Dublin, Ireland. While the case was in litigation, the CLOUD Act became law, providing that service providers must comply with orders to turn over the contents of electronic communications regardless of whether they are stored inside or outside of the country. The government obtained another warrant under that act and, on appeal, the Court held that there was no longer a live dispute between the parties.

Political Questions • Even when the Court has jurisdiction over a properly framed suit, it may decline to rule because it decides that a case raises a political question that should be resolved by other political branches. Like other jurisdictional doctrines, the political-question doctrine means what the justices say it means.

The doctrine has its origin in the following observation by Chief Justice Marshall in *Marbury v. Madison* (1803): "The province of the Court, is, solely, to decide on the rights of individuals. . . . Questions in the nature political, or which are, by the constitution and laws, submitted to the executive can never be made in this Court." Yet, as Alexis de Tocqueville noted in the 1830s, "Scarcely any political question arises in the United States that is not resolved, sooner or later, into a judicial question." Litigation that reaches the Court is often political, and the justices decide what and how to decide cases on their docket.

The Taney Court first developed the political question doctrine in *Luther v. Borden* (1849).[39] There, the Court was called on to decide whether Rhode Island had a "republican form of government," as guaranteed by Article IV of the Constitution. Chief Justice Taney reasoned that Article I gave Congress, not the Court, "the right to decide." Subsequent rulings elaborated other reasons for the doctrine besides deference to separation of powers, such as that the Court may lack information needed for a ruling. In some areas, as in foreign policy and international relations, the Court lacks both adequate standards for resolving disputes and the means to enforce its decisions.

For many decades the Court relied on the doctrine to avoid entering the "political thicket" of state representation and malapportionment.[40] Yet when blacks and other minorities in urban areas were denied equal voting rights, the Court finally responded and reversed itself in *Baker v. Carr* (1962).[41] The Court reasserted its power to decide what is and is not a "political question" when it held that disputes over malapportionment were within its jurisdiction and justiciable, and led to the Warren Court establishing the principle of "one person, one vote."

The doctrine's logic is admittedly circular. "Political questions are matters not soluble by the judicial process; matters not soluble by the judicial process are political questions. As an early dictionary explained," political scientist John Roche observed, "violins are small cellos, and cellos are large violins."[42]

Nevertheless, as the Columbia Law professor Louis Henkin pointed out, even when denying review because of a political question, "the court does not refuse judicial review; it exercises it. It is not dismissing the case or the issue as nonjusticiable; it adjudicates it. It is not refusing to pass on the power of the political branches; it passes upon it, only to affirm that they had the power which had been challenged and that nothing in the Constitution prohibited the particular exercise of it."[43]

Stare Decisis *and Other Policies* • The justices also occasionally rely on other self-denying policies to avoid reaching issues. They may, for example, invoke what has been called the doctrine of "strict necessity" and thereupon decide only the narrowest ground—a position that Chief Justice Roberts has championed.

The doctrine of *stare decisis* ("let the prior decision stand") is not a mechanical formula. It is, rather, a judicial policy that promotes "the certainty, uniformity, and stability of the law." "*Stare decisis* is usually the wise policy," Justice Brandeis remarked, "because in most matters it is more important that the applicable rule of law be settled than that it be settled right."[44] On constitutional matters, however, Justice Douglas, among others, emphasized that "*stare decisis*—that is, established law—was really no sure guideline because what did. . . . the judges who sat there in 1875 know about, say, electronic surveillance? They didn't know anything about it."[45]

The Rehnquist Court's deference to *stare decisis* bearing on constitutional questions became a matter of major controversy on and off the bench. The justices debated the value of adhering to the doctrine of *stare decisis* in several cases, most notably in their abortion rulings in *Webster v. Reproductive Health Services* (1989) and *Casey*, as well as in *Payne v. Tennessee* (1991);[46] the latter decision overruled two earlier rulings that prohibited the use of "victim-impact statements" during the sentencing stage in capital murder trials.[47] When granting *Payne v. Tennessee*, the

Court directed the parties to address the question of whether it should overturn prior decisions barring the use of victim-impact statements. In 1987 when that issue was initially addressed in *Booth v. Maryland*, Justice Powell cast the crucial fifth vote for barring the use of victim-impact statements. Following his retirement and the arrival of his successor, Justice Kennedy, the Court reconsidered the issue in *South Carolina v. Gathers* (1989), but this time Justice White switched sides and voted with a bare majority to reaffirm *Booth*. After Justice Brennan's retirement in 1990 and the arrival of Justice Souter, the Court's composition changed again. And by a 6–3 vote, with White again switching his position without explanation, *Payne v. Tennessee* reversed both *Booth* and *Gathers*.

In handing down *Payne*, Chief Justice Rehnquist observed that "*Stare decisis* is not an inexorable command" and set forth some guidelines for adhering to the doctrine of *stare decisis*. Precedents dealing with property and contract rights deserve great respect but "the opposite is true in cases such as the present one involving procedural and evidentiary rules." Moreover, Rehnquist deemed especially open to reconsideration precedents in areas of civil rights and liberties that commanded the support of only a bare majority. By contrast, dissenting Justice Marshall charged that "Power, not reason, is the new currency of this Court's decision making," and pointed out, "Neither the law nor the facts supporting *Booth* and *Gathers* underwent any change in the last four years. Only the personnel of this Court did."

The Court's reversal of prior rulings reflects the politics of the changing composition of the bench. In historical perspective, the Court reversed itself on average about once each term. In the nineteenth century reversals were more infrequent, if only because there were fewer decisions to overturn. Notably, though, when the Court's composition changes dramatically in a short period of time, or a pivotal justice leaves the bench, the Court tends to overturn prior rulings. The Warren Court (1953–1969) was even more activist than the Roosevelt Court in reversing forty-five precedents. The Roosevelt Court, with FDR's eight successive appointees and the elevation of Justice Harlan Stone to the chief justiceship, overturned thirty precedents between 1937 and 1946. During Chief Justice Burger's tenure (1969–1986), the Court gradually became more conservative, particularly in the area of criminal procedure. As its composition changed, the Burger Court also continued reconsidering precedents—though typically liberal ones—reversing a total of fifty-five prior rulings. The Rehnquist Court's initial rush to overrule liberal precedents abated, however, as more moderate centrists came to command a majority due to Clinton's appointees. Whereas in the first seven terms of the Rehnquist Court, twenty-five precedents were abandoned, after Justices Ginsburg and Breyer joined the Court and its composition stabilized, only fourteen precedents were overturned in the following eleven terms. Chief Justice Roberts strives to avoid overturning precedents and to decide cases on the narrowest possible ground; yet, sixteen precedents have been overturned.

Besides rapid changes in the Court's composition in a short period of time (as with FDR's New Deal appointees), justices may limit precedents to justify the legitimacy of policy choices of the Court's new majority. Indeed, Justices Scalia and Thomas criticized the trend toward narrow rulings and refusal to overturn precedents in *CBOCS West, Inc. v. Humphries* (2008)[48] and *Hein v. Freedom from Religion Foundation, Inc.* (2007).[49] Dissenting in *CBOCS West*, Justice Thomas criticized the majority for "retreat[ing] behind the figleaf of ersatz *stare decisis*." On the Roberts Court, Justice Thomas appears the least respectful of precedents; in the words of Justice Scalia, "He doesn't believe in *stare decisis*, period."[50]

It remains important, perhaps, to highlight the difference between precedents bearing on constitutional issues and those on statutory interpretation. The latter have a "special force" because "'Congress remains free to alter what [the Court has] done'"[51] whereas a constitutional precedent may only be overruled by the Court or a constitutional amendment. Recently, when asked to overturn a precedent dealing with patents for a Spider-Man toy, Justice Kagan writing for the Court declined to do so, emphasizing that *stare decisis* has enhanced force with respect to statutory rulings since (1) Congress could have overridden the prior decision, (2) the prior ruling's underpinnings had not been eroded, and (3) the precedent had not proven unworkable. However, in that case, Chief Justice Roberts and Justices Thomas and Alito dissented.[52]

It also bears emphasizing that most precedents are not reversed, obviously (see the table "Decisions of the Supreme Court Over-ruled" in Chapter 1). Of those overruled, empirical studies find that about half did not survive more than twenty years.[53] Moreover, as illustrated earlier, reversals tend to occur when there is a sharp change in the composition of the bench. Studies, furthermore, support Chief Justice Rehnquist's observation in *Payne v. Tennessee* that precedents "decided by the narrowest of margins, over spirited dissents"—that is, decisions handed down by bare majorities or pluralities with multiple concurring or dissenting opinions—are more likely to be overturned than those unanimously decided and which have longevity.[54]

Still, it is important to underscore that precedents are neither fixed in stone, nor provide inflexible, mechanical rules. Precedents may come to be deemed so erroneous as to render them no longer "good" law, or instead of being expressly overturned, simply abandoned without the Court's saying so, and no longer followed or applied. *Buck v. Bell* (1927), for example, held that the government may sterilize "feebleminded" men and women without violating the due process. Although never expressly overruled, that decision has been so thoroughly discredited as to be no longer precedential.

The Court may also decline to overrule even watershed precedents but hold that they no longer apply to particular cases and controversies. The Warren Court did that with the doctrine of "separate but equal" in holding that it no longer applied to segregated public schools. Rather than a sweeping ruling reversing *Plessy v. Ferguson* (1896) in *Brown v. Board of Education* (1954), the Court simply observed that *Plessy*'s doctrine of "separate but equal" no longer applied to dual public school systems; questions about racial segregation in other areas of public accommodations were thus left for another day.

Prior decisions may also remain precedential but so diminished by subsequent exceptions to their holdings that their rationales are fundamentally undermined. *Mapp v. Ohio* (1961), for instance, was highly controversial in holding that incriminating evidence must be excluded at trials if obtained in violation of the Fourth Amendment's "exclusionary rule." In the following decades, however, the Court carved out exceptions—such as the "good faith" exception and the "inevitable discovery rule"— permitting the use of illegally obtained evidence, thereby circumscribing the scope of the exclusionary rule, if not completely eliminating its utility and underlying rationale. So too, the "bright line rules" for police interrogations of criminal suspects, laid down in *Miranda v. Arizona* (1965), are no longer bright or even clear due to the Court's reinterpretation of *Miranda* and carving out exceptions to its central holding. In other words, precedents may be *said* to hold up, even when in fact they don't, and much of their reasoning has been eroded or rejected in subsequent cases.

In short, the precedential value of prior rulings, as Justice Jackson in half-jest quipped, "are accepted only at their current valuation and have a mortality rate as high as their authors."[55] Or as Justice Alito observed, "*Stare decisis* is like wine. If it's really new, you don't want to drink it, it has to age for a while. If it's really old, it is very valuable, or it has possibly turned to vinegar. There's this magical period in between. It [is] not difficult for a judge to make the *stare decisis* inquiry come out however the judge wants it [to] come out."[56]

FORMAL RULES AND PRACTICES

Except for corporate and government attorneys, few people pay any attention to the technical rules of the Court. Yet the rules are an exercise of political power and determine the nation's access to justice. They govern the admission of attorneys to the Supreme Court's bar, the filing of appeals, and the presentation of oral arguments. They stipulate the fees, forms, and length of filings, as well as the size of pages submitted. Most important, they explain the Court's formal grounds for granting and disposing of cases.

There are no fixed rules, however, for a justice's recusal, nor do the justices even have to explain why they think they might have a potential financial or personal conflict of interest that disqualifies them from voting on a case. Justice O'Connor, for instance, withdrew from consideration in a case because she "learned that [her] mother's estate, in which I have a remainder interest, includes some AT&T stock." In another case, O'Connor recused herself after finding that her "sister's husband participated as a judge in the lower court."[57] In her first couple of terms Justice Kagan recused herself from cases that she participated in when serving as solicitor general (SG). Moreover, in some corporate law cases all the justices would have to disqualify themselves due to their stock holdings, as Justice Blackmun once pointed out, because "counsel have put the case together in such a way that it represents almost the entire heavy industrial structure in the United States."[58] Justice White tracked the number of recusals and found that, with one exception, justices did not offer an explanation for their recusals and some recused themselves from a high number of cases (Justice Kennedy in fourteen), while others rarely did (Chief Justice Rehnquist and Justice Brennan each in one case per term).[59]

To expedite the process of deciding what to decide, the Court periodically revises its rules. For example, even after the Judiciary Act of 1925 expanded the Court's discretionary jurisdiction, the justices still felt burdened by mandatory appeals. Accordingly, in 1928 the Court required the filing of a jurisdictional statement, explaining the circumstances of an appeal, the questions presented, and the reasons that the Court should grant review. The requirement, as Justice Stone explained, "enabled us to dispose of many questions without bringing counsel to argue them, but it has also helped to enlighten counsel as to the nature of our jurisdiction and the burden which always rests on an appellant to establish jurisdiction."[60]

One of the reasons for granting *certiorari* that the Court's rules give is that "a federal court of appeals has rendered a decision in conflict with the decision of another federal court of appeals on the same matter." This rule is especially advantageous for the federal government. The Department of Justice has a relitigation policy. If it receives an adverse ruling from a circuit court of appeals, it may relitigate the same issue in other circuits in order to generate a conflict among the circuits, which then may be brought to the Court. One function of the Court, in Chief Justice Vinson's words, has become the resolution of "conflicts of opinion on federal questions that have arisen among lower courts."[61]

Yet, each term, the Court denies review to many such conflicts.[62] The rule for granting circuit conflicts does not control mechanically the granting of review. The Rehnquist Court was less willing than the Burger Court to grant cases involving alleged conflicts among the circuit courts. A case must typically present, as Justice Ginsburg emphasized, a "deep conflict," involving more than two circuit courts in order for it to be granted review. In general, the Court does not grant cases review unless there is a genuine conflict on an important issue. The circuit conflict also must be neither too old nor too new, too narrow, or in need of "percolation" among the circuits, and it must be a conflict that cannot be resolved by Congress or an administrative agency.

Moreover, there are some notable exceptions to the rule on intercircuit conflicts. Even though there was no intercircuit conflict, the Court granted review in *United States v. Windsor* (2013),[63] which struck down the provision in the Defense of Marriage Act of 1996 that barred federal recognition of and benefits for same-sex couples. By contrast, the Court denied numerous appeals of appellate court decisions invalidating state constitutional bans on same-sex marriage. Once the Court of Appeals for the Sixth Circuit upheld four such state bans, creating an intercircuit conflict, the Court granted review in *Obergefell v. Hodges* (2015),[64] in which a bare majority declared that, under the Fourteenth Amendment, there was a "fundamental right to marry" and, thus, states could no longer bar same-sex marriages.

Most crucial in granting *certiorari* is simply agreement on the national importance of the issue presented. The Court underscored that when changing Rule 10 to indicate that *certiorari* would be granted for only "important" matters or for "compelling reasons." This fact is also underscored by the justices' screening process. The justices rely primarily on law clerks' memos when granting *certiorari*. But these memos only summarize the facts, questions, and arguments presented. On that basis, they recommend whether a case should be granted or denied. Clerks' memos do not fully explore whether an alleged conflict is "real," "tolerable," or "square" and must be decided. The workload once often precluded such an examination until a case had already been granted and set for oral argument. In some instances the Court dismisses cases as improvidently granted. With the computerization of the Court's docket and past years' *cert.* memos available, it has become easier to determine whether there is a true circuit conflict that needs to be decided or whether a conflict should be allowed to percolate among the circuits.

That the Court's rules for granting or denying cases do not dictate judicial behavior should not be surprising. But we should not conclude that justices do not take the rules seriously. A majority of the Court has firmly indicated that it will no longer abide "frivolous" petitions filed by indigents. For the first time, in 1989, a bare majority took the extraordinary step of denying an individual the right ever to again file an *in forma pauperis* (Ifp) petition.[65] Subsequently, after denying several other indigents the right to file Ifp petitions, the Court amended its rule governing motions to proceed *in forma pauperis* to provide for their denial whenever a majority deemed a petition frivolous or malicious.[66] Although admitting that "frequent filers" did not consume any of the justices' conference time, Chief Justice Rehnquist and Justice Scalia spearheaded the change in the rules because they "consume the time of law clerks and of the Clerk's office." Dissenting Justices Marshall, Stevens, and Blackmun, however, lamented the political symbolism of that action. In the words of Marshall, "This Court once had a great tradition [echoed in the oath taken by the justices when sworn into office]: 'All men and women are entitled to their day in Court.' That guarantee has now been conditioned on monetary worth. It now will read: 'All men and women are entitled to their day in Court only if they have the *means* and the *money*.'"

Setting the Agenda

The justices' interpretations of jurisdictional rules govern access to the Court. But the justices also need flexible, informal procedures for screening cases and deciding what to decide. The Court is a collegial institution in which all nine justices have an equal vote, and so justices need room for compromise. Attempts at streamlining the process and imposing strict procedures, however, can get in the way of compromise and divide the justices.

Justice Frankfurter's unsuccessful efforts to persuade his brethren to adopt formal rules for conducting deliberations illustrate the dynamics of the Court. A persistent meddler, Frankfurter circulated a memorandum every year from 1951 until his last term in 1961, proposing formal procedural rules for conducting the Court's deliberative process (often the same each year but with minor editorial changes).[67] Always a hyper-self-conscious law professor, he became increasingly concerned with the fact of life in the Court that Justice Brandeis pointed out to him in 1923, while Frankfurter was still a professor at Harvard. "Nothing is decided without consideration," Brandeis told him, "but hardly anything is decided with adequate consideration. . . . [Y]ou must constantly bear in mind the large part played by personal considerations and inadequacy of consideration."[68] Once on the bench, Frankfurter campaigned for procedures he thought would ensure "adequate consideration" of the Court's business. He succeeded only in distancing himself from Chief Justice Warren and the others.[69] In particular, Douglas protested:

If we unanimously adopted rules on such matters we would be plagued by them, bogged down, and interminably delayed. If we were not unanimous, the rules would be ineffective. I, for one, could not agree to give anyone any more control over when I vote than over how I vote.[70]

Likewise, Black opposed the adoption of formal rules. "I am satisfied with our present flexible procedures," he wrote Frankfurter, adding, "The majority, I suppose, could not by mechanical rules bind individual Justices as to the exercise of their discretion."[71]

SCREENING CASES

When any appeal or *certiorari* petition arrives, it immediately goes to the clerk's office. There, staff determine whether it satisfies requirements regarding form, length, and fees and, if the filing is from an indigent, whether there is an affidavit stating that the petitioner is too poor to pay fees. All unpaid cases are assigned numbers in the order they arrive and placed on what is called the Miscellaneous Docket. Paid cases are also assigned numbers but placed on the Appellate Docket. Briefs on the merits, after *certiorari* has been granted, must be filed within forty-five days, with forty copies. The other party, or respondent, must file a brief in response within thirty days. After receiving briefs from respondents, the clerk circulates to the justices' chambers a list of cases ready for consideration and a set of briefs for each case.

For much of the Court's history, every justice was responsible for reviewing each case. The justices did not delegate responsibility for screening cases to others. That is no longer true. As the size of the docket grew, so did the amount of paperwork and demands on the justices' time in screening cases. In the 1930s Attorney General Homer Cummings observed that the number of filings was so large that every justice in reviewing them would have to read the equivalent of *Gone with the Wind* every day before breakfast. In the last 40 years the number of filings and amount of paperwork so dramatically increased that the justices have delegated much of the responsibility for screening cases to their law clerks. The justices or their clerks must now consider before selecting those few cases granted review an enormous amount of material, as estimated here:

250,000 pages of appeals and petitions for review
 62,500 pages of responses opposing review
 25,000 pages of replies favoring review
 37,500 pages of law clerks' memoranda on the cases

That amounts to over 375,000 pages of filings that must be reviewed, in addition to the briefs on the merits of the roughly seventy cases now granted oral arguments each term.[72]

Changes in the screening of cases began because of the increasing number of unpaid petitions. In historical perspective, the number of unpaid filings fluctuates with changes in the Court's direction and in the criminal justice system, along with socioeconomic forces in the country. Before the 1930s the number of unpaid filings was negligible, fewer than eighty a year. But as the Court began to review more cases involving the rights of the accused, unpaid filings incrementally increased during the 1940s and 1950s. By Chief Justice Warren's first year on the bench (1953) the number of unpaid and paid cases was about the same (618 unpaid and 884 paid cases). By 1968, after the Warren Court forged its "revolution in criminal procedure," the number of unpaid cases swelled to 1,947, while paid cases grew to only 1,324.

The rising tide of unpaid filings went unabated in the 1970s, but so did that of paid cases. By 1979 paid cases slightly outnumbered unpaid cases, and that remained so until the mid-1980s. Since then, however, the number of "jailhouse lawyers" and indigents filing petitions has steadily grown, largely due to the dramatic increase in prison populations as a result of tougher sentencing laws and the "war on drugs." Unpaid filings now outnumber paid cases.

Each justice traditionally received copies of the briefs in all paid cases. But beginning with the Taft Court (1921–1930), justices deferred to the chief justice and his law clerks' recommendations on whether unpaid cases should be granted. While the number was still manageable in the 1930s, Chief Justice Hughes examined all unpaid petitions and orally reported his findings at conference. He was highly solicitous of indigents' petitions, which led Justice Frankfurter to complain that he was "the leader of the legal aid movement."[73] Only exceptional cases were distributed to other justices. Chief Justice Stone initially continued the practice, but in conference, rather than briefly stating his views, he read his law clerks' memos on each petition. "After two or three Stone terms a spontaneous feeling developed among [the justices] that instead of having Stone merely read the memorandum, full as it was, by his law clerk, it would be better to have multiple copies made of it for circulation among the brethren prior to conference."[74] During his last two years, Stone had copies of his clerks' memos sent to all the justices. At conference, the justices discussed only those Stone or others placed on a "take-up list" appended to the conference Discuss List that included appeals and other paid cases. Chief Justices Vinson and Warren continued that practice, except that gradually petitions in death penalty and other extraordinary cases were routinely circulated to all justices and discussed at conference. Only those unpaid cases thought to be important by a chief justice or another justice were discussed at conference. All other unpaid cases were placed on the Dead List and formally denied at conference. Under Chief

PAID AND UNPAID FILINGS, 1935–2015

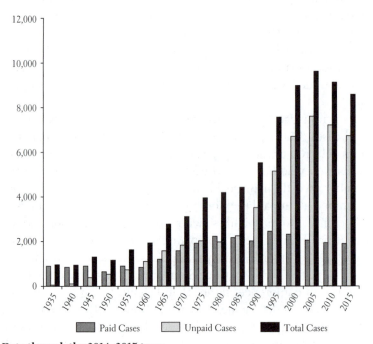

Paid Cases   Unpaid Cases   Total Cases

Data through the 2014–2015 term.

Justice Roberts, however, the Dead List no longer circulates to the justices, but prior to conference they may still request that a case be discussed at conference.

When Burger arrived at the Court in 1969, the number of unpaid cases constituted almost half of the total docket. He immediately sought congressional approval for nine additional law clerks but succeeded in obtaining only three. These three "general" law clerks, along with one of the chief's, wrote memos on all unpaid cases. Their memos were photocopied (on the Court's newly acquired and, at the time, only copier) and sent to the other justices. This "inordinate burden" on the chief justice's chambers, however, was not one that Burger was "willing to bear, along with an average of at least 20 hours a week on administrative duties."[75]

During his first term, Burger had the National Archives and Records Service (NARS) study the paperwork involved in processing the caseload and estimate the cost-effectiveness of alternative practices. At conference Burger proposed three alternatives: (1) establish a revolving panel of senior judges to act as "special masters" who would review all unpaid cases and recommend a few for the justices' consideration; (2) divide all the unpaid cases among the justices, with each examining one-ninth; and (3) copy and circulate all unpaid cases, along with paid cases, to each chamber. There was vehement opposition to the first proposal. The justices refused to give up control over their docket and agenda setting. The second alternative also met opposition, and NARS estimated that it would be the most expensive alternative and greatly increase the workload of each chamber. The conference settled on the third option of having all unpaid cases circulated to each chamber. The increased workload was offset by the addition of one law clerk per justice.[76]

Subsequently, at the suggestion of Justice Powell, the "*cert.* pool" was established in 1972. Initially, only five justices shared their collective law clerks' memos on all paid and unpaid cases. The four most senior and liberal justices—Justices Douglas, Stewart, Brennan, and Marshall—refused to join. In particular, Douglas staunchly opposed on the grounds that petitions would receive inadequate attention and that the *cert.* pool amounted to a "Junior Supreme Court." Basically, the *cert.* pool accomplished internally what Paul Freund's Study Group proposed in 1973 as an external solution to the Court's workload problem—namely, the creation of a national appellate court to screen appeals. Freund, who had clerked for Brandeis in the 1930s, took the "moral stance" that a separate appellate court was preferable to having law clerks do the screening, since such a court would be more "professional, visible, and institutionally accountable."[77] Nonetheless, with the exception of Justice Stevens, almost every justice appointed since the mid-1970s has joined the pool, including Chief Justice Roberts and Justice Alito, although after one term the latter dropped out of the *cert.* pool; Gorsuch is also not in the pool.

The clerks' memos have a strict format. Besides summarizing the issues presented, each contains the docket number, case name, court below, and citation; the author of the opinion below and that of any dissenting or concurring judges; if a federal case, whether there is an intercircuit conflict; and if a criminal case, what penalty was imposed. Each recommends whether the case should be granted and is signed and dated by the clerk. There is also a prescribed use of abbreviations, such as "atty" for "attorney," "conc" for "concurring," "1A" for "First Amendment," and "CA1" for "the U.S. Court of Appeals for the First Circuit." After the justices periodically complained about too-lengthy memos, they became limited to a maximum of thirteen pages. All memos are available in a computerized *cert.* pool memo file-sharing system, which facilitates comparison of cases raising the same or similar issues from prior terms. Each week, the memos are circulated by Thursday noon before the chief justice's composition and circulation of the conference Discuss List on the following Tuesday morning. The chief justice oversees the operation of the *cert.* pool; and Rehnquist and Roberts rode herd on problems ranging from reminding clerks about the length and timeliness of memos to their discarding used memos in "burn bags," not as recycled material, and to reprimanding clerks for swapping cases, unless a case came from a court on which a clerk previously worked, so as not to undermine the random assignment of cases.[78]

The expanded role of clerks in screening cases is significant and problematic. Although bright, the clerks are much less experienced than the justices. As Justice Harlan noted, "Frequently the question whether a case is 'cert. worthy' is more a matter of 'feel' than of precisely ascertainable rules."[79] And for precisely that reason his predecessor, Justice Jackson, lamented the growing role of law clerks in the Court's work, for as he put it, "I do not think judging can be a staff job and I deplore whatever tendency there may be . . . to make it such."[80] Indeed, the *cert*. pool and the justices' delegation of so much of their work to clerks has been sharply criticized, even by former clerks. Kenneth W. Starr, for one, who clerked for Burger, urged the Court to "[d]isband the *cert*. pool," because it exerted too much influence with the consequence that there was not enough independent review by the justices and important cases were passed over.[81] Even within the Court, some justices have expressed concerns. At the time of Justice Thomas's nomination, Justice Kennedy urged the chief justice to encourage the new justice to join the pool but added, "[t]hat would mean, though, that only John [Stevens] would be reviewing the petitions without the use of a pool memo." He thus proposed a change in the *cert*. pool—namely, for each case one justice would not receive a pool memo and instead would prepare a separate one, resulting in two memos. "This suggestion would impose a slight additional burden," he conceded, "but the benefit of an alternative form of review within the pool system may justify the extra effort." Justice Blackmun agreed. "So long as there are three or four not in the pool," he explained, "there was a brake against errors that might be committed by pool members." For his part, Rehnquist admitted the "obvious weakness" in the *cert*. pool "as the number of justices who participated in it grows."[82] Yet neither he nor others were moved to change the system. Justice Stevens, though, concluded that clerks may wield too much influence and prove "risk averse" when recommending whether or not to grant cases. Stevens, who clerked for Justice Rutledge in 1947–1948, also admitted that then he "had a lot less responsibility than some of the clerks now. They are much more involved in the entire process now."[83] Justice Alito, however, has disagreed that the *cert*. pool is responsible for the Court's declining docket of granted cases because "There are plenty of cases where the clerks recommend a grant, and we deny, and plenty where they recommend we deny, and we grant."[84] Nevertheless, studies show a strong correlation

Justice Clarence Thomas with his law clerks in 2002. (*David Hume Kennerly/Getty Images*)

between *cert.* pool clerks' recommendations and whether the Court grants or denies a case (as discussed in the last chapter).[85]

The problems of relying too much on clerks are apparent at the beginning of each term. The term runs from October to the end of June, but filings come in year round. Until justices delegated to their clerks the responsibility of screening filings, bags of petitions and appeals were sent out by the clerk throughout the summer to the justices wherever they were vacationing. This was done when Hughes spent his summers in Jasper Park, Canada, and Douglas made an annual trek to the Pacific Northwest. Many of the justices now spend at least part of their summers in Europe, often teaching courses for law schools or participating in conferences. The justices now initiate their clerks, who come aboard in July, by having them write memos on the filings that arrive during the summer. The justices review these memos before their conference at the beginning of the term. Yet these memos are written by clerks who have little experience with the Court's rules and norms.

Moreover, law clerks in their initial two or three months screen about one-fourth of the cases for a term. The number of filings has grown so much that the Court now has a docket of over 2,000 cases before it even starts its term. As the caseload increased, the justices' initial conference grew longer and carried over for several days during the last week of September before the start of a new term.[86] The Burger Court found it necessary to begin meeting the last week of September, before its formal opening on the first Monday in October. During this preterm conference the justices dispose of about 2,000 cases, discussing fewer than 100. In Burger's years as chief justice, the conference usually lasted four or five days. But Chief Justices Rehnquist and Roberts managed to get the conference to pass on about the same number of cases in typically one day. Thus, before the start of its term, the Court has already disposed of approximately one-fourth of its entire docket. Over four-fifths of those cases are screened out by law clerks and never collectively discussed and considered by the justices.

CONFERENCE DISCUSSIONS

The justices meet alone in conference to decide which cases to accept and discuss the merits of those few cases on which they heard oral arguments. Throughout the term, during the weeks in which the Court hears oral arguments, it holds conferences on Wednesday afternoons to take up the cases argued on Monday, and then on Fridays to discuss new filings and the cases on which it heard oral arguments on Tuesday and Wednesday. In May and June, when the Court does not hear oral arguments, conferences are held on Thursdays, from ten in the morning until about lunchtime or mid-afternoon if necessary.

Summoned by a buzzer five minutes before the hour, the justices meet in the conference room, located directly behind the courtroom itself and next to the chief justice's chambers. The oak-paneled room is lined with *United States Reports*, containing the Court's decisions. Over the mantel of an exquisite fireplace at one end hangs a portrait of Chief Justice John Marshall. The justices' large oblong table at which conferences are held used to sit next to the fireplace, with the chief justice sitting at the east end of the table. But in 2009 the table was rearranged so that now it sits on a north–south axis in the center of the room. Chief Justice Roberts now sits at the south end of the table, closest to his chambers. The senior associate justice (Thomas) sits at the opposite end, in front of the fireplace. Along the chief justice's right side sit the three justices with the most seniority and on the left side sit the four with less seniority, with the most junior sitting next to the conference room door in order to answer any knocks.[87]

Although the seating of the justices has traditionally been on the basis of seniority, variations have occurred. In the late nineteenth century, for instance, Justice Peckham grew accustomed to the seat at the foot of the table, and on Justice McKenna's appointment, he refused to move over one seat and thus retained the junior justice's place. Sitting closest to the outside double door, the junior justice by tradition receives and sends messages that come and go by knocks on the door—a tradition that led Tom Clark to comment wryly, "For five years I was the highest paid doorkeeper in the world."[88] At his first conference, when Justice Alito was slow to answer a knock, Breyer, who had been the junior justice for eleven years, started to answer the door. Chief Justice Roberts told him to stay put, and reminded Alito of his new responsibility. Justice Kagan, when the most junior justice, has said that besides answering the door, she took notes and reported to the clerk the cases granted review, as well as chaired the Court's cafeteria committee—taking pride in the fact that in 2010 it acquired a yogurt machine for the cafeteria.

Two conference lists used to be circulated to each chamber by noon on the Tuesday before the Friday conference. They structure conference discussion and enable the justices to get through their caseload. On the first list—the Discuss List—are jurisdictional statements, petitions for *certiorari*, and motions that are ready and deemed by the chief justice worth discussing. The Discuss List typically includes forty to fifty cases for each conference. In addition, the chief justice circulates another weekly memorandum with summaries and recommendations for miscellaneous motions to be discussed at conference.[89] Some favored ending the practice of placing all motions in capital cases on the Discuss List, but a majority decided against that change, though most are not discussed unless a justice specifically asks for a discussion of a case.[90] It was once the practice for the chief justice to also circulate a second list—called the "Dead List"—containing those cases considered unworthy of conference time. However, Chief Justice Roberts no longer circulates that list, though justices may still ask for cases to be moved to the Discuss List. The overwhelming number of cases, thus, are automatically denied without discussion, and most of those on the Discuss List are denied as well.[91]

Each conference begins with the customary shaking of hands, which reminded Justice Byrnes of "the usual instruction of the referee in the prize ring, 'Shake hands, go to your corner and come out fighting.'"[92] A typical conference begins with those cases for which opinions have already been written and are ready to be announced the following week and moves to a consideration of motions and finally to those cases on which oral arguments were heard earlier in the week.[93] The chief justice begins discussions, which then pass from one justice to another in order of their seniority. In the absence of the chief justice, the senior associate justice leads the conference.[94]

Chief justices have significant opportunities for structuring and influencing conference discussions. As Rehnquist put it, "what the conference shapes up like is pretty much what the chief justice makes it."[95] Chief justices vary in their skills, style, and ideological orientations. Hughes is widely considered to have been the greatest chief justice in the twentieth century. "Warren was closer to Hughes than any others." And in Justice Douglas's view, "Burger

The justices' private conference room. (*Steve Petteway, Collection of the Supreme Court of the United States*)

was close to Vinson. Stone was somewhere in between."[96] Both Rehnquist and Roberts are considered major improvements over Burger.

Hughes's photographic memory, authoritative demeanor, and personal charisma made him a respected task and social leader. He strove to limit discussion by giving crisp three-and-a-half-minute summaries of each filing. His "machine gun style" was largely successful. Justice Owen Roberts recalled that "so complete were his summaries that in many cases nothing needed to be added by any of his associates."[97] But Chief Justice Stone, a former Columbia law professor always interested in a searching examination of every issue, took a different view. He found it annoying that Hughes conducted conferences "much like a drill sergeant."[98] When Stone was elevated to chief justice, he encouraged lengthy discussions, at the cost of prolonging conferences and carrying unfinished business over to the next week. Personally inclined to debate every point, Stone was not disposed to cut short the debates that erupted from disagreements. As a result, under Stone, Douglas observed, the justices were "almost in a continuous Conference." Chief Justice Vinson was not as intellectually equipped or interested in the law as Stone. But he was more business minded, though Douglas claimed that "he would filibuster for hours to have his way on a case."

Chief Justice Earl Warren was more of a politician with great personal charm. "We all loved him," Justice Stewart fondly recalled. But when Warren first arrived, he was totally unprepared and unfamiliar with Court ways. Frankfurter immediately tried to bring him under his sphere of influence and to some extent succeeded in the first couple of terms. But by the end of the 1956 term Warren had grown wary of Frankfurter. Warren then developed a warm working relationship with Brennan. They had a practice of meeting in Brennan's chambers on Thursday afternoons to discuss the cases that would be taken up at the Friday conference. And Warren gradually came into his own at conference. Though not a legal scholar, he showed that he was more than a skilled politician and that he had more intellectual ability than many critics gave him credit for.

Chief Justice Burger was more like Vinson. Outside of the area of criminal procedure, Justice Powell felt that he did not have a "legal mind" or a "taste for the law."[99] He was more interested (and his great accomplishments lie) in judicial administration. At conference Burger tended to rely heavily on his clerks' memos when running conference discussions. He claimed to make a conscious attempt not to mention every point raised in a case in order to let the others pick up on those points and contribute to the discussion. Yet, his discussion of cases left several justices feeling that he was "the least prepared member of the Court." Justice Stevens recalls that Burger was "less well prepared, and less articulate, than either of the men [Rehnquist and Roberts] who held the position after him."[100] Moreover, Justice Powell recalled that with Chief Justice Burger, "the justices at conference [had] a great deal of latitude. You could speak as long as you wanted, and you could interrupt another justice if you wanted to." Rehnquist, who was a junior associate justice during the Burger Court years, often felt there was little for him to say by the time it came for him to give his views at conference. And after becoming chief justice, Rehnquist discouraged such exchanges in the belief that it is "very important for every one of the members of the Court to speak once on a subject before there is cross questioning . . . or second bites of the apple."[101] That is the practice that Roberts tries to follow.

During Burger's years, conference discussions occasionally became heated. Following one such conference, Rehnquist wrote his brethren, "I had a feeling that at the very close of today's Conference we may have fitted Matthew Arnold's closing lines in 'Dover Beach' wherein he refers to those 'Swept with confused alarms of Struggle and flight Where ignorant armies clash by night.' "[102] Confusion occasionally resulted over who voted how and which justices later switched votes.[103] But Burger's lack of precision, contributing to confusion at conference, permitted him to later assign the opinion for the Court, thereby allowing him to continue to try to influence the outcome.

With Rehnquist's elevation from associate to chief justice, conferences greatly improved. Even liberal Justices Brennan and Marshall praised him as a "splendid" chief justice. This is in part because Burger was not equipped to lead conference discussions. By contrast, Rehnquist had the intellectual and temperamental wherewithal to be a leader, in Marshall's words, "a great chief justice." Rehnquist moved conferences along quickly, and as Blackmun observed, "He [got] through the agenda in a hurry" and "cut down [on the] interchange between the justices and always says, well, that can come out in the writing."[104] Justice Thomas agreed, noting that at conference Rehnquist simply said, "What is your vote?"[105] Unlike Burger, Rehnquist did not allow other justices to interrupt or engage in cross-exchanges until all the justices had spoken once, in descending order of seniority. As a result, conference deliberations consumed much less time, and the post-conference opinion-writing and circulation process became even more pivotal to the decision-making process.

By virtually all accounts, Rehnquist's success as chief justice was attributable to his strong "social" and "task" leadership, in addition to his sense of humor and congenial manner. Rehnquist also succeeded in bringing the Court's annual term to a close by the end of June. He did so by adopting certain opinion-assignment rules and by establishing the norm that *"all* majority opinions are expected to circulate by June 1, and *all* dissents by June 15."[106] As for his opinion assignments, Rehnquist sought to "give everyone approximately the same number of assignments of opinions for the Court during any one term," except that after the midterm point he gave more weight to whether a justice (1) already had for a month or more an uncirculated majority opinion, or (2) an uncirculated dissenting opinion, and (3) had not "voted in a case in which both majority and dissenting opinions [had] circulated."[107] Although his strategy for managing the Court's work largely succeeded, it drew some criticism. Justice Stevens complained that "although the prompt completion of a Supreme Court opinion is important, the quality of our work product is even more so. Too much emphasis on speed can have an adverse effect on quality." Moreover, Stevens pointed out that justices usually work on several opinions at once, and the chief justice's deadlines could "adversely affect the orderly production of a group of opinions."[108]

Chief Justice Roberts has reportedly been deemed a very good chief. He, of course, came to the Court with the experience of clerking for Rehnquist during the Burger Court years and then maintaining a long relationship with Rehnquist. Like Rehnquist, Roberts has a sense of humor and better managerial skills than Burger. He is an active questioner during oral arguments and allows somewhat greater discussion in conferences.[109] Justice Stevens has said that Roberts is "always a well-prepared, fair, and effective leader. . . . He also welcomed more discussion of the merits of the argued cases than [Chief Justice

Rehnquist]. . . ."[110] He also places greater weight on reaching consensus than either Burger or Rehnquist, who were not bothered by 5–4 or double- or even triple-header opinions for the Court—that is (as further discussed in the next chapter), opinions in which two or more justices deliver opinions announcing the opinion of the Court on different issues in the same case. In Roberts's words, "Division should not be artificially suppressed, but the rule of law benefits from a broader agreement. The broader the agreement among the justices, the more likely it is a decision on the narrowest possible grounds." In his view, that has real benefits like "clarity and guidance for lawyers and for the lower courts trying to figure out what the Supreme Court meant."[111] Accordingly, at conferences Roberts frames the issues as narrowly as possible in order to promote consensus. In his words, "In most cases, I think the narrower the better, because people will be less concerned about it." Still, he admits, "A chief justice's authority is really quite limited, and the dynamic among all the justices is going to affect whether he can accomplish much or not."[112]

Although there once was a good deal of give-and-take in conference, that is no longer possible in light of the growing caseload. Even in the 1950s justices like Jackson and Frankfurter complained about the lack of conference deliberations. In Jackson's words, "Anything like a thorough discussion, a thorough consideration of those cases, in conference is impossible. That I think is one of the reasons why there's so much disagreement in the Court. . . . An ideal court, in my opinion, would have more time devoted to conference, but we don't seem to be able to work it out."[113] The problem has only grown in the last eighty years with the increase in the size of the docket, in spite of the Court's granting review to fewer cases. Some justices have found this disturbing and hoped for "more of a roundtable discussion." "In fact," Scalia once observed, "to call our discussion of a case a conference is really something of a misnomer. It's much more a statement of the views of each of the nine justices."[114] Lengthier discussions, however, he conceded, would probably not lead justices to change their minds when voting on cases. That is because the justices confront similar issues year after year, and as Rehnquist noted, "it would be surprising if [justices] voted differently than they had the previous time."[115] Justice Breyer also observed that "there are two great unwritten rules" about conferences: "Rule one, nobody speaks twice until everyone has spoken once. That is a fabulous rule for any small group of people. The people at the end [of the conference table discussion] don't feel they're not being listened to. Second rule, tomorrow is another day. You and I might have been the greatest allies on case one that's ever been. And we get to case two, and we're totally at loggerheads. And the fact that you were an ally on case one does not affect the decision on case two. . . . Tomorrow is another day."[116]

The justices come to conference prepared to vote and to explain very briefly their position on each case. "By the time that everyone has had his say," Justice White explained, "the vote is usually quite clear; but, if not, it will be formally taken."[117] The justices once voted in ascending order of seniority. Justice Clark, for one, gave the following rationale for that manner of voting: "Ever since Chief Justice Marshall's day the formal vote begins with the junior Justice and moves up through the ranks of seniority, the Chief Justice voting last. Hence the juniors are not influenced by the vote of their elders."[118] A quaint rationale, but that procedure has not been consistently followed since Hughes was chief justice. A number of the justices have noted that that procedure broke down during Stone's time as chief justice (1941–1946) because he was unable to control conference discussions. But there are also indications that his successor, Chief Justice Vinson (1946–1953), tried to continue that practice.[119] Still, in interviews neither Brennan nor Burger could recall when that procedure was last strictly adhered to by the Court. In any event, the caseload is now so heavy that there is no longer time for each justice to discuss and deliberate over what the others have said, and then vote on each case.

As Black emphasized, it is "a fiction that everybody always waits for the youngest man to express himself, or vote, as they say. Well that's fiction."[120] Likewise, Blackmun affirmed, "we vote by seniority, as you know, despite [the fact] that some texts say we vote by juniority."[121] Moreover, shortly after Rehnquist was elevated to the chief justiceship in 1986, Justice Stevens, when approving certain changes in the docket book, jested, "Since we now have a Chief Justice who experienced the disadvantage of speaking only after most of his colleagues had already voted," perhaps "he might be sympathetic to considering a return to the Court's old practice of having the discussion of argued cases proceed down the ladder but have the voting then go up the ladder?"[122] Yet Blackmun, reflecting back on service as a junior justice, emphasized that when "the vote is four to four and it gets down to you then you realize that there is a burden on you and that your vote will determine the fate of the case."[123] Likewise, Justice Alito observed that as the junior justice and last to vote, "By the time they got to me, I was either irrelevant or I was very important, depending on how the vote had come out."[124] Justice Sotomayor has described the conferences conducted by Chief Justice Roberts: "The chief [justice] will start, and his is usually the most forceful explanation. He'll come up and say 'Well, this is the way that I'm voting, but I'm a little bit unsure, and this is what's still troubling me,' . . . He also explains why some counterarguments don't convince him. What happens is then we go down in descending order, around the room, in descending order of seniority. . . . By the end of the discussion, we all sort of know what each is thinking."[125]

Immediately after conference, the chief justice traditionally reported the votes on granted cases to the Clerk of the Court. Burger delegated this task to a junior justice, in part because he occasionally made mistakes recording conference votes.[126] All the justices have large docket books in which they may note votes and discussions for their personal records. But now the junior justice takes notes on conference votes and tells the Clerk of the Court which cases have been granted oral arguments and which have been denied. "When we have a conference," Justice Alito observed, "the votes can go kind of fast. So I have to make sure I've got the outcome correct because at the end of the conference everybody else leaves and the clerk's office contingent comes in and I go through them case by case."[127] The clerk then notifies both sides in a case granted review. The petitioner has forty-five days to file briefs on the merits, and the respondent then has thirty days.

Considering the volume of the Court's business and the justices' ideological differences, unanimity in case selection is remarkably high. Unanimity is a rather consistent pattern in case selection, regardless of the Court's composition. One study found that during the chief justiceships of Vinson and Warren, on the basis of a study of Justice Burton's docket books for the period 1947–1957, 82 percent of all cases were unanimously disposed; and of these, 79 percent were denied and 3 percent were granted review.[128] During that period, the Court disposed of approximately 1,500 cases each term.

The Court's docket is now over six times bigger, but an examination of Brennan's docket book for the 1973 term nevertheless reveals comparable unanimity. Almost 79 percent of all petitions and appeals were initially unanimously disposed. Some 72 percent of the denials of *certiorari* were unanimous. But the number of petitions unanimously granted dropped by half, to fewer than 2 percent.

Despite the Court's increasing caseload, its internal norms for discussing a limited number of cases and granting fewer cases review were only strengthened. During his time on the bench, Justice White periodically had his clerks keep track of the flow of the Court's business. For the October 1985–1986 term, for instance, he determined that on average only 26 percent of the cases on the Court's conference lists were discussed and just 3 percent of the total cases were granted review.[129]

In addition, as the caseload steadily increased and Congress expanded the Court's discretionary jurisdiction by further eliminating mandatory appeals under the 1988 Act to Improve the Administration of Justice, the number of petitions unanimously denied rose to over 88 percent, registering the institutional norm or consensus that only a limited number of cases may be granted. The extent of greater unanimity in case selection is illustrated in the table on below.[130]

What explains the patterns of unanimity in case selection, despite the changing composition of the Court? Agreement on case selection reflects the interplay of a number of factors. Most important, institutional norms promote a shared conception of the role of the Court as a tribunal for resolving only issues of national importance. With their increasing caseloads, the justices came to accept the view expressed by Chief Justice Taft:

No litigant is entitled to more than two chances, namely, to the original trial and to a review, and the intermediate courts of review are provided for that purpose. When a case goes beyond that, it is not primarily to preserve the rights of the litigants. The Supreme Court's function is for the purpose of expounding and stabilizing principles of law for the benefit of the people of the country, passing upon constitutional questions and other important questions of law for the public benefit.[131]

Justices agree that the overwhelming number of cases are "frivolous" and only a few may be given full consideration.

DISPOSITION IN CASE SELECTION, 1990–1991 TERM

Disposition	Unanimous (%)	Divided (%)	Total Number (%)
Denied petition	3,852 (88.0)	222 (5.0)	4,074 (93.1)
Granted petition	70 (1.6)	97 (2.2)	168 (3.8)
Appeal accepted	3 (0.06)		3 (0.06)
Appeal affirmed	2 (0.04)	2 (0.04)	4 (0.09)
Appeal dismissed	1 (0.02)	1 (0.02)	2 (0.04)
Miscellaneous	117 (2.67)	5 (0.01)	122 (2.78)
Total	4,046 (9.25)	327 (7.47)	4,373

These factors tend to overshadow ideological divisions in case
selection. Ideological differences appear less pronounced in voting on case selection than in voting on the merits of cases disposed by written opinions. The selection process may appear as
"the first battleground on the merits,"[132] but principally for those
justices at either end of the ideological spectrum. They may vote
to deny a case review as a "defensive denial" to avoid granting
cases that might result in outcomes with which they disagree.

The Rule of Four and What It Means

When Congress initially gave the Court discretionary jurisdiction in the Court of Appeals Act of 1891 and then the Judiciary
Act of 1925, by substituting petitions for *certiorari* for mandatory appeals, the justices developed the informal rule of four to
decide which petitions to grant.[133] During conference, at least
four justices must agree that a case merits oral argument.

The "rule of four" evolved in a flexible, collegial manner. When
urging Congress to pass the Judiciary Act of 1925, Justice Van
Devanter contended that the rule of four would ensure that
important cases would still be granted. "We always grant the petitions when as many as four think that it should be granted and
sometimes when as many as three think that way. We proceed
upon the theory," he explained, "that, if that number out of the
nine are impressed with the thought that the case is one that
ought to be heard and decided by us, the petition should be
granted."[134]

When the caseload was lighter than today, exceptions were
sometimes made to the rule of four. Influential justices and persuasive arguments occasionally won cases a hearing on fewer than
four votes. Even during the 1930s under Chief Justice Hughes,
the rule was rather loosely followed. As he explained, "*certiorari*
is always granted if four justices think it should be, and not infrequently, when 3, or even 2, justices strongly urge the grant."[135]

After a conference vote denying a case, three justices may
still find or persuade another to vote to grant a case at the next

conference.[136] A strategy justices sometimes employ to win votes to grant *cert.* is the circulation of dissents from the denial of *certiorari*. Such a tactic may be particularly effective if it is joined by one or more justices. It also became a rather common practice in the 1970s and 1980s after some justices regularly began to publish their votes to grant and dissents from the denial of *cert.* In the 1940s and 1950s when Justices Black and Douglas occasionally noted their dissents from denial, they provoked debate within the Court.[137] Frankfurter, for one, complained that such dissents threatened the "integrity of the *certiorari* process."[138] Nevertheless, dissents from denials greatly increased in the 1970s and 1980s, largely due to Justice Douglas's making it a practice to publish every dissent from denial of review. He did so in opposition to the creation of the *cert.* pool in 1972, and some others followed his practice. Notably, Justice White started publishing his dissents in 1973 and continued doing so throughout his career.[139] He did so largely to flag cases in which he identified a conflict among circuit court rulings that he deemed to demand resolution.

Dissents from the denial of *cert.* and the casting of Join-3 votes are strategic, with potentially dramatic consequences as illustrated by *Bowers v. Hardwick* (1986), which upheld Georgia's law criminalizing sodomy. A decade earlier, the Court had summarily affirmed a district court decision upholding Virginia's criminal sodomy law, in *Doe v. Commonwealth's Attorney for the City of Richmond* (1976). In *Bowers* the appellate court reasoned that since *Doe* was a summary affirmance it was not a controlling precedent and, hence, struck down Georgia's law. When the justices initially discussed *Bowers v. Hardwick* in conference, there were not four votes to grant *cert.* But after conference Justice White circulated a proposed dissent from the denial of *cert.*, emphasizing that the appellate court's decision conflicted with other circuits' rejection of claims to constitutional protection for homosexual sodomy. That drew quick responses from Brennan and Rehnquist, who both joined his dissent. At conference the next day, Marshall also agreed and thus there were four votes to grant review. Yet, conference discussions also suggested to Brennan that the justices would be sharply divided on the merits. He could count on Marshall, Blackmun, and Stevens to vote for extending protection to individuals' sexual autonomy, while White and Rehnquist were steadfastly opposed, as were Burger and O'Connor. That left Powell with the pivotal vote. On the merits of the case, Brennan worried, a majority might go the other way. After discussions with his law clerks, Brennan circulated a memo changing his vote to deny review—a defensive denial aimed at possibly avoiding a ruling rejecting the privacy claim. The next day, though, Burger responded with a memo changing his vote to a Join-3 vote to grant the case. (A Join-3 vote provides a fourth vote if others vote to grant review, but is otherwise considered as a vote to deny.) At that week's Friday conference there were thus four votes to grant: Burger, Marshall, Rehnquist, and White, while the remaining five voted to deny *cert.* Following oral arguments in the spring, the justices remained sharply split, with Justice Powell tentatively siding with the four to strike down Georgia's law. Still, he remained torn by the fact that Michael Hardwick had not been tried and convicted, and yet if he had been he faced a twenty-five-year sentence, which appeared "cruel and unusual punishment." As draft opinions subsequently circulated, Powell then switched his vote to uphold Georgia's law.[140] And Blackmun's draft for the majority became a dissenting opinion from White's opinion for the Court, which was later overruled in *Lawrence v. Texas* (2003).

But with the retirement of White and subsequently others, the publication of dissents from denial largely fell out of practice; such dissents are now rarely published (fewer than 20 a term), except when justices want to record strong opposition to the denial of *cert.* In 2015, for example, Thomas, along with Scalia, issued a lengthy dissent from the denial of a petition appealing a decision upholding a California ordinance forbidding the possession of handguns in a residence unless (1) they were "stored in a locked container or disabled with a trigger lock" approved by the state or (2) the handgun is carried on a person over the age of eighteen.[141] They vigorously protested the refusal to review the lower court's decision because it was inconsistent with the rulings in *District of Columbia v. Heller* (2008)[142] and *McDonald v. Chicago* (2010),[143] both of which struck down similar regulations for running afoul of individuals' "right to keep and bear arms" for self-defense in their homes.

Justice Thomas again dissented in 2018 from the Court's denial of an appeal of an appellate court's upholding of California's law requiring a ten-day waiting period for firearms sales, observing that the majority was turning the Second Amendment into a "disfavored right."[144]

Today, the rule of four operates only in a fraction of cases due to the increasing caseload. Whereas in 1941 the Court acted on 951 petitions, that number had doubled by 1961; it doubled again, with a total of 4,066 petitions, by 1981, and then rose to 5,191 in 1990–1991,[145] and in the last decade rose to over 9,000 petitions a year. Justice Stevens estimated, on the basis of the docket books of Harold Burton, that during the Vinson Court in 1946–1947, over 25 percent of the cases granted had the support of no more than four justices. Brennan's docket book for 1973 reveals that 19 percent of the cases accepted for oral argument received less than a majority vote. Of those cases granted, 80 percent were on the basis of a vote of five or more of the justices, and only 27 percent as the result of a bare majority. By contrast, in the 1990–1991 term the number of cases granted by less than a majority rose to 22 percent, and 77 percent were granted on the basis of a vote of five or more justices, of which only 19 percent were the result of a bare majority vote.[146]

Still, the small number of petitions granted on the rule of four raises two important questions. First, if the rule of four operates in only a small number of cases, is it still useful? Second, because less than 1 percent of *all* petitions are granted on less than a majority vote, what is the meaning of a denial of *certiorari*?

The caseload and institutional norms push toward limiting the operation of the rule of four. But the rule remains useful, particularly if there is a bloc of justices who share the same ideological orientation. The rule of four is also instrumental in establishing a threshold for granting cases and thus managing the Court's plenary docket. In the early 1980s when the Court was granting and deciding over 180 cases a year, Justice Stevens proposed abandoning the rule of four and instead granting petitions only on a majority vote.[147] He did so as a counter to Burger's proposal that Congress establish a special tribunal to which cases might be referred (and thereby relieve the justices' workload). Stevens estimated that abandoning the rule of four would eliminate as many as one-fourth of the cases granted.

Justice Stevens's proposal for discarding the rule of four met strong opposition, however. In particular, Justice Marshall contended that the Court could not abandon the rule without consulting Congress, because Van Devanter and others had promised to abide by it when pressing for the Judiciary Act of 1925.[148] But as Stevens noted, "Since [the Judiciary Act of 1925] the Court has made a number of changes—most notably abandoning the practice of discussing every petition at conference and making extensive use of law clerks' memoranda—without worrying about congressional approval, and I see no reason why we could not decide to adopt a Rule of Five if we thought it prudent to do so."[149]

Given the diminished plenary docket over the last couple of decades, Stevens no longer favored abandoning the rule of four.[150] Yet his proposal remains instructive, for it highlights the importance of the rule of four as a threshold for granting cases. As Stevens repeatedly reminded his colleagues who complained about the workload, "if we simply acted with greater restraint during the case selection process, we might be able to manage the docket effectively under the Rule of Four."

What Stevens did not mention at the time was that other justices were casting so-called Join-3 votes. As noted earlier, a Join-3 vote is a vote to provide a fourth vote if others vote to grant review,

NOTATIONS OF VOTES TO GRANT AND DISSENTS
FROM THE DENIAL OF REVIEW, 1981–2015

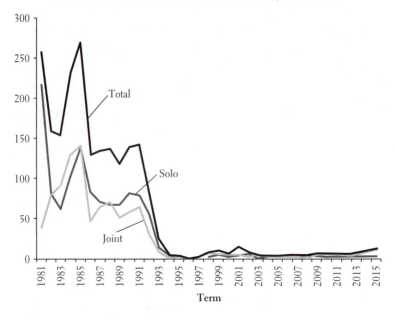

Total notations of votes to grant and dissents from the denial of review include the number of individual and joint notations and dissents. Excluded are statements about the denial of review and concurring opinions. The data include the 2014–2015 term.

but is otherwise considered as vote to deny. The rule of four was firmly in place until the Burger Court years, though neither Chief Justice Rehnquist nor Justices Blackmun and Stevens recalled "any definitive discussion about the use of the [Join-3] vote."[151] One explanation for the practice of casting Join-3 votes was that when leading conferences, Burger began voting to join three and others did the same. He may have done so because his discussion of cases was often vague and he felt pressured to fill the expanded space on the oral argument calendar once the time allotted each

JUSTICES CASTING JOIN-3 VOTES, 1979–1990

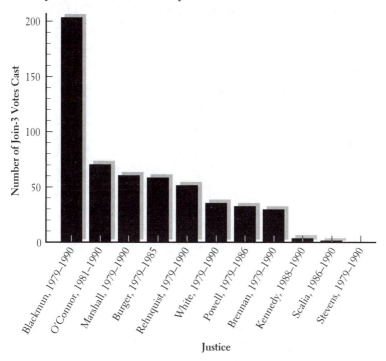

Justice

side was reduced from one hour to thirty minutes in 1970, permitting the granting of more cases. In addition, as noted earlier, in response to the creation of the *cert.* pool in 1972, several justices began threatening and publishing dissents from denial, often joined by one or more other justices. In anticipation of them, Burger and others may have been inclined to cast Join-3 votes. In any event, it is clear from Justice Marshall's bench memos and docket books that some justices cast a large number of Join-3 votes, whereas others rarely (if ever) did, as indicated in the graph on page 226.

Join-3 votes arguably lowered the threshold for granting cases, thereby weakening the self-discipline imposed by the

CASES GRANTED PLENARY REVIEW AND ORALLY ARGUED FROM THE WARREN COURT TO THE ROBERTS COURT, 1968–2018

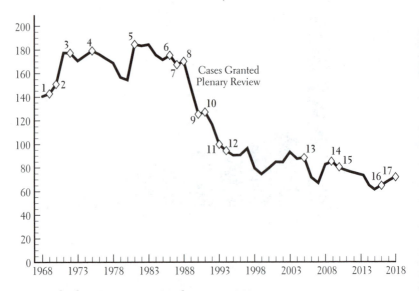

1. Chief Justice Burger joins the Court, 1969.
2. The oral argument calendar is expanded, 1970.
3. The *cert.* pool is created, 1972.
4. Justice Stevens's first full term, 1975.
5. Justice O'Connor joins the Court, 1981.
6. Rehnquist's first term as chief justice and Justice Scalia joins the Court, 1986.
7. Justice Kennedy joins the Court, 1987.
8. Act to Improve the Administration of Justice expands discretionary jurisdiction, 1988.
9. Justice Souter joins the Court, 1990.
10. Justice Thomas joins the Court, 1991.
11. Justice Ginsburg joins the Court, 1993.
12. Justice Breyer joins the Court, 1994.
13. Chief Justice Roberts and Justice Alito join the Court, 2005–2006.
14. Justice Sotomayor joins the Court, 2009.
15. Justice Kagan joins the Court, 2010.
16. Justice Gorsuch joins the Court, 2017.
17. Justice Kavanaugh joins the Court, 2018.

rule of four and contributing to the inflation of the plenary docket in the 1970s and early 1980s, when between 150 and 180 cases were decided annually. The plenary docket in turn, then, declined since the 1990s and 2000s in part because of the retirements of those who cast such votes and their replacement on the bench with justices who simply vote to grant or deny review.

What remains the significance of the Court's denial of *certiorari*?[152] Denial of *certiorari* purportedly "imparts no expression of opinion upon the merits of the case."[153] The Court, however, is "not quite of one mind on the subject," as Justice Jackson observed. "Some say denial means nothing, others say it means nothing much. Realistically, the first position is untenable and the second is unintelligible."[154]

Justice Frankfurter explained the orthodox view that "a denial no wise implies agreement" on the merits of a case: "It simply means that fewer than four members of the Court deemed it desirable to review a decision of the lower court as a matter of 'sound judicial discretion.' Pertinent considerations of judicial policy here come into play."[155]

Justices may have any number of reasons for denying *certiorari*. But as Jackson observed, "Because no one knows all that a denial means, does it mean that it means nothing?"[156] A denial cannot mean "nothing much." The Court does not grant *certiorari* to review the facts of cases. Do denials thus imply approval of the lower-court ruling? In *Brown v. Allen* (1953), involving federal courts' jurisdiction over *habeas corpus* appeals, three justices indicated that when issues are repetitiously raised, denials should be understood as affirming the lower court's ruling. Yet if a grant or a denial is based on the justices' view of the merits of a case, then a paradox results in voting on case selection. Because only four justices can grant a case, a minority binds the majority to deciding the merits of a case that they do not think need to be considered. In all other respects, the Court operates by majority rule. "Even though a minority may bring a case here for oral argument," Frankfurter contended, "that does not mean that the majority has given up its right to vote on the ultimate disposition of the case as conscience dictates."[157] Frankfurter made a practice of refusing to vote on the merits of cases that he thought the Court had improperly granted.[158] If Frankfurter's practice were widely accepted, the rule of four would be superfluous. As Douglas objected, "If four can grant and the opposing five dismiss, then the four cannot get a decision of the case on the merits. The integrity of the four vote rule would then be impaired."[159]

Because the Court declines to take a case, it does not follow that "[i]t means nothing else."[160] The denial of *certiorari* cannot be considered completely meaningless, for a number of reasons. Justice Brennan's docket books show that 98 percent of the cases were granted or denied on the basis of a vote of a majority or more. Stevens's proposal for replacing the rule of four by a majority vote simply would have acknowledged what already basically occurs in practice. Also, adoption of a rule of five would legitimize the view that denials amount to passing on the merits of cases. Denials inevitably send signals as to what kinds of cases "do not present questions of sufficient gravity."[161]

Why don't the justices explain what they are doing, why they are denying review? They don't, because the power to deny review enables the Court to dispose of its caseload, and to explain each denial would increase their workload. As Stone explained, "to state a reason which would be accurately expressed and would satisfy the members of the Court, would require an amount of time and energy that is simply impossible to give."[162] A denial without explanation also gives greater flexibility in agenda setting. Justices may let an issue percolate in the lower courts and then take it up in a later case without feeling bound by their earlier denial.

Denial of *certiorari* remains an important technique for managing the caseload. But its meaning in particular cases is usually far from clear. And the rule of four is not inflexible. In 1980, in two capital punishment cases, *four* justices issued dissenting opinions from the denial of review. Each justice indicated that, but for one more vote, the case should have been granted, the ruling below vacated, and the case remanded to the lower court.[163]

Four justices dissented from the majority's denial of an application to stay an injunction against protesters claiming that they were denied their First Amendment right of freedom of speech in *Hirsh v. City of Atlanta* (1990).[164] Again, four justices dissented from the denial of *certiorari* in *McCleary v. Navarro* (1992), which appealed a decision concerning whether a police officer, who had a warrant but broke into the wrong house, was entitled to immunity from being sued.[165] The appellate court's ruling came down just a few days after the Court announced in *Hunter v. Bryant* (1991) a new legal standard for determining immunity in such cases. By denying *certiorari* in *McCleary* the majority left the lower court's decision and reliance on a standard rejected in *Hunter* undisturbed.[166]

More recently, Justices Breyer, Ginsburg, Sotomayor, and Kagan dissented from the denial of *cert.* and petitions for stays of execution.[167] After *Baze v. Rees* (2008)[168] upheld lethal injections, for instance, controversy arose over the drugs used, midazolam, in particular, in a three-drug "cocktail" that causes the heart to stop. There were also several well-publicized botched executions in which a drug cocktail was used. In *Warner v. Gross* (2015), the Court denied to stay the execution of four inmates challenging the protocol—one of which was executed the next day. Justices Ginsburg, Breyer, and Kagan joined a sharp dissent by Justice Sotomayor. Three days later, however, the Court granted another case raising the same Eighth Amendment challenge presumably due to the four dissenting votes in *Warner*, and possibly one or more other votes to resolve the controversy. A bare majority, then, in *Glossip v. Gross* (2015)[169] upheld the protocol because the inmates failed to (1) prove that the drug was "sure or likely to result in needless suffering" and (2) show that states had better options than using midazolam. Justices Breyer and Sotomayor each issued bitter dissents, joined by Justices Ginsburg and Kagan.

In sum, as the rule of four has evolved it now rather strictly applies only to granting petitions plenary consideration. Even if four justices think that an application ought to be treated like a *certiorari* petition (as in *Hirsh*), a petition for *habeas corpus* or for a stay of an injunction, or a summary judgment entered instead of denying *certiorari* (as in *McCleary*), they must acquiesce silently in or dissent from the majority's disposition. In addition, a majority may override the rule of four, after a case has been granted and oral arguments heard, with a vote to "DIG"— that is, to "dismiss as improvidently granted."[170] Not surprisingly, when that occurs the other four may dissent. One such controversy led Justices Brennan and Rehnquist to suggest a procedure for handling "DIGs and the Rule of Four." While rejecting the view that "there *should* be an absolute rule against" such dismissing, they agreed that "comity to our colleagues and respect for the Rule of Four should make DIG'ing . . . relatively rare." They therefore proposed that "the five voting to DIG set out their reasons in a published opinion," but also that "our policy on this issue is a matter best left unpublished and should be treated as an internal rule."[171]

When four justices join a dissenting opinion from the denial of review, they obviously underscore their profound disagreement with the direction of the Court. Thus, in *In re Kevin Nigel Stanford* (2002),[172] Justices Stevens, Souter, Ginsburg, and Breyer joined a dissenting opinion from the denial of a *habeas* petition in order to highlight their opposition to the execution of individuals who are under the age of eighteen at the time of their offense, and that they would overturn a bare majority's holding contrariwise in *Stanford v. Kentucky* (1989),[173] which was finally overruled by a bare majority in *Roper v. Simmons* (2005).[174] If four justices vote to grant *cert.* in a death penalty case, the Court's recent practice has been for a "courtesy fifth vote" to be provided in order to stay a pending execution and to give the case further consideration; but if four justices vote to stay an execution, no "courtesy fifth" will be given. Under the Court's rules, five votes are needed to grant petitions for a rehearing and also for direct appeals, as under the Voting Rights Act, for example.

Thus the rule of four has come to operate only with regard to granting cases oral argument, and on all other matters the majority prevails. Although enabling the Court to manage its business, denials invite confusion and the suspicion, as Justice Jackson once observed, "that this Court no longer respects impersonal rules of law but is guided in these matters by personal impression which from time to time may be shared by a majority of the justices."

DECIDING CASES WITHOUT FULL CONSIDERATION

The distinction between mandatory and discretionary review of appeals and *certiorari* petitions has basically disappeared from the process of deciding what to decide. Before Congress eliminated virtually all the remaining mandatory appeals in 1988, fewer than 20 percent of all appeals were granted oral argument. Instead of giving mandatory appeals the full-dress treatment, however, the Court summarily decided them. In other words, without hearing oral arguments, the Court simply affirmed, vacated, or reversed the lower-court ruling. As the caseload grew, the number of summary decisions increased until 1988, when Congress replaced most provisions for mandatory appeals with provisions for *certiorari* petitions. Since then they have become increasingly more infrequent.

The justices also occasionally *grant certiorari, vacate* the judgment below, and *remand* the case to the lower court, or, as it is known within the Court, summarily dispose of cases with a "GVR" order. This is done with cases raising an issue that has been decided in another case, and thus they are granted, vacated, and remanded for reconsideration in light of the Court's recent ruling on the issue. The Court has also made it clear that it will issue GVRs when the federal government confesses making an error in the lower court and switches its position on the issues presented.[175]

Agenda for Policy Making—Who Benefits, Who Loses?

The power to decide what to decide entails more than merely selecting a manageable number of cases for oral argument. The Court also sets its own substantive agenda for policy making. The Court did not always have the power to set its own agenda, nor did its docket include the kinds of major issues of public policy that arrive today. During its first decade, the Court had little important business. Over 40 percent consisted of admiralty and prize cases, about 50 percent raised issues of common law, and the remaining 10 percent dealt with matters such as equity, including one probate case.[176] Not until the chief justiceship of John Marshall did the Court assert its power of judicial review. Still, only a tiny fraction of its business raised important issues of public policy. By the late nineteenth century the Court's business had gradually changed in response to the Industrial Revolution and other developments in American society. The number of admiralty cases, for instance, had by 1882 dwindled to fewer than 4 percent of the total. Almost 40 percent of the decisions handed down still dealt with either disputes at common law or questions of jurisdiction and procedure in federal courts. Over 43 percent of the Court's business, however, involved interpreting congressional statutes. And less than 4 percent of the cases raised issues of constitutional law. The decline in admiralty and common law litigation and the increase in statutory interpretation reflected the impact of the Industrial Revolution and the growing governmental regulation of social and economic relations. In the twentieth century the trend continued. Throughout the 1980s and 1990s about 47 percent of the cases decided by opinion involved matters of constitutional law; around 38 percent dealt with the interpretation of congressional statutes; and the remaining 15 percent resolved issues of administrative law, taxation, patents, and claims. By contrast, the Roberts Court (2005–) has tended to grant far more cases involving jurisdiction, practice, and procedure, as well as statutory interpretation, than cases raising constitutional questions. However, it still decides several high-profile cases each term, like *Obergefell v. Hodges* (2015). The table on page 236 illustrates the changing nature of the Court's business.[177]

The contemporary Court's power to pick the cases it wants from a very large docket enables it to assume the role of a super legislature. The overwhelming number of cases on the docket involve indigents' claims and issues of criminal procedure. Yet, as is indicated below, few are granted review. Cases raising other issues of constitutional law have a better chance of being selected; so do cases involving statutory, administrative, and regulatory matters. These are all areas in which the government has an interest in legitimating its policies. The Court thus functions like a roving commission, selecting and deciding only issues of national importance for the governmental process.

The Court directly and indirectly encourages interest groups and the government to litigate issues of public policy.[178] The Court selects and decides "only those cases which present questions whose resolution will have immediate importance far beyond the particular facts and parties involved." Attorneys whose cases are accepted by the Court "are, in a sense, prosecuting or defending class actions"; as Chief Justice Vinson emphasized, "you represent your clients, but [more crucially] tremendously important principles, upon which are based the plans, hopes and aspirations of a great many people throughout the country."[179]

For the poor and minorities, as the Warren Court observed in *NAACP v. Button* (1963), "litigation may well be the sole practicable avenue open to a minority to petition for redress of grievances."[180] Interest-group litigation, however, is by no means confined to the poor and minorities. Pointing to the successes of the American Civil Liberties Union (ACLU), Powell, shortly before his appointment to the Court, urged the Chamber of Commerce of the United States to consider that "the judiciary may be the most important instrument for social, economic and political change."[181] And over the last several decades it has aggressively done so.

The Business of the Supreme Court, October Terms, 1825–2015

Subject of Court Opinions	1825	1875	1925	1935	1945	1955	1965	1975	1985	1995	2005	2015
Admiralty	2	5	8	1	3	1	0	0	2	3	1	0
Antitrust	0	0	2	3	2	2	8	3	4	1	2	0
Bankruptcy	0	13	9	9	7	1	5	0	1	2	2	5
Bill of Rights (civil liberties; except rights of accused)	0	2	3	3	9	6	15	8	22	9	6	10
Commerce Clause												
1. Constitutionality *and* construction of federal legislation, regulation, and administrative action	0	0	31	13	28	28	13	31	36	13	0	1
2. Constitutionality of state regulation	0	2	2	11	4	1	8	27	2	2	0	1
Common law	10	81	11	3	3	0	0	0	2	2	0	1
Miscellaneous statutory interpretation	4	16	15	16	9	16	12	4	1	11	22	24
Due Process												
1. Economic interests	0	0	20	8	3	1	0	0	3	3	1	1
2. Procedure of rights of accused contained in Bill of Rights	0	2	3	2	5	7	18	34	41	16	14	9
Impairment of contract/just compensation	0	1	4	6	1	0	1	0	1	1	1	0
Native Americans	0	0	7	0	2	1	0	4	4	1	2	0
International law, war, and peace	2	5	6	2	12	3	0	1	2	2	1	1
Jurisdiction, procedure, and practice	4	30	29	27	27	17	16	4	27	16	16	10
Land legislation	0	11	3	3	0	0	0	0	1	0	0	0
Patents, copyright, and trademarks	1	8	4	5	2	1	1	1	0	2	2	5
Slaves	3	0	0	0	0	0	0	0	0	0	0	0
Other suits against the government and officials	0	12	17	1	2	0	5	16	8	3	4	1
Suits by states	0	0	8	5	0	2	5	6	0	4	1	3
Taxation (federal and state)	0	5	27	40	19	7	5	4	5	1	0	2

Interest groups from the entire political spectrum look to the Court to decide issues of public policy. "This is government by lawsuit," Justice Jackson once observed. "These constitutional lawsuits are the stuff of power politics in America."[182] Interest-group and public-interest law firms offer a number of advantages for litigating policy disputes. They command greater financial resources than the average individual. A single suit may settle a large number of claims, and the issues are not so likely to be compromised or settled out of court. Interest-group law firms typically specialize in particular kinds of lawsuits. They are therefore able to litigate more skillfully and over a longer period of time. There are also tactical opportunities: litigants may be chosen to bring "test cases," and those cases may be coordinated with other litigation and the activities of other organizations.

Interest-group litigation proliferated on the theory that politically disadvantaged groups are more successful in achieving their legal-policy goals through litigation than through the political process. Studies, however, suggest that interest-group litigation may not fare any better than individual and nongroup lawsuits.[183] Interest groups also may simply champion litigation in order to command media attention, maintain or attract supporters, or make or keep an issue such as abortion salient in electoral politics.[184]

In addition, interest groups may enter litigation as third parties by filing *amicus curiae* briefs, which are no longer neutral or friendly, but partisan. In recent years the U.S. Chamber of Commerce, the National Association of Defense Lawyers, and both conservative and liberal legal foundations are active and successful in filing *amicus* briefs. In the reverse discrimination case of *Regents of the University of California v. Bakke* (1978), 120 organizations joined 158 *amicus* briefs filed before the Court. The number of *amicus* briefs filed in *Bakke*, however, was exceeded during the abortion controversy over *Webster v. Reproductive Health Services* (1989) when 78 briefs were filed,[185] then again in the 2003 affirmative action cases *Grutter v. Bollinger* and *Gratz v. Bollinger*, in which 107 *amicus curiae* briefs were filed.[186]

Some 136 organizations and states filed *amici* briefs in the Affordable Health Care case, *National Federation of Independent Business v. Sebelius* (2012).[187] But those records were exceeded in *Obergefell v. Hodges* (2015), in which 149 *amicus* briefs were filed for hundreds of individuals and organizations, including nineteen states opposing and twenty-one states supporting bans on same-sex marriage.

Since the introduction of *amici* briefs in 1823,[188] the number has dramatically increased, particularly in the latter half of the twentieth century—rising from an average of fewer than one per case granted review in the 1950s, to two per case in the 1970s, and to almost six per case in recent years.[189] Under the Court's Rule 37, potential *amicus* must file a motion for permission to file a brief if one of the parties in a case withholds consent. In the last half century there has been a rather dramatic increase in the filing of such briefs. In the 1940s and 1950s, for instance, *amicus* briefs were filed in about 45 percent of the cases annually granted review, but by 1986 they rose to 86 percent and more recently were filed in close to 100 percent of the cases granted plenary review.[190]

The justices also increasingly cite *amicus* briefs in their opinions, and most justices have their law clerks review them first. Justice Ginsburg, for one, has her clerks divide them into three categories: "read, skim, and skip."[191] Indeed, in highly controversial cases such as *Citizens United v. Federal Election Commission* (2010),[192] challenging a federal ban on corporations' buying ads in support or opposition of candidates for federal office, numerous interest groups may join *amici* briefs that in terms of pages are overwhelming for the justices and their clerks. In *Citizens United*, nearly 100 interest groups, twenty-six states, and several members of Congress, among others, joined *amici* briefs totaling almost 2,000 pages—more than Leo Tolstoy's *War and Peace* (1,225 pages). Although in recent years the filing of *amicus curiae* briefs has increased by an estimated 800 percent,[193] the justices and their clerks increasingly conduct their own fact-finding research on the Internet and cite material that goes beyond that presented in the briefs.[194] Moreover, the Court's references to *amicus* briefs and other material found on the Internet has risen sharply. About one-third of the majority opinions cited one or more *amicus* briefs,[195] and citations to sources on the Internet are now listed each term on the Court's website.

Do justices select cases because they are brought by particular interest groups? There is no evidence that they do and considerable evidence that they do not. Some political scientists hypothesize that justices select cases on the basis of certain "cues" in the filings.[196] According to the "cue theory," justices disproportionately grant cases in which one or more of the following cues are present: (1) a civil liberties issue, (2) disagreement in lower courts, and (3) the involvement of the federal government as the petitioner. Studies of justices' docket books and of samples drawn from the petitions granted and denied, however, indicate that the strongest correlation between any of these cues and granting review of a case is the participation of the federal government. Although justices' attitudes toward upperdogs (the government and corporations) or underdogs (individuals and minorities) may predispose their voting on whether to grant a case, the overwhelming number of filings are unanimously denied.[197] As earlier discussed, institutional norms promote a shared conception of the work appropriate for the Court. Besides, the justices tend not to look for cues to reduce their workload but increasingly have come simply to rely on their clerks to screen cases. The justices in turn tend to grant review when they disagree with the lower court's ruling and in cases in which the federal government is participating.

The federal government has a distinct advantage in getting cases accepted, but its higher rate of success is not surprising. Since the creation of the office in 1870, the SG has been responsible for representing the federal government. From the Court's perspective, the SG performs an invaluable service—a "gatekeeping" function. He or she screens all prospective federal appeals and petitions and decides which should be taken to the Court. Unlike any other petitioner, the SG has the advantage of selecting from a large number of cases around the country and appealing only those likely to win Court approval. Since the SG's office argues all government cases before the Court, it has intimate knowledge of the justices and has been characterized as the Court's "ninth-and-a-half" member because of filing a large number of cases that are granted review as well as filing *amicus* briefs.[198] Given these tactical advantages, the SG is the most frequent and successful litigant before the Court, and in recent years about 70 percent of the SG's petitions were granted.[199] The SG also participates in about one-half of all cases decided on merits, and in the last half of the twentieth century the Court annually decided more than 50 percent of the cases in favor of the government.[200] Because of the position and the high reputation of the attorneys working in the office of the SG, the justices often defer and simply vote to "go with the S.G."[201] The justices may also invite the SG to present a brief on petition for *certiorari*— "CVSGs" ("calls for the view of the solicitor general")—though in recent years the SG has filed more *amicus* briefs but met with a somewhat declining success rate.[202]

Notably, in the last couple of decades there has been a reemergence of an elite group of attorneys who specialize in Supreme Court litigation. The contemporary "Supreme Court bar"—a "legal elite" of "repeat players"—as Chief Justice Roberts has noted, is composed of former law clerks at the Court, solicitors general, deputy solicitors general, and law professors.[203] Since World War II the Court has annually admitted more than 2,000 attorneys to its bar, yet the overwhelming majority never argue a case before the justices. A study of lawyers who filed appeals found that less than 1 percent (66 of 17,000) were involved in 43 percent of cases granted review between 2004 and 2012. These elite lawyers largely represent corporate interests and work in the largest and top law firms. Almost half formerly clerked at the Court and almost another half had clerked or worked in the SG's office. As Michael Luttig, who clerked for Chief Justice Burger and sat on the Court of Appeals for the Fourth Circuit, observed, "It has become guild, a narrow group of elite justices and elite counsel talking to each other"; the Court and its bar have become more insular, "detached and isolated from the real world."[204]

By contrast, indigents are unlikely to have their cases given full consideration. With the increasing number of unpaid cases, the percentage of those granted has declined sharply. During the Vinson and Warren Courts, the number dropped from around 9 percent to less than 3 percent and then to about 1 percent during the Burger and Rehnquist Courts, and even further during the Roberts Court.

The decline in the number of *in forma pauperis* (Ifp) petitions granted is due to a number of factors. First and foremost is simply the reality that the more filings, the more that are considered "frivolous." Second, justices no longer individually consider indigents' petitions. Instead, they rely on their law clerks' *certiorari* memos and recommendations. Third, most are deemed "frivolous" and prepared without the assistance of counsel. Finally, the Burger, Rehnquist, and Roberts Courts, unlike the Warren Court, became increasingly less sympathetic to claims brought by indigents.

The transformation of the Court's agenda registers the interplay between changes in its composition and the issues brought by litigants and broader socioeconomic forces. On economic issues, for example, changes in the composition of the bench led to eras in which the Court pursued alternatively conservative or liberal policy making. From 1790 to 1835 the Court staunchly defended property rights. But from the presidency of Andrew Jackson and his appointments of Chief Justice Taney and four other justices, through the Civil War and Reconstruction—as well as the period of the Industrial Revolution (1836–1890)—the Court generally supported governmental regulation of economic interests. That period was in turn followed by a second conservative era (1890–1937) in which the Court defended laissez-faire capitalism against progressive legislation. The Court's "switch in time that saved nine" in 1937 and FDR's subsequent appointments then ushered in a second era of liberal economic judicial philosophy. Fewer economic regulation cases were granted, even though the number of such cases arriving on the docket did not decline, and those decided upheld, rather than overturned, governmental regulations.[205] The Court's agenda generally changes incrementally, though sudden shifts may take place. Over the long haul it also registers policy-making cycles. During such cycles the Court commits itself to a new legal-policy area—such as school desegregation, affirmative action, or capital punishment—and opens a window of opportunity for some litigants. For a time (sometimes several decades) the Court continues addressing related "spillover" issues—challenges to legislation passed in response to its rulings, conflicts generated in the lower courts over applying its holdings to different fact patterns—and fine-tunes its doctrinal jurisprudence. In time the Court either comes to regard particular legal areas settled and redirects attention to other issues or, as its composition changes, reconsiders prior rulings and charts a new course.

Review Denied, Justice Denied?

The Court now decides fewer than 1 percent of the cases annually arriving on its docket. That is far less than forty years ago when about 3 percent of a much smaller docket were granted and decided. Some forty years ago the docket was just reaching 5,000 cases, and the justices decided between 150 and 180 cases a term. The docket now hovers around 9,000, yet the justices decide fewer than eighty a year. That is about the same number decided by the Court in 1955 when the docket remained under 2,000.

Even some of the justices have been "amazed" by the trend and have speculated on possible explanations. It "just happened," according to Justice Souter. "Nobody set a quota; nobody sits at the conference table and says, 'We've taken too much. We must pull back.' . . . It simply has happened."[206] Even if the Court had continued to grant as many cases as it once did, the percentage would have declined, of course, due to the continued growth in the case-load. Still, the diminished plenary docket is striking and probably reflects a combination of factors internal and external to the Court. As discussed earlier in this chapter, these factors undoubtedly contributed to the inflation of the plenary docket during the Burger Court years (1969–1986) and its contraction thereafter. Early in his chief justiceship, Burger expanded the size of the oral argument calendar in order to accommodate more cases, because of his concern over the Court's declining supervisory capacity. During Burger's tenure, the discipline imposed by the rule of four was also weakened with the emerging practice of casting Join-3 votes and the increased circulation of dissents from denial of review. As the Court's composition changed from the 1990s to the 2010s, so did the justices' voting practices: fewer Join-3 votes are cast and dissents from denial have become less common. In addition, virtually all remaining nondiscretionary appellate jurisdiction was eliminated, thereby increasing the Court's "managerial capacity" for controlling the plenary docket by denying review to more cases. Justice Stevens, among others, underscored that the institutionalization of the *cert.* pool over the last half century undoubtedly contributed in several ways: more justices rely, and rely to a greater degree than before, on their clerks' *cert.* memos, and thus there is less independent review of petitions by the justices themselves. As Stevens emphasized, the clerks tend to be "risk averse" when recommending that cases be granted.[207] Finally, Chief Justice Roberts has speculated that the continuing decline in the plenary docket may be due to less sweeping congressional legislation in recent years and in turn to less litigation involving statutory interpretation (though the Roberts Court tends to grant primarily statutory appeals, with the exception of "hot button" cases involving controversies over same-sex marriage and the like).

Even when the Court granted more cases and its total docket was smaller, the question often arose: Is this not a matter of review denied, justice denied? Justice Black once offered a partial response to that question:

I don't think it can fairly be said that we give no consideration to all who apply. I think we do. . . . Frequently I'll mark up at the top [of a petition] "Denied—not of sufficient importance." "No dispute among the circuits," or something else. And I'll go in and vote to deny it. Well, I've considered it to that extent. And every judge does that same thing in [our] conference.[208]

As Black indicated, every case is given some consideration, though now decidedly more by law clerks than by the justices. No case, of course, is entitled to unlimited review. And the justices appear to agree that the Court no longer functions to correct errors in particular cases, but rather to resolve only controversies of nationwide importance.

No less crucial, the justices generally agree that the vast majority of filings are frivolous. Testifying before Congress in 1937, Chief Justice Hughes observed:

I think that it is safe to say that almost 60 percent of the applications for *certiorari* are wholly without merit and ought never to have been made. There are probably about 20 percent or so in addition which have a fair degree of plausibility, but which fail to survive critical examination. The remainder, falling short, I believe, of 20 percent, show substantial grounds and are granted.[209]

Ideologically opposed justices agree that more "than nine-tenths of the unpaid petitions [are] so insubstantial that they never should have been filed" and that "more than one-half of all appeals are so untenable that they never should have been filed." In Rehnquist's words, "a lot of the filings are junk."[210]

But what are "frivolous" cases? Clarence Brummett, for one, repeatedly asked the Court to assist him in a war of extermination he vowed to wage against Turkey.[211] Brennan gave further illustrations of the kinds of frivolous cases that arrive at the Court:

Are the federal income tax laws unconstitutional insofar as they do not provide a deduction for depletion of the human body? Is the 16th Amendment unconstitutional as violative of the 14th Amendment?

and . . . Does a ban on drivers turning right on a red light constitute an unreasonable burden on interstate commerce?[212]

To be sure, the largest category of frivolous cases comes from "jailhouse lawyers" such as the Reverend Clovis Green, founder of the Church of the New Song and the Human Awareness Universal Life Church, who, from his prison cell, alone filed an estimated 700 petitions in federal and state courts.[213] In amending its rule for granting *in forma pauperis* petitions, the Court emphasized that it does not look kindly on such petitions and would summarily deny those deemed "frivolous or malicious."

But which cases appear frivolous and which merit the Court's attention, of course, depend on the justices. In *Cohen v. California* (1971), for example, the Court overturned as inconsistent with the First Amendment the criminal conviction of a man who wore in a courthouse a jacket bearing the words "Fuck the Draft" as a protest to the draft and the Vietnam War. The Court established the important First Amendment principle that four-letter words are not obscene per se and may symbolically express political ideas as well. But in a circulated and unpublished dissent, Chief Justice Burger protested

that this Court's limited resources of time should be devoted to such a case as this. It is a measure of a lack of a sense of priorities. . . . It is nothing short of absurd nonsense that juvenile delinquents and their emotionally unstable outbursts should command the attention of this Court. The appeal should be dismissed for failure to present a substantial federal question.[214]

Ultimately, whether justice is denied depends on who sits on the Court and the process of deciding what to decide. In Justice Douglas's words, "The electronics industry—resourceful as it is—will never produce a machine to handle these problems. They require at times the economist's understanding, the poet's insight, the executive's experience, the political scientist's understanding, the historian's perspective."[215]

FIVE

Deciding Cases and Writing Opinions

T HE COURT now grants a full hearing to only about eighty of the over 9,000 cases annually on the docket. When cases are granted full consideration, attorneys for each side submit briefs "on the merits," setting forth their arguments and how they think the case should be decided. The Clerk of the Court circulates the briefs to each chamber and sets a date for the attorneys to argue their views orally before the justices. After hearing oral arguments, the justices vote in private conference on how to decide the issues presented in a case.

Cases are decided by majority rule on the basis of a tally of the justices' votes. But conference votes by no means end the work or resolve conflicts. Votes are tentative until an opinion announcing the Court's decision is handed down. After conference, a justice assigned to write the Court's opinion circulates drafts to all the other justices for their comments and then usually revises the opinion before delivering it in open Court. Justices are free to switch their votes and to write separate opinions concurring in or dissenting from the Court's decision. They thus continue after conference to compete for influence on the final decision and opinion.

"The business of the Court," Justice Potter Stewart once said, "is to give institutional opinions for its decisions."[1] The Court's opinion communicates an institutional decision. It also should convey the politically symbolic values of certainty, stability, and impartiality in the law. In most cases, justices therefore try to persuade as many others as possible to join an "opinion for the Court." Sometimes when the justices cannot agree on an opinion for their decision, or in minor cases, an unsigned (*per curiam*) opinion is handed down.[2]

Contemporary justices, however, rarely work together to reach an institutional decision and opinion. Justice Brennan recalled only a couple of times that they did so in his time on the bench (1956–1990).[3] Chief Justice Roberts has placed a premium on reaching a consensus but largely failed, especially with highly controversial decisions. But the historical trend has been toward less consensus on the Court's rulings. The justices are often divided over their decisions, and individual opinions have become more highly prized than institutional opinions. The Court now functions more like a legislative body relying simply on a tally of the votes to decide cases, rather than like a collegial body working toward collective decisions and opinions.

The Role of Oral Argument

For those outside the Court, the role of oral argument in deciding cases is vague, if not bewildering. Visitors at the Court often stand in line for an hour or more—sometimes days before oral arguments in high-profile cases—before they are seated in the courtroom to hear oral arguments. There is also a separate line for attorneys and members of the Supreme Court bar, but in 2015 the Roberts Court restricted that to only lawyers arguing cases on the day of oral argument, and no longer permits lawyers to hire "line standers" in order to secure a seat in the courtroom. The public is typically given only three or four minutes to listen and watch attorneys argue cases before they are ushered out. That is because the courtroom has only about 300 seats for the public, the news media, and members of the Court's bar. Only by special request, and subject to available seats, may members of the public hear entire arguments in a case. There are reserved seats for the press, and in major cases reporters may be allocated additional seats from the public section. Approximately 50,000 people annually view oral arguments during the Court's term, and about 1 million annually visit the Court.

The importance of oral argument, Chief Justice Hughes observed, lies in the fact that often "the impression that a judge has at the close of a full oral argument accords with the conviction which controls his final vote."[4] The justices hold conference and take their initial, usually decisive vote on cases within a day or two after hearing arguments, so oral arguments come at a crucial time. They focus the minds of the justices and present the possibility for fresh perspectives. "Often my idea of how a case shapes up is changed by oral argument," Brennan once observed, adding, "I have had too many occasions when my judgment or a decision has turned on what happened in oral argument."[5]

The role of oral argument was more prominent in the business of the Court in the nineteenth century.[6] Virtually unlimited time for oral argument was once allowed. In the important case of *Gibbons v. Ogden* (1824), there were twenty hours of oral arguments over five days.[7] In *Gibbons*, the Marshall Court held that Congress's power over interstate commerce limits the power of states to regulate commerce and transportation within their borders. By contrast, cases are now given only one hour, unless time is extended.

The Court began cutting back on time for oral arguments in 1848. The 1848 rule allowed eight hours per case. In 1871 the Court cut the time in half, permitting two hours for each side. Subsequently, in 1911, each side got an hour and a half. In 1925, time was further limited to one hour per side. Finally, in 1970 arguments were limited to thirty minutes per side. The Court, however, occasionally makes exceptions to its current practice of giving cases one hour for oral arguments. Recently, the Roberts Court devoted almost six hours to oral arguments in the Affordable Care Act (ACA) case, *National Federation of Independent Business v. Sebelius* (2012); in *Obergefell v. Hodges* (2015) the Court heard two-and-a-half hours—one-and-a-half hours on the question of whether the Fourteenth Amendment requires states to issue marriage licenses to same-sex couples and one hour on whether that amendment requires states to recognize same-sex marriages granted in other states. Still, in *Brown v. Board of Education*, the Court heard about thirteen-and-a-half hours of oral argument—an apparent record for the modern Court.

The Court's argument calendar once permitted the hearing of between 150 and 180 cases each year. The Roberts Court, however, now annually takes fewer than eighty and its calendar allows for eighty-four hours of argument, though in extraordinary cases more time may be added. For fourteen weeks each term, from the first Monday in October until the end of April, oral arguments are heard from ten to twelve and occasionally (rather than routinely, as in the past) from one to three on Monday, Tuesday, and Wednesday about every two weeks. Although the amount of time per case has been substantially reduced, more cases may be heard than forty years ago. At the turn of the twentieth century, the Court heard between 170 and 190 cases. After the Judiciary Act of 1925 enlarged the Court's power to deny cases review, the number of cases granted oral argument dropped. During the chief justiceship of Vinson, the Court heard an average of 137 cases each term, and during that of Warren, about 138. By cutting back on the time allowed for oral arguments, the Burger Court increased the number of cases it could hear to between 150 and 180 each term. But after a few years the justices began complaining they were deciding too many cases. During Rehnquist's tenure as chief justice (1986–2005), the Court gradually cut back on the number of cases granted oral arguments. That practice has continued with the Roberts Court (2005–).

Oral argument usually takes place four months after a case has been accepted. The major exception is in cases granted after February. By then the Court's calendar typically already has been filled, so the case may be put over to the next term. Occasionally, in very pressing cases, the Court will advance a case for oral argument. It did so in the Little Rock School case *Cooper v. Aaron* (1958), which was argued three days after the petition was filed, and in *United States v. Nixon* (1974), which was heard less than six weeks after being granted.

New York Times Co. v. United States (1971), in which the Nixon administration sought to suppress publication of the *Pentagon Papers*, a history of America's involvement in Vietnam, was also a case of a rushed oral argument.[8] The Court moved at a "frenzied" pace to decide the case over the protests of Burger and others. On the morning of Thursday, June 24, 1971, the Court received the *New York Times*'s petition, and that of the government arrived later that day. The following morning Chief Justice Burger called Solicitor General Erwin N. Griswold, who argued the case for the government, and told him that the Court had granted the petition and scheduled oral arguments for ten in the morning the next day, Saturday, June 26. The briefs on the merits of the case arrived just minutes before oral argument took place. Four days later, in a single-paragraph *per curiam* opinion, the Court upheld the First Amendment right to publish without prior restraint. But all nine justices filed separate opinions—six concurring and three dissenting—for a total of ten opinions!

No less dramatic was the decision on Friday, December 8, 2000, by a bare majority of the Rehnquist Court—all of the conservative justices—voted to stay the Florida State Supreme Court's order of a statewide manual recount of votes cast in the 2000 presidential election and to hear oral arguments in *Bush v. Gore* the following Monday. The four dissenters—Justices Stevens, Souter, Ginsburg, and Breyer—shot back with an unusual dissenting opinion, sharply criticizing the majority's stay of the recount for "inevitably cast[ing] a cloud on the legitimacy of the election." The day after hearing oral arguments, at ten in the evening, the Court issued sixty-five pages of opinions: a *per curiam* opinion, reversing the state supreme court; a concurring opinion by Chief Justice Rehnquist, which Justices Scalia and Thomas joined; and four separate dissents by Justices Stevens, Souter, Ginsburg, and Breyer.

The reduction in the amount of time devoted to oral arguments was only partly due to an increasing caseload. No less important, some justices had grown dissatisfied with the quality of advocacy.

For most of the nineteenth century, a relatively small number of attorneys, such as Daniel Webster, argued before the Court and excelled in the art of oratory. The difficulties of transportation precluded many attorneys from traveling to Washington, D.C. to argue their cases. Hence, attorneys hired D.C. lawyers to make oral arguments. The Court's bar was small, and there was usually a close friendship between the justices and counsel. Daniel Webster epitomized the best of nineteenth-century oratory and the mutual respect of the Court and its bar. At issue in one of his early cases, *Dartmouth College v. Woodward* (1819), was whether, without abridging the contract clause of the Constitution, New Hampshire could revise a college charter, granted originally by the British Crown, to replace the board of trustees with one more to its liking.[9] With his sonorous and histrionic power, Webster concluded his argument in a grand manner:

Sir, you may destroy this little institution. It is weak. It is in your hands! I know it is one of the lesser lights in the literary horizon of the country. You may put it out. But if you do so, you must carry through your work. You must extinguish, one after another, all those great lights of science which, for more than a century, have thrown their radiance over our land.

It is, Sir, as I have said, a small college and yet, there are those who love it. . . .

Sir, I care not how others may feel, but, for myself, when I see my Alma Mater surrounded, like Caesar in the senate-house, by those who are reiterating stab on stab, I would not, for this right hand, have her turn to me, and say *et tu quoque, mi fili!*[10]

Webster's oratory won the day, as it often did. He described his feelings when later arguing *Gibbons v. Ogden* (1824), the landmark case on the regulation of interstate commerce, before Chief Justice Marshall: "I think I never experienced more intellectual pleasure arguing [a] novel question to a great man who appreciates it and takes it in; and he did take it in, as a baby takes in its mother's milk."[11]

As travel became easier in the late nineteenth century, attorneys journeyed more often to the District of Columbia for the publicity of arguing cases before the highest court in the land. But their lack of experience became all too evident. As the quality of advocacy declined, oral presentations seemed to Justice John Clarke to "stretch out as if to the crack of doom."[12] Holmes used the time to write letters, confessing, "[W]e don't shut up bores, one has to listen to discourses dragging slowly along after one has seen the point and made up one's mind. That is what is happening now and I take the chance to write as I sit with my brethren. I hope I shall be supposed to be taking notes."[13] Once Frankfurter passed a note to Black asking, "You are more indulgent of poor advocacy than I am—so please tell me why a lawyer having limited time wastes 10 minutes before he comes to the point 'on which the case turns'?"[14] Indeed, Rehnquist once lectured the ABA on sloppy, "slipshod" advocacy and warned lawyers to be prepared for hypotheticals during oral arguments.[15] Justice Blackmun even graded advocates on an eight-point scale; the solicitor general and former law clerks generally received higher grades than private practitioners and state attorneys general.

Even before time was limited to thirty minutes per side, a number of justices agreed that the best arguments were those presented in half an hour. In Frankfurter's words, "A number of lawyers think it is a constitutional duty to use an hour when they have got it."[16]

Oral argument remains the only opportunity for attorneys to communicate directly with the justices. Except when standing at a podium while making their oral arguments, counsel sit at tables facing the high bench, with their backs to visitors in the courtroom. On the bench, the chief justice sits in the center chair, and associate justices sit in alternating order of seniority on the chief's right and left. At separate tables at the ends of the bench sit the Clerk of the Court on the chief's right, and the marshal on the left.

Two basic factors appear to control the importance of oral argument. As Justice Rutledge observed, "One is brevity. The other is the preparation with which the judge comes to it."[17] The justices have enforced their interest in brevity in several ways. Chief Justice White invented what was called the summary docket: if an appeal could not be dismissed but the Court did not deem a case worth full argument time, each side was allowed thirty minutes. Chief Justice Taft had a practice of announcing, "The Court does not care to hear the respondent," if the appellate or petitioner failed to sustain his contention in opening argument.[18] A rigorous enforcer of rules governing oral arguments, Chief Justice Hughes reportedly called time on a lawyer in the middle of the word *if*. But the Court became somewhat "more liberal," Chief Justice Burger claimed, "We allow a lawyer to finish the sentence that is unfolding when the red light goes on, provided, of course, the sentence is not too long." However, after Rehnquist became chief justice, he once let an attorney go over time, and a couple of the justices walked off the bench. Chief Justice Roberts on a number of occasions also permitted attorneys to go over the allotted time, perhaps because he once argued before the Court and feels that more time is often needed. He recalled that as an attorney arguing before the Court, he "once had more than 100 questions [posed by the justices] in a half hour."[19] Indeed, Justice Ginsburg noted that the contemporary Court has a "hot bench" because the justices ask more questions than they used to. Although the amount of time given oral arguments is about half that of fifty years ago, the justices' questioning from the bench has increased by 24 percent, while attorneys' arguments have decreased by 46 percent.[20]

Central to preparation and delivery is a bird's eye view of the case, the issues and facts, and the reasoning behind legal developments. Crisp, concise, and conversational presentations are what the justices want. An attorney must never forget, in Rehnquist's words, that "he is not, after all, presenting his case to some abstract, platonic embodiment of appellate judges as a class, but . . . [to] nine flesh and blood men and women." Oral argument is definitely not a "brief with gestures."[21] Chief Justice Roberts has likewise advised lawyers to become more "attuned" to questions asked from the bench. Reflecting on his experience of arguing thirty-nine cases before the Court (winning about 70 percent), he observed, "I would try today to be much more receptive, try to process more effectively, 'Now what does that question tell me about what that judge is thinking?' and respond rapidly rather than trying to stick to my script."[22] Justice Alito has said that oral arguments are "considerably better" than when he served in the office of the solicitor general during the Reagan administration,[23] although he feels they are "a small part of the Court's work."[24] From his experience, prior to oral arguments justices usually have a "pretty strong idea of [their] position," and though oral arguments may sometimes "make a difference," their importance lies in the fact that they are "the first time that any of us get an idea about what other [justices] think." Hence, Alito advises attorneys to "read the Court," and "most important[ly] answer questions from the bench" and if there is an "accident" or "traffic jam" stay on course in making two or three main points.[25]

The Court's clerk sends lawyers a booklet offering advice on preparing and presenting oral arguments. Among the recommendations, "*Never under any circumstance* interrupt a Justice when he or she is addressing you. Give the Justice your attention while being addressed by the Justice! If you are speaking and a Justice interrupts you, you should cease talking immediately and listen." Attorneys are advised to "[m]ake every effort to answer the questions directly. If at all possible, use 'yes' or 'no' and then expand upon your answer." They are also counseled on responding to hypotheticals: "In the past, attorneys have responded, 'But those aren't the facts in this case!' Please be advised that the Justice who poses the hypothetical question is aware that there are different facts in your case, but the Justice wants your answer to the posed hypothetical question." Finally, the booklet warns, "Attempts at humor usually fall flat. The same is true for attempts at familiarity. For example, do not say something like this: 'This is similar to a case argued when I clerked here.' "[26]

In his book, *Making Your Case: The Art of Persuading Judges*, Justice Scalia offered these additional recommendations when arguing cases: "Look the judges in the eye. Connect. . . . Be conversational but not familiar. . . . Never read an argument."[27] He underscored that point in 2014 when interrupting a nervous first-timer before the Court by asking, "Counsel, you are not reading this, are you?" The attorney froze and had no response, until Justice Breyer broke the tension with "It's all right."[28]

Justices differ in their own preparation. Douglas insisted that "oral arguments win or lose a case," but Warren found them "not highly persuasive."[29] By contrast, Holmes rarely found oral arguments influential; if not writing letters, he took catnaps while on the bench. Both Frankfurter and Douglas claimed never to read briefs before oral arguments, but once they were on the bench their styles and strategies varied markedly. Frankfurter consumed large segments of time with questions, exasperating counsel and other justices. Frankfurter once interrupted a lawyer ninety-three times during a 120-minute oral argument.[30]

Most justices now come to hear oral arguments armed with bench memos drafted by their law clerks. Bench memos identify the central facts, issues, and possible questions raised by a case. Because of the workload, Scalia once explained, "you have to have done all the work you think is necessary for that case before you hear the argument." He no longer thought, as he did before his appointment, of oral arguments as "a dog and pony show," and he went over each case with clerks before hearing oral arguments. "Things," he once said, "can be put in perspective during oral argument in a way that they can't in a written brief." Justice Kennedy also emphasized, "When the people come . . . to see our arguments, they often see a dialogue between the justices asking a question and the attorney answering it. And they think of the argument as a series of these dialogues. It isn't that. As John [Stevens] points out, what is happening is the Court is having a conversation with itself through the intermediary of the attorney."[31] Justice Sotomayor echoed that view, observing that oral arguments serve two purposes: first is for lawyers to clarify misunderstandings and second, "for justices to hear what's bothering each other."[32] So too, Chief Justice Roberts asks aggressive questions in order to get advocates to "come up with a good answer that might help respond to [an]other justice's concern."[33] Justice Sotomayor emphasizes that "Through our individual questions our colleagues are understanding each other."[34] So, too, Justice Kagan underscored that, "Often the justices aren't really asking you questions. They don't really care about the answers you give. They're making points to their colleagues."[35]

To be sure, over time justices differ in their styles and approaches to questioning of attorneys. Consequently, oral arguments have a different flavor depending on the Court's composition. In the 1970s and early 1980s, for instance, very few justices on the Burger Court asked questions from the bench. Indeed, questioning from the bench has increased over the last couple of decades, and studies suggest that justices ask more questions of attorneys with whom they disagree or whose briefs they find weak.[36] With the exception of Justice Thomas, every justice on the Roberts Court routinely and aggressively asks questions. Indeed, Thomas has asked only a couple of questions during over two decades on the bench. He has explained, "I don't see the need for all those questions. I think justices, 99 percent of the time, have their minds made up when they go to the bench."[37] By contrast, Justice Sotomayor immediately proved a sharp and active questioner from the bench. Justices Scalia, Souter, and Breyer have been called "masters of the hypothetical" for their sometimes convoluted, even off-the-wall questions.[38] Scalia, like Frankfurter before him, earned a reputation for outspokenness, which some justices and attorneys found irritating. Conceding his overbearing manner, Scalia explained, "It is the academic in me. I fight against it. The devil makes me do it."[39] Likewise, Justice Gorsuch in his first terms emerged as an aggressive questioner from the bench.

"Does oral argument make a difference? Of course it makes a difference," according to Justice Kennedy. "It has to make a difference. That's the passion and the power, and the poetry of the law—that a rhetorical case can make a difference, because abstract principles have to be applied in a real-life situation. And that's what the lawyer is there to remind the Court about." Justice Breyer has said that oral arguments change justices' points of view in a "significant number of cases," explaining, "I usually say if you say less than five percent, you're too low, if you say more than ten or fifteen, you're too high. But if you ask the question differently, how often does it change the way you look at the case, then the answer is quite a lot. And that matters, because we're writing an opinion." By contrast, Justice Thomas, who rarely asks questions, explains, "I don't see [how asking questions] advances anything. . . . I don't like to badger people. . . . I see no need for all of that. Most of that is in the briefs, and there are a few questions around the edges [of the arguments in the brief]."[40] Nonetheless, justices often cite transcripts of oral arguments in their opinions in opposing the position of one party in a suit, in explaining the relevant law or laying out specific facts, or in discrediting the majority's opinion.

Conference on Merits

The justices hold private conferences on Wednesday afternoons to discuss the merits of the cases heard on Monday, and then again on Friday to discuss the cases they heard on Tuesday and Wednesday. But the Court meets only on Thursdays in May and June, for about twenty-four conferences during a term. Conference discussions are secret, except for revelations in justices' opinions, off-the-bench communications, or, when available much later, in their private papers. "The integrity of decision making would be impaired seriously if we had to reach our judgments in the atmosphere of an ongoing town meeting," Justice Powell claimed. "There must be candid discussion, a willingness to consider arguments advanced by other Justices, and a continuing examination and reexamination of one's own views."[41]

Since conference discussions are not revealed, their importance apart from the voting on cases is difficult to determine. But the significance of conference discussions has certainly changed with the increasing caseload. "Our tasks involve deliberation, reflection and mediation," Douglas observed.[42] But, those tasks no longer take place at conference; they now revolve around the activities in and among the chambers after conference. Justice Alito has underscored, "almost all communications are done in writing" after conferences, and conferences are "not open-ended discussions." Chief Justice Roberts "does not speak for a long time," basically stating only whether he would affirm or reverse the lower court, and "even less was said" during Rehnquist's chief justiceship.[43]

Conference discussions do not play the role they once did. In the nineteenth century, when the docket was smaller, conferences were integral to the justices' collective deliberations. Cases were discussed in detail and differences hammered out. The justices not only decided how to dispose of cases but also reached agreement on an institutional opinion for the Court. As the caseload grew, conferences became largely symbolic of past collective deliberations. Now they only discover how the justices line up. There is no longer time for justices to reach agreement and compromise on opinions for the Court.

With the limited time available, Douglas observed, "[c]onference discussion sometimes changes one's view of a case, but usually not."[44] Rehnquist agreed that persuading others to change their

positions is "the exception." When examining the Court's workload in the late 1950s, the Harvard Law School professor Henry
Hart estimated that the justices heard oral arguments about 140
hours and deliberated in conference about 132 hours each term.[45]
The Court's docket then included around 2,000 cases, meaning
that each case could have been given an average of three to four
minutes at conference. A large number, however, were never brought
up for discussion. If we assume (on the basis of the discussion of the
Court's screening process in Chapter 4) that over 80 percent of the
cases are not discussed, each remaining case could have been
given at most eleven minutes. Assuming further (and unrealisti-
cally) that the Court devoted entire conferences to only those
cases argued and decided on merits (around 125 cases at the time),
each case would have received at most seven minutes of conference discussion per justice. Even in the 1950s, however, Justice
Jackson lamented the lack of deliberation, estimating "at the average conference an average of five minutes per item, or about 33
seconds of discussion per item by each of the nine justices."[46]

Conference discussion, as Justice Scalia further explained,
"is not really an exercise in persuading each other; it's an exercise
in stating your views while the rest of us take notes. That's its
function. You take notes so that if you get assigned the opinion,
you know how to write it in a way that will get at least four other
votes besides your own."[47]

Some cases undoubtedly are discussed at greater length and
even at more than one conference. But conference discussions
have less significance in the Court's decision making. The result
of devoting less time to collective deliberation and consensus
building contributes to more divided decisions. Because the justices no longer have the time or inclination to agree on opinions
for the Court, they file a greater number of separate opinions. The
reality of more cases and less collective deliberation in turn dis-
courages the reaching of compromises necessary for institutional
opinions. Ideological and personal differences among the justices
remain and perhaps are reinforced.

STRATEGIES DURING CONFERENCE

Justices vary in the weight they place on conference deliberations. They all come prepared to vote, but some have little interest in discussions, while others take copious notes. Much depends
on a justice's intellectual ability, self-confidence, and style. At conference, some junior justices have been said to experience a
"freshman effect." That is, because senior justices speak first,
newly appointed members may be somewhat circumspect. Hughes
once observed that "it takes three or four years to get the hang of
it, and that so extraordinary an intellect as Brandeis said that it
took him four or five years to feel that he understood the jurisdictional problems of the Court."[48] Justice Thomas agrees that it
took "three to five years to adjust to the work of the Court." Calling his first five years his "rookie year," he added, "In your first
five years, you wonder how you got here. After that you wonder
how your colleagues got here."[49]

Justice Scalia recalled that his "biggest surprise" on arriving
at the Court was "the enormity of the workload. I don't think I
worked as hard in my life," he adds, "including first-year law
school, as I did my first year on the Court." Yet Scalia did not
give any indication of experiencing a freshman effect; far from
being circumspect, he quickly staked out his sharply conservative positions.[50] Likewise, Chief Justice Roberts and Justices
Ginsburg, Breyer, Sotomayor, Kagan, and Gorsuch gave no indication of experiencing a freshman effect in their first terms;
Ginsburg, Breyer, Sotomayor, Gorsuch, and Kavanaugh had over
a decade of experience on the appellate bench before their
elevation to the Court.

The justices' interaction at conference has been analyzed in
terms of small-group behavior, specifically the role of the chief
justice, distinguishing between two kinds of influence—"task"
and "social" leadership.[51] Task leadership relates to managing the
workload, even at the cost of ignoring personal relations among

the justices. By contrast, social leadership addresses the interpersonal relations among the justices that are crucial for a collegial body. Some chief justices are oriented more to either task or social leadership, few assume both roles, and some fail at both.

Though the chief justice is the titular head of the Court, it by no means follows that he has a monopoly on leadership. Taft was good humored but, recognizing his intellectual limitations, relied on Van Devanter for task leadership.[52] Warren, likewise socially oriented, found it useful to consult with Brennan when planning conferences. On the Burger Court, Powell showed considerable task leadership with suggestions for expediting the processing of the growing caseload. Rehnquist was a strong taskmaster with a quick wit that eased relations and made him a good social leader. Roberts apparently tries to follow that practice, but has been described as a little too "chiefie" at times.

Still, any justice may assume task or social leadership. He or she also may assert a third kind of leadership—policy leadership. Justices demonstrate policy leadership by persuading others to vote in ways (in the short and long run) favorable to their policy goals. Some justices deny the possibility of such influence. "It may well be that, since the days of John Marshall, an individual Justice or Chief Justice cannot 'lead,'" Blackmun suggested. "The Court pretty much goes its own way."[53] Likewise, Frankfurter observed, "A member of the Supreme Court is at once a soloist and part of an orchestra."[54] But all three kinds of influence— task, social, and policy—are intertwined and present various strategic opportunities for trying to influence the outcome of decisions.

On especially controversial cases, one strategy may be simply to confer but not to vote. Forcing a vote may sharply divide the justices and foreclose negotiations. The Warren Court adopted that approach with *Brown v. Board of Education* (1954). When Warren arrived at the Court in 1953, *Brown* had already been on the docket for more than a year. Oral arguments were held in

November 1953, but he carried the case over week after week at conference. No vote was taken until the middle of February 1954. Frankfurter and Jackson reinforced Warren's inclination to hold off voting and pushed for a unanimous ruling. If *Brown* had been decided when it first arrived, the vote might have been 6–3; Vinson was still chief justice then. As Justice Burton noted in his diary, Warren did a "magnificent job in getting a unanimous Court. (This would have been impossible a year ago—probably 6–3 with the Chief Justice at that time one of the dissenters)."*[55] But, Warren cultivated the justices from the Deep South—Justices Black, Clark, and Reed—for the unanimous decision.[56]

The strategy of postponing a vote is open not only to the chief justice. Since the chief justiceship of Vinson, the practice has been "to pass any argued case upon the request of any member of the Court."[57] Obviously, there are limits to how often this can be done if the Court is to complete its work. Vinson's experience indicates that less than 9 percent of the cases were decided "upon votes not cast at the first conference following argument."[58]

Another strategy may provide more opportunities to influence others. "The practice has grown up," according to Burger, "of assigning one Justice to simply prepare a memorandum about the case, and at that time all other Justices are invited if they want to submit a memorandum; and then out of that memorandum usually a consensus is formed and someone is identified who can write an opinion that will command a majority of the Court."[59] The practice sharpens the confrontation between opposing policy

---

*Although Warren managed to bring the Court's full prestige to the ruling, opposition to *Brown* was nevertheless intense and widespread, as will be further discussed in Chapter 6; and perhaps, as Justice Stevens once observed, a nonunanimous decision would have been preferable because southerners might have felt that at least some of the members of the Court understood their traditions and the inexorable problems of ending segregation. (Author interview with Justice Stevens, April 5, 1985.)

For my friend and colleagues
William O. Douglas who will always
climb new mountains as long
as they are there.
                    With best wishes
                            Warren E. Burger

Chief Justice Warren Burger (right) and Justice William O. Douglas. (*Collection of the Supreme Court of the United States*)

preferences. This occurred, for instance, with the circulation of rival opinions in the important obscenity case *Miller v. California* (1973).[60] Burger and Brennan directly competed for votes to support their respective draft opinions. In the end, a bare majority accepted Burger's analysis and more restrictive definition of obscenity, based on local community standards of what appeals to a prurient interest in sex.[61]

A justice who decides to draft a memorandum on a case for conference discussion gains time to refine ideas and to try to persuade others. This strategy so appealed to Frankfurter that he often circulated memos on cases pending before conference. The disadvantage of such preconference reports was the inevitable increase in the workload. Such a practice, Douglas thought, would also "launch the Court into the law review business, multiplying our volumes, and load them with irrelevances."[62] But the practice of circulating memos prior to conference deliberations largely disappeared during the Rehnquist and Roberts Courts.

At conference justices may try to reason with each other, but there is little time for that, considering the Court's current workload. Their success depends on how much time they have and their style as much as on the reasons they offer. Frankfurter was inclined to monopolize discussions, occasionally standing up and lecturing. Stewart recalled telling him "that he held forth for exactly fifty minutes, the length of a law school class period at Harvard."[63] Once, when Frankfurter refused to answer one of Douglas's questions, the latter protested, but added, "We all know what a great burden your long discourses are. So I am not complaining."[64] Frankfurter's tendency to monopolize conference discussions so irritated Douglas that on occasion, recalled Brennan, he "would rise from his seat, approach the chief justice and say, 'When Felix finishes, Chief, I'll be back,' and leave the conference."[65] In contrast, Justice Harlan never talked at great length. He always focused on the facts he thought controlling and frequently concluded, "Now that we have the whole case before us it is clear this is a 'peewee' but it is here and we should deal with it."[66]

Justices may also appeal to emotions and egos rather than to reason. Jackson once observed of another that "you just can't disagree with him. You must go to war with him if you disagree."[67] Actual physical aggression, of course, is rare. However, Douglas recalled one time when Chief Justice Vinson became so perturbed that he got up from the conference table and headed around the room, shouting at Frankfurter, "No son-of-a-bitch can ever say that to Fred Vinson."[68] Personal animosities sometimes prevail. The most extreme were those of Justice McReynolds. He was anti-Semitic, and whenever Brandeis spoke at conference, he would get up and walk out of the conference room. But he would leave the door open a crack and peek in until Brandeis was through, then come back. For the most part, justices do not let professional differences become personal, as a number of present justices have said. They must disagree without being disagreeable.

When discussions become heated, humor may prove useful. As Rehnquist put it, the only effective power a chief justice has at conference is that of "making a frown" to cut down on heated debates. There is also the story of Holmes's interrupting one of Harlan's discourses, violating the unwritten rule against interruptions. "But that just won't wash," he said, outraging Harlan. Thereupon Chief Justice Fuller quickly mimed a washboard motion with his hands and said, "But I just keep scrubbing away, scrubbing away."[69] During another heated debate at conference, Frankfurter and Chief Justice Stone squared off. Again, humor helped relieve the tension. After Stone made one of his long presentations on a case, Frankfurter snapped, "I suppose you know more than those who drafted the Constitution." To which Stone shot back, "I know some things better than those who drafted the Constitution," to which Frankfurter quipped, "Yes, wine and cheese," drawing laughter from the justices.[70]

At other times, justices may more or less subtly appeal to each other's egos. Personally offended by a remark at a conference, Justice Murphy passed a note to Black stating, "Hugo: I appreciate your sentiments because you are the bravest and keenest man on this Court."[71] By contrast, Justice Minton thought Black a "Demagogue" after he made "one of his inflammatory outbursts at Conference."[72]

Even ideological foes, such as Black and Frankfurter, may nonetheless appeal to, if not retain, each other's self-esteem. Black once wrote to the latter:

More than a quarter of a century's close association between us in the Supreme Court's exacting intellectual activities had enabled both of us, I suspect, to anticipate with reasonable accuracy the basic position both are likely to take on questions that importantly involve the public welfare and tranquility. Our differences, which have been many, have rarely been over the ultimate and desired, but rather have related to the means that were most likely to achieve the end we both envisioned. Our years together, and these differences, have but added to the respect and admiration that I had for *Professor* Frankfurter even before I knew him— his love of country, steadfast devotion to what he believed to be right, and to his wisdom.[73]

TENTATIVE VOTES

Voting presents opportunities to negotiate on which issues to decide and how. "*Votes* count," one of Black's colleagues reminded him in a note passed at conference. "I vote to reverse, if there were two more of my mind there would be a reversal."[74] But the justices' votes are always tentative until the day the Court hands down its decision. Before, during, and after conference, justices may use their votes in strategic ways to influence the disposition of a case. "The books on voting are never closed until the decision actually comes down," Harlan explained. "Until then any member of the Court is perfectly free to change his vote, and it is not an unheard of occurrence for a persuasive minority opinion to eventuate as the prevailing opinion."[75]

At conference, a justice may vote with others if they appear to constitute a majority, even though disagreeing with their treatment of a case. The justice may then bargain and try to minimize the damage, from his or her policy perspective. Alternatively, justices may threaten dissenting opinions or try to form a voting bloc and thereby influence the final decision.

The utility of such voting strategies depends on how the justices line up at conference. They may prove quite useful if the initial vote is 5–4 or 6–3. But their effectiveness also depends on institutional norms and practices. The importance of voting strategies at conference is also conditioned by the complexity of the issues presented and their divisiveness. Complex cases may result in confusion at conference. When there is a vacancy on the bench, as happened after Justice Scalia's death in 2016, the justices may split 4–4, thereby leaving the lower court's decision intact, or work toward forging a compromise 5–3 ruling, as they did in upholding the University of Texas at Austin's affirmative-action program in *Fisher v. University of Texas at Austin* (2016).

The circulation of draft opinions also reinforces the strategic use of tentative votes and the importance of post-conference deliberations. Not only are opinion assignments and the circulation of draft opinions central to the contemporary Court's decision-making process, they also provide opportunities for holding on to or enlarging a majority supporting the decision (as discussed in the next section); and when justices are closely divided, the circulation of drafts may result in an outcome that differs from the vote at conference. In *Heller v. Doe* (1993), for example, the justices divided 5–4.[76] Subsequently, Justice Souter circulated a draft opinion for the Court striking down Kentucky's statute, providing for different standards and commitment procedures for the mentally disabled and the mentally ill, as a denial of the equal protection of the law. But Justice Kennedy immediately responded with a proposed dissenting opinion that upheld Kentucky's law. Eventually, Kennedy's opinion commanded a majority because Justice White switched positions and joined Kennedy's opinion. As Justice White explained when joining Kennedy's dissent, "I was tentatively the other way, but I find that I am more comfortable with what you have written and you may count me in."[77]

Opinion-Writing Process

Opinions justify or explain votes at conference. The opinion for the Court is the most important and most difficult to write because it represents a collective judgment. Writing the Court's opinion, as Holmes put it, requires that a "judge can dance the sword dance; that is he can justify an obvious result without stepping on either blade of opposing fallacies."[78] Holmes often complained about the compromises he had to make when writing an opinion for the Court. "I am sorry that my moderation," he wrote Chief Justice White, "did not soften your inexorable heart—But I stand like St. Sebastian ready for your arrows."[79]

Justice Blackmun agreed that opinions must often be revised "because other justices say, if you put in this kind of a paragraph or say this, I'll join your opinion. So you put it in. And many times the final result is a compromise. I think the public doesn't always appreciate this, but many times the final result is not what the author would originally have liked to have. But five votes are the answer and that's what the coached judgment is. So you swallow your pride and go along with it if you can."[80]

Since conference votes are tentative, the assignment, drafting, and circulation of opinions are crucial to the Court's rulings. At each stage, justices compete for influence in determining the Court's final decision and opinion.

OPINION ASSIGNMENT

The power of opinion assignment is perhaps a chief justice's "single most influential function" and, as Justice Clark emphasized, an exercise in "judicial-political discretion."[81] In a tradition dating back to the Marshall Court (1801–1835), when the chief justice is in the majority, he assigns the Court's opinion. Prior to that there was not a set practice—sometimes the English practice of *per curiam* (unsigned) and *seriatim* (individual) opinions was followed, but more often the justice announced the opinion "by the Court."[82] The practice became that of issuing "opinions for the Court" because Chief Justice Marshall insisted on unanimous decisions in order to establish the Court's institutional legitimacy, or forced the appearance of unanimity by rigorously establishing the practice of delivering the Court's opinions. Marshall did so in order to (1) establish the legitimacy of the Court, and (2) provide lower courts and the bar with guidance and assurance as to what the law was. And he largely prevailed, delivering the vast majority of opinions for the Court, even when he disagreed with the outcome. During his thirty-four-year tenure, Chief Justice Marshall wrote 547 opinions, whereas Justice Gabriel Duvall (1811–1835), for instance, wrote fifteen and Justice Thomas Todd (1807–1826) wrote fourteen.[83] There were also few dissents in Marshall's time, throughout the nineteenth century, and into the 1930s and 1940s (as discussed further in this chapter). The English tradition of *seriatim* opinions, thus, gave way to institutional opinions for the Court, which was then reinforced by the publication of the official *U.S. Reports* of decisions and the justices' recognition that they were writing opinions for publication and guidance for not just the bar but other institutions and the public.

Today, if the chief justice does not vote with the majority, then the senior associate justice in the majority either writes the opinion or assigns it to another. If chief justices are in the majority they may, of course, keep cases for themselves. This is in the tradition of Chief Justice Marshall, but as modified by the workload and other justices' expectations of equitable opinion assignments. In landmark cases, chief justices often self-assign the Court's opinion. "The great cases are written," Justice John Clarke observed, "as they should be, by the Chief Justice."[84] But chief justices differ. Fuller, even against the advice of other justices, frequently "gave away" important cases[85]; by contrast, Taft retained 34 percent, Hughes 28 percent, and Stone 11 percent of "the important cases."[86] Various considerations may lie behind a chief justice's self-assignment, such as how much time he already invested in a case and his final vote.

Chief justices also have approached opinion assignment differently. Hughes tended to write most of the Court's opinions and was "notoriously inclined to keep the 'plums' for himself." Between

1930 and 1938, Hughes wrote an average of twenty-one opinions for the Court, whereas other justices averaged only sixteen. Hughes also made all assignments immediately after conference. Typically, "assignments would arrive at each justice's home within a half hour or so" of his return from the Court.[87] Because conferences tended to drag on under Stone, he was not so prompt in his assignments. Like Hughes, however, Stone tended to take more of the opinions for himself. He averaged about nineteen, whereas other justices wrote only about fifteen opinions for the Court every term.

The inequities in opinion assignments by Hughes and Stone angered some justices. When Vinson became chief justice, he strove to distribute opinions more equitably. The increase in the business of the Court also led Vinson to safeguard against justices' piling up of too many opinions and forcing the Court to sit for extra weeks before the term ended. On a large chart, he kept track of the opinions assigned, when they were completed, and which remained outstanding.[88] Vinson was remarkably successful in achieving parity in opinion assignments. All justices on the Vinson Court averaged about ten opinions for the Court every term. Warren largely followed that practice.[89] Burger likewise paid attention to equity in opinion assignments, but tended to write slightly more opinions for the Court each term than the others.[90]

By comparison, Chief Justice Rehnquist strove for an even more equal distribution of the workload.[91] In a memorandum, he said that "the principal rule" in his opinion assignments was "to give everyone approximately the same number of assignments of opinions for the Court during any one term." However, this policy did not take into account the difficulty of a case or the work backed up in different chambers, and Rehnquist explained that he, therefore, gave additional weight to whether "(1) A chambers has one or more uncirculated majority opinions that were assigned more than four weeks previously; (2) A chambers has one or more uncirculated dissenting opinions in which the majority opinion has circulated more than four weeks previously; and (3) A chambers has not voted in a case in which both majority and dissenting opinions have circulated."[92] This way, Chief Justice Rehnquist achieved both equity in and expeditious processing of opinions for the Court.

Likewise, Chief Justice Roberts tries to spread opinion assignments evenly in terms of the number and difficulty of cases. "I can't take all the good ones for myself," he has said, "and I have to take my share of the dogs." He also tries to assign opinions that may command a broad consensus on a narrow opinion because, he has said, that is "the way the law ought to proceed."[93] A study of his opinion assignments found that Roberts made certain that each justice had almost exactly the same number of majority opinions, and on that score his record was "unmatched" by all prior chief justices.[94] However, when it came to "major" cases he kept about a third and assigned another third to Kennedy, followed by Alito (with 16 percent) and the remaining (18 percent) to other justices (except for Sotomayor). Notably, he tended to assign opinions to Kennedy because that reduced "the risk of the swinging justice swinging" and would lock in the conference vote. Alito received more assignments than Scalia (his senior) because he was trusted to write more narrowly than Scalia, who also tended to write bolder and broader opinions. Still, like prior chief justices, Roberts self-assigns opinions in the most controversial cases, like that on the Affordable Care Act (Obamacare) of 2010 in *National Federation of Independent Business v. Sebelius* (2012). The justices split 1–4–4, with Roberts delivering the opinion of the Court, on upholding the "individual mandate" that requires most Americans to have "minimum essential" health coverage or pay a penalty, but striking down the provisions that would have extended Medicaid. In a separate concurring opinion, Justice Ginsburg, joined by Justices Breyer, Sotomayor, and Kagan, would have upheld the entire law; while dissenting Justices Scalia,

Kennedy, Thomas, and Alito would have struck down the law in
its entirety.

Although parity in opinion assignment now generally prevails,
the practice of assigning opinions immediately after conference,
as Hughes did, or within a day or two, as Stone did, ended with
Vinson's tenure as chief justice. Chief Justice Roberts follows the
practice of Warren, Burger, and Rehnquist in assigning opinions
after each two-week session of oral arguments and conferences.
With more assignments to make at any given time, chief justices
thus acquired greater flexibility in distributing the workload, as
well as enhanced their own opportunities for influencing the final
outcome through opinion assignment.

Assignment of opinions is complicated in controversial cases.
Occasionally, a justice assigned to write an opinion discovers that
it "just won't write," and it must be reassigned.[95] Chief Justice Taft
once assigned himself an opinion but wrote it reversing the vote
taken at conference, explaining, "I think we made a mistake in
this case and have written the opinion the other way. Hope you
will agree."[96]

Sometimes other justices switch votes after an opinion has
been assigned. Rather dramatically in the course of writing an
opinion for a bare majority in *Garcia v. San Antonio Metropolitan Transit Authority* (1985),[97] Justice Blackmun changed his
mind and wrote an opinion that instead of extending an earlier
5–4 ruling handed down in *National League of Cities v. Usery*
(1976),[98] called into question that precedent and reached a result
opposite of the vote at conference. Rehnquist's opinion in *Usery*
was divisive because the Court had not limited Congress's power
under the commerce clause since striking down much of the early
New Deal legislation, which precipitated the "constitutional crisis" of 1937. Yet Rehnquist managed to persuade Blackmun, along
with three others, to strike down Congress's setting of minimum
wage and maximum hour standards for all state, county, and
municipal employees under the Fair Labor Standards Act. He did
so on a novel reading of the Tenth Amendment guarantee that

powers not delegated to the federal government "are reserved to the States" and by claiming that the Court should defend states' sovereignty against federal intrusions on their "traditional" and "integral" state activities. The justices remained sharply divided on Rehnquist's position in *Usery*.[99] Finally, when assigned *Garcia*, Blackmun changed his mind about the wisdom of Rehnquist's earlier opinion and attempt to draw a line between "traditional" and "nontraditional" state activities. So his draft in *Garcia* was in line with the views of the four dissenters in *Usery*, though it stopped short of overruling that earlier decision. Because he did not circulate the draft until two weeks before the end of the term and reached a result contrary to the conference vote, a majority decided to carry *Garcia* over to the next term and hear rearguments, specifically addressing whether *Usery* should be overturned. Blackmun, along with Brennan, Marshall, and Stevens, opposed that, and he warned that as a result *Usery* "just might end up being overruled."[100] The rearguments strengthened Blackmun's resolve, and his revised draft in *Garcia* expressly overturned *Usery*.

Justice Kennedy likewise switched his vote when working on the opinion for the Court in *Lee v. Weisman* (1992), and the ultimate outcome was contrary to the original conference vote.[101] At conference, the justices split 5–4 to reverse a lower-court decision holding that the First Amendment barred school-sponsored prayer at high school graduation ceremonies. Chief Justice Rehnquist assigned the opinion for the Court to Kennedy, who appeared to hold the pivotal vote. But when drafting the opinion he changed his mind and wrote an opinion going the other way. As he explained to Blackmun, who was the senior associate justice in the minority:

After writing to reverse in the high school graduation prayer case, my draft looked quite wrong. So I have written it to rule in favor of the objecting student, both at middle school and high school exercises. The Chief said to go ahead and circulate, and I thought as the senior member of those who voted for this result you should have brief advance notice. I will accompany the draft with a memo confirming that I circulate with the Chief's consent, though he had desired a different result.[102]

Subsequently, Rehnquist gave the opinion assignment to Blackmun, who as senior associate justice in the minority reassigned the opinion to Kennedy. Kennedy's draft thus remained the opinion for the Court but reaffirmed for a bare majority that school-sponsored prayers run afoul of the First Amendment.

Dramatic instances of vote switching and opinion reassignment, however, are rare. Changes in voting alignments usually only increase the size of the majority.[103] The unpublished opinions of the second Justice Harlan reveal that of some sixty-one undelivered opinions only nine were abandoned because of a reversal of a majority on the treatment of a case. Typically, Harlan withdrew a draft of a concurrence or a dissent because the author of the Court's opinion accommodated his views. Harlan did so in twelve cases. In thirteen cases, he substantially revised his initial separate opinion in light of changes made in the opinion for the Court. In four cases, he abandoned an initial vote in favor of joining another. About one case each term, Harlan suppressed an opinion because the Court was so divided that the final vote was to issue a brief *per curiam* opinion, affirming the lower-court ruling by an equally divided Court, or to carry the case over to the next term.[104]

Because justices may switch their votes and opinions for the Court require compromise, chief justices may assign opinions on the basis of a "voting paradox" or "assign the case to the justice whose views are closest to the dissenters on the ground that his opinion would take a middle approach upon which both majority and minority could agree."[105] The chief justice or an associate justice in the majority may also take on writing an opinion for the Court but then switch their positions and write an opinion contrary to their vote at conference, as Chief Justice Roberts apparently did when upholding the ACA ("Obamacare") as within Congress's spending and taxing power, though not based on its power to regulate interstate commerce.[106]

Some chief justices employ the strategy of assigning opinions to pivotal justices more than others do. Hughes, Vinson, and Warren tended to favor justices likely to hold on to a majority. Taft and Stone were not so inclined.[107] Assigning opinions to pivotal justices presents a chief justice with additional opportunities for influencing the final ruling.

Chief justices may take other factors into account when assigning opinions. What kind of reaction a case is likely to engender may be important. Hughes apparently took this into account when giving Frankfurter the first flag-salute case, *Minersville School District v. Gobitis* (1940), because he was a Jewish immigrant.[108] There the Court, with only Stone dissenting, denied the Jehovah's Witnesses' claim that requiring schoolchildren to salute the American flag at the start of classes violates the First Amendment. But three years later, in a second case, the Court reversed itself. Stone, now chief justice, assigned the opinion to Justice Jackson and in *West Virginia State Board of Education v. Barnette* (1943) the Court held that the First Amendment prohibits states from compelling schoolchildren to recite the pledge of allegiance to the flag.[109]

Hughes also was inclined to give "liberal" opinions to "conservative" justices to defuse opposition to rulings striking down early New Deal legislation. Later, when the Court decided the Texas white primary case *Smith v. Allwright* (1944), ruling that blacks may not be excluded from voting in state primary elections, Stone assigned the Court's opinion to Frankfurter.[110] But Jackson immediately expressed concerns about the assignment. Frankfurter was a Vienna-born Jew, raised in New York, and a former professor at Harvard Law School. Stone and Frankfurter were persuaded to the wisdom of reassigning the opinion to Reed, a native-born Protestant from Kentucky, long associated with the Democratic Party. The justices thought that they might thereby diminish opposition in the South to the ruling.[111]

A number of other cases illustrate how public relations may enter into a chief justice's calculations. The leading civil libertarian on the Court at the time, Justice Black, wrote the opinion in *Korematsu v. United States* (1944), upholding the constitutionality of the relocation of Japanese Americans during World War II.[112] A former attorney general experienced in law enforcement, Tom Clark, wrote the opinion in the landmark exclusionary rule case *Mapp v. Ohio* (1961), holding that evidence obtained in violation of the Fourth Amendment's requirements for a reasonable search and seizure may not be used against criminal suspects at trial.[113] Blackmun, a former counsel for the Mayo Clinic and experienced in the law of medicine, was assigned the abortion case *Roe v. Wade* (1973).

These examples also suggest that chief justices may occasionally look for expertise in particular areas of law. Taney gave Peter Daniel a large number of land, title, and equity cases, but few involving constitutional matters.[114] Taft was especially likely to assign opinions on the basis of expertise: John Clarke and Joseph McKenna wrote patent cases; Brandeis, tax and rate opinions; McReynolds was "the boss on Admiralty"; while Van Devanter and Sutherland, both from "out West," were given land and Indian disputes.[115] Burger tended to give First Amendment cases to White and Stewart and those involving federalism to Powell or Rehnquist. By contrast, Warren expressly disapproved of specialization. He thought that it both discouraged collective decision making and might make a "specialist" defensive when challenged.[116] Yet Brennan wrote the watershed opinions on the First Amendment during the Warren Court.

Senior associate justices, when they are in the majority, may also self-assign opinions and carve out a niche and their place in history. Justice Kennedy appears to have done that during the last two decades in recognizing the rights of the LGBTQ community. In *Romer v. Evans* (1996)[117] he struck down a Colorado state constitutional amendment forbidding localities from enacting ordinances outlawing discrimination against gays and lesbians. In

Chief Justice nominee John Roberts (front, right) carrying the coffin of Chief Justice Rehnquist into the Supreme Court on September 6, 2005. (*AP Photo/ Kevin Wolf*)

Lawrence v. Texas (2003)[118] he wrote for the Court, overturning *Bowers v. Hardwick* (1986),[119] striking down Texas's law criminalizing homosexual (but not heterosexual) sodomy. Those two rulings reinforced the movement for the constitutional recognition of same-sex marriages. Kennedy then struck down a provision of the Defense of Marriage Act of 1996 that denied recognition of and federal benefits for same-sex couples in *United States v. Windsor* (2013).[120] And for another bare majority, Kennedy extended constitutional protection to same-sex marriages in *Obergefell v. Hodges* (2015).[121]

Some political scientists argue that in their first couple of years on the bench "freshman justices" are assigned to write fewer opinions for the Court.[122] By tradition, new justices are usually given a unanimous decision to write as their first opinion for the Court, a tradition that continues. Justice Gorsuch's first opinion, for instance, was for a unanimous Court in a debt collection case.[123] And some justices—Murphy, O'Connor, and Souter, for instance—wrote significantly fewer opinions in their first year on the bench. However, a major study of opinion assignment ratios of senior and junior justices found no confirmation for the theory that junior justices are necessarily less likely to write opinions for the Court or assigned difficult opinions.[124]

"During all the years," Warren claimed, "I never had any of the Justices urge me to give them opinions to write, nor did I have anyone object to any opinion that I assigned to him or anyone else."[125] Warren's experience was exceptional, but he also often conferred with other justices before making opinion assignments.[126] Black and Douglas, for instance, urged Warren to assign Brennan the landmark case on reapportionment, *Baker v. Carr* (1962). They did so because Brennan's views were closest to those of Stewart, the crucial fifth vote, and his draft would most likely command a majority.[127] Most chief justices have found themselves lobbied, to a greater or lesser degree, when they assign opinions, but recent chief justices have also paid greater attention to equality in opinion assignments.[128]

WRITING AND CIRCULATING OPINIONS

Writing opinions is the justices' most difficult and time-consuming task. As Frankfurter once put it when appealing to Brennan to suppress a proposed opinion, "psychologically speaking, voting is one thing and expressing views in support of a vote quite another."[129] Justice Thomas tells his clerks, "Look, the genius is having a ten-dollar idea in a five-cent sentence, not having a five-cent idea in a ten-dollar sentence."[130]

Justices differ in their styles and approaches to opinion writing. They now delegate responsibility to their clerks for drafting opinions. However, Justice Stevens regularly did the first draft of his opinions; he did them, he said, "for self-discipline." For opinions in cases deemed important, Justice Scalia also used to undertake his own first drafts and said that they then go through revisions "at least five times."[131] The first drafts of all the other justices' opinions are now usually prepared by their clerks. Nevertheless, only after a justice is satisfied with a draft does it go to the other justices for their reactions.

The circulation of opinions among the chambers added to the Court's workload and changed the process of opinion writing. The practice of circulating draft opinions began around the turn of the twentieth century with the expanded use of typewriters and soon became pivotal in the decision-making process. The circulation of opinions provides more opportunities for the shifting of votes and further coalition building or fragmentation within the Court. Chief Justice Marshall, with his insistence on unanimity and nightly conferences after dinner, achieved unsurpassed unanimity. Unanimity, however, was based on the reading of opinions at conferences. No drafts circulated for other justices' scrutiny. Throughout much of the nineteenth century when the Court's sessions were shorter and the justices had no clerks, opinions were drafted in about two weeks and then read at conference.[132] If at least a majority agreed with the main points, the opinion was approved.

In the twentieth century the practice became that of circulating draft opinions, initially carbon copies, later photocopies, and now electronic files for each justice's chamber's review. Because they and their clerks gave more attention to each opinion, the justices found more to debate. The importance of circulating drafts and negotiating language in an opinion was underscored when Jackson announced from the bench, "I myself have changed my opinion after reading the opinions of the members of the Court. And I am as stubborn as most. But I sometimes wind up not voting the way I voted in conference because the reasons of the majority didn't satisfy me."[133] Similarly, Brennan said, "I converted more than one proposed majority into a dissent before the final decision was announced. I have also, however, had the more satisfying experience of rewriting a dissent as a majority opinion for the Court." In one case, he "circulated 10 printed drafts before one was approved as the Court's opinion."[134]

As the amount of time spent on considering proposed opinions grew, so did the workload. More law clerks were needed, and they were also given a greater role in opinion writing. Though clerks are now largely responsible for drafting opinions, they remain subordinates when it comes to negotiating opinions for the Court. Even with clerks assuming more responsibility for working on opinions, the justice ultimately must account for what is circulated.

How long does opinion writing take? On an average case, Justice Clark observed, about three weeks' work is required before an opinion circulates, "Then the fur begins to fly." The time spent preparing an opinion depends on how fast a justice and his or her clerks work,[135] what his or her style is, how much use of law clerks he or she makes, and how controversial the assigned case is. Holmes and Cardozo wrote opinions within days after being assigned, with little assistance from law clerks. Indeed, Chief Justice Hughes held back assignments from Cardozo because the justice's law clerk, Melvin Segal, complained that Cardozo would spend his weekends writing his opinions and thus he had little to do during the week. Cardozo later gave his clerk responsibility for checking citations and proofreading drafts. But Cardozo still overworked himself, and Hughes continued to hold back assignments for fear that the bachelor's health would fail.[136] By comparison, Frankfurter relied a great deal on his clerks and was still notoriously slow. As he once apologized for the delay in circulating a proposed opinion, "The elephant's period of gestation is, I believe, eighteen months, but a poor little hot dog has no such excuse."[137]

A number of factors affect how long it takes a justice to complete opinion assignments. A study of the Vinson Court

(1946–1952) found confirmation for Black's and Douglas's repu-
tations as expeditious opinion writers, and for Frankfurter consistently taking more time than his colleagues to complete his
opinions. They also found that over the years Chief Justice Vinson,
while striving to equalize his opinion assignments, tended to favor
"speedy" writers such as Black and Douglas, despite his ideological disagreements with them. Other factors associated with prolonging the time taken to produce an opinion for the Court are:
(1) the importance and divisiveness of a case, (2) the size of the
voting majority at conference, (3) whether the initial vote was to
affirm rather than reverse a lower court, (4) whether one or more
of the justices later switched their votes, and (5) whether a case
had to be reassigned or carried over for another term.[138]

The interplay of professional and psychological pressures on
a justice writing the Court's opinion is a complex but crucial part
of the decision-making process. In the 1920s and 1930s when the
practice was to return comments within twenty-four hours after
receipt of a draft, the pressures were especially great. There are
no time limits now, but the pressures persist, especially during
the last two months of a term, when the justices concentrate on
opinion writing.[139]

Whether drafting or commenting on a proposed opinion, justices differ when trying to influence each other. They may look
for emotional appeals, and sometimes personal threats. Justice
Clark thought that Warren was the greatest chief justice in the
history of the Court and sought his approval of a revised opinion.
But he received this disturbing response: "Tom: Nuts. E. W."[140]
Shortly after coming to the Court, Brennan wrote Black, "I welcome, as always, every and any comment you will be good enough
to make on anything I ever write—whether we vote together at
the time or not."[141] By contrast, Justice Marshall tended to simply scribble "B.S." on drafts circulated by Rehnquist.[142]

Justice Douglas could be a real charmer—if he wanted to
be—when appealing for modifications in proposed opinions. "I
would stand on my head to join with you in your opinion," he told

Justice Byrnes, though continuing, "I finally concluded, however, that I cannot." His strategy was that of the "Yes, but game." This is evident in his response to one of Reed's drafts: "I like your opinion in No. 18 very much. You have done an excellent job in a difficult field. And I want to join you in it. *But*—"[143] He then set forth the changes that he thought would have to be made.

By contrast, McReynolds was abrupt, sometimes rude, and usually left little room for negotiation. "This statement makes me sick," he once wrote.[144] Frankfurter's approach also could be irritating. He was not above making personal attacks. To threaten his ideological foe Hugo Black, Frankfurter circulated, but did not publish, the following concurring opinion:

> I greatly sympathize with the essential purpose of my brother (former Senator) Black's dissent. His roundabout and turgid legal phraseology is a *cris de coeur.* "Would I were back in the Senate," he seems to say, "so that I could put on the statute books what really ought to be there. But here I am, cast by Fate into a den of judges devoid of the habits of legislators, simple fellows who have a crippling feeling that they must enforce the laws as Congress wrote them and not as they ought to have been written."[145]

Frankfurter nonetheless usually tempered his criticisms by making fun of his own academic proclivities: "What does trouble me is that you do not disclose what you are really doing." He wrote Douglas, "As you know, I am no poker player and naturally, therefore, I do not believe in poker playing in the disposition of cases. Or has professing for twenty-five years disabled me from understanding the need for these involutions?"[146]

More typically, when commenting on circulated drafts, justices appeal to professionalism and jurisprudential concerns. Even McReynolds, perhaps at the prompting of Taft, once appealed to Stone's basic conservatism: "All of us get into a fog now and then, as I know so well from my own experience. Won't you 'Stop, Look, and Listen'?"[147] Such appeals may carry subtly or explicitly the threat of a concurring or dissenting opinion. In one instance,

Stone candidly told Frankfurter, "If you wish to write [the opinion] placing the case on the ground which I think tenable and desirable, I shall cheerfully join you. If not, I will add a few observations for myself."[148] Frankfurter was more caustic when he wrote Reed that "all talk about 'jurisdictional facts' and 'constitutional facts' seems to be rubbish—worse than rubbish, misleading irrelevancies."[149]

Justices may suggest minor editorial or major substantive changes. Before joining one of Justice Goldberg's opinions, Harlan requested that the word "desegregation" be substituted for "integration" throughout the opinion. As he explained, "'Integration' brings blood to Southerners' eyes for they think that 'desegregation' means just that—'integration.' I do not think that we ought to use the word in our opinions."[150] Likewise, Stewart strongly objected to some of the language in Fortas's proposed opinion in *Tinker v. Des Moines School District* (1969), which upheld the right of students to wear black armbands in protest of the government's involvement in Vietnam.[151] "At the risk of appearing eccentric," Stewart wrote, "I shall not join any opinion that speaks of what is going on in Vietnam as a 'war' [since Congress never formally declared a war in Vietnam]."[152]

Justice O'Connor's circulated draft in *Shaw v. Reno* (1993), the leading decision in a series of rulings striking down the creation of "minority-majority" congressional districts, drew similar criticism from two justices in her bare majority.[153] Rehnquist agreed to join her opinion if she dealt "with two non-substantive concerns" that in fact challenged her characterization of the history and role of the Fourteenth Amendment. As the chief justice explained:

First, on page 7 you say that the Civil War was fought in part to secure the elective franchise to black Americans. One can certainly say that the Civil War was fought to end slavery, but I don't think it is an accurate statement to say that it was fought to secure the elective franchise for blacks. This view gained majority support only during the period of Reconstruction after the Civil War was over.

Second, on page 23, you say that the Fourteenth Amendment embodies "the goal of a fully integrated society." The Fourteenth Amendment prohibits discrimination; it does not require integration, and I think it is a mistake to intimate that it does even as a "goal."[154]

Justice Scalia followed with some other "nit-picky suggestions" that also resulted in important changes in her opinion.[155]

Editorial suggestions thus may be directed at a justice's word choice, use of precedents, and even basic conceptualization. Brennan, for instance, sent a twenty-one-page list of revisions on Chief Justice Warren's initial draft of *Miranda v. Arizona* (1966), which upheld the right of criminal suspects to remain silent at the time of police questioning.[156] At the outset, Brennan expressed his feeling of guilt "about the extent of the suggestions." But he emphasized the importance of careful drafting, "[T]his will be one of the most important opinions of our time and I know that you will want the fullest expression of my views."[157]

Occasionally, proposed changes lead to a recasting of the entire opinion. Douglas was assigned the Court's opinion in *Griswold v. Connecticut* (1965), in which he announced the creation of a constitutional right of privacy based on the "penumbras" of various guarantees of the Bill of Rights.[158] His initial draft, however, did not develop this theory. Rather, Douglas sought to justify the decision on the basis of earlier cases recognizing a First Amendment right of associational privacy. The analogy and precedents, he admitted, "do not decide this case." "Marriage does not fit precisely any of the categories of First Amendment rights. But it is a form of association as vital in the life of a man or a woman as any other, and perhaps more so." Both Black and Brennan strongly objected to Douglas's extravagant reliance on First Amendment precedents. In a three-page letter, Brennan detailed an alternative approach, as the following excerpt indicates:

I have read your draft opinion in *Griswold v. Connecticut*, and, while I agree with a great deal of it, I should like to suggest a substantial change in emphasis for your consideration. It goes without saying, of course, that your rejection of any approach based on *Lochner v. New York* is absolutely right. [In *Lochner* (1905), a majority read into the Fourteenth Amendment a "liberty of contract" in order to strike down economic legislation. Although the Court later abandoned the doctrine of a "liberty of contract," *Lochner* continues to symbolize the original sin of constitutional interpretation—that is, the Court's creation and enforcement of unenumerated rights.] And I agree that the association of husband and wife is not mentioned in the Bill of Rights, and that that is the obstacle we must hurdle to effect a reversal in this case.

But I hesitate to bring the husband-wife relationship within the right to association we have constructed in the First Amendment context. . . . In the First Amendment context, in situations like *NAACP v. Alabama* [1964], privacy is necessary to protect the capacity of an association for fruitful advocacy. In the present context, it seems to me that we are really interested in the privacy of married couples quite apart from any interest in advocacy. . . . Instead of expanding the First Amendment right of association to include marriage, why not say that what has been done for the First Amendment can also be done for some of the other fundamental guarantees of the Bill of Rights? In other words, where fundamentals are concerned, the Bill of Rights guarantees are but expressions or examples of those rights, and do not preclude applications or extensions of those rights to situations unanticipated by the Framers.[159]

The restriction on the dissemination and use of contraceptives, Brennan explained,

would, on this reasoning, run afoul of a right to privacy created out of the Fourth Amendment and the self-incrimination clause of the Fifth, together with the Third, in much the same way as the right of association has been created out of the First. Taken together, those amendments indicate a fundamental concern with the sanctity of the home and the right of the individual to be alone.

"With this change of emphasis," Brennan concluded, the opinion "would be most attractive to me because it would require less departure from the specific guarantees and because I think there is a better chance it will command a Court." Douglas subsequently revised his opinion and based the right of privacy on the penumbras of the First, Third, Fourth, Fifth, and Ninth Amendments.[160] But Brennan, nonetheless, joined Justice Goldberg's concurring opinion in *Griswold*.

In order to accommodate the views of others, the author of an opinion for the Court must negotiate language and sometimes bargain over substance. "The ground you recommend was not the one on which I voted 'no'—But I think that, as a matter of policy, you are clearly right; and I am engaged in redrafting the opinion on that line," Brandeis wrote Van Devanter, adding, "May I trouble you to formulate the rule of law, which you think should be established?"[161]

At times, justices may not feel that a case is worth fighting over. "Probably bad—but only a small baby. Let it go," Sutherland noted on the back of one of Stone's drafts. Hughes was a bit more graphic when responding to another proposed opinion: "I choke a little at swallowing your analysis, still I do not think it would serve any useful purpose to expose my views."[162] Similarly, Pierce Butler agreed to go along with one of Stone's opinions, though noting, "I voted to reverse. While this sustains your conclusion to affirm, I still think reversal would be better. But I shall in silence acquiesce. Dissents seldom aid in the right development or statement of the law. They often do harm. For myself I say: 'Lead us not into temptation.'"[163]

Justices sometimes join an opinion with which they disagree, perhaps with the hope that in some later case other justices will reciprocate and not threaten a dissenting vote or opinion. This tactic was not lost on Stone, who explained to Frankfurter, "I voted the other way in this case but I shall acquiesce in the decision unless some of my brethren see the light and point out that you cracked the law in order to satisfy your moral scruples."[164] Disturbed by one of Holmes's draft opinions, Justice McKenna wrote, "It may be that there is some defect in my mental processes for I can't appreciate the reasoning. But I will not dissent alone."[165]

Justice William J. Brennan Jr. in his chambers. (© *CORBIS/Corbis via Getty Images*)

Another of Holmes's circulated opinions prompted Justice Pitney to respond, "Cannot agree, but will say nothing."[166]

More than a willingness to negotiate is sometimes required. Judicial temperament and diplomacy are also crucial, as is illustrated by the deliberations behind the landmark decision inaugurating the reapportionment revolution. *Baker v. Carr* (1962) raised two central issues: first, whether the malapportionment of a state legislature is a nonjusticiable "political question" for which courts have no remedy; second, the merits of the claim that individuals have a right to equal votes and equal representation. With potentially broad political consequences, the case was divisive, being carried over and reargued for a term. The extreme positions within the Court remained firm, but the center was soft. Allies on judicial self-restraint, Frankfurter and Harlan were committed to their view, expressed in *Colegrove v. Green* (1946), that the "Court ought not to enter this political thicket."[167] At conference, Clark and Whittaker supported their view that the case presented a nonjusticiable political question. By contrast, Warren, Black, Douglas, and Brennan thought that the issue was justiciable and were prepared to address the merits of the case. The pivotal justice, Potter Stewart, considered the issue justiciable but adamantly refused to address the merits of the case. He would vote to reverse the lower-court ruling that the issue was a political question only if the decision was limited to holding that the lower court had jurisdiction to decide the dispute. Stewart did not want the Court to decide the merits of the case.

Assigned the task of drafting the opinion, Brennan had to hold on to Stewart's vote and dissuade Black and Douglas from writing opinions on the merits that would threaten the loss of the crucial fifth vote. After circulating his draft and incorporating suggested changes, he optimistically wrote Black, "Potter Stewart was satisfied with all of the changes. The Chief also is agreed. It, therefore, looks as though we have a court agreed upon this as circulated."[168] It appeared that the decision would come down on the original 5–4 vote.

Clark, however, had been pondering the fact that in this case the population ratio for the urban and rural districts in the state was more than nineteen to one. As he put it, "city slickers" had been "too long deprive[d] of a constitutional form of government."[169] Clark concluded that citizens denied equal voting power had no political recourse; their only recourse was to the federal judiciary. Clark wrote an opinion abandoning Frankfurter and going beyond the majority to address the merits of the claim.

Brennan faced the dilemma of how to bring Clark in without losing Stewart, which would enlarge the consensus. Further negotiations were necessary but limited. Brennan wrote his brethren:

The changes represent the maximum to which Potter will subscribe. We discussed much more elaborate changes which would have taken over a substantial part of Tom Clark's opinion. Potter felt that if they were made it would be necessary for him to dissent from that much of the revised opinion. I therefore decided it was best not to press for the changes but to hope that Tom will be willing to join the Court opinion but say he would go further as per his separate opinion.[170]

Even though there were five votes for deciding the merits, the final opinion in *Baker v. Carr* was limited to the jurisdictional question. Douglas refrained from addressing the merits in his concurring opinion. Stewart joined with an opinion emphasizing the limited nature of the ruling. Clark filed an opinion explaining his view of the merits. Whittaker withdrew from the case, retiring from the Court two weeks later. Only Frankfurter and Harlan were left dissenting.

The Value of Judicial Opinions

Published opinions for the Court are the residue of conflicts and compromises among the justices. But they also reflect changing institutional norms. In historical perspective, changes in judicial norms have affected trends in opinion writing, the value of judicial opinions, and the Court's contributions to public law and policy.

OPINIONS FOR THE COURT

During the nineteenth century and down through the early part of the twentieth century there were few separate, concurring, or dissenting opinions from the opinion announcing the Court's decision.[171] That is not to say that justices did not disagree with each other. There is considerable evidence that they did.[172] But they suppressed their disagreements when issuing opinions for the Court.

The norm of consensus on opinions for the Court was forged by Chief Justice Marshall, who believed that unanimous decisions would build the Court's legitimacy. He therefore discouraged dissenting opinions and wrote the overwhelming number of the Court's opinions, even when he disagreed with a ruling.[173] The Taney Court and subsequent Courts in the nineteenth century and early twentieth century generally emulated that practice, and the appearance of consensus became an institutional norm.

Dissenting opinions were deemed "injurious,"[174] "useless and undesirable,"[175] and justices often "acquiese[d] for the sake of harmony & the Court."[176] They sometimes noted their disagreement, but did not file a concurring or dissenting opinion, or withheld a draft dissent.

That norm broke down in the late 1930s and 1940s with the publication of increasing numbers of individual opinions. As the graph on page 292 underscores, throughout the nineteenth century opinions for the Court accounted for 80 to over 90 percent of all opinions annually issued.[177] That changed dramatically, however, with the percentage falling throughout the 1940s and thereafter never again rising above 50 percent, with the exception of a couple of terms. In other words, in the nineteenth century individual opinions amounted to less than 20 percent of the Court's total opinion production. In the second half of the twentieth and the early twenty-first centuries, however, institutional opinions constituted less than half of the Court's annual output of opinions.

Moreover, although unanimity remains high on case selection (over 80 percent, as discussed in Chapter 4), unanimity on opinions dropped to below 35 percent. Even though the business of the Court is to give institutional opinions, as Justice Stewart observed, "that view [came] to be that of a minority of the justices."[178] When compared to the Court's practice over half a century ago, there are approximately ten times the number of concurring opinions, four times more dissenting opinions, and seven times the number of separate opinions in which the justices explain their personal views and why they partially concur in and/or dissent from the Court's opinion.

What explains the rise of individual opinions? In his pioneering work, *The Roosevelt Court: A Study in Judicial Politics and Values*, political scientist C. Herman Pritchett identified the rise in individual opinions with the appointments made by FDR between 1937 and 1943.[179] "Looking backward," he pointed out,

"the 1941–1942 term was definitely a turning point." Disagreement rates increased and the percentage of opinions for the Court
of the total opinions issued plunged from 81 percent in Hughes's
last term to 67 percent in Stone's first term as chief justice. The
percentage continued to fall sharply throughout Stone's chief justiceship as well as those of his successors. Pritchett offered two
principal explanations: First, the New Deal justices quickly began
working out their competing judicial philosophies. Second, the
1941 term "saw the debut of Stone as Chief Justice" and, as
Pritchett observed, "it seems to be agreed that as presiding officer
he lacked some of the talents of his very able predecessor."

Subsequent studies attributed the erosion of the Court's consensual norm primarily to Stone.[180] But the rise of individual opinions (as further illustrated in the graph on page 292) appears
largely due to the impact of changes in the Court's composition
and more complex than simply Stone's lack of leadership skills. For
one thing, concurring opinions were on the rise before Stone's
chief justiceship.[181] Moreover, the percentage of unanimous decisions began dropping before his chief justiceship and continued
to decline during the following decades.[182] Furthermore, the drop
in the percentage of opinions for the Court of the total number
issued began during the last four years of the Hughes Court,
coinciding with the arrival of FDR's first five appointees (Black,
Reed, Frankfurter, Douglas, and Murphy). The traditional norm
of consensus, in other words, began failing to hold in the last four
years of Hughes's chief justiceship and continued to erode as individual opinions came to predominate over institutional opinions
for the Court. Chief Justice Hughes "believed that unanimity of
decision contributed to public confidence in the Court" and he
generally was willing to acquiesce "in silence rather than expose
his dissenting views."[183] He nonetheless supported published
dissenting opinions as a sign of judicial independence; in his
words, "because what must ultimately sustain the court in public confidence is the character and independence of the judges."[184]

PERCENTAGE OF OPINIONS FOR THE COURT OF THE
TOTAL OPINIONS ISSUED, 1801–2018

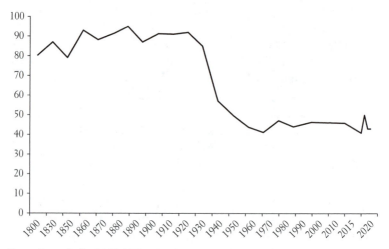

Data through the 2017–2018 term.

Indeed, by 1947 the votes of each justice in all cases were published in the *U.S. Reports*—identifying who wrote or joined a majority, concurring, or dissenting opinion, and signaled the demise of earlier tradition of justices joining the opinion for the Court in "silent acquiescence."[185]

Why did the norm of consensus collapse with the arrival of the New Deal justices? Simply put, they brought the full force of American legal realism and liberal legalism to bear on the Court. FDR's appointees not only constituted a majority but also embodied the intellectual forces of a generation of progressives who revolted against the legal formalism of the old conservative order. American legal realism, though, was not so much a school of thought as an intellectual movement or "intellectual mood,"[186] embracing diverse, though generally progressive and pragmatic, positions on judging and legal reform. Legal realism highlighted

OPINION WRITING, 1937–2018

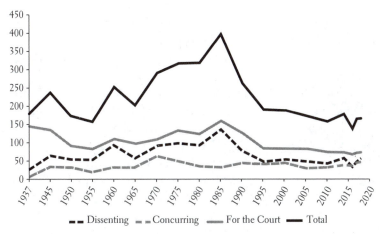

Data through the 2017–2018 term.

the indeterminacy of law, taught that judges make law, and advocated judicial pragmatism or the balancing of competing values. Instead of relying on fixed formulas and tests, legal realism—about matters of degree and judicial balancing—made consensus more difficult and raised the premium on justifying the decisions.

In addition, liberal legalism lacked coherence. At bottom, as Pritchett explained, were "the short-comings of American liberalism as a social and economic philosophy." On the bench, liberal legalism, inherited from Holmes and Brandeis and perpetuated by FDR's appointees, fragmented the justices. Holmes stood for judicial self-restraint and deference to legislatures, whereas Brandeis championed progressive legal reforms. Although dominating the Court, FDR's New Deal justices split into two camps: Frankfurter, Reed, and Jackson stood for judicial self-restraint and became more conservative during their time on the bench; whereas Black, Douglas, Murphy, and Rutledge pushed toward greater progressive judicial activism. These two camps in turn further fragmented over where and how to draw the line between judicial self-restraint and activism in constitutional interpretation. As a result of their disagreements, the New Deal justices were inclined to articulate their distinctive views in individual opinions.

Besides these intellectual currents sweeping the Court came other changes in its operation that contributed to the rise of individual opinions. First, throughout most of the nineteenth century the author of the Court's opinion did not circulate drafts. Instead, drafts were read at conference, where other justices basically agreed only on the key points of the opinion. Under Chief Justice Fuller (1888–1910), the justices began circulating drafts of opinions before conference, which became routine by the 1930s. The justices thus had more time to study the actual wording of opinions and make suggestions for changes, or write separately. Second, coinciding with higher disagreement rates was the Court's move into its own building. Before the completion of the building in 1935 (as discussed in Chapter 3), the justices worked alone at home. With their move into the marble temple, the institutional life of the Court changed. The building initially brought about greater interaction and, perhaps, intensified their psychological interdependence and independence. Finally, along with settling into the marble temple, the number of law clerks gradually began to increase, and individual opinion writing subsequently proliferated.[187]

In sum, the demise of the norm of consensus on institutional opinions preceded Stone's chief justiceship. The New Deal justices infused legal realism and liberal legalism into the Court, but they were not of one mind. They quickly began pursuing their conflicting tenets of liberal legalism in individual opinions. The continued increase in individual opinions long after Stone's departure further undercuts the theory that Stone bears "much of the responsibility for changing the operational norms of the Court."[188] Post–New Deal justices, then, were socialized into higher rates of individual expression. By the end of the Warren Court, the New Deal justices had effectively transformed the Court's norm of consensus into one of individual expression.

Although the percentage of opinions for the Court of the total annually issued increased slightly with the Rehnquist Court, there is no indication of a return to the norm of consensus, though even Chief Justice Roberts expressed concerns about the tendency to hand down too many divided opinions. At conference, little time remains for more than a mere tally of votes. Another indication of the devaluation of consensus is the larger number of plurality opinions announcing the decision of the Court. A plurality opinion is an opinion for the Court that fails to command a majority, even though at least five justices agree on the decision. For example, a bare majority may decide a case, but only three justices agree on an opinion announcing the decision. The other two justices in the majority usually file separate concurring opinions, explaining why they think the case was correctly decided but how they disagree with the rationalization in the (plurality) opinion announcing the ruling.

Between 1800 and 1900 only ten opinions commanded the support of less than a majority of the Court. Between 1901 and 1969, the last year of Chief Justice Warren, fifty-one cases were decided by plurality opinions. By contrast, during the Burger Court years a total of 116 plurality opinions were handed down, more plurality opinions than rendered in the entire history of the Court.[189]

Under Chief Justice Rehnquist, the Court tended to hand down fewer plurality opinions. But for the first time, the Court handed down what Rehnquist dubbed "doubleheaders or twins": cases in which there were two opinions announcing different (and somewhat contradictory) parts of the Court's ruling for two different majorities in a *single* case. In the "coerced confession" case of *Arizona v. Fulminante* (1991),[190] for instance, Chief Justice Rehnquist's opinion for the Court commanded four votes for holding that the admission of a coerced confession at a trial may be excused as a "harmless error" when it can be shown that other evidence adequately supports a guilty verdict. Justice Souter provided the key vote in joining the four Reagan appointees to form a majority on that issue. But the lineup changed and was complicated by the justices' stands on other questions raised in the case. Justice White delivered another opinion announcing the Court's decision on two other aspects of the ruling. White deemed the circumstances of Oreste Fulminante's confession to constitute a coerced confession, whereas Rehnquist, O'Connor, Kennedy, and Souter disagreed. On that issue, Scalia joined White's opinion, which was also joined by Blackmun, Marshall, and Stevens. Moreover, on the final question of whether the use of Fulminante's confession was harmless beyond a reasonable doubt, White commanded a majority for affirming the judgment of the court below and remanding the case back for a new trial at which Fulminante's confession could not be used against him, despite the broader ruling permitting the use of such confessions handed down in Rehnquist's opinion for the Court. On that issue, White was joined by Blackmun, Marshall, Stevens, and Kennedy; Rehnquist, O'Connor, and Scalia dissented; and Souter gave no indication of how he had voted on that issue.

Notably, the Rehnquist Court continued handing down doubleheaders, reflecting the diminished value of achieving agreement on a single opinion for the Court.[191] Indeed, in the complex case challenging the constitutionality of the Bipartisan Campaign Reform Act (BCRA) of 2002, *McConnell v. Federal Election Commission* (2003),[192] no fewer than four justices in three separate opinions delivered the opinion of the Court. Justices Stevens and O'Connor together delivered the opinion upholding the BCRA's bans on "soft money" and "issue ads," Chief Justice Rehnquist delivered the opinion striking down the law's ban on campaign contributions from individuals under the age of eighteen, and Justice Breyer issued the opinion upholding the BCRA's requirements for broadcasters to maintain publicly available records of campaign requests. In addition, Stevens and Rehnquist wrote dissenting opinions, and Kennedy, Scalia, and Thomas each produced opinions in part concurring and dissenting, for a total of almost 300 pages of opinions.

Trends and changes in the justices' consensus building and opinion writing register basic changes in judicial behavior and the Court's composition, as well as the value of institutional and individual opinions. When individual opinions are more highly prized than opinions for the Court, consensus declines and the Court's rulings appear more fragmented, less stable, and less predictable. Yet as discussed in the following section, even conservative justices, like Scalia, have defended the filing of individual concurring and dissenting opinions.

SEPARATE, CONCURRING, AND DISSENTING OPINIONS

The tension between institutional and individual opinions is part of a deeper conflict in judicial behavior between the norms of interdependence and independence. "I defend the right of any justice to file anything he wants," Douglas observed.[193] Yet the proliferation of individual opinions comes at the cost of certainty and stability in the law.

In contrast to the author of an opinion for the Court, a justice writing separate, concurring, or dissenting opinions does not carry the burden of massing other justices. In extraordinary circumstances a separate opinion may prove necessary as the only practical way of obtaining a ruling for the Court. Perhaps Frankfurter put it best in a letter: "A member of the Supreme Court is at once a soloist and part of an orchestra. While [concurring and] dissenting opinions seem like solo performances, even that is not always true and, in any event, the private rehearsals, as it were, behind the impenetrable draperies of judicial secrecy may tell much more about the soloist and the rest of the orchestra than the public performance even remotely reveals."[194]

Justices usually write concurring opinions to explain how the Court's decision could have been otherwise rationalized. Some are defensible because a compromised opinion would be meaningless. They also may be required because of a "greater institutional interest in the forthrightness of differing justices' views."[195] At other times, justices try to send signals to lower courts about the direction of the Court's policy making. Such concurring opinions, in the view of some justices, are objectionable because they amount to "advisory opinions."

Concurring opinions were rare for most of the nineteenth and early twentieth centuries, but are no longer uncommon. Every justice now usually writes anywhere from four to twelve concurrences each term. Ideological differences do not appear to have any bearing on whether justices publish concurrences. Advocates of judicial self-restraint and activism are just as likely to publish concurring opinions. "Centralists" such as Powell, O'Connor, and Kennedy tended to write a few more, because their votes are often pivotal to the Court's decisions. In addition, what was once true of dissents may now be true about concurrences: "Associate Justices are remembered chiefly by their dissenting opinions, in which they wrote their views without restraint," as Justice John Clarke observed.[196]

Dissenting opinions are more understandable and defensible. Dissenting opinions, in the view of Hughes, who rarely wrote dissents, appeal "to the brooding spirit of the law, to the intelligence of a future day, when a later decision may possibly correct the error into which the dissenting judge believes the Court to have been betrayed."[197] Dissents may appeal for more immediate legislative action: Justice Iredell's dissent in *Chisholm v. Georgia* (1793)[198] invited the adoption of the Eleventh Amendment, overturning the Court's decision; and the dissenters' arguments in *Dred Scott v. Sandford* (1857) lent support to the passage of the Thirteenth, Fourteenth, and Fifteenth Amendments after the Civil War.[199]

Occasionally, though infrequently, a dissenter may eventually prevail and write an opinion for the Court vindicating his or her position. Justice Stevens, for one, dissented from Rehnquist's opinion for a bare majority upholding a ban on advertising casino gambling in *Posadas de Puerto Rico v. Tourism Company of Puerto Rico* (1986).[200] Yet, a decade later he commanded a unanimous Court (including Rehnquist) to overturn *Posadas* and to strike down a ban on the advertising of the price of alcohol, tobacco, and other "vices" in *44 Liquormart, Inc. v. Rhode Island* (1996).[201]

A dissenting opinion is a way of undercutting the Court's decision and opinion. The threat of a dissent may thus be useful for a justice trying to persuade the majority to narrow its holding or tone down the language of its opinion. Brandeis, who often dissented, complained, "The Court does not heed dissents sufficiently."[202] Yet he himself at times "suppressed dissents for tactical reasons." "I think this case is wrongly decided," he wrote Holmes. "But you have restricted the opinion so closely to the facts of this case, that I am inclined to think it will do less harm to let it pass unnoticed by dissent."[203]

There is a crucial difference, nonetheless, between threatening a dissent and publishing it. A number of considerations enter into a decision to publish a dissent. A revised opinion struck Justice Pitney as "still indefensible." "But the revision of the opinion," he wrote William Day, "has eliminated some errors of statement, construction, and reasoning that would have wrought far-reaching mischief in the general administration of the law. In view of this, possibly [it would be] better to submit in silence, consoling ourselves that the injustice to the individual defendant in error will, in all human probability, be rectified upon a new trial."[204]

Threats of dissents now carry less force. Although in the nineteenth and early twentieth centuries justices might threaten (and bargain with) a dissent, they usually withheld publication. Chief Justice Marshall observed, "I should now, as is my custom, when I have the misfortune to differ from this Court, acquiesce silently in its opinion."[205] Similarly, Chief Justice Chase noted in his diary that he seldom filed dissents because he thought "that except in very important causes [filing a] dissent [was] inexpedient."[206] Justices, to be sure, still sometimes withhold draft dissents. Justice Ginsburg has said that she will occasionally go along with the majority in a tax case, explaining: "Even though I disagree, I will bury my dissent. We call that a graveyard dissent." But she added: "I will never compromise when it's a question of, say, freedom of speech or press, gender equality."[207]

Lower dissent rates in the nineteenth century do not reflect, as earlier noted, more agreement within the Court,[208] only that institutional decisions were more highly prized and justices, perhaps, more willing to compromise. As Chief Justice Taft, who suppressed more than 200 dissents during his service on the high bench, explained, "I don't approve of dissentings generally, for I think in many cases where I differ from the majority, it is more important to stand by the Court and give its judgment weight than merely to record my individual dissent where it is better to have the law certain than to have it settled either way."[209]

Published dissents are a manifestation of "institutional disobedience."[210] But justices differ in how far they carry that disobedience. Holmes and Brandeis were among the "great dissenters." Yet Holmes was "reluctant to [dissent] again after he had once had his say on a subject."[211] Likewise, Tom Clark would dissent once from the Court's rulings with which he disagreed and thereafter in similar cases silently acquiesce.[212] In contrast, Black and Douglas noted every dissent and frequently issued dissenting opinions, even when they had previously made clear their disagreements with the majority. In Black's words, "Dissents keep the boys on their toes." For Black, a dissenter was an advocate. He once told Blackmun, "That's the way to do it, Harry—strike for the jugular, strike for the jugular."[213] Perhaps the most extreme instance of institutional disobedience was the uniquely unsigned dissent by four justices from Chief Justice Roberts's opinion upholding the ACA in *National Federation of Independent Business v. Sebelius* (2012), in which Roberts reportedly drafted "most of the material in the first three quarters of the joint dissent" before switching his vote to uphold the law.[214]

As the publishing of dissenting opinions gradually spread, the practice became an acceptable form of institutional disobedience.

The change in judicial norms is underscored by a comparison of current rates of dissenting opinions with those of the "great dissenters"—those who wrote a disproportionate number of dissents during earlier periods. Although the number of dissenting opinions rose dramatically during the 1970s and early 1980s, after Chief Justice Burger left the bench in 1986, dissenting justices tended to more frequently join each other in a single dissent, rather than file multiple dissents. In their last years on the Court as senior associate justices in dissent, Brennan and Marshall often assigned themselves or others to write a joint dissent, except in especially controversial and important cases.[215] However, in *Cruzan by Cruzan v. Director, Missouri Department of Health* (1990), for instance, the Court split when confronting the claim of a constitutional "right to die,"[216] and Brennan, Marshall, Blackmun, and Stevens found themselves outvoted at conference. Brennan wrote the other three: "We four are in dissent in [*Cruzan*]. I suggest that, because of the significance of this case, perhaps each of us might want to write his own."[217] Still, as O'Connor noted, the prevailing practice became for the senior associate justice in the minority to assign an author to write a dissent to the majority's ruling.[218] Justice Ginsburg continued that practice on the Roberts Court.

Notably, Justice Scalia's dissents were frequently the most acerbic and sarcastic.[219] He blasted opinions for the Court's majority as "incoherent" and "nothing short of ludicrous";[220] "entirely irrational";[221] as "nothing short of preposterous" and with "no foundation in American constitutional law, and barely pretends to."[222] Dissenting from the bare majority's ruling on same-sex marriages in *Obergefell v. Hodges* (2015), he snidely observed that "today's decree is not of immense personal importance to me," and then ridiculed the "majority of the nine lawyers on the Supreme Court" for an opinion full of "mummeries and straining-to-be-memorable passages," along with "showy profundities [that] are often profoundly incoherent," and concluded, "The world does not expect logic and precision in poetry or inspirational pop-philosophy; it demands them in the law. The stuff contained in today's opinion has to diminish the Court's reputation for clear thinking and sober analysis."[223]

The proliferation of separate dissenting and concurring opinions concerned some of the justices and has been criticized by the practicing bar and scholars. But several justices have defended the practice of dissenting opinions. Justice Ginsburg, for one, emphasized their "in-house impact." In her words, "nothing is better than an impressive dissent to improve an opinion for the Court. A well reasoned dissent will lead the author of the majority opinion to refine and clarify her initial circulation. An illustration: I wrote for the Court in the Virginia Military Institute case, which held that VMI's denial of admission to women violated the Equal Protection Clause. The published opinion was ever so much better than my first draft, thanks to Justice Scalia's attention-grabbing dissent."[224]

Justice Scalia also staunchly defended the practice of filing dissenting and concurring opinions. In T. S. Eliot's *Murder in the Cathedral*, when Thomas à Becket is tempted by the devil to resist Henry II, he responds, "That would be greatest treason, to do the right deed for the wrong reason." Scalia maintained that the same principle applies to judicial opinions. In his words, "to get the reasons wrong is to get it all wrong, and that is worth a dissent, even if the dissent is called a concurrence." Like Ginsburg, Scalia praised separate opinions for their internal and external consequences. "The most important internal effect of a system permitting dissents and concurrences is to improve the majority opinion." The prospect of a dissent may make the majority's opinion writer receptive to suggested changes, and a draft dissent "often causes the majority to refine its opinion, eliminating the more vulnerable assertions." Moreover, he maintained that "dissents augment rather than diminish the prestige of the Court. When history demonstrates that one of the Court's decisions has been a truly horrendous mistake, it is comforting—and conducive of respect for the Court—to look back and realize that at least some of the Justices saw the danger clearly, and gave voice, often eloquent voice, to their concern." "A second external consequence of a concurring or dissenting opinion is that it can help change the law," as well as "inform the public in general, and the bar in particular, about the state of the Court's collective mind." Finally, Scalia stressed, "By enabling, indeed compelling, the Justices of our Court, through their personally signed majority, dissenting and concurring opinions, to set forth clear and consistent positions on both sides of the major legal issues of the day, it has kept the Court in the forefront of the intellectual development of the law. . . . The Court itself is not just the central organ of legal *judgment*; it is center stage for significant legal *debate*."[225]

The force of a dissent may also be underscored by a justice reading portions of his or her dissent from the bench when the Court's decision is announced.[226] Among other notable instances, for example, all four dissenters—Chief Justice Roberts and Justices Scalia, Thomas, and Alito—read portions of their dissents from the Court's ruling striking down state bans on same-sex marriages in *Obergefell v. Hodges* (2015), the only time that Roberts did so in his first decade as chief justice.

Institutional and Individual Opinions

The devaluation of opinions for the Court and the greater premium placed on individual opinions, though, may affect compliance with the Court's rulings. Even Black, who had no qualms about threatening or filing separate opinions, recognized the importance of institutional opinions. Black wrote Tom Clark about one of his proposed opinions:

I have no idea what troubles you about my treatment of the [case]. . . . It is rather bad I think to have less than a majority for a court opinion. Consequently, I would be glad to see if your objections, whatever they are, can be met. I feel so strongly that one should have a court opinion that I would be willing to have the case reassigned if that would help.[227]

COMPARISON OF DISSENT RATES: THE GREAT DISSENTERS°

Justice	Number of Dissenting Opinions	Average per Term
J. Catron, 1837–1865	26	0.9
W. Johnson, 1804–1834	30	1.0
O. W. Holmes, 1902–1932	72	2.4
N. Clifford, 1858–1881	60	2.6
L. D. Brandeis, 1916–1939	65	2.9
J. M. Harlan, 1877–1911	119	3.5
H. F. Stone, 1925–1946	93	4.6
H. L. Black, 1937–1971	310	9.1
W. H. Rehnquist, 1972–2005	333	10.0
H. Blackmun, 1970–1994	245	10.2
F. Frankfurter, 1939–1962	251	10.9
J. M. Harlan, 1955–1971	242	15.1
J. P. Stevens, 1975–2010	678	18.8
W. O. Douglas, 1939–1975	783	21.7

°In recent decades, justices have averaged fewer than ten dissenting opinions per term, with the exception of Justices William J. Brennan (1956–1990) and Thurgood Marshall (1967–1991), though in the last few terms Justice Clarence Thomas (1991–) has also written more dissents.

By contrast, Frankfurter, among others, came to value individual expression more than the compromises necessary for achieving institutional opinions. "Unanimity is an appealing abstraction," Frankfurter concluded, but "a single Court statement on important constitutional issues and other aspects of public law is bound to smother differences that in the interests of candor and of the best interest of the Court ought to be expressed."[228]

A number of realities lie behind the changing norms and patterns of institutional and individual opinions. Individual opinion writing, as noted earlier, became institutionalized after the arrival of the New Deal justices. In addition, personal and ideological differences contribute. The contemporary Court's virtually complete discretionary jurisdiction also enables it to select primarily cases of national importance for public law and policy. The Court now decides principally major questions of constitutional and statutory interpretation. These are areas in which the justices are most likely to disagree and to be least inclined to compromise. Constitutional interpretation, in Frankfurter's words, "is not at all a science, but applied politics," and thus proves especially divisive.[229] Cases granted oral argument and decided by opinion are also the most thoroughly researched and considered cases. They are the ones to which the justices devote most of their time, and hence have clarified their own thinking and differences.

The increasing caseload may also have contributed to changes in norms of opinion writing. The "proliferation of concurring opinions and even some dissenting opinions is a result of these pressures" of a greater workload, Burger claimed, "and the consequent lack of time to try to hammer out differences."[230] In the nineteenth and early twentieth centuries the justices spent more time in conference discussing each case and were more inclined to try to reach compromises. There is now less direct communication and more formal, written exchange. The justices' "isolation" in their chambers also may play a part, for, according to Justice Thomas, "there is no going to each other's chambers," as they once did to hammer out differences.[231] There are more law clerks as well, along with greater delegation of responsibility for drafting concurring and dissenting opinions. Justices in turn are less willing to withdraw concurring or dissenting opinions because of the time their clerks have devoted. As one justice put it, even though his concerns had been accommodated in the majority's opinion, "it would break [his] law clerk's heart" to suppress his concurring opinion.[232]

Accompanying the trend toward more separate opinions has been "the ascendency of the law-review type of opinion" and an "increased length of opinions."[233] Opinions have become not merely more numerous but longer. Opinions in 1938 averaged about eight pages, by 1970 slightly more than nine pages, and by the 1980s eleven pages. That increase may seem small, but the justices were also writing more than twice as many opinions each term as they did fifty years earlier.[234] The Rehnquist Court cut back on the number of cases decided by full written opinion as well as the length of some of its opinions. Nevertheless, the reduction in the number of cases did not lead to a corresponding decline in the length of opinions.[235] In the 1950s the median length of decisions was about 2,000 words, whereas the Roberts Court's annual median runs between 4,700 to 8,000 words.[236]

The justices' opinions also contain a large amount of "boilerplate"—restatement of facts and discussions of nonconstitutional matters, even in constitutional cases. Justice Ginsburg tries "to write an opinion so that no one will have to read a sentence twice to get what it means. I generally open an opinion with a kind of a press-release account of what the case is about, what legal [issue] the case presents, how the Court decides it, and the main reason why."[237] An analysis of the content of opinions written by Rehnquist and Brennan in constitutional cases found that about half of the paragraphs dealt either with the case's facts or matters other than constitutional interpretation. Furthermore, those two ideologically opposed justices were just as likely to marshal the same kinds of constitutional arguments, though for different ends. As a judicial conservative, Rehnquist championed an *interpretivist* approach to constitutional interpretation, while Brennan was labeled a *noninterpretivist*. Interpretivists generally hold that constitutional interpretation should be confined to the text and historical context of provisions of the Constitution, or as Scalia and Thomas have championed, "original textualism"—that is, interpreting provisions in light of their "original public understanding."[238] By contrast, noninterpretivists maintain that constitutional interpretation frequently requires going beyond text and historical context to structural arguments grounded in the Constitution and broader principles of constitutional politics. Neither approach is inexorably wedded to either a

Comparative Constitutional Approaches in Opinions

Type of Argument Advanced in Opinions	Number of Paragraphs (%)	
	Rehnquist	*Brennan*
Doctrinal	1,492 (34.2)	1,513 (37.7)
Statements of facts	1,320 (30.2)	1,045 (26.0)
Nonconstitutional	942 (21.6)	934 (23.3)
Extrinsic (nontextual)	391 (8.9)	389 (9.7)
Textual	77 (1.7)	34 (0.8)
Structural	73 (1.6)	42 (1.0)
Historical	67 (1.5)	49 (1.2)
Total	4,362 (99.7)	4,006 (99.7)

conservative or a liberal political philosophy,[239] and the difference between the two is a matter of degree, not a difference in kind. A comparison of opinions by Rehnquist and Brennan reveals that, respectively, 51 and 49 percent of the paragraphs in their opinions were devoted to nonconstitutional matters. When the kinds of constitutional arguments made in their opinions were compared, both overwhelmingly advanced arguments based on *stare decisis* and developing legal doctrines.[240] Besides writing opinions consisting largely of statements of facts and drawing on doctrinal arguments, Rehnquist did not significantly appeal to history any more often than Brennan, nor were the latter's opinions significantly more likely to advance noninterpretivist arguments.

Still, less agreement and more numerous and longer opinions invite uncertainty and confusion about the Court's rulings, and interpretation of law. As individual opinions came to predominate, they also became more idiosyncratic. "It is a genuine misfortune to have the Court's treatment of the subject be a virtual Tower of Babel, from which no definite principles can be clearly drawn," Rehnquist once lamented in a dissent, adding, "I regret even more keenly my contribution to this judicial clamor, but find that none of the views expressed in the other opinions written in the case came close enough to mine to warrant the necessary compromise to obtain a Court opinion."[241] Indeed, in a decision upholding the EPA's regulation of greenhouse effects, for example, the syllabus for the Court's opinion read:

> SCALIA, J., announced the judgment of the Court and delivered an opinion. Parts I and II of which were for the Court. ROBERTS, C.J., and KENNEDY, J., joined that opinion in full; THOMAS and ALITO, JJ., joined as to parts I, II-A, and II-B-1; and GINSBURG, BREYER, SOTOMAYOR, and KAGAN, JJ., joined as to Part II-B-2. BREYER, J., filed an opinion concurring in part and dissenting in part, in which GINSBURG, SOTOMAYOR, and KAGAN, JJ., joined. ALITO, J., filed an opinion concurring in part and dissenting in part, in which THOMAS, J., joined.[242]

In sum, despite Chief Justice Roberts's efforts to achieve greater consensus, five-to-four splits and individual and plurality opinions continue, and continue to invite confusion about, and more litigation over, what the Court actually held.

SIX

The Court and American Life

"WHY DOES the Supreme Court pass the school desegregation case?" asked one of Chief Justice Vinson's law clerks in 1952. *Brown v. Board of Education of Topeka, Kansas* had arrived on the Court's docket in 1951, but it was carried over for oral argument the next term and then consolidated with four other cases and reargued in December 1953. The landmark ruling did not come down until May 17, 1954. "Well," Justice Frankfurter explained, "we're holding it for the election"—1952 was a presidential election year. "You're holding it for the election?" the clerk persisted in disbelief. "I thought the Supreme Court was supposed to decide cases without regard to elections." "When you have a major social political issue of this magnitude," timing and public reactions are important considerations, and, Frankfurter continued, "we do not think this is the time to decide it."[1] Similarly, Justice Tom Clark recalled that the Court waited, over Douglas's dissent, for additional cases from the District of Columbia and other regions, so as "to get a national coverage, rather than a sectional one." Frankfurter and Jackson also wanted to await the view of the incoming administration of Dwight David Eisenhower. Such political considerations are by no means unique. "We often delay adjudication. It's not a question of evading at all," Clark concluded. "It's just the practicalities of life—common sense."[2]

Denied the power of the sword or the purse, the Court must cultivate its institutional prestige. The power of the Court lies in the persuasiveness of its rulings and ultimately rests with other political institutions and public opinion. As an independent force, the Court has no chance to resolve great issues of public policy. *Dred Scott v. Sandford* (1857) and *Brown v. Board of Education* (1954) illustrate the limitations of the Supreme Court in ruling on major political controversies. The "great folly," as Senator Henry Cabot Lodge characterized *Dred Scott*, was not the Taney Court's constitutional interpretation or the unpersuasive moral position that blacks were not citizens. Rather, "the attempt of the Court to settle the slavery question by judicial decision was simple madness." As Lodge explained:

Slavery involved not only the great moral issue of the right of one man to hold another in bondage and to buy and sell him but it involved also the foundations of a social fabric covering half the country and caused men to feel so deeply that it finally brought them beyond the question of nullification to a point where the life of the Union was at stake and a decision could only be reached by war.[3]

Over a hundred years later, political struggles within the country and, notably, presidential and congressional leadership in enforcing the school desegregation ruling saved the moral appeal of *Brown* from becoming another "great folly." Yet, *Brown*'s mandate, due to changes in the Court's composition and the country, was also transformed from ending dual systems of racially segregated schools to achieving the more ambiguous and ambitious goal of integration.

Because the Court's decisions are not self-executing, public reactions sometimes weigh on the justices. Justice Stone, for one, was furious at Chief Justice Hughes's rush to hand down *Powell v. Alabama* (1932), involving the fairness of a trial without the assistance of an attorney for nine young black men accused of raping two white women before an all-white jury in Scottsboro, Alabama.[4] Picketers protested the "Scottsboro boys" conviction and death sentences. Stone attributed the rush to judgment to Hughes's "wish to put a stop to the [public] demonstrations around the Court."[5] Opposition to the school desegregation ruling in *Brown* led to bitter, sometimes violent confrontations. In Little Rock, Arkansas, Governor Orval Faubus encouraged disobedience, and the National Guard had to be called out to maintain order. The school board in Little Rock unsuccessfully pleaded in *Cooper v. Aaron* (1958) for postponement of compliance with *Brown*.[6] In the midst of the controversy, Frankfurter worried that Chief Justice Warren's attitude became "more like that of a fighting politician than that of a judicial statesman." In such confrontations "the transcending issue," Frankfurter reminded the others, remains that of preserving "the Supreme Court as the authoritative organ of what the Constitution requires."[7] When the justices move too far or too fast in their interpretation of the Constitution, they threaten public acceptance not only of the Court's rulings but also of its legitimacy.

The Court's institutional prestige and role in American politics occasionally wears on the justices, particularly when confronting major controversies. The plurality opinion issued by Justices Kennedy, O'Connor, and Souter in *Planned Parenthood of Southeastern Pennsylvania v. Casey* (1992), declining to overrule "the essence of *Roe v. Wade*" while rejecting much of its analysis (as discussed in Chapter 1), illustrates that concern. As the plurality in *Casey* explained, "the Court cannot build support for its decisions by spending money and . . . it cannot independently coerce obedience to its decrees. The Court's power lies, rather, in its legitimacy."

The political struggles of the Court (and among the justices) continue after the writing of opinions and final votes. Announcements of decisions trigger diverse reactions from the media, interest groups, lower courts, Congress, the president, and the general public. Their reactions may enhance or thwart compliance and reinforce or undermine the Court's prestige. Opinion days thus may reveal something of the political struggles that might otherwise remain hidden within the marble temple. They also may mark the beginning of larger political struggles in the country.

Opinion Days

The justices announce their decisions in the courtroom, typically crowded with reporters, anxious attorneys, and curious spectators. When several decisions are to be handed down, the justices delivering the Court's opinions make their announcements in reverse order of seniority, except that the chief justice is always considered the most senior. Authors of concurring or dissenting opinions are free to give their views orally as well, but usually only in cases they feel especially strongly about.

Before 1857 decisions were announced on any day the Court was in session. Thereafter the practice was to announce decisions only on Mondays, but in 1965 the Court reverted to its earlier practice. In 1971 the Court further broke with the late nineteenth-century tradition of "Decision Mondays." On Mondays, the Court generally released only orders and summary decisions and admitted new attorneys to its bar. That practice was followed until 1995 when the Court decided that it would immediately release (but not announce in the courtroom) which cases were granted after the Friday conference, instead of waiting until Mondays so it could speed up the announcement of opinions and hear oral arguments.

When oral arguments are heard (from October through April), opinions are typically announced on Tuesdays and Wednesdays, and then on any day of the week during the rest of the term (May and June). By tradition, there is no prior announcement as to when cases will be handed down; though there have been breaches of secrecy (as discussed in Chapter 3). Since 2012 the Roberts Court has released its orders and summary decisions at nine-thirty in the morning, prior to its ten o'clock sessions. On opinion days, the justices now generally summarize "bench opinions" and a "slip opinion" is published in print and on the Court's website, with minor corrections; the final "official" version (again, if necessary, with corrections) is then published in the *United States Reports*.

As late as 1969, entire days were devoted to the delivery of opinions and admission of attorneys.[8] In 1971 Burger managed to persuade the others to make only brief summary announcements. But he failed to get the justices to agree to put an end to what he considered an "archaic practice" of orally announcing opinions from the bench.[9] Justices now announce, in reverse order of seniority, most opinions in two to four minutes, merely stating the lineup of the justices and the result in each case, though there are occasional exceptions.

The erosion of the practice of reading the full text of opinions was only partly due to its time-consuming nature. The practice sometimes occasioned caustic exchanges, publicly dramatizing the struggles within the Court. Once, when vigorously dissenting, McReynolds hit the bench with his fist, exclaiming, "The Constitution is gone!" and then explained why he thought so. Frankfurter tended to monopolize opinion days, just as he liked to dominate oral arguments and conferences. In one instance, after he ad-libbed at length when delivering the Court's opinion, Chief Justice Stone snidely remarked, "By God, Felix, if you had put all that stuff in the opinion, never in my life would I have agreed to it."[10] On another occasion, Frankfurter took nearly fifteen minutes to attack the majority's ruling as nonsense. His sharp criticism prompted Chief Justice Warren, who had not even written an opinion in the case, to offer a rebuttal in open Court. Warren then turned to Frankfurter and invited him to respond. Not to be outdone, the latter told the courtroom, "The Chief Justice urges me to comment on what he said, but of course I won't. I have another case."[11] Such heated exchanges are rare now, with the prevalence of summary announcements. Dissents announced from the bench occur only a handful of times each term.[12] Chief Justice Roberts, for instance, did not read from any of his dissents during his first decade on the bench until dissenting in *Obergefell v. Hodges* (2015).

Communicating Decisions to the Media

The Court's opinions, Justice Brennan once observed, "must stand on their own merits without embellishment or comment from the judges who write or join them."[13] Justice White was notorious for simply announcing that the lower court was reversed or affirmed "for reasons on file with the Clerk." By contrast, Justice Ginsburg usually announces a decision from a prepared text that is given later to reporters. Likewise, Justice Kagan, who has a reputation for clear, crisp, and uncompromising language, along with a touch of sarcasm, has said her goal in writing and delivering opinions is to "figure out [how] to communicate complicated ideas to people who know a lot less than you do about a certain subject" and to find "vivid ways of explaining that will stick with people."[14]

Justices appreciate that compliance with their decisions depends on the public's understanding of their opinions. Sometimes they are particularly sensitive to this consideration. Chief Justice Hughes, for instance, permitted FDR to run a telephone line from the White House to the Court to learn immediately the Court's decision in the *Gold Clause* cases (1935).[15] That decision was vital to the New Deal in upholding FDR's removal of the gold standard and the devaluation of the dollar. In Frankfurter's view, Hughes "established the very bad precedent of pandering to journalist impatience" by pushing for quick decisions and brief opinions.[16] When *Brown v. Board of Education* was decided, Chief Justice Warren insisted that "the opinion should be short, readable by the lay public, non-rhetorical, unemotional and, above all, non-accusatory."[17]

Media coverage of the Court grew in the mid-twentieth century. In the 1930s less than half a dozen reporters covered the

Court on a regular basis. During Hughes's chief justiceship, a "Press Office" was established in the Office of the Marshal. The single "press officer" (a former reporter) announced those cases on the Court's conference list and those set for oral argument. In the 1940s, he began distributing an edited list of the cases. Reporters had six small cubicles on the ground floor, where they received copies of opinions sent down through a pneumatic tube.[18] By the late 1950s there were full-time reporters from all the major newspapers, and a couple of more specialized legal periodicals, such as *U.S. Law Week*. But since the 1970s the number of reporters has steadily decreased. All three major television networks, along with the Cable News Network (CNN), once had regular reporters at the Court but dropped them in the late 1980s and 1990s. However, the Internet has made access to the Court's decisions and processes more readily available. The Court's website at www.supremecourt.gov now provides the full text of opinions shortly after they have been handed down along with audio recordings of oral aurguments. In addition, an extremely useful blog covering cases granted and decisions as they are handed down is SCOTUSblog at www.scotusblog.com.

The Court has sometimes been accused of indifference to the problems of journalists covering the Court. Shortly after coming to the Court, for example, Burger was confronted with a petition of grievances of reporters. They presented "an outline of some problems which [they perceived to be] of mutual concern to the Court and to the press" and suggested changes "so that the public may be better informed about the Court." But the Court was unreceptive to the demands for providing reasons justices sometimes disqualify themselves from cases and for permitting journalists "access to the staff of the justices." The Court also rejected a proposed media privilege of having—"on a confidential basis"—advance notification and copies of the opinions to be handed down.[19]

Still, changes have been made, though not without occasional opposition from some justices. On opinion days, journalists now receive copies of the headnotes (prepared by the reporter of decisions) summarizing the lineup from some justices of the justices and the main points of a decision. Justice Black disapproved on the ground that "the press will understand the opinions better."[20] The Court also has a Public Information Office, which makes available conference lists and final opinions, as well as speeches made by the justices—all of which may also be accessed on the Court's website. Reporters (and the public) thus may follow cases from the time of filing to acceptance for oral argument, and then listen to or read transcripts of oral arguments, as well as immediately read the opinions. Even so, as discussed in Chapter 3, no cameras are permitted in the courtroom and that does not appear likely to change in the near future. Justice Kennedy, among others, expressed concern over having colleagues "saying something for a sound bite"; likewise, Scalia contended that cameras in the courtroom would "miseducate and misinform" because most people would hear only "15-second sound takeouts on the network news."

In light of such changes, Chief Justice Burger felt that "except for its decision conferences, the Supreme Court literally operates 'in a goldfish bowl.'"[21] Some reporters feel differently. They do not have the kind of access that they do to Congress and the executive branch. For some, the secrecy within the marble temple is disturbing, though others are less troubled. As Lyle Denniston, who reported on the Court for over half a century, put it: "It's an institution that virtually does most of its work in the open. And as they like to say, the work comes in the front door and goes out the front door" (from the filing of cases to the final decision).[22]

Some of the difficulties of covering the Court are inherent in the business of journalism—deadlines and the problems of condensing and explaining complex decisions. The problem was magnified in the initial coverage by Fox News and CNN of the Roberts Court's ruling on the Affordable Care Act (ACA) in *National Federation of Independent Business v. Sebelius* (2012).[23]

In rushing to provide "breaking news" on the widely anticipated ruling, both mistakenly stated that Chief Justice Roberts had struck down the "individual mandate" for health insurance. They based their reporting on the bottom of the second page of the Court's syllabus for the decision, which stated that Congress had exceeded its power under the Commerce and Necessary and Proper Clauses. After a few minutes and CBS's correctly reporting (based on the third page) that the "individual mandate" was upheld based on Congress's Taxing and Spending power, Fox News and CNN corrected their mistakes. The Court's opinion appeared half an hour later on its website.

The public, moreover, learns through the media about only a few of the rulings each term. Studies of media coverage indicate that major networks report on no more than half of the most important decisions each term,[24] though anyone interested may go to the Court's website or SCOTUSblog, and other websites.

Regardless of whether reporters have a legal background, interpreting opinions is sometimes difficult. Some problems are of the Court's own making. Since the Court's decisions must have the approval of a majority of the justices, ambiguity results from the compromises necessary to reach agreement. Hughes, for instance, met opposition to one of his opinions because of "the insertion of the word 'reasonable' in certain places," even though he "put in the word out of abundant caution" to qualify the Court's holding. Since it was not "worthwhile to have a division in the Court over its use in the present case," he omitted the word.[25] Ambiguities may also be strategic, leaving problems open for later cases, and the Court preserves its policy-making options. Reporters, school boards, and citizens, for example, celebrated or cursed *Brown v. Board of Education* for not mandating integration rather than merely ending segregation. But the justices had no doubt about that "big distinction." Some justices would never have gone along with a ruling mandating integration. As Chief Justice Warren later emphasized, the justices "decided only that the practice of segregating children in public schools solely because of their race was unconstitutional. This left other questions to be answered"—in later cases, after the justices gauged public reactions and the Court's composition changed.[26]

Misunderstanding also results when opinions include extraneous matter and other forms of *dicta*—words entirely unnecessary for the decision. These problems are exacerbated by longer, more heavily footnoted opinions. Furthermore, the justices invite confusion when they divide 5–4 and issue plurality opinions and numerous concurring and dissenting opinions.

Still, over the last two decades justices have been more willing to engage with the media (both on and off the record), even explaining their view of pending cases and final decisions.[27] Justices O'Connor, Thomas, and Sotomayor published autobiographies and went on book tours while serving on the bench. Justices Breyer and Scalia published books explaining their respective judicial philosophies and promoted them in interviews, even appearing together in public forums. Almost all of the justices now frequently give interviews and lectures, which are made accessible on the Internet.

Implementing Rulings and Achieving Compliance

When deciding major controversies, justices consider strategies for gaining public acceptance of their rulings. When striking down the doctrine of "separate but equal" schools in *Brown v. Board of Education* (*Brown* I),[28] for instance, the Warren Court waited a year before issuing, in *Brown* II,[29] its mandate for "all deliberate speed" in ending racial segregation in public education. All of the justices knew that there would be major opposition, school closings, and massive resistance.

Resistance to the social policy change announced in *Brown* I was expected. A rigid timetable for desegregation would only have intensified opposition. During oral arguments on *Brown* II, devoted to the question of what kind of decree should be issued to enforce *Brown* I, Warren confronted the hard fact of southern resistance. The attorney for South Carolina, S. Emory Rogers, pressed for an open-ended decree—one that would not specify when and how desegregation should take place. He boldly proclaimed:

Mr. Chief Justice, to say we will conform depends on the decree handed down. I am frank to tell you, right now [in] our district I do not think that we will send—[that] the white people of the district will send their children to the Negro schools. It would be unfair to tell the Court that we are going to do that. I do not think it is. But I do think that something can be worked out. We hope so.

"It is not a question of attitude," Warren shot back, "it is a question of conforming to the decree." Their heated exchange continued as follows:

CHIEF JUSTICE WARREN: But you are not willing to say here that there would be an honest attempt to conform to this decree, if we did leave it to the district court [to implement]?

MR. ROGERS: No, I am not. Let us get the word "honest" out of there.

CHIEF JUSTICE WARREN: No, leave it in.

MR. ROGERS: No, because I would have to tell you that right now we would not conform—we would not send our white children to the Negro schools.[30]

The exchange reinforced Warren's view "that reasonable attempts to start the integration process is [*sic*] all the court can expect in view of the scope of the problem, and that an order to immediately admit all negroes [into] white schools would be an absurdity because [it would be] impossible to obey in many areas. Thus, while total immediate integration might be a reasonable order for Kansas, it would be unreasonable for Virginia, and the district judge might decide that a grade a year or three grades a

The Warren Court in 1953–1954. Front row (from the left): Felix Frankfurter, Hugo Black, Earl Warren, Stanley F. Reed, and William O. Douglas. Second row (from the left): Tom C. Clark, Robert H. Jackson, Harold Burton, and Sherman Minton. (*George Tames/New York Times Co./Getty Images*)

year is reasonable compliance in Virginia."[31] Six law clerks were assigned to prepare a desegregation research report. They summarized available studies, discussed how school districts in different regions could be desegregated, and projected the effects and reactions to various desegregation plans.

The Court's problem, as one of Justice Reed's law clerks put it, was to frame a decree "so as to allow such divergent results without making it so broad that evasion is encouraged."[32] The clerks agreed that there should be a simple decree but disagreed on whether there should be guidelines for its implementation. One clerk opposed any guidelines, while the others thought that their absence "smacks of indecisiveness, and gives the extremists more time to operate." The problem was how precise a guideline should be established. What would constitute "good-faith" compliance? "Although we think a 12-year gradual desegregation plan permissible," they confessed, "we are not certain that the opinion should explicitly sanction it."[33]

At conference, Warren repeated these concerns. Black and Minton thought that a simple decree, without an opinion, was enough. As Black explained, "the less we say the better off we are." The others disagreed. A short, simple opinion seemed advisable for reaffirming *Brown* I and providing guidance for dealing with the inevitable problems of compliance. Justice Harlan wanted *Brown* II expressly to recognize that school desegregation was a local problem to be solved by local authorities. Others also insisted on making clear that school boards and lower courts had flexibility in ending segregation. In Burton's view, "neither this Court nor district courts should act as a school board or formulate the program" for desegregation.

Agreement emerged that a short opinion-decree should be issued. In a memorandum, Warren summarized the main points of agreement. The opinion would simply state that *Brown* I held racially segregated public schools to be unconstitutional. *Brown* II would acknowledge that the ruling created various administrative problems, but emphasize that "local school authorities have the primary responsibility for assessing and solving these problems; [and] the courts will have to consider these problems in determining whether the efforts of local school authorities" are in good-faith compliance. The cases, he concluded, should be remanded to the lower courts "for such proceedings and decree necessary and proper to carry out this Court's decision." The justices agreed, and along these lines Warren drafted a short opinion-decree.[34]

An "Impeach Earl Warren" sign in 1962. The sign was constructed by those
who thought the Warren Court had gone too far in defending civil rights and
liberties. (*Duane Howell*/The Denver Post *via Getty Images*)

The phrase "all deliberate speed" was borrowed from Holmes's
opinion in *Virginia v. West Virginia* (1911),[35] a case dealing with
when and how much of the state's public debt Virginia ought to
receive when West Virginia broke away and became a state. It was
inserted in the final opinion in *Brown* II at the suggestion of
Frankfurter. Forced integration might lead to a lowering of educational standards. Immediate, court-ordered desegregation, Frankfurter warned, "would make a mockery of the Constitutional
adjudication designed to vindicate a claim to equal treatment to
achieve 'integrated' but lower educational standards." The Court,
he insisted, "does its duty if it gets effectively under way the right-
ing of a wrong. When the wrong is a deeply rooted state policy the
court does its duty if it decrees measures that reverse the direction
of the unconstitutional policy so as to uproot it 'with all deliberate

speed.' "[36] As much an apology for not setting precise guidelines as a recognition of the limitations of judicial power, the phrase
symbolized the Court's bold moral appeal to the country. As
University of Chicago Law School professor Dennis Hutchinson
perceptively pointed out: "*Brown* I was a clarion, *Brown* II's
ambivalence impicitly diminished the moral importance of the
first decision."[37]

Ten years later, after school closings, massive resistance, and
continuing litigation, Black complained, "There has been entirely
too much deliberation and not enough speed" in complying with
Brown. "The time for mere 'deliberate speed' has run out."[38]
Brown's moral appeal amounted to little more than an invitation
for delay. At the beginning of the school year in 1964, President
Johnson was apprised of the piecemeal progress and continuing
resistance:

ARKANSAS: Desegregation expanded in schools in Little Rock and
Fort Smith. About 870 Negroes reported in previously white schools,
compared to 390 last year. Twenty-one districts desegregated, compared
to 13 last year. . . .

MISSISSIPPI: Biloxi—Seventeen Negro children attended integrated classes in four previously all-white elementary schools, after
10 years of angry resistance. . . .

VIRGINIA: Virginia will have 25 newly-desegregated districts this
year—including Prince Edward County [which had previously closed
rather than desegregate its schools]—making 80 of 128 in the State
with some integration. About 6,000 Negroes are attending once-white
schools.[39]

With no federal leadership, implementation of *Brown* was
slow and uneven. Ruby Martin, an attorney for the U.S. Commission on Civil Rights, recalled that "the work of the lawyers from
1954 to 1964 resulted in two percent of the Negro kids in the
Southern states attending schools with white students."[40] The
Department of Justice (DoJ) had little role in ending school segregation before the passage of the Civil Rights Act of 1964. The

Civil Rights Division within the DoJ was created after Congress passed the Civil Rights Act of 1957, which expanded federal jurisdiction over voting rights and was the first such legislation in eighty-seven years. But the division had virtually no authority, expertise, or resources to enforce *Brown* until the passage of the 1964 act.[41]

Even after the DoJ assumed a role in enforcing school desegregation, it initially gave little attention to areas outside the South or to problems other than ending *de jure* segregation—segregation enforced by laws prohibiting the integration of public schools. The DoJ paid almost no attention to *de facto* segregation caused by socioeconomic conditions such as housing patterns in the North and the West. LBJ was advised by the attorney general, "There are no current federal programs directly related to the problem of *de facto* school segregation. Title VI of the Civil Rights Act is of doubtful applicability." Attorney General Nicholas de B. Katzenbach admitted, "[O]ne of our difficulties is that we don't know enough about *de facto* segregation."[42] The Department of Health, Education, and Welfare (HEW) was subsequently given responsibility for the federal government's role in ending segregated schools. It had authority to issue guidelines for integration. More important, HEW had the power to cut off federal funding if school districts refused to comply with desegregation plans.

By the late 1960s the DoJ and HEW had assumed leadership in implementing *Brown*. But it took time to build evidence of segregation in northern and western school districts. Not until the summer of 1968 did the outgoing Johnson administration initiate the first school desegregation cases in the North and the West and try to achieve the national coverage that the Court envisioned in *Brown*.[43]

In 1969 Justice Black impatiently observed, "There is no longer the slightest excuse, reason, or justification for further postponement of the time when every public school system in the United States will be a unitary one."[44] In *Alexander v. Holmes County Board of Education* (1969), the Burger Court agreed on a brief *per curiam* opinion holding that the Fifth Circuit Court of Appeals should deny further requests for delay from southern school districts. In its opinion, the Court observed that the "standard allowing 'all deliberate speed' for desegregation is no longer constitutionally permissible." *Alexander* sent a message that "the obligation of every school district is to terminate dual school systems at once and to operate now and hereafter only unitary schools."[45]

The message in *Alexander,* like that in *Brown,* was still ambiguous. Justice Marshall could not win agreement on setting a "cut-off" date for desegregation. Black threatened a dissenting opinion noting that "all deliberate speed," as Frankfurter had understood when suggesting the Holmesian phrase, connoted delay, not speed. Black concluded that the Court's emphasis on "all deliberate speed" had been a "self-inflicted wound." "The duty of this Court and of the others," he implored, "is too simple to require perpetual litigation and deliberation. That duty is to extirpate all racial discrimination from our system of public schools NOW." On the Court less than four months, Burger vigorously opposed setting any final cut-off date. Brennan sought consensus, but the justices could not agree on a more precise order than that of proceeding with desegregation plans "here and now."[46]

The shortcomings of *Alexander* came to light when the court of appeals delayed yet again. The Court, in *Carter v. West Feliciana Parish School Board* (1970),[47] scolded the lower courts about the continued failure to proceed with desegregation. This time Burger, Rehnquist, and Stewart voiced their disagreement, insisting on maintaining a flexible approach to implementation.

Twenty years after *Brown,* some schools remained segregated. Secretary of HEW David Mathews reported to President Ford the results of a survey of half of the nation's primary and secondary public schools, enrolling 91 percent of all students: 42 percent had an "appreciable percentage" of minority students; 16 percent had undertaken desegregation plans, whereas 26 percent had not; and 7 percent of the school districts remained racially segregated.[48]

For over four decades, problems of achieving compliance with *Brown* persisted. Litigation by civil rights groups forced change, but it was piecemeal, costly, and modest. The judiciary alone could not achieve integration. Evasion and resistance were encouraged by the reluctance of presidents and Congress to enforce the mandate. Refusing publicly to endorse *Brown*, Eisenhower did not take steps to enforce the decision until violence erupted in Little Rock, Arkansas. He then did so "*not* to enforce integration but to prevent opposition by violence to orders of a court."[49] Later the JFK and LBJ administrations lacked congressional authorization and resources to enforce school desegregation. Not until 1964 when Congress passed the Civil Rights Act did the executive branch have such authorization. The election of Nixon in 1968 then brought changes both in the policies of the executive branch and the composition of the Court.

Enforcement and implementation required the cooperation and coordination of all three branches. Little progress could be made, as Assistant Attorney General Stephen Pollock explained, "where historically there had been slavery and a long tradition of discrimination [until] all three branches of the federal government [could] be lined up in support of a movement forward or a requirement for change."[50] The simplicity and flexibility of *Brown* I and II invited evasion. It produced a continuing struggle over measures, such as gerrymandering school district lines and busing, because the mandate itself had evolved from one of ending segregated schools to one of securing integrated schools—a much more ambitious and ambiguous objective.

Over forty years after *Brown* more than 500 school desegregation cases remained in the lower federal courts. At issue in most was whether schools had achieved integration and were free of the vestiges of past segregation. Although lower courts split over how much proof school boards had to show to demonstrate that present *de facto* racial isolation was unrelated to past *de jure* segregation, the Court declined to review major desegregation cases from the mid-1970s to the end of the 1980s. During that time the dynamics of segregation in the country changed, as did the composition and direction of the Court.

In the 1980s support for integration waned. The Reagan and George H. W. Bush administrations encouraged localities to escape the "burdens" of *Brown* by fighting courts' desegregation orders. The federal bench also grew more conservative and integration proved ever more elusive. By the 1990s resegregation was on the rise in many parts of the country, particularly in the Midwest and Northeast for blacks and in the West for Hispanics. And by 2000, the proportion of blacks attending white-majority schools declined by 13 percent, reaching the lowest level since 1968.[51]

The war over *Brown*'s mandate for ending state-imposed *de jure* segregation was won. But the battles over achieving integration continued because of demographic changes pushing toward renewed *de facto* segregation, profound disagreement over how much could and should be done to root out the vestiges of past discrimination, and the apparent futility of court-ordered integration in regions that were fast becoming racially resegregated. Support for the judiciary's continued efforts to force integration also quietly ebbed with each change in the Court's composition. *Missouri v. Jenkins* (1990) (*Jenkins* I) upheld the authority of federal judges to order school boards to raise taxes to pay for desegregation plans.[52] But Reagan's four appointees—Rehnquist, O'Connor, Scalia, and Kennedy—stood together in disagreeing with the majority's analysis. With the retirements of Brennan in 1990 and Marshall a year later, the Rehnquist Court signaled a gradual end to the *Brown* era.

Following the appointment of Justice Souter to replace Brennan, Chief Justice Rehnquist commanded a bare majority in *Board of Education of Oklahoma City Public Schools v. Dowell* (1991),[53] holding that school districts that once intentionally segregated may achieve unitary status and court-ordered busing may stop. Despite the fact that some schools remained overwhelmingly black or white, a majority of the Rehnquist Court reasoned that if schools had complied with court orders over a reasonable period of time, they had for all practical purposes eliminated the vestiges of prior discrimination. But in one of his last dissents, Marshall, joined by Blackmun and Stevens, took a widely different view of *Brown's* legacy and the "vestiges of past segregation." They would have ruled that the persistence of racially identifiable schools per se demonstrated that the vestiges of racial discrimination had not been eliminated.

Dowell was not the last word from the Rehnquist Court. Like that in *Brown*, the ruling in *Dowell* was ambiguous, though pointing in an opposite direction. *Brown's* mandate for "all deliberate speed" provided no guidance for how far lower courts' remedial decrees should go. *Dowell* offered little guidance for when courts may withdraw and return full responsibility to local school boards. Both the majority and the dissenters in *Dowell* reaffirmed the Warren Court's last major desegregation case, *Green v. New Kent County School Board* (1968), which held that lower courts should examine "every facet of school operations," including student assignments, faculty, staff, transportation, extracurricular activities, and facilities.[54] But *Dowell* left undecided the most important issues: how much proof school districts had to show in demonstrating that racially isolated schools were unrelated to past intentional discrimination, and whether other factors such as housing patterns promote the vestiges of past segregation and, hence, justify continued judicial supervision.

Barely a month after *Dowell*, the Rehnquist Court agreed to review several other desegregation cases, including *Freeman v. Pitts*, in order to clarify its new stance.[55] *Freeman* raised the question of how long federal courts should supervise desegregation in DeKalb County, Georgia. The DeKalb County School District, Georgia's largest with 80,000 students, had a population that was 57 percent black. Half of the black students attended schools that were at least 90 percent black, while a quarter of the white students attended schools in which over 90 percent of the students were white. A federal district court, nevertheless, concluded that DeKalb County's schools were integrated and no longer bore responsibility for continuing supervision. But the appellate court reversed, holding on the basis of *Green* that no school could be declared fully integrated until "it maintains at least three years of racial equality in six categories: student assignment, faculty, staff, transportation, extracurricular activities and facilities."

On the opening day of the 1991 term, just days before the Court's scheduled date for oral arguments in *Freeman v. Pitts*, Justice Marshall abruptly retired in order not to have to hear the arguments, even though he had earlier said that he would retire upon his successor's confirmation. Since Justice Thomas had not yet been confirmed, he did not participate in the case. Although unanimous in their decision, the justices were not of one mind on how quickly or on what basis lower courts should halt their desegregation orders. Kennedy's opinion for the Court, which only Rehnquist, White, Scalia, and Souter joined, was a rough compromise on the closing of the *Brown* era.

In reversing the appellate court's decision in *Freeman*, Kennedy held that lower courts may withdraw from supervising discrete categories of school operations, as identified in *Green*, once school districts showed compliance with desegregation orders. Lower courts need neither wait for a period of years before doing so, nor await desegregation in all areas of a school system. Yet his opinion did not go far enough for Scalia, who in a concurrence urged an immediate end to all judicial supervision of schools that no longer intentionally discriminated. At the same time, Kennedy's opinion went too far for Blackmun, Stevens, O'Connor, and Souter. They countered in separate concurrences that lower courts should undertake a probing analysis of a school district's record before abandoning desegregation orders. *Dowell* and *Freeman* thus charted a new course, pointing to a new period of litigation—a period not unlike that immediately after *Brown*, but in which lower courts would gradually move to relinquish, rather than assert, control over public schools.

The new course signaled in *Dowell* and *Freeman* was further underscored in *Missouri v. Jenkins* (1995) (*Jenkins* II).[56] There, writing for a bare majority, Chief Justice Rehnquist ruled that a lower federal court exceeded its power in ordering the creation of magnet schools and greater funding for the Kansas City school district, which was predominantly black, due to "white flight," in order to make the city's schools more attractive to white students living in the suburbs. By contrast, Stevens, Souter, Ginsburg, and Breyer disagreed. "Given the deep, inglorious history of segregation in Missouri," in Ginsburg's words, "to curtail desegregation at this time and in this manner is an action at once too swift and too soon."

By the fiftieth anniversary of *Brown* numerous desegregation orders had been lifted, and most school districts had reverted to some version of neighborhood schools. *Dowell, Freeman,* and *Jenkins* II, indeed, signaled the end of the post-*Brown* era of court-ordered desegregation. In the two decades following those rulings the percentage of southern blacks attending white-majority schools fell from over 40 percent to 30 percent, about the level in 1969.[57] States and local school districts faced growing problems of the resegregation of black students in southern and border states, the increasing segregation of Latino students in the West, as well as finding ways to equalize financial funding for public schools.[58] Indeed, recent stories conclude that schools in Florida and elsewhere have grown more segregated since the 1990s.[59]

In response to the problems of maintaining integration following the rulings in *Freeman v. Pitts* and *Jenkins* II, however, an "adequacy movement" emerged with interest groups turning to state courts and state constitutions, which often mandate equal public education, to force increases in public school financing and make adequate educational resources "available to all on equal terms."

Some local school boards, moreover, adopted race-based assignment policies to maintain integrated schools. Those policies were in turn challenged in light of the Court's rulings in *Gratz v. Bollinger*,[60] which invalidated the University of Michigan undergraduate affirmative-action program based on a point system; and *Grutter v. Bollinger* (2003),[61] which upheld the University of Michigan Law School's "holistic" affirmative-action admissions program by a 5–4 vote (with Justice O'Connor casting the crucial vote) in holding that race may be a factor in admissions to achieve diverse student bodies.

The Roberts Court reconsidered those rulings and the use of race in student assignments in public schools in *Parents Involved in Community Schools v. Seattle School District No. 1* (2007).[62] That case presented a challenge to a policy of giving racial preferences in school assignments. Under the program, students indicated their preference for a high school, but the district assigned them with a goal of having a mix of between 40 percent white students and 60 percent racial minorities so as to offset racially segregated housing patterns. If too many white students applied for the same school, priority was given to those with a sibling at the school. Otherwise, racial preference was used as a "tiebreaker" in school assignments. A federal district court upheld the program as narrowly tailored to achieving the district's goal of integrated schools, and the Court of Appeals for the Ninth Circuit affirmed.

A bare majority of the Roberts Court in *Parents Involved in Community Schools v. Seattle School District No. 1* (2007) reversed the lower court's decision. Chief Justice Roberts wrote for a plurality striking down the school district's programs for impermissibly adopting race-conscious student assignments. In his words, "The way to stop discrimination on the basis of race is to stop discriminating on the basis of race." Kennedy's concurring opinion, however, disagreed, contending that race may be a consideration in order to achieve and maintain integration in schools when, for example, drawing attendance zones, but not in individual students' school assignments. In a seventy-page dissenting opinion, Breyer, joined by Stevens, Souter, and Ginsburg, rejected the majority's analysis of the history of integration efforts and of the problems of addressing increasingly racially isolated schools. Subsequently, a solid majority of the Roberts Court, in *Schuette v. Coalition to Defend Affirmative Action, Integration and Immigrant Rights and Fight for Equality By Any Means Necessary (BAMN)* (2014),[63] signaled the end to court-approved affirmative-action programs in education and, more generally, government. Following the Court's rulings in *Gratz v. Bollinger* (2003),[64] striking down the University of Michigan's race-conscious undergraduate admissions process that assigned points for various factors, such as race, legacy, and geography, and *Grutter v. Bollinger* (2003),[65] upholding the University of Michigan Law School's "holistic" admissions process, Michigan voters approved a state constitutional amendment barring governmental preferential treatment "on the basis of race, sex, color, ethnicity, or national origin." That amendment was upheld by the Roberts Court in its ruling in *Schuette*. In a plurality opinion, joined only by Roberts and Alito, Kennedy emphasized that "This case is not about how the debate about racial preferences should be resolved. It is about who may resolve it. There is no authority in the Constitution of the United States or in this court's precedents for the judiciary to set aside Michigan laws that commit this policy determination to the voters." Dissenting Justice Sotomayor, joined by Ginsburg (with Kagan recusing herself), sharply criticized Kennedy's opinion. The Court's majority, in her view, failed to recognize the persistence of racial bias and the fact that minorities could not enact a constitutional amendment permitting affirmative action policies and, thus, were disadvantaged and denied the equal protection of the law. Indeed, Sotomayor singled out Chief Justice Roberts's observation, in *Parents Involved in Community Schools v. Seattle School District No. 1*, that "The way to stop discrimination on the basis of race is to stop discriminating on the basis of race." Sotomayor, who describes herself as "an affirmative action baby," countered that "The way to stop discrimination on the basis of race is to speak openly and candidly on the subject of race, and to apply the Constitution with eyes open to the unfortunate effects of centuries of racial discrimination." "Race matters," she explained, because of the "long history of racial minorities being denied access to the political process," and because "of the slights, the snickers, the silent judgments that reinforce the most crippling of thoughts: 'I do not belong here.'"

In response to *Parents Involved in Community Schools*, a number of districts adopted "class-based integration" policies, whereby a certain percentage of student school assignments are based on low-income status, not race. But many other major cities were not be able to integrate their schools by race or class due to residential demographics. In Los Angeles, California, for instance, 85 percent of students in public schools are black or Latino.[66] In Boston public schools only 12 percent of the students are white, though Boston's schools are better integrated than Chicago and Dallas public schools, with only 8.8 and 4.8 percent white students, respectively. Public schools are not only increasingly racially separate but unequal in facilities because of property taxes and funding. Indeed, white students comprise less than half of all students in increasingly racially isolated public schools.[67] In short, the controversy over integration persists, due to increasingly racially isolated housing patterns in large parts of the country.

"By itself," the political scientist Robert Dahl observed, "the Court is almost powerless to affect the course of national policy."[68] Gerald Rosenberg goes much further in claiming that "courts can *almost never* be effective producers of significant social reform."[69] *Brown's* failure to achieve immediate and widespread desegregation is instructive, Rosenberg reasons, in developing a model of judicial policy making on the basis of two opposing theories of judicial power. On the theory of a "Constrained Court," three institutional factors limit judicial policy making: "[t]he limited nature of constitutional rights," "[t]he lack of judicial independence," and "[t]he judiciary's lack of powers of implementation." On the other hand, a "Dynamic Court" theory emphasizes the judiciary's freedom "from electoral constraints and [other] institutional arrangements that stymie change," thus enabling the courts to take on issues that other political institutions might not or cannot. But neither theory is completely satisfactory, according to Rosenberg, because occasionally courts do bring about social change. The Court may do so when the three institutional restraints identified with the Constrained Court theory are absent, and at least one of the following conditions exists to support judicial policy making: other political institutions and actors offer either (a) incentives or (b) costs to induce compliance; (c) "judicial decisions can be implemented by the market"; or (d) the Court's ruling becomes "a shield, cover, or excuse, for persons crucial to implementation who are *willing to act.*" On the historical basis of resistance and forced compliance with *Brown's* mandate, Rosenberg concluded, "*Brown* and its progeny stand for the proposition that courts are impotent to produce significant social reform."

Brown, nonetheless, dramatically and undeniably altered the course of American life. Neither Congress nor President Eisenhower would have moved to end segregated schools in the 1950s, as their reluctance for a decade to enforce *Brown* underscores. The Court lent moral force and legitimacy to the civil rights movement and to the eventual move by Congress and LBJ to enforce compliance with *Brown*.[70] More importantly, to argue that the Court is impotent to bring about social change overstates the case. Neither Congress nor the president, any more than the Court, could have single-handedly dismantled racially segregated public schools. Just as presidential power ultimately rests on a president's power of persuasion,[71] the Court's power depends on the persuasiveness of its rulings and the magnitude of social change mandated.

The claim that the Court is a "hollow hope" for bringing about social change has also been challenged by another political scientist, Matthew E.K. Hall.[72] Analyzing the influence of 59 Supreme Court rulings, Hall makes two crucial theoretical presuppositions: (1) there is a difference between rulings that (a) are implemented primarily by lower courts ("vertical" rulings that primarily depend on lower courts' compliance) and (b) require the support or acquiescence of other political institutions (these are "lateral" rulings that depend more on other institutions than the lower courts for implementation); and (2) public opinion supports the Court's decision and, hence, pushes legislatures and executives to implement policy changes. Accordingly, *Roe v. Wade* (1973) was a vertical but very politically contentious decision; and *Baker v. Carr* (1962) was a lateral and very popular, pro-democracy ruling; whereas *Brown v. Board of Education* (1954) was a lateral and extremely unpopular decision. In other words, the Court's impact on American life is less likely when it hands down rulings that are unpopular on a lateral issue requiring other institutions' implementation, but may have a greater impact when its decisions bear on basically vertical issues that require primarily lower court compliance and also command widespread public support.

There is no doubt that the Court raises the ante in its bid for compliance when it appeals for massive social change through a prescribed course of action, in contrast to simply saying "no" when striking down a law. The unanimous but ambiguous ruling in *Brown* reflected the justices' awareness that their decisions are not self-enforcing, especially when dealing with highly controversial issues and rulings heavily dependent on other institutions for implementation. Moreover, the ambiguity of *Brown*'s remedial decree was the price of achieving unanimity. Unanimity appeared necessary for the Court to preserve its institutional prestige while pursuing revolutionary change in social policy. The justices sacrificed their own policy preferences for more precise guidelines, while the Court tolerated lengthy delays in recognition of the costs of open defiance, and gaining public acceptance.

But in the following decades, *Brown*'s mandate was transformed from a simple decree ending state-imposed segregation into the more vexing one of achieving integrated public schools. With that transformation the political dynamics of the controversy over race evolved, along with a changing Court and country.

Public opinion curbs the Court when it threatens to go too far or too fast in its rulings. The Court has usually been in step with major political movements, except during transitional periods or critical elections.[73] It would nevertheless be wrong to conclude, along with Finley Peter Dunne's fictional Mr. Dooley, that "th' supreme court follows th' iliction returns."[74] To be sure, the battle over FDR's "Court-packing" plan and the Court's "switch in time that saved nine" in 1937 left that impression. Shortly afterward, however, FDR's close friend and soon-to-be nominee for the Court, Frankfurter, wrote Justice Stone, confessing that he was "not wholly happy in thinking that Mr. Dooley should, in the course of history turn out to have been one of the most distinguished legal philosophers."[75] Frankfurter, of course, knew that justices do not simply follow the election returns. But the fact that the Court abandoned its opposition to the New Deal significantly undercut public support for FDR's Court-packing plan. Gallup polls taken during the spring of 1937 revealed that the Court's switch influenced the shift in public opinion away from FDR's proposed reforms. Yet, as noted in Chapter 2, the "switch in time that saved nine"—the actual vote to uphold New Deal legislation—took place in conference in December 1936, *before* FDR introduced his Court-packing proposal.[76] Even so, the publication of the Court's decision upholding progressive legislation in the spring was timely and influential.

Life in the marble temple is not immune to shifts in public opinion.[77] For one thing, Scalia once emphasized, "it's a little unrealistic to talk about the Court as though it's a continuing, unchanging institution rather than to some extent necessarily a reflection of the society in which it functions. Ultimately, the justices of the Court are taken from the society, [and] if the society changes, you are going eventually to be drawing judges from that same society, and however impartial they may try to be, they are going to bring with them those societ[al] attitudes."[78]

Justice Antonin Scalia (1986–2016), appointed to the Supreme Court by Ronald Reagan. (*AP Photo/Charles Dharapak*)

The justices, of course, deny being directly influenced by public opinion. In an interview on ABC's *Nightline*, for instance, Blackmun twice mentioned public support for capital punishment when discussing his opposition to the death penalty. But when asked, "Why would public opinion have any impact on the thinking of a Supreme Court justice on an issue as vital as the death penalty?" Blackmun responded, "Well, the reference . . . I have made because I disagree with it. I don't agree with it, and I am not influenced by it."[79]

The Court nonetheless occasionally cites or takes "judicial notice" of public opinion in its own opinions. Sometimes the Court takes notice of pertinent state laws as an indirect measure of public opinion and "traditional societal values," as Rehnquist did when noting a public consensus against physician-assisted suicide in *Vacco v. Quill* (1997) and *Washington v. Glucksberg* (1997).[80] Likewise, Kennedy noted the changes in state laws criminalizing homosexual sodomy after the ruling in *Bowers v. Hardwick* (1986),[81] in his opinion overruling *Bowers* in *Lawrence v. Texas* (2003).[82]

The Court's prestige rests on preserving the public's view that justices base their decisions on interpretations of the law rather than personal policy preferences. Studies indicate that the public understands that the justices' ideology plays a role, but the Court's legitimacy flows from the belief that the justices' discretion is exercised in a principled fashion.[83] Of course, justices' complete indifference to public opinion would be the height of judicial arrogance. Even one so devoted to the law as Frankfurter was not above appealing to the forces of public opinion. When the Warren Court debated the landmark reapportionment case, *Baker v. Carr*, Frankfurter asked Stewart—who had the pivotal vote—to consider that this case could

bring the Court in conflict with political forces and exacerbate political feeling widely throughout the Nation on a larger scale, though not so pathologically, as the Segregation cases have stirred. The latter . . . resulted in merely regional feeling against the Court, with the feeling of most of the country strongly in sympathy with the Court. But if one is right about the widely scattered assailable apportionment disparities, . . . clash and tension between Court and country and politicians will assert themselves within a far wider area than the Segregation cases have aroused.

Baker v. Carr, Frankfurter feared, would turn the whole country against the Court. But after there was a clear majority for the overturning of laws that denied equal voting rights, Justice Douglas pushed for an early announcement of the decision with the comment, "This is an election year."[84]

Changes in the composition of the high bench, as Justice Scalia once suggested, appear to reflect broader changes in the country. A number of political scientists draw on various kinds of data to support the hypothesis that the Court usually registers public opinion in legitimating policies of the prevailing national coalition, rather than playing the role of a "counter-majoritarian institution" over the long haul.[85] But studies of the Court's relationship to public opinion encounter theoretical and methodological problems, because they often indirectly measure public opinion.[86] For example, they may focus on polls covering only a few landmark rulings, lack consistent data, and fail to control for the effects of variable responses elicited by questions that may be phrased or framed in different ways when asking about the same complex issue. Studies matching national polls with the Court's rulings reveal considerable congruence, though levels of agreement vary from one policy area to another.[87] Still, such aggregate analyses do not answer the vexing causal question of whether the Court reacts to public opinion or whether the latter is shaped by the Court; nor do they address the extent to which other political forces intervene or the linkages between the Court and its approval ratings among various constituents.[88]

The question of whether the Court should or does stay in step with the opinion of dominant national political coalitions remains problematic in other ways as well. As an unelected body, the Court basically has a counter-majoritarian role and, therefore, whether it ought to "stay in tune with the times" is highly debatable.[89] Whether the Court assumes the role of a majoritarian-reinforcing institution seems doubtful. Vacancies on the bench occur almost randomly and at times are unrelated to shifts in electoral politics. Moreover, it is unclear that the Court always confers legitimacy on the policies of other nationally democratically accountable institutions.

The Court's correlation with shifts in the electorate and public opinion also reveals no historically determined role. American electoral politics periodically undergoes partisan realignment coinciding with the rise and fall of majority parties.[90] The Federalist-Jeffersonian period of the early Republic ran from 1789 to 1828 and then gave way to the Jacksonian era (1828–1860). Abraham Lincoln's election in 1860 marked the beginning of a

Republican era that ended in 1896, followed by a second Republican era lasting until 1932. With FDR's election in 1932 the New Deal–Democratic Party coalition came together and prevailed until the late 1960s. Since that coalition's breakup, divided government has more or less persisted. These periods of realignment and dealignment arose from issues cutting deeply across existing lines of ideological division, resulting in sharply polarized electorates and parties' redefinition. Cleavages emerged over slavery in the 1850s; between rich and poor in the 1880s and 1890s; over progressive economic regulations in the 1930s; due to the quest for racial equality, combating rising crime, and cultural clashes over lifestyle choices in the 1960s; and, more recently, government regulation of the economy. The party system and dominant national political coalitions have thus been transformed by critical elections and a series of dealigning elections.

During critical elections in 1860, 1896, 1932, 1960, and 1964, some political scientists argue, the Court supported the reigning party by helping shape its positions on critical issues.[91] Other political scientists, however, contend that after critical elections the Court stands firm and battles with the newly emergent majority party. Yet, "neither role appears inevitable," nor has the Court played the same role in each realignment.[92]

Before the 1860 election, *Dred Scott* fanned the flames of sectional conflict over slavery. Even so, after Lincoln's 1860 victory and his securing a new majority of Republican justices on the bench, the Court invariably did not side with him or his party's policies. Before the 1896 election the Court reinforced the laissez-faire economic policies of the old Republican Party by overturning federal income tax legislation and restricting enforcement of antitrust laws. Before the New Deal realignment the Court sent mixed signals on progressive economic policies, yet after the 1932 election it virtually went to war with FDR and Congress over the New Deal. During the subsequent constitutional crisis in 1937 the Court abruptly reversed course, despite no changes in membership. In the 1960s the Warren Court's rulings reinforced the liberal-egalitarian social policies promoted by the Democratic Party, thereby contributing to the defection of white middle-class voters, especially in the South, and to the breakup of the old New Deal coalition. Already angry over LBJ pushing the Civil Rights Act of 1964 through the Democratic-controlled Congress, voters grew increasingly bitter over forced integration, rising crime rates, affirmative action, and higher taxes. "Liberal judicial activism," "crime control," and quotas became powerful symbols for Republican presidential candidates from Nixon to George W. Bush. In short, the Court has not played a prescribed role either before or after partisan realignments.

The relationship between the Court and public opinion remains subtle and difficult to measure. Unlike *Brown, Roe, Casey, Citizens United,* and *Obergefell* most of the Court's decisions attract neither media nor widespread public attention. The public tends to identify with the Court's institutional symbolism as a temple of law rather than politics. Yet there is a strong relationship between public support for the Court and agreement with its recent rulings, political ideology, and partisanship.[93] The Court continues to be held in relatively high regard by the public, though its prestige has declined over the last thirty years, along with that of the government in general.[94] Moreover, over the last two decades public approval has also become more polarized, with about 49 percent approving and 46 percent disapproving of the Court's rulings. After the Roberts Court's rulings upholding the ACA and extending protection to same-sex marriages, Democrats' approval surged to 76 percent, while Republicans' approval plummeted to a record low of 18 percent. In short, Democrats and Republicans tend to change their opinions based on the most recent high-profile rulings,[95] and the fact remains that the justices and the Court "are a mystery to many Americans."[96]

Does the Court influence public opinion or does the latter influence the Court? There is no simple answer. Much depends on the Court's composition, what and how it decides particular issues, and its salience for the public in the short and long run. In sum, "Sometimes opinion moves against the Court; at other times it follows the Court; and at still others it scarcely moves at all."[97] A 2018 Pew Research Center poll, however, underscores that public opinion does gradually shift with the Court's changing composition and rulings. Over the last decade, for instance, the percentage of those who believe the Constitution should be interpreted based on what it "means in current times" grew to 55 percent, while those who believe it should be interpreted on what it "meant as originally written" declined to 41 percent.[98]

CONSTITUENTS AND PUBLICS

Less concerned about public opinion than elected public officials, justices are sensitive to the attitudes of the Court's immediate constituents: the solicitor general; the attorney general; the DoJ; counsel for federal agencies, states' attorneys general, and the legal profession. Their responses to the Court's rulings in turn shape public understanding and may determine the extent of compliance.

The solicitor general, the attorney general, and agency counsel interpret the Court's decisions and advise the White House and agencies on compliance; in turn justices may find a favorable or unfavorable reception from the executive branch. The attorney general and agency counsel are more directly involved in trying to extend or thwart the Court's rulings. They do so through advisory opinions, litigation strategies, and development of agency policy and programs.

The reactions of the fifty state attorneys general are no less important. They have a pivotal role in advising governors, mayors, police chiefs, and others in their states. Their responses tend to reflect state and local reactions to the Court's rulings. Regional differences were evident, for example, in responses to the Court's school prayer decisions, after the Court struck down a state-composed prayer in *Engel v. Vitale* (1962)[99] and the reciting of the Lord's Prayer in public schools in *Abington School District v.*

Schempp (1963).[100] Long-standing practices of school prayer in
the East and the South were not easily relinquished. Voluntary
school prayer, silent meditation, and the "objective study of the
Bible and of religion" were viewed as still permissible. Where
school prayer received support in state constitutions or legislation,
state and local officials denied the legitimacy of the Court's
decrees and refused to obey.

Local and regional opposition to rulings like those on school
desegregation and school prayer does not emerge from a vacuum.
Opposition tends to reflect broader national political debates.
Southern resistance to *Brown* was encouraged in 1957 by 101 U.S.
senators and representatives who signed the "Southern Manifesto," challenging the authority of the Court and declaring:

> We pledge ourselves to use all lawful means to bring about a reversal
> of this decision [*Brown v. Board of Education*] which is contrary to the
> Constitution and to prevent the use of force in its implementation.
>
> In this trying period, as we seek to right this wrong, we appeal to our
> people not to be provoked by the agitators and trouble makers invading
> our states and to scrupulously refrain from disorder and lawlessness.[101]

Similarly, congressional and presidential responses to the
school prayer rulings have at times tended to legitimize opposition
to the Court's decisions. Within three days after *Engel*, more than
fifty proposed constitutional amendments to override or limit the
decision were introduced in Congress, and two decades later the
number swelled into the hundreds. Both the House of Representatives and the Senate at various times voted in favor of constitutional amendments but failed to achieve their ratification.
Compliance with *Engel* remained uneven. Twenty-two states had
laws calling for silent or voluntary prayers at the beginning of the
school day in public schools. Arizona, Connecticut, and Rhode
Island permitted classes to begin with a moment of silent meditation. But in *Wallace v. Jaffree* (1985), the Court reaffirmed its
earlier rulings.[102] There, the Court struck down an Alabama law
requiring each school day to begin with a moment of silent prayer

or meditation. The majority held that states may not require silent prayer, though meditation may be allowed so long as states do not expressly try to promote religion in the classroom.

Seven years after *Wallace*, the Rehnquist Court reconsidered the issue of prayer in public schools in *Lee v. Weisman* (1992).[103] That case posed a challenge to school authorities allowing the inclusion of brief prayerful mentions of God in invocations and benedictions during graduation ceremonies. The George H. W. Bush administration joined the suit in an *amicus* brief, asking the Court to jettison earlier rulings barring prayer in public schools and legitimate "the practice under assault [as a] non-coercive, ceremonial acknowledgement of the heritage of a deeply religious people." However, in a somewhat surprising decision, given the changes in the Court's composition, a bare majority held that even nonsectarian benedictions violate the First Amendment's bar to government establishment of religion.

Justice Kennedy announced *Lee v. Weisman*, because he cast the deciding vote in a ruling that otherwise split the justices 4–4 (as discussed in Chapter 5). The school district's supervision of graduation ceremonies, according to Kennedy, "places public pressure, as well as peer pressure, on attending students to stand as a group or, at least, maintain respectful silence during the Invocation and Benediction. This pressure, though subtle and indirect, can be as real as any overt compulsion." And he concluded that under any of the Court's First Amendment tests "the government may not coerce anyone to support or participate in religion or its exercise." Kennedy's opinion, though, held out the possibility that government may endorse religion in other ways, and that he would join the four dissenters here in other cases allowing governmental financial support for religious schools in the form of computers, teachers for students with disabilities, and vouchers.[104]

Subsequently, in two companion cases on the public display of the Ten Commandments, the Court split 5–4. In *Van Orden v. Perry* (2005), the majority held that the erection of a six-foot granite monument with the Ten Commandments did not violate the First Amendment, but in *McCreary v. ACLU* (2005), it held that the display of the commandments in courthouses ran afoul of the First Amendment.[105] In both cases Justice Breyer cast the pivotal vote. He did so on pragmatic grounds, reasoning that the Texas granite monument had stood unopposed for over forty years, whereas the Kentucky courthouse displays sparked immediate controversy and clearly appeared to be aimed at endorsing religion in violation of the (dis)establishment clause.

The Roberts Court will not escape recurring controversies over the (dis)establishment clause, because localities continue to adopt policies and practices endorsing religion that in turn invite new litigation. In a major ruling in *Town of Greece, New York v. Galloway* (2014),[106] for instance, a bare majority held that prayers—predominately Christian prayers—before town council meetings are permissible. Writing for a plurality, Kennedy shifted the test for "the separation of church and state" from the "endorsement test" for a particular religion to the "coercion test" that he earlier proposed in *Lee v. Weisman*. He reinterpreted and extended the ruling in *Marsh v. Chambers* (1983),[107] which upheld the practice of prayers before sessions of Congress and state legislatures, to local governments. His opinion was a kind of middle ground between that of Justices Scalia and Thomas, on the one hand, and the four dissenters. Kennedy's ruling—that prayers may be given not only at the opening sessions of Congress but all state and local governmental meetings—was narrow and came with a number of limitations: (1) prayers may be given only during the ceremonial part of the governing body's session; (2) anyone in the community must be allowed to deliver a prayer; (3) governing bodies may not dictate the prayer message; (4) the prayers may not "proselytize"—promote one faith as the true path—or criticize other faiths; (5) the prayers are permissible when most of the audience is made up of adults, unlike in *Lee v. Weisman*; and finally (6) in reviewing challenges to governmental prayer practices courts should examine "the pattern of prayers" and not second-guess the content of individual prayers. Justices Scalia and Thomas maintained that the (dis)establishment clause did not even apply to the states, and that states and localities should be free to include or exclude prayers from their meetings. By contrast, Kagan, joined by Ginsburg, Breyer, and Sotomayor, disputed Kennedy's "reinterpretation" of *Marsh* and criticized the failure to appreciate the differences between prayers at the opening sessions of Congress and state legislatures—bodies in which the public may only observe—versus town hall meetings in which members of the public may actively participate and hence find more offensive. The Court's ruling is certain to perpetuate the controversy over governmental endorsement of religion and invite further litigation.

The justices, though, may also give great weight to the anticipated reactions of the immediate audience of their rulings, as they did in *Brown*. Another example is that of Chief Justice Warren in *Miranda v. Arizona* (1966), holding that police must read suspects their Fifth and Sixth Amendment rights to remain silent and to consult and have an attorney present during police questioning.[108]

When working on *Miranda*, Warren recalled a controversy involving a law professor's seminar for Minneapolis-area police and Minnesota's state attorney general (and later senator and vice president) Walter Mondale. At the seminar, police were told how to adhere to the Court's decisions and still maintain past interrogation practices. "For instance, you're supposed to arraign a prisoner before a magistrate without unreasonable delay," the law professor advised. "But if the magistrate goes hunting for the weekend on a Friday afternoon at 3:00 P.M., you can arrange to arrest your suspect at 3:30. That way you've got the whole weekend." Mondale took the law professor to task. At a news conference, he responded, "Some persons claim the Supreme Court has gone too far. Others claim to know how constitutional protections may be avoided by tricky indirection. Both viewpoints are wrong—this [seminar] was called to assist us in better fulfilling our sworn duty to uphold the Constitution. It was not called to second guess the Supreme Court." Warren knew full well that not all state attorneys general and police supported the Court's rulings on criminal procedure. He therefore strove to outline in *Miranda* a code for police procedures governing the interrogation of criminal suspects that police could not easily evade. There was considerable antagonism toward the *Miranda* warnings, but they became widely accepted in police practice.[109]

Policy considerations such as the cost of compliance also may persuade the justices to limit the scope of their decisions, as with some of their rulings on police searches. In another controversial decision, *Mapp v. Ohio* (1961),[110] the Warren Court reversed an earlier holding in *Wolf v. Colorado* (1949).[111] In *Wolf*, the Court had held that the Fourth Amendment's prohibition against "unreasonable searches and seizures" applied to the states and the national government. However, in *Wolf* the Court refused to extend to the states the Fourth Amendment's exclusionary rule, which forbids the use at trial of evidence obtained in violation of requirements for a proper search and seizure. *Mapp* reversed *Wolf* by holding that the exclusionary rule applies in state as well as federal courts. The decision raised the possibility that all convictions secured in state courts before 1961 on the basis of illegally obtained evidence would be challenged and new trials demanded.

The Court's decisions traditionally have applied retroactively, permitting retrials for individuals who were convicted based on the same constitutional violation. In *Linkletter v. Walker* (1965),[112] however, the Court refused to apply *Mapp* retroactively. Justice Clark reasoned that the exclusionary rule was designed to deter police misconduct and that retrials "would tax the administration of justice to the utmost." The Burger Court subsequently developed what became known as its "ambulatory retroactivity doctrine" in other areas of criminal law. "That doctrine," Harlan explained, "was the product of the Court's disquietude with the impacts of its fast-moving pace in constitutional innovation in the criminal field." But he also objected that the doctrine merely

rationalizes the Court's freedom "to act, in effect, like a legislature, making its new constitutional rules wholly or partially ret-
roactive or only prospective as it deems wise."[113]

In *Teague v. Lane* (1989), the Court established guidelines for
when new decisions apply retroactively.[114] Under *Teague*, an old
ruling applies both on direct and collateral (an independent challenge to overturn a judgment) review. A new rule overturning a
precedent applies only to cases still on direct review and applies
retroactively in collateral proceedings only if it (1) is substantive
or (2) has a watershed bearing on "the fundamental fairness and
accuracy of the criminal proceeding," such as the Sixth Amendment right to counsel decision in *Gideon v. Wainwright* (1963).
That decision was unanimously reaffirmed by the Roberts Court
in *Wharton v. Bockting* (2007).[115] Writing for the Court in *Wharton*, however, Justice Alito further limited the retroactivity doctrine to apply only to watershed rulings on "substantive rights,"
as in *Gideon* (discussed in Chapter 3), in contrast to new rulings
on "procedural rights." Justice Alito, then, reaffirmed that ruling
on the retroactivity of watershed decisions on substantive rights
versus those on procedural rights in *Davis v. United States*
(2011).[116] Subsequently, in *Montgomery v. Louisiana* (2016),[117]
Justice Kennedy held that the holding in *Miller v. Alabama*
(2012),[118] that sentencing a juvenile to life without the possibility
of parole without considering mitigating factors violates the Eighth
Amendment, applies retroactively because it was a ruling on substantive rights; Justices Scalia, Thomas, and Alito disagreed and
dissented.

The Court has no direct means of mobilizing support for its
rulings. Justices may appeal to the legal profession for understanding and assistance, as Frankfurter unsuccessfully did during the
Little Rock school desegregation crisis in *Cooper v. Aaron*. He
felt compelled to do so because many of his former students at
Harvard Law School were leading members of the southern bar
and because the ex-justice (and governor of South Carolina) James
Byrnes had called on the country to curb the Court. Byrnes pub-

lished an attack on *Brown* and against an article written by one
of Frankfurter's favorite former law clerks, Alexander Bickel. As
a clerk, Bickel had prepared a lengthy research report on school
desegregation when the Court first considered *Brown*. Later,
Bickel revised and published it in the *Harvard Law Review*. Given
Byrnes's attack, Frankfurter personally felt the need to lecture
southern lawyers on the legitimacy of the ruling in *Brown*.[119]

Still, the Court inevitably leaves (or cannot anticipate) numerous unanswered questions about the ramifications of its rulings
on major controversies, as in *Brown*, *Roe*, and *Obergefell*. And
as earlier noted, if the Court goes too fast and too far ahead of
public opinion it may encounter decades of opposition, as several members of the Roberts Court have concluded based on
the opposition to the rulings in *Brown* and *Roe*. Public support
for *Brown* only gradually rose during the following 50 years
from just above 50 percent to over 85 percent. Whereas support
for *Roe v. Wade* has fluctuated during most of the last half
century, with the public remaining sharply divided, a 2018
Galluppoll found that 48 percent identify themselves as "pro-
choice" and the same percentage as "pro-life"; while 43 percent
think abortion should be legal in all (29 percent) or most (14 percent) circumstances, a majority (53 percent) claim it should be legal
in few (35 percent) or no (18 percent) circumstances.[120] By contrast, public support for same-sex marriages rose rather dramatically from about 27 percent in 1995 to over 60 percent by 2015.[121]

In sum, the Court is an instrument of law and political power,
but the justices remain dependent on the attitudes and actions of
their immediate constituents and elected officials, along with the
dynamics of pressure-group politics and public opinion. Implementation and compliance largely depend on lower courts, Congress, and the president.

COMPETITION AND COMPLIANCE IN LOWER COURTS

The Court's "bare bones" decree in *Brown* II maximized flexibility. "Local passions aroused by [*Brown* I] would thereby be

absorbed or tempered," Frankfurter insisted, but also pointed out, "local conflicts would be left on the doorsteps of local judges." The Court left the job of achieving compliance to the lower courts. Unloading "responsibility upon lower courts most subject to community pressures without any guidelines for them except our decision of unconstitutionality," Frankfurter prophetically observed, "would result in drawn-out, indefinite delay without even colorable compliance."[122]

Lower-court judges bore the burdens of opposition to *Brown*. Initially, for many southern judges, social ostracism became a fact of life. They were forced "to discontinue the public listing of their telephone number to avoid anonymous and obscene telephone calls made round the clock. Their mail [was] loaded with threatening letters. Some [were] forced to seek police protection for themselves and their families."[123] Others were denied elevation from district to circuit courts.

When trial judges decide wide-ranging disputes over desegregation or the environment, community pressures may confront them with hard choices. The more responsive judges are to local community values, the more threatened is their legitimacy as dispassionate enforcers of national law. Circuit court of appeals judges are, to an extent, geographically removed from local community pressure. Still, the decentralized structure of the federal judiciary encourages them to apply the Court's decisions in ways that accommodate local values. They fashion a law of the circuit and, as a result, "[i]nformal norms are national in scope but regionally enforced."[124] Unlike southern circuit judges after *Brown*, for instance, northern appellate court judges ordered massive busing and redistricting of school lines in order to achieve integration. Appellate court judges thus regionalize public law and policy.

Compliance with the Court's decisions on politically explosive issues by lower courts is invariably uneven. These courts may extend or limit decisions in anticipation of later rulings by the high court. Following the watershed ruling on privacy in

Griswold v. Connecticut (1965), lower courts interpreted the newfound constitutional right of privacy to justify striking down a wide range of laws, from those limiting the length of employees' hair to those forbidding the use of marijuana. Subsequently, the Court rejected the extension of the right of privacy in many such areas.

A simple model of compliance is not very useful because decisions bearing on major issues of public policy are not necessarily applied by lower courts. Plurality or 5–4 decisions invite lower courts to pursue their own policy goals. Crucial language in an opinion may be treated like *dicta*. Differences between the facts on which the Court ruled and the circumstances of a case at hand may be emphasized so as to distinguish or reach a result opposite of the Court's decision. Lower courts may thereby effectively delay implementation and compliance.

Lower courts also may make "exceptions" when applying the Court's rulings in anticipation of a change in the composition of the high bench, thinking the justices will eventually approve of them and thereby limit earlier rulings. For example, lower courts, and finally the Supreme Court, carved out a "good faith exception" to the Fourth Amendment's exclusionary rule. In two rulings, *Massachusetts v. Sheppard* and *United States v. Leon* (1984), the Burger Court upheld the good faith exception in holding that the exclusionary rule does not bar the use of evidence that police found when conducting a search based on a warrant that they believed to be good but was later found to be defective.[125] Subsequently, in *Arizona v. Evans* (1995), the Rehnquist Court expanded the good faith exception to the exclusionary rule to include police reliance on mistaken computer records of outstanding arrest warrants,[126] and the even more conservative Roberts Court further cut back on the exclusionary rule.[127]

Open defiance to the Court's rulings is infrequent but not unprecedented. In *Jaffree v. Board of School Commissioners* (1983), for example, a federal district court judge in Alabama directly challenged the legitimacy of the Court.[128] The judge upheld the daily recitation of prayers in public schools and expressly rejected the twenty-year-old rulings in *Engel* and *Abington* that the First Amendment's ban on the establishment of religion applies to the states and that compulsory school prayer violates the establishment clause. A majority of the Court rebuffed the lower court when it decided an appeal of the ruling and struck down the "moment of silence" law in *Wallace v. Jaffree* (1985).[129]

The Court, however, may deny review or summarily reverse lower court decisions that limit its precedents, as the Roberts Court has done, over the dissents of Justices Scalia and Thomas,[130] with lower court rulings upholding regulations banning semi-automatic firearms and large-capacity magazines, as used in recent mass murders, and thus limiting the scope of the Court's decisions recognizing a Second Amendment right to bear arms for self-defense in one's home.[131]

On the other hand, lower federal courts may anticipate the Court's future rulings on the basis of recent changes in its direction in what has been termed "anticipatory compliance." In *Brzonkala v. Virginia Polytechnic Institute and State University* (1999), for example, based on the Court's rulings on federalism handed down after the passage of the Violence Against Women Act of 1994, a federal appellate court struck down provisions of that law.[132] Subsequently, a bare majority of the Court affirmed that decision and extended its previous rulings limiting congressional power in *United States v. Morrison* (2000).[133]

Even more dramatically, state and federal courts anticipated the Court's extension of constitutional protection to same-sex marriages. After the ruling in *Lawrence v. Texas* (2003), the supreme court of Massachusetts in 2004 recognized same-sex marriages under its state constitution and ignited a national backlash, with eventually 30 states enacting prohibitions of same-sex marriages. But by 2012 three states had legitimated such marriages, and, then, writing for a bare majority in *Windsor v. United States* (2013), Justice Kennedy struck down the Defense of

Marriage Act of 1996 that barred federal recognition of same-sex couples. What followed was a firestorm of federal and state court rulings striking down state constitutional bans on same-sex marriage. Within a little over a year, 36 states, as a result of judicial and legislative action, recognized same-sex marriages and public opinion approval reached over 65 percent by the time *Obergefell v. Hodges* (2015) was handed down.

Federal and state judges also express disagreements with the Court's rulings in their opinions, at judicial conferences, bar association meetings, and in news conferences, as well as in their correspondence. The Conference of State Chief Justices in 1958 went so far as to pass a resolution condemning the Warren Court for its erosion of federalism and its tendency "to adopt the role of policymaker without proper judicial restraint."[134] The Warren Court's rulings in such cases as *Gideon, Mapp,* and *Miranda* revolutionized criminal procedure by holding that the rights of the accused guaranteed in the Bill of Rights apply in state no less than in federal courts. The Warren Court thus drew intense criticism from state judges. That criticism is exemplified by the reaction to *Katz v. United States* (1967).[135] *Katz* held that the Fourth Amendment "protects people, not places" and that police must obtain a search warrant before tapping telephone lines, even those of a public telephone booth. Writing to Harlan, one of the most conservative members of the Court at the time, Georgia State Supreme Court Chief Justice William Duckworth castigated the ruling and expressed the views of many critics of the Warren Court:

By such nearsighted decisions you victimize the innocent public and force them to endure crime, solely because some individual officer personally violated rights of the criminal. . . . If your court would recognize that State courts are capable of honestly and intelligently enforcing criminal laws—and by experience know more than most of you about how to do it within the Constitution, the flood-tide of crime would abate. No honest judge can or will deny that the Constitution is the Supreme Law. But Justices of the Supreme Court, although given the final word, are not superior in qualification, dedication and honor in deciding cases.[136]

Surprised by the frankness of the criticism, Harlan responded that "the great debates that have been taking place, both within and without the judiciary, [are] the product of the extraordinary era in which we are living and not of any change in the basic point of view of the federal judiciary."[137]

Some state court judges on occasion still rebel. In anticipation of the ruling on same-sex marriages in *Obergefell v. Hodges* (2015), the Supreme Court of Alabama asserted its power to interpret the Constitution when upholding its state bans on same-sex marriages. After *Obergefell* came down, that court's chief justice, Roy S. Moore, denounced the decision as "judicial tyranny" and directed probate judges—the only state officials empowered to issue marriage licenses—to deny licenses to same-sex couples. But a federal district court issued an injunction against the enforcement of Alabama's ban on same-sex marriages, and the Supreme Court refused to stay that injunction, thereby forcing compliance.[138] (By contrast, the Louisiana state supreme court permitted the adoption of a child by a same-sex couple because "the matter was no longer a justiciable controversy" after *Obergefell*, though over two bitter dissents.) Subsequently, the Roberts Court, in *Pavan v. Smith* (2018),[139] overturned the Arkansas state supreme court's decision that the state could require the name of the biological father placed on birth certificates, because it discriminated against LGBTQ couples of adopted children. A brief *per curiam* opinion reaffirmed *Obergefell*'s holding that state laws are unconstitutional "to the extent they treated same-sex couples differently from opposite-sex couples." However, as dissenting Justices Thomas and Alito in *Obergefell* emphasized, the majority's holding invited opposition from those who believe their religious opposition to same-sex marriages is protected by the First Amendment guarantees for free speech and religious exercise. When confronted with that inevitable controversy—over a baker's refusal to make a wedding cake for a same-sex couple due to his religious convictions, and for which he was found to violate a state antidiscrimination law—in *Masterpiece Cakeshop v. Colorado Civil Rights Commission* (2018),[140] a majority of the Roberts Court failed to address the First Amendment claims. Writing for the Court, Justice Kennedy reversed the state court's decision and remanded the case for reconsideration, upon concluding that the Colorado Civil Rights Commission had not considered Masterpiece Cakeshop's claims with religious neutrality. Justices Kagan, Gorsuch, and Thomas each issued separate concurring opinions, while Justices Ginsburg and Sotomayor dissented. Such issues are certain to return to the Court.

Opposition and defiance by federal and state judges to the Court's decisions, of course, reflects their own policy preferences, the political currents, and public pressures of the time. When the Warren Court handed down *Mapp v. Ohio* (1961), the California state attorney general (and later state supreme court justice) Stanley Mosk told Justice Douglas, "Thank the good Lord for *Mapp v. Ohio.*" He explained that a bare majority of the California state supreme court had just interpreted its state constitution to incorporate the exclusionary rule, and its decision was attacked by local politicians. Mosk explained that "with the system of elective judges they have in California, pressure on the trial courts was very, very great not to apply [the decision] or to find there were more exceptions to it, or in others, try to get around it." *Mapp*, Douglas reported, took "the pressure off the local judges to create exceptions and to follow the exclusionary rule and all its ramifications."[141]

Whether state judges oppose or embrace the Court's rulings depends on their political views and the direction of the Court's policy making. During the Warren Court revolutions in school desegregation, criminal procedure, and reappointment, state judges like Georgia's Chief Justice Duckworth complained about the nationalization of public law and policy. The autonomy of state judges appeared to be eroded by the Court's rulings.

Miranda's safeguards against coerced confessions, for example, and *Obergefell*'s ruling on same-sex marriages established a "*federal minimum floor*" or threshold requirement for all fifty states.

State courts may still guarantee more procedural safeguards and rights than recognized by the Court—that is, above the federal minimum floor as defined by the Court—based on their state constitutions. During the last few decades the direction of the Court gradually changed in many areas, reflecting the more conservative views of the appointees of Nixon, Reagan, George H. W. Bush, George W. Bush, and Donald Trump. Although not always outright reversing Warren and Burger Court rulings, the Rehnquist and Roberts Courts refused further extensions and achieved retrenchment in some areas. More liberal state supreme courts accordingly refused to follow the more conservative rulings of the Court. "Why should we always be the tail being wagged by the Federal dog?" asked former New Hampshire State Supreme Court Justice Charles Douglas and other state judges. "Liberal state courts have taken the doctrines of federalism and states' rights, heretofore associated with [conservatives] like George C. Wallace," California's Justice Stanley Mosk explained, "and adapted them to give citizens more rights under their state constitutions rather than to oppress them." Thus a *new judicial federalism* emerged based on state supreme courts interpreting their state bills of rights to give greater protection than the Supreme Court's interpretation of the federal Bill of Rights.

Indeed, state supreme courts have handed down hundreds of rulings vindicating rights broader than or left unprotected by the Court. State supreme courts, for example, led the way in recognizing same-sex marriages before the Court's ruling in *Obergefell v. Hodges* (2015), and in refusing to follow the Court's rulings in other areas as well. In *Prescott v. Oklahoma Preservation Commission* (2015), for instance, Oklahoma's supreme court refused to follow the Court's ruling in *Van Orden v. Perry* (2005) that upheld the placing of a Ten Commandments monument on

Texas's state capitol grounds over First Amendment objections. Based on its state constitutional provision for the separation of government and religion, the Oklahoma Supreme Court ruled that placing a virtually identical monument on its state capitol grounds was impermissible.

Such developments in state constitutional law, in the view of some, are a sign of "the strength of our federal system." By contrast, conservative justices have sought to bring state courts into line by reversing decisions vindicating broader constitutional rights than approved by the Court. In *Michigan v. Long* (1983), for instance,[142] the Court announced that when state courts defend rights broader than what has been approved by the Court, they must clearly and explicitly make a "plain statement" that their decisions rest on "adequate and independent state grounds"—that is, their state constitutions or state constitutional rulings. Otherwise, the Court assumes that state courts are relying on federal constitutional law and feels free to reverse those decisions with which it disagrees.

CONGRESSIONAL ACTION AND REACTION

Legislators frequently "have gone after the Supreme Court because it doesn't cost anything," Attorney General Nicholas Katzenbach once observed.[143] On the floor of the Senate or the House of Representatives, rhetoric is cheaper than building coalitions.

Major confrontations between Congress and the Court have occurred a number of times. With the election of Thomas Jefferson in 1800, the Republicans gained control of Congress. Before Jefferson was inaugurated, the defeated President John Adams and the outgoing Federalists in Congress retaliated by passing the Judiciary Act of 1801, creating new circuit court judgeships and stipulating that when the next vacancy on the Court occurred, it should go unfilled. That attempt to maintain influence in the judiciary was quickly countered. In 1802 the Republican Congress repealed the act of 1801, abolishing the judgeships and returning the number of Supreme Court justices to six. Congress also post-poned the Court's next term in order to preclude it from imme-diately hearing a challenge to its repealing legislation in *Stuart v. Laird* (1803).[144] In *Stuart*, the Court upheld Congress's power to repeal the Judiciary Act of 1801. And in response the Jeffer-sonian Republicans impeached Justice Samuel Chase for expound-ing Federalist doctrine. Though the Senate acquitted him, it would not confirm nominees for federal judgeships unless they were Jeffersonian Republicans.

The Marshall Court approved the expansion of national governmental power, but in response, Congress in the 1820s and 1830s threatened to remove the Court's jurisdiction over dis-putes involving states' rights. After the Civil War, Congress suc-ceeded in repealing the Court's jurisdiction over certain denials of writs of *habeas corpus*—orders commanding that a prisoner be brought before a judge and that cause be shown for his or her imprisonment. In *Ex parte McCardle* (1869), the Court upheld the repeal of its own jurisdiction and thus avoided deciding a controversial case attacking the constitutionality of Reconstruc-tion legislation.[145]

At the turn of the twentieth century, progressives in Congress unsuccessfully sought to pressure the Court, which was domi-nated at the time by advocates of laissez-faire social and eco-nomic policy. They proposed requiring a two-thirds vote by the justices when striking down federal statutes, and permitting Con-gress to overrule the Court's decisions by a two-thirds majority. This confrontation escalated with the Court's invalidation of the early New Deal program in the 1930s. Although Congress refused to go along with FDR's Court-packing plan, it passed legislation allowing justices to retire after ten years of service at age seventy, with full rather than half salary. Congress thus made retirement more financially attractive, which in turn gave FDR opportuni-ties to appoint justices who shared his political philosophy. Later, the Warren Court faced persistent attempts to curb its jurisdiction and reverse specific decisions. And the Burger Court's rulings on abortion generated numerous proposals to curb the Court's jurisdiction and overturn or modify its decisions (as discussed in Chapter 1).

On the other hand, since the Civil War the Court has increasingly challenged Congress, invalidating legislation based primarily on the Interstate Commerce Clause and the First Amendment. Still, the Court more generally has tended to support Congress, except during the 1960s and 1990s.[146]

Congress may put pressure on the Court in a number of ways. The Senate may try to influence judicial appointments or impeach justices, but more often, Congress uses institutional and jurisdictional changes as weapons against the Court. Congress has tried to pressure the Court when setting its terms and size and authorizing appropriations for salaries, law clerks, secretaries, and office technology. Only once, in 1802, when repealing the Judiciary Act of 1801 and abolishing a session for a year, did Congress actually set the Court's term in order to delay and influence a particular decision.

The size of the Court is not preordained, and changes generally reflect attempts by Congress to influence the direction of its rulings. The Jeffersonian Republicans' quick repeal of the act passed by the Federalists in 1801 reducing the number of justices was the first of several attempts to influence the Court. Presidents James Madison, James Monroe, and John Quincy Adams all claimed that the country's geographical expansion warranted enlarging the size of the Court. But Congress refused to do so until the last day of Andrew Jackson's term in 1837. During the Civil War the number of justices increased to ten, ostensibly because of the creation of a tenth circuit in the West. This gave Abraham Lincoln his fourth appointment and a chance to secure a pro-Union majority on the bench. Antagonism toward President Andrew Johnson's Reconstruction policies led to a reduction from ten to seven justices. After General Ulysses S. Grant was elected president, Congress again authorized nine justices—the number that has prevailed. In the nineteenth century Congress successfully denied presidents additional appointments in order to preserve the Court's policies.

Although Article III of the Constitution forbids reducing justices' salaries, Congress may withhold salary increases as punishment, especially in times of high inflation.

Even so, more direct attacks appear possible. Under Article III, Congress is authorized "to make exceptions" to the appellate jurisdiction of the Court. That authorization has been viewed as a way of denying the Court review of certain kinds of cases. Congress succeeded with the 1868 repeal of jurisdiction over writs of *habeas corpus*, which the Court upheld in *Ex parte McCardle* (1869). More recently, in response to the rulings that "enemy combatants" held at Guantánamo Bay, Cuba, had a right to file a writ of *habeas corpus* and be tried by independent tribunals in *Rasul v. Bush* and *Hamdi v. Rumsfeld* (2004), Congress enacted the Detainee Treatment Act (DTA) of 2005.[147] That law withdrew federal court jurisdiction over *habeas* writs filed by aliens detained outside of the United States. However, in *Hamdan v. Rumsfeld* (2006),[148] without ruling on the constitutionality of the DTA, the Court held that enemy detainees whose *habeas* applications were pending at the time of the enactment of the DTA could invoke the judiciary's jurisdiction, and ruled that they must be tried by civilian courts, courts martial, or military commissions as authorized by Congress. Congress then passed the Military Commissions Act of 2006, which denied federal courts jurisdiction over all *habeas* applications filed by "unlawful enemy combatants." When the constitutionality of that law was challenged, the Roberts Court initially denied review, but subsequently granted review and in *Boumediene v. Bush* (2008), by a 5–4 vote, struck down Congress's stripping of *habeas corpus* review of the basis for detention.[149] Writing for the majority, Justice Kennedy emphasized, "The laws and Constitution are designed to survive, and remain in force, in extraordinary times." Chief Justice Roberts and Justices Scalia, Thomas, and Alito dissented.

In short, Court-curbing legislation is not a very effective weapon.[150] Rather than limiting judicial review, Congress has given the Court the power to set its own agenda and decide major issues of public law and policy—precisely the kinds of issues that Congress then seeks to deny the Court review. The Court has also suggested that it would not approve repeals of its jurisdiction that were merely attempts to dictate how particular kinds of cases should be decided. But most proposals to curb the Court, of course, are simply that.[151] During the Cold War era, for instance, the Republican Senator William Jenner spearheaded a drive to forbid review of cases challenging legislative committees investigating un-American activities. Another unsuccessful attempt was made in 1968 to amend the Omnibus Crime Control and Safe Streets Act, which would prevent the Court from reviewing state criminal cases raising *Miranda* issues. Given the overwhelming failure of Court-curbing attempts, C. Herman Pritchett pointed out, "Congress can no longer claim with good conscience the authority granted by Article III, Section 2, and every time proposals to exercise such authority are rejected, the Court's control over its appellate jurisdiction is correspondingly strengthened."[152] Indeed, of almost 400 Court-curbing bills introduced in Congress since 1937, only a couple were successful.[153]

Congress has had somewhat greater success in reversing the Court by constitutional amendments. Congress must pass a constitutional amendment, which three-fourths of the states must then ratify. The process is cumbersome, and thousands of amendments to overrule the Court have failed. But six decisions have been expressly overturned by constitutional amendment. *Chisholm v. Georgia* (1793), holding that citizens of one state could sue another state in federal courts, was reversed by the Eleventh Amendment, guaranteeing sovereign immunity for states from suits by citizens of another state.[154] The Thirteenth and Fourteenth Amendments, abolishing slavery and making blacks citizens of the United States, technically overturned the ruling in *Dred Scott v. Sandford* (1857). With the ratification in 1913 of the Sixteenth

Amendment, Congress reversed *Pollock v. Farmers' Loan and Trust Co.* (1895), which had invalidated a federal income tax.[155] In 1970 an amendment to the Voting Rights Act of 1965 lowered the voting age to eighteen for all elections. Within six months in *Oregon v. Mitchell* (1970), a bare majority of the Court held that Congress had exceeded its power by lowering the voting age for state and local elections.[156] Less than a year later the Twenty-Sixth Amendment was ratified, extending the franchise to eighteen-year-olds in all elections.

In addition, the Nineteenth Amendment in 1920 extended voting rights to women and basically nullified *Minor v. Happersett* (1874), which had rejected the claim that women could not be denied the right to vote under the Fourteenth Amendment's equal protection clause.[157] The Twenty-fourth Amendment ratified in 1964 prohibits the use of poll taxes as a qualification for voting, and thus invalidated the Court's rejection of a Fourteenth Amendment challenge to poll taxes in *Breedlove v. Suttles* (1937).[158] Finally, it bears noting that several leaders in the Reconstruction Congress maintained that provisions of what became the Fourteenth Amendment in 1868 would effectively override *Barron v. Baltimore* (1833) and apply the Bill of Rights to the states as well as the federal government.[159] Shortly after that amendment's ratification, however, the Court rejected that interpretation of the amendment in *The Slaughterhouse Cases* (1873).[160] But in the early and mid-twentieth century the Court selectively incorporated the major guarantees of the first eight amendments into the Fourteenth Amendment and applied them to the states.

More successful than constitutional amendments have been congressional enactments that rewrite legislation in response to the Court's rulings. For example, the Court held in *Pennsylvania v. Wheeling and Belmont Bridge Co.* (1852) that a bridge built across the Ohio River obstructed interstate commerce and violated a congressionally approved state compact.[161] Congress immediately passed a law declaring that the bridge did not obstruct interstate commerce.

Congressional reversals usually relate to nonstatutory matters involving administrative policies. Congressional reversals of the Court's statutory interpretations have historically been less frequent, though far greater in number than constitutional amendments. Congress usually has been constrained by the lobbying efforts of beneficiaries of the Court's rulings. Between 1967 and 1990 Congress overrode 121 of the Court's statutory decisions; by contrast, between 1945 and 1957 only 21 rulings were overridden. Moreover, Congress increasingly overrules lower federal court decisions as well.[162]

Congress cannot overturn the Court's interpretations of the Constitution by mere legislation. But Congress can enhance or thwart compliance with the Court's rulings. After the Warren Court's landmark decision in *Gideon v. Wainwright* (1963) that indigents have a right to counsel, Congress provided attorneys for indigents charged with federal offenses. By contrast, in the Crime Control and Safe Streets Act of 1968, Congress permitted federal courts to use evidence obtained from suspects who had not been read their *Miranda* rights if their testimony appeared voluntary on the basis of the "totality of the circumstances" surrounding their interrogation. Congress thus attempted to return to a pre-*Miranda* standard for the questioning of criminal suspects. But the DoJ under both Democratic and Republican administrations declined to follow that provision. When that statute was challenged in *Dickerson v. United States* (2000) the Rehnquist Court reaffirmed the constitutionality of *Miranda*, rebuffing Congress's attempt to make an end run around its ruling, with only Scalia and Thomas dissenting.[163]

The Court underscored its power in *City of Boerne v. Flores* (1997), striking down sections of the Religious Freedom Restoration Act of 1993 (RFRA), which Congress enacted in an attempt to override the Court's 1990 decision in *Employment Division, Department of Human Resources of Oregon v. Smith*.[164] In *Smith*, the Court set aside the balancing test for religious minorities laid down in *Sherbert v. Verner* (1963), holding instead that the First Amendment guarantee for the free exercise of religion does not require making exceptions for religious minorities from generally applicable laws such as education, traffic, and unemployment compensation regulations.[165] A broad coalition of religious organizations persuaded Congress to reestablish the *Sherbert* test as a matter of federal law in RFRA. But in striking down sections of the RFRA, the Court ruled that Congress does not have the power, under the Fourteenth Amendment's enforcement power in Section 5, to enforce constitutional rights broader than those recognized by the Court. Congress has the power under Section 5 only to provide remedies for violations of rights that the Court recognizes.[166] Yet, Congress again pushed back by enacting the Religious Land Use and Institutionalized Persons Act (RLUIPA) of 2000, reestablishing, though with more limited application, that a burden on a prisoner's free exercise of religion must be the least restrictive means to further a compelling governmental interest. The Roberts Court upheld the application of RLUIPA in several cases, including *Holt v. Hobbs* (2015)—involving a Muslim prison inmate who, following Allah's dictate, wanted to keep a half-inch beard over prison officials' objections.[167]

Notably, the Court has curbed Congress by invalidating legislation that aims to expand rights beyond those it has recognized or that have exceeded its interpretation of congressional power. *City of Boerne*, for instance, was extended in *United States v. Morrison* (2000),[168] striking down a section of the Violence Against Women Act of 1994 that allowed victims to sue their attackers for damages. Also, *Kimel v. Florida Board of Regents* (2000) held that Congress exceeded its powers in amending the Age Discrimination in Employment Act to allow state employees to sue for age discrimination.[169] The reasoning was that age discrimination had not been held by the Court to violate the Fourteenth Amendment, and Congress's power under Section 5 is limited to remedying constitutional violations but does not include the power to broaden its protections.

Congress may, nonetheless, on occasion openly defy the Court's rulings. When holding that Congress may not delegate decision-making authority to agencies and still retain the power of vetoing decisions with which it disagrees in *Immigration and Natural-ization Service v. Chadha* (1983), the Court invalidated over 200 provisions for one-house vetoes of administrative actions. Congress responded by deleting or substituting joint resolutions for one-house veto provisions. But in the years since *Chadha*, Congress also passed over 400 new provisions for legislative vetoes.[170]

Congress indubitably has the power to delay and undercut implementation of the Court's rulings. Congress delayed imple-mentation of *Brown* by not authorizing the executive branch to enforce the decision before the Civil Rights Act of 1964. Then, by cutting back on appropriations for the DoJ and HEW during the Nixon and Ford administrations, Congress registered increas-ing opposition to court-ordered busing and other attempts to achieve integrated public schools. "What the Congress gave in Title VI of the 1964 Civil Rights Acts," former HEW secretary Joseph Califano observed, "it took away in part through the annual HEW appropriations bills by forbidding the use of any funds to bus school children."[171]

On major issues of public policy, Congress is likely to prevail or at least temper the impact of the Court's rulings. In a study of the Court's invalidation of legislation, Robert Dahl found that Congress ultimately prevailed 70 percent of the time. Congress was able to do so by reenacting legislation and because of changes in the composition and direction of the Court.[172] Still, the Court forges public policy not only by invalidating federal legislation but also by overturning state and local laws and practices, an impor-tant fact that Dahl failed to take note. The continuing controver-sies over decisions striking down state laws on school prayer, abortion, and same-sex marriages are a measure of how the Court's policy making may elevate issues to the national political agenda and influence American life.

Charged with the responsibility of taking "care that the laws be faithfully executed," the president is the chief executive officer under the Constitution. As the only nationally elected public official, the president ostensibly represents the views of the dominant national political coalition. A president's obligation to faithfully execute the laws, including decisions of the Court, may thus collide with his own perceived electoral mandate.

The Court often has been the focus of presidential campaigns and power struggles. But presidents have seldom openly defied particular decisions by the Court. Presidential defiance is perhaps symbolized by the famous remark attributed to Andrew Jackson: "John Marshall has made his decision, now let him enforce it." Jackson's refusal to enforce the decision in *Worcester v. Georgia* (1832),[173] which denied state courts jurisdiction over crimes committed on Indian lands, in fact simply left enforcement problems up to the lower courts and state legislatures. During the Civil War, Lincoln ordered his military commanders to refuse to obey writs of *habeas corpus* issued by Chief Justice Taney. On less dramatic occasions, presidents have instructed their attorneys general to refuse to comply with other court orders.

In major confrontations, presidents have yielded to the Court. Nixon complied with the ruling in *New York Times Co. v. United States* (1971), striking down, as a prior restraint on freedom of the press, an injunction against the publication of the *Pentagon Papers*—a top-secret report detailing the history of America's involvement in Vietnam. Then he submitted to the decision in *United States v. Nixon* (1974), ordering the release of White House tape recordings pertinent to the trial of other presidential assistants for conspiracy and obstruction of justice, which ultimately led to Nixon's resignation in the face of impeachment.

Although presidents seldom defy the Court outright, their reluctance to enforce rulings may effectively thwart implementation. Eisenhower's reaction to the school desegregation decision was quite similar to Jackson's earlier one. *Brown* was "a hot potato handed to [him] by the judiciary," Attorney General Herbert Brownell recalled. "After the Court decision [the president] realized that it then became his job as head of the executive branch of government to enforce it. And he went about doing that in what he thought was the right way—it was a long-term way."[174] Eisenhower would not assume leadership for enforcing *Brown*. He disapproved of the Court's bold attempt to mandate a change in the way of life of many Americans. "Laws are rarely effective unless they represent the will of the majority," and, he reasoned, *Brown* removed the "cloak of legality to segregation in all its forms," which the Court itself had given in *Plessy v. Ferguson* (1896), when proclaiming the doctrine of "separate but equal" in public transportation.[175] "After three score years of living under these patterns," Eisenhower concluded, "it was impossible to expect complete and instant reversal of conduct by mere decision of the Supreme Court."[176]

Styles and strategies of political leadership vary, but presidential persuasion can significantly influence compliance with the Court's rulings. By the late 1960s considerable progress had been made toward ending segregated public schools. This was due largely to the leadership of JFK and LBJ. In the 1968 presidential campaign, though, Nixon won the southern vote with antibusing pledges and promises to take a "middle-of-the-road" approach to school desegregation as well as return "law and order" to the country. After his election, he observed, "[T]here are those who want instant integration and those who want segregation forever. I believe that we need to have a middle course between these two extremes."[177] Surprised by the unanimous decision in *Alexander v. Holmes County School Board* (1969),[178] he became the first president to disagree publicly with one of the Court's rulings on school desegregation. *Alexander* did not deter Nixon from keeping his campaign promises. His strategy was to return the problems of compliance to the courts by curtailing the DoJ's prosecution of school districts that refused to desegregate and to cut back on the funding and jurisdiction of HEW for enforcing integration.

In both the short and the long run, presidents may undercut the Court's policy making. By issuing contradictory directives to federal agencies and assigning low priority to enforcement by the DoJ, they may limit the Court's decisions. Although most of the early New Deal program was invalidated by the Court, after 1937 FDR persuaded Congress to reenact major provisions of his social and economic policies. Presidents may also make broad moral appeals in response to the Court's rulings, and those appeals may transcend their limited time in office. The Court put school desegregation and abortion on the national agenda, but it was JFK's appeal for civil rights that captivated a generation and encouraged public acceptance of the Court's rulings. Similarly, Reagan's opposition to abortion legitimated resistance to *Roe v. Wade*, as did Trump's rhetoric, judicial appointments, and legislative agenda. And George W. Bush helped keep the controversy alive in 2003 by signing into law a federal ban on performing "partial-birth abortions," even though the Court had struck down similar state laws in *Stenberg v. Carhart*. A bare majority of the Roberts Court subsequently upheld that federal restriction in *Gonzales v. Carhart* (2007) (as discussed in Chapter 1).

Presidential influence over the Court in the long run remains largely contingent on appointments to the Court. Vacancies occur at the rate of one in about every two years. Four presidents—including Jimmy Carter and George W. Bush in his first term—had no opportunities to appoint members of the Court. There is also no guarantee on how a justice will vote or that the addition of his or her vote will prove instrumental in limiting or reversing past rulings with which a president disagrees. But through their appointments (as discussed in Chapter 2), especially when they fill a number of seats in short order or replace a pivotal justice, presidents may leave their mark on the Court and possibly align the Court and the country, or precipitate later confrontations. Major controversies such as those over desegregation, abortion, affirmative action, and same-sex marriages tend to play out over several generations.

The Supreme Court and American Life

"The powers exercised by this Court are inherently oligarchic," Frankfurter once observed when pointing out that "[t]he Court is not saved from being oligarchic because it professes to act in the service of humane ends."[179] Judicial review is antidemocratic and counter-majoritarian. But the Court's power stems from its duty to give authoritative meaning to the Constitution and rests with the persuasive forces of reason, institutional prestige, the cooperation of other political institutions, and, ultimately, public opinion. The country, in a sense, saves the justices from being an oligarchy by curbing the Court when it goes too far or too fast. Violent opposition and resistance, however, threaten not merely the Court's prestige but the very idea of a government under law.

Some Court watchers, and occasionally even some justices, warn of "an imperial judiciary" and a "government by the judiciary."[180] Still others contend that in major controversies the Court's rulings engage the country in a "vital national seminar."[181] For much of the Court's history, though, the work of the justices has not involved major issues of public policy. In most areas of public law and policy, the fact that the Court decides an issue is more important than what it decides. Relatively few of the many issues of domestic and foreign policy that arise reach the Court. When the Court does decide major questions of public policy, it does so by bringing political controversies within the language, structure, and spirit of the Constitution. By deciding only immediate cases, the Court infuses constitutional meaning into the resolution of the larger surrounding political controversies. But the Court by itself cannot lay major controversies to rest.

The Court nonetheless profoundly influences American life. As a guardian of the Constitution, the Court sometimes invites controversy by challenging majoritarian sentiments to respect the rights of minorities and the principles of a representative democracy. The Court's influence is usually more subtle and indirect, varying over time, and from one policy issue to another. In the end, the Court's influence on American life cannot be measured precisely, because its policy making is inextricably bound up with that of other political institutions. Major confrontations in constitutional politics, such as those over school desegregation, school prayer, abortion, and discrimination against minorities, are determined as much by what is possible in a system of free government and pluralistic society as by what the Court says about the meaning of the Constitution. At its best, the Court appeals to the country to respect the substantive value choices of human dignity and self-governance embedded in our written Constitution.

Appendix: Members of the Supreme Court of the United States

	Appointing President	Dates of Service
CHIEF JUSTICES		
Jay, John	Washington	1789–1795
Rutledge, John	Washington	1795–1795
Ellsworth, Oliver	Washington	1796–1800
Marshall, John	Adams, J.	1801–1835
Taney, Roger Brooke	Jackson	1836–1864
Chase, Salmon Portland	Lincoln	1864–1873
Waite, Morrison Remick	Grant	1874–1888
Fuller, Melville Weston	Cleveland	1888–1910
White, Edward Douglass	Taft	1910–1921
Taft, William Howard	Harding	1921–1930
Hughes, Charles Evans	Hoover	1930–1941
Stone, Harlan Fiske	Roosevelt, F.	1941–1946
Vinson, Frederick Moore	Truman	1946–1953
Warren, Earl	Eisenhower	1953–1969
Burger, Warren Earl	Nixon	1969–1986
Rehnquist, William Hubbs	Reagan	1986–2005
Roberts, John G., Jr.	Bush, G. W.	2005–

(Continues)

	Appointing President	Dates of Service
ASSOCIATE JUSTICES		
Rutledge, John	Washington	1790–1791
Cushing, William	Washington	1790–1810
Wilson, James	Washington	1789–1798
Blair, John, Jr.	Washington	1790–1796
Iredell, James	Washington	1790–1799
Johnson, Thomas	Washington	1792–1793
Paterson, William	Washington	1793–1806
Chase, Samuel	Washington	1796–1811
Washington, Bushrod	Adams, J.	1799–1829
Moore, Alfred	Adams, J.	1800–1804
Johnson, William	Jefferson	1804–1834
Livingston, Henry Brockholst	Jefferson	1807–1823
Todd, Thomas	Jefferson	1807–1826
Duvall, Gabriel	Madison	1811–1835
Story, Joseph	Madison	1812–1845
Thompson, Smith	Monroe	1823–1843
Trimble, Robert	Adams, J. Q.	1826–1828
McLean, John	Jackson	1830–1861
Baldwin, Henry	Jackson	1830–1844
Wayne, James Moore	Jackson	1835–1867
Barbour, Philip Pendleton	Jackson	1836–1841
Catron, John	Jackson	1837–1865
McKinley, John	Van Buren	1838–1852
Daniel, Peter Vivian	Van Buren	1842–1860
Nelson, Samuel	Tyler	1845–1872
Woodbury, Levi	Polk	1845–1851
Grier, Robert Cooper	Polk	1846–1870
Curtis, Benjamin Robbins	Fillmore	1851–1857
Campbell, John Archibald	Pierce	1853–1861
Clifford, Nathan	Buchanan	1858–1881
Swayne, Noah Haynes	Lincoln	1862–1881
Miller, Samuel Freeman	Lincoln	1862–1890
Davis, David	Lincoln	1862–1877
Field, Stephen Johnson	Lincoln	1863–1897
Strong, William	Grant	1870–1880
Bradley, Joseph P.	Grant	1870–1892
Hunt, Ward	Grant	1873–1882
Harlan, John Marshall	Hayes	1877–1911
Woods, William Burnham	Hayes	1881–1887
Matthews, Stanley	Garfield	1881–1889

(*Continues*)

	Appointing President	*Dates of Service*
Gray, Horace	Arthur	1882–1902
Blatchford, Samuel	Arthur	1882–1893
Lamar, Lucius Quintus C.	Cleveland	1888–1893
Brewer, David Josiah	Harrison	1890–1910
Brown, Henry Billings	Harrison	1891–1906
Shiras, George, Jr.	Harrison	1892–1903
Jackson, Howell Edmunds	Harrison	1893–1895
White, Edward Douglass	Cleveland	1894–1910
Peckham, Rufus Wheeler	Cleveland	1896–1909
McKenna, Joseph	McKinley	1898–1925
Holmes, Oliver Wendell	Roosevelt, T.	1902–1932
Day, William Rufus	Roosevelt, T.	1903–1922
Moody, William Henry	Roosevelt, T.	1906–1910
Lurton, Horace Harmon	Taft	1910–1914
Hughes, Charles Evans	Taft	1910–1916
Van Devanter, Willis	Taft	1911–1937
Lamar, Joseph Rucker	Taft	1911–1916
Pitney, Mahlon	Taft	1912–1922
McReynolds, James Clark	Wilson	1914–1941
Brandeis, Louis Dembitz	Wilson	1916–1939
Clarke, John Hessin	Wilson	1916–1922
Sutherland, George	Harding	1921–1938
Butler, Pierce	Harding	1923–1939
Sanford, Edward Terry	Harding	1923–1930
Stone, Harlan Fiske	Coolidge	1925–1941
Roberts, Owen Josephus	Hoover	1930–1945
Cardozo, Benjamin Nathan	Hoover	1932–1938
Black, Hugo Lafayette	Roosevelt, F.	1937–1971
Reed, Stanley Forman	Roosevelt, F.	1938–1957
Frankfurter, Felix	Roosevelt, F.	1939–1962
Douglas, William Orville	Roosevelt, F.	1939–1975
Murphy, Frank	Roosevelt, F.	1940–1949
Byrnes, James Francis	Roosevelt, F.	1941–1942
Jackson, Robert Houghwout	Roosevelt, F.	1941–1954
Rutledge, Wiley Blount	Roosevelt, F.	1943–1949
Burton, Harold Hitz	Truman	1945–1958
Clark, Thomas Campbell	Truman	1949–1967
Minton, Sherman	Truman	1949–1956
Harlan, John Marshall (II)	Eisenhower	1955–1971
Brennan, William Joseph, Jr.	Eisenhower	1956–1990
Whittaker, Charles Evans	Eisenhower	1957–1962
Stewart, Potter	Eisenhower	1958–1981

(Continues)

	Appointing President	Dates of Service
White, Byron Raymond	Kennedy	1962–1993
Goldberg, Arthur Joseph	Kennedy	1962–1965
Fortas, Abe	Johnson, L.	1965–1969
Marshall, Thurgood	Johnson, L.	1967–1991
Blackmun, Harry A.	Nixon	1970–1994
Powell, Lewis Franklin, Jr.	Nixon	1972–1987
Rehnquist, William Hubbs	Nixon	1972–1986
Stevens, John Paul	Ford	1975–2010
O'Connor, Sandra Day	Reagan	1981–2006
Scalia, Antonin	Reagan	1986–2016
Kennedy, Anthony	Reagan	1988–2018
Souter, David H.	Bush, G. H. W.	1990–2009
Thomas, Clarence	Bush, G. H. W.	1991–
Ginsburg, Ruth Bader	Clinton	1993–
Breyer, Stephen G.	Clinton	1994–
Alito, Samuel, Jr.	Bush, G. W.	2006–
Sotomayor, Sonia	Obama	2009–
Kagan, Elena	Obama	2010–
Gorsuch, Neil	Trump	2017–
Kavanaugh, Brett	Trump	2018–

Notes

ABBREVIATIONS FOR PRIMARY SOURCES

BHLUM	Bentley Historical Library, University of Michigan, Ann Arbor, Michigan
BLUC	Bancroft Library, Oral History Project, University of California, Berkeley, California
CPL	William J. Clinton Presidential Library, Little Rock, Arkansas
CLE	Clemson University, Cooper Library, Clemson, South Carolina
CU	Columbia University, Butler Library, New York, New York
CUOHP	Columbia University, Oral History Project, New York, New York
CWM	College of William and Mary, Williamsburg, Virginia
EPL	Dwight David Eisenhower Presidential Library, Abilene, Kansas
FPL	Gerald R. Ford Presidential Library, Ann Arbor, Michigan
HI	Hoover Institution, Stanford University, Stanford, California
HLS	Harvard Law School, Manuscripts Room, Cambridge, Massachusetts
HPL	Herbert Hoover Presidential Library, West Branch, Iowa
HWBPL	George H. W. Bush Presidential Library, College Station, Texas
JPL	Lyndon Baines Johnson Presidential Library, Austin, Texas
KPL	John F. Kennedy Presidential Library, Waltham, Massachusetts
LC	Library of Congress, Manuscripts Division, Washington, D.C.
MHL	Minnesota Historical Library, St. Paul, Minnesota
MLPU	Seeley G. Mudd Library, Princeton University, Princeton, New Jersey
NACP	National Archives, College Park, Maryland
NARS	National Archives and Records Service, Washington, D.C.
RPL	Franklin D. Roosevelt Presidential Library, Hyde Park, New York
RRPL	Ronald Reagan Presidential Library, Simi Valley, California
SC	Supreme Court of the United States, Washington, D.C.
TPL	Harry S. Truman Presidential Library, Independence, Missouri
UK	University of Kentucky, Special Collections Library, Lexington, Kentucky

UT	University of Texas, Manuscripts Room, Law School Library, Austin, Texas
UV	University of Virginia, Alderman Library, Charlottesville, Virginia
WHCF	White House Central Files
WLLS	Washington and Lee Law School, Lexington, Virginia
YA	Yale University Library, New Haven, Connecticut
YU	Yeshiva University, Cardozo School of Law, New York, New York

ONE

A Struggle for Power

1. Quoted by L. Shearer, "Intelligence Report," *Parade* magazine (January 23, 1983). See also Norma McCorvey, *I Am Roe: My Life*, Roe v. Wade, *and Freedom of Choice* (New York: HarperCollins, 1994).
2. C. Rowan television interview, *In Search of Justice*, WUSA (September 14, 1987); "Jane Roe Speaks Out," *Village Voice*, April 11, 1989, 44.
3. See, generally, James Mohr, *Abortion in America: The Origins and Evolution of National Policy* (New York: Oxford University Press, 1978); Leslie J. Reagan, *When Abortion Was a Crime: Women, Medicine, and Law in the United States, 1867–1973* (Berkeley: University of California Press, 1997); Linda Greenhouse and Reva Siegel, *Before* Roe v. Wade: *Voices That Shaped the Abortion Debate Before the Supreme Court's Ruling* (New Haven, Conn.: Yale Law Library, 2d ed., 2012); Mary Ziegler, *After Roe: The Lost History of the Abortion Debate* (Cambridge: Harvard University Press, 2015); Linda Greenhouse and Reva Siegel, "*Casey* and Clinic Closings: When 'Protecting Health' Obstructs Choice," 125 *Yale Law Journal* 1428 (2016); Melissa Murray, Katherine Shaw, and Reva Siegel, eds., *Reproductive Rights and Justice Stories* (St. Paul, Minn.: West Academic, 2019); and Carol Sanger, *About Abortion: Terminating Pregnancy in Twenty-First-Century America* (Cambridge: Harvard University Press, 2017).
4. A. L. Goodstein, "'Jane Roe' Renounces Abortion Movement," *Washington Post*, August 15, 1995, F1.
5. Docket Book, William J. Brennan Jr. Papers, Box 417, LC.
6. Sarah Weddington, *A Question of Choice* (New York: The Feminist Press at CUNY, 2013).
7. The discussion of the oral arguments in *Roe v. Wade* is based on recordings of the arguments available at NARS and transcripts in P. Kurland and G. Casper, eds., *Landmark Briefs and Arguments of the Supreme Court of the United States* (Arlington, Va.: University Publications of America, 1974). *Roe v. Wade*, 410 U.S. 113 (1973).
8. Docket Book, Brennan Papers, Box 420A, LC.
9. Memos, December 18 and 20, 1971, Brennan Papers, Box 281, LC.
10. Memos, May 18 and 19, 1972, from Douglas and Brennan, and Memos to Conference, May 18 and 25, 1972, from Blackmun, Brennan Papers, Box 281, LC.
11. Memorandum to the Conference, May 31, 1972, Brennan Papers, Box 281, LC.
12. Memo to Blackmun, May 31, 1972, Brennan Papers, Box 281, LC.
13. Memorandum for Conference, June 1, 1972, Brennan Papers, Box 281, LC.
14. Memo to Chief Justice Burger, June 1, 1972, Brennan Papers, Box 281, LC.
15. Memo from Chief Justice Burger to Justice Douglas, July 27, 1972, Harry A. Blackmun Papers, Box 151, LC.
16. Memo to Blackmun, January 4, 1973, Brennan Papers, Box 281, LC.

17. Memorandum to Conference, December 15, 1972, Blackmun Papers, Box 151, LC.
18. Memorandum to Conference, January 16, 1973, Brennan Papers, Box 281, LC.
19. Memos, January 16 and 17, 1973, Blackmun Papers, Box 151, LC.
20. Quoted in "Statements by 2 Cardinals," *New York Times*, January 23, 1973, A20.
21. Quoted in "Statements by 2 Cardinals," p. A20.
22. See, e.g., *Planned Parenthood v. Danforth*, 428 U.S. 52 (1976) (written consent of woman, after doctor's explanation of dangers of abortion, permissible; but spousal consent unconstitutional if husband is allowed to prohibit abortion); *Bellotti v. Baird*, 443 U.S. 622 (1979) (parental veto of minor's abortion unconstitutional); *H. L. v. Matheson*, 450 U.S. 398 (1981) (upheld requirements that parents be notified of minor's decision to have an abortion); and *Bigelow v. Virginia*, 421 U.S. 809 (1975) (states may not ban advertisements for abortion clinics).
23. See *Poelker v. Doe*, 432 U.S. 519 (1977) (upholding city's policy of refusing nontherapeutic abortions in public hospitals); *Beal v. Poe*, 432 U.S. 438 (1977), and *Maher v. Roe*, 432 U.S. 464 (1977) (upholding restrictions on the funding of nontherapeutic abortions).
24. *Harris v. McRae*, 448 U.S. 297 (1980).
25. *City of Akron v. Akron Center for Reproductive Health*, 462 U.S. 416 (1983).
26. *Thornburgh v. American College of Obstetricians & Gynecologists*, 476 U.S. 747 (1986).
27. *Webster v. Reproductive Health Services*, 492 U.S. 490 (1989).
28. *Planned Parenthood of Southeastern Pennsylvania v. Casey*, 500 U.S. 833 (1992).
29. Memorandum to Conference from Justice Souter, January 15, 1992, Blackmun Papers, Box 601, LC.
30. Memos from Justices Souter and Stevens, January 15 and 16, 1992, Blackmun Papers, Box 601, LC.
31. *Planned Parenthood of Southeastern Pennsylvania v. Casey*, 502 U.S. 1052 (1992).
32. Based on Justice Blackmun's notes in Docket Book, Blackmun Papers, Box 602, LC.
33. First Draft, May 27, 1992, Blackmun Papers, Box 602, LC.
34. Draft opinions for the Court and note from Justice Kennedy to Justice Blackmun, Blackmun Papers, Box 602, LC.
35. *Stenberg v. Carhart*, 530 U.S. 914 (2000).
36. *Gonzales v. Carhart*, 550 U.S. 124 (2007).
37. Guttmacher Institute, "More State Abortion Restrictions Were Enacted in 2011–2013 Than in the Entire Previous Decade" (Washington, D.C.: Alan Guttmacher Institute, January 2, 2014).
38. *Whole Woman's Health v. Hellerstedt*, 136 S. Ct. 2292 (2016).
39. *National Institute of Family and Life Advocates v. Becerra*, 139 S. Ct.__ (2018).
40. *Rust v. Sullivan*, 500 U.S. 173 (1991).
41. Edward D. White, "The Supreme Court of the United States," 7 *American Bar Association Journal* 341–343 (July 1921).

TWO

The Cult of the Robe

1. Memorandum to the President, January 6, 1965, John Macy Papers, Box 726, "Judgeships File," JPL.
2. Felix Frankfurter Oral History Interview, at 52–53, KPL. See also Letter, May 15, 1964, Charles Wyzanski Papers, Box 1, File 26, HLS.

3. Letter to Alexander Bickel, March 18, 1963, Felix Frankfurter Papers, Box 206, HLS.

4. H. Abraham, "A Bench Happily Filled: Some Historical Reflections on the Supreme Court Appointment Process," 66 *Judicature* 282, 286 (1983).

5. *Jacobellis v. Ohio*, 378 U.S. 184, 197 (1964).

6. Based on Leon Friedman and Fred Israel, eds., *Justices of the United States Supreme Court*, 4 Vols., 4th ed. (New York: Facts on File, 2013).

7. Letter, October 9, 1928, Harlan F. Stone Papers, Box 24, LC.

8. Letter, Box 24, LC.

9. Quoted in "The Second Woman Justice: Ruth Bader Ginsburg Talks Candidly about a Changing Society," *ABA Journal* 40 (October 1993), at 41.

10. White House Counsel's Office, Decision Memo: DC Cir Kagan (6/17/99), OA/ID No. 22016; and Kagan- FBI Draft 4/99, OA/ID 14688, CPL.

11. Letter, February 20, 1932, WHCF, Box 878, HPL.

12. WHCF, Box 193, HPL. (The undated note from Justice Stone appears in a file of endorsements of Hughes for chief justice. Justice Stone may have also suggested Cardozo for the chief justiceship; but the note, with President Hoover's notations, appears to have been intended for filling Justice Sanford's vacancy.) See also Benjamin Cardozo Papers, Box 11, CU and YU.

13. See materials on the Parker nomination, WHCF, Boxes 192 and 193, HPL; and Stone Papers, Box 17, LC.

14. Homer Cummings Diaries, UV; and WHCF-PSF, Box 231, TPL.

15. See C. Cameron, A. Cover, and J. Segal, "Senate Voting on Supreme Court Nominees: A Neoinstitutional Model," 84 *American Political Science Review* 525 (1990).

16. See J. Massaro's excellent study, *Supremely Political: The Role of Ideology and Management in Unsuccessful Supreme Court Nominations* (Albany, N.Y.: SUNY Press, 1990).

17. W. Mitchell, "Appointment of Federal Judges," 17 *American Bar Association Journal* 569 (1931). See also William Mitchell Papers, Box 7, MHS; and WHCF, Box 441, HPL.

18. See Lee Epstein and Jeffrey Segal, *Advice and Consent: The Politics of Judicial Appointments* (New York: Oxford University Press, 2005); CRS Report RL 33225, "Supreme Court Nominations, 1789–2005" (Washington, D.C.: Congressional Research Service, January 5, 2006); and Margaret Williams and Lawrence Baum, "Supreme Court Nominees before the Senate Judiciary Committee," 90 *Judicature* 73 (2006).

19. Letter, October 17, 1975, WHCF-FG, Box 50; Letter from Baroody, November 19, 1975, WHCF-FG, Box 51; Telephone Logs, WHCF-FG, Box 17, FPL. For further discussion, see D. O'Brien, "The Politics of Professionalism: President Gerald Ford's Appointment of John Paul Stevens," 21 *Presidential Studies Quarterly* 103 (1991).

20. See ABA, *Standing Committee on Federal Judiciary: What It Is and How It Works* (ABA, 1983). See also WHCF-GF, Box 67, EPL.

21. Letter to Thomas Reed Powell, October 15, 1928, Stone Papers, Box 24, LC.

22. Records of the Department of Justice, Harold Burton Files, NARS; William O. Douglas Interview with Walter Murphy, MLPU; Tom C. Clark Oral History Interview, TPL; and WHCF-CF, Box 5, TPL.

23. See, generally, D. Danelski, *A Supreme Court Justice Is Appointed* (New York: Random House, 1964).

24. Letter to the President, November 12, 1938, Hugo Black Papers, Box 63, LC.
25. File on Wiley Rutledge, Records of the Attorney General, Department of Justice, NARS; also, Papers as President, PSF, Box 186, RPL.
26. Douglas Interview, at 86–89, MLPU.
27. Quoted in William H. Honan, "Roman L. Hruska Dies at 94; Leading Senate Conservative," *New York Times*, April 27, 1999, B8.
28. See, e.g., Memos to the President on Lower Court Appointments, WHCF-FG, Box 505; Larry Temple Papers, Box 1; Barefoot Sanders Papers, Box 1; and John Macy Oral History Interview, Tape 3, at 13, JPL.
29. L. R. Wilfry to the President, October 31, 1910, Edward White Papers, LC.
30. See Memorandum for the Attorney General, November 27, 1942, and Comparative List Showing Religion of Judges Appointed during the Periods of 1922–1933 and 1933–1942, Francis Biddle Papers, Box 2, RPL.
31. Note on telephone conversation with Attorney General Brownell, September 9, 1956, Dwight David Eisenhower (DDE) Diaries, Box 11, EPL.
32. Quoted in Memorandum on Confirmation of Justice Louis Brandeis, WHCF, Fortas/Thornberry Series, Chron. File, JPL. See, generally, A. T. Mason, *Brandeis: A Free Man's Life* (New York: Viking Press, 1946).
33. Kennedy Interview, at 319, KPL.
34. Letter to the President, July 19, 1965, WHCF-FG, Box 535, JPL.
35. Justice Ruth Bader Ginsburg, "From Benjamin to Breyer: Is There a Jewish Seat?" 24 *The Supreme Court Historical Quarterly* no. 3 (2003).
36. Letter from Paul Carrington, March 13, 1967, to Joseph Califano, Records of Department of Justice, NARS.
37. Quoted in Mark V. Tushnet, *Making Civil Rights Law: Thurgood Marshall and the Supreme Court, 1961–1991*, at 9 (New York: Oxford University Press, 1994).
38. *Brown v. Board of Education of Topeka, Kansas*, 347 U.S. 483 (1954).
39. Thurgood Marshall Oral History Interview, at 7, JPL.
40. See, generally, Wil Haygood, *Showdown: Thurgood Marshall and the Supreme Court Nomination That Changed America* (New York: Knopf, 2015).
41. *Adarand Constructors, Inc. v. Pena*, 515 U.S. 200, 241 (1995) (Thomas, J., con. Op.).
42. WHCF-OF, 41A, Box 212, TPL.
43. Macy Papers, Box 726, JPL.
44. R. Nixon, *RN: The Memories of Richard Nixon* 423 (New York: Grosset & Dunlap, 1978).
45. Ginsburg, *ABA Journal*, supra note 9, at 41.
46. Letter to Thomas Reed Powell, October 15, 1928, Stone Papers, Box 24, LC.
47. *West Coast Hotel v. Parrish*, 300 U.S. 379 (1937).
48. *National Labor Relations Board v. Jones & Laughlin Steel Corporation*, 301 U.S. 1 (1937). See letter from Justice Frankfurter to Charles Fairman (December 27, 1945), Frankfurter Papers, Box 184, HLS. See also Justice Frankfurter letter to Paul Freund (October 18, 1953), Frankfurter Papers, Box 184, HLS.
49. "The Black Controversy," Robert Jackson Papers, LC.
50. Statement Appended to Letter to Virginia Hamilton, April 7, 1968, Black Papers, Box 31, LC. (I am grateful to Professor Howard Ball for directing me to this note.) See also materials in Black Papers, Box 234, LC; and Cummings Diaries, UV.
51. Cummings Diaries, UV; Stanley Reed Interview, 3–35, CUOHP; and Stanley Reed Papers, Boxes 282 and 370, UK.

52. Cummings Diaries, UV.
53. Henry Morgenthau Diaries, vol. 69, p. 308, RPL; and G. Kanin, "Trips to Felix," *Atlantic Monthly* 55, 60 (1964).
54. Interview Session, Justice Felix Frankfurter and Gerald Gunther, Frankfurter Papers, Box 201, HLS; and Cummings Diaries, UV.
55. Papers as President, PSF, Box 77, RPL.
56. Douglas Interview, at 2–15; MLPU. See also President Roosevelt's correspondence with Senator Schwellenbach, Papers as President, PSF, Box 186, RPL.
57. Cummings Diaries, UV.
58. Robert Jackson Interview, at 779, CUOHP; and Jackson Papers, LC.
59. On Hughes's appointment, compare M. Pusey, *Charles Evans Hughes*, vol. 2, at 651 (New York: Macmillan, 1951), with F. B. Wiener, "Justice Hughes' Appointment—The Cotton Story Re-examined," *Yearbook of the Supreme Court Historical Society* 78 (1981). Apart from the conjectures in the above article and book, there is also evidence that Justices Holmes and Brandeis conferred with President Hoover before his nomination of Hughes and may have indicated their preference for the appointment of Hughes rather than for the elevation of Justice Stone. Herbert Hoover Papers, Boxes 62 and 317, HI; Mitchell Papers, Box 7, MHL; WHCF, Boxes 22 and 191, HPL; Appointment Books and Telephone Logs, HPL; PPS, Box 370, HPL; Frankfurter Papers, Box 169, HLS; and Stone Papers, Box 13, LC.
60. Notes on "H. F. S. & C. J. ship," Frankfurter Papers, Box 172, HLS.
61. Jackson Interview, at 1086–87, CUOHP; and Jackson Papers, LC.
62. Fred Vinson Papers, Box 218, UK; Reed Papers, Box 325, UK; WHCF-PSF, Boxes 221 and 231, and OF, Box 212, TPL; Eban Ayers Papers, 1947 Diary in Box 26, TPL; and Jackson Papers, LC.
63. Letter, June 11, 1946, reprinted in *Off the Record: The Private Papers of Harry S. Truman*, ed. R. Ferrell (New York: Harper & Row, 1980), 90.
64. Clark Oral History Interview, at 16, UK.
65. William Rogers Oral History Interview, UK.
66. Douglas Interview, at 265–66, MLPU.
67. There is no doubt that Nixon and Knowland found the appointment fortunate. See letter from Senator Knowland to the President, September 25, 1953 (the letter arrived at the White House after the appointment of Warren was announced), WHCF-OF, Box 371, EPL.
68. Herbert Brownell Oral History Interview, at 6–11, EPL; Herbert Brownell Interview, at 60–65, BLUC; and DDE Diary, Box 4, EPL.
69. October 8, 1953, DDE Diary, Box 4; and letter to Edgar Eisenhower, WHCF-NS, Box 11, EPL.
70. Bernard Shanley Papers, Box 1, EPL.
71. Letter, WHCF-NS, Box 11, EPL.
72. Nixon, supra note 46, at 419–20.
73. Memorandum for H. R. Haldeman (March 25, 1969), WHCF-FG 50, Box 1; and Memorandum for the President (May 6, 1969), WHCF-EXFG 51, Box 1, Nixon Presidential Materials, NACP.
74. Letter to the President (May 8, 1969), Nixon Presidential Materials, WHCF-EXFG 51, Box 1, NACP.
75. For further discussion, see D. M. O'Brien, "Federal Judgeships in Retrospect," in *The Reagan Presidency*, eds. W. Elliot Brownlee and Hugh Davis Graham (Lawrence: University Press of Kansas, 2003), 327–54.

76. Quoted and discussed by D. M. O'Brien, *Judicial Roulette* (New York: Twentieth Century Fund, 1988).
77. "Reagan-Bush Committee News Release," in Fred F. Fielding Files, CFOA 941942, RRPL. See also "Judicial Selection Criteria" (June 18, 1981), in Fielding Files, CFOA 941942, RRPL; and Memorandum from Max Friedersdorf (July 6, 1981), in Fielding Files, CFOA 941942, RRPL.
78. Memorandum, in Peter Wallison Files, OA 14286, RRPL.
79. "Proposed Nominees," in Arthur (A.B.) Culvahouse Files, OA 15065, RRPL. See also Edwin Meese III Files, OA 2408, RRPL; and Alan Raul Papers, OA 19157 Series III B, RRPL.
80. For a listing of solo dissenters from 1953 to 1991, see L. Epstein, J. Segal, H. Spaeth, and T. Walker, *The Supreme Court Compendium: Data, Decisions, & Developments*, 2nd ed. (Washington, D.C.: CQ Press, 2001), 502.
81. Statement from Justice Powell, Thurgood Marshall Papers, Box 406, LC.
82. For further discussion, see O'Brien, "Epilogue: The Bork Controversy," *Judicial Roulette*, loc. cit., at 99.
83. See Culvahouse Files, OA 15065, RRPL.
84. Press Conference by the President (July 1, 1991), Thomas, OA/ID CF 00153, John Sununu, Subject File, White House Chief of Staff, Bush Presidential Records, HWBPL.
85. "Bill Clinton Reveals for the First Time that Former New York Governor Mario Cuomo Rejected Supreme Court Nomination," *New York Daily News*, June 6, 2012.
86. White House, office of Press Secretary, "Background Briefing by Senior Administrative Officials," June 14, 1993, CPL.
87. Memos to White House Counsel Bernard Nussbaum on Judge Ginsburg's Opinions, Legal Scholarship, and Views on Selected Areas, Folder Ruth Bader Ginsburg, OA/Box No. 6066; and Breyer Confirmation Memoranda, Counsel's Office, OA/Box No. 4774, CPL.
88. See Stephen Breyer, *Active Liberty: Interpreting Our Democratic Constitution* (New York: Knopf, 2005).
89. See Jo Becker and Barton Gelman, "The Cheney Vice Presidency: A Strong Push from Backstage," *Washington Post*, June 26, 2007, A10.
90. Roberts Confirmation Hearings (September 12 and 13, 2005), available at http://www.washingtonpost.com/wp-dyn/content/article/2005/09/13/Ar2005091300876.html. AR2005091301469.html. AR2005091300693.html. AR2005091301981.html.
91. See William Blake, "Umpires as Legal Realists," *PS: Political Science and Politics* 271 (2012).
92. *Obergefell v. Hodges,* 135 S. Ct. 2584 (2015).
93. For further discussion see Jan Crawford Greenburg, *Supreme Conflict: The Inside Story of the Struggle for Control of the United States Supreme Court* (New York: Penguin, 2007).
94. Interview, "Supreme Court Week," C-SPAN, October 4, 2009.
95. See Lori A. Ringhand and Paul M. Collins Jr., "Neil Gorsuch and the Ginsburg Rules," 93 *Chicago-Kent Law Review* 475 (2018), and more generally, their book *Supreme Court Confirmation Hearings and Constitutional Change* (New York: Cambridge University Press, 2013).
96. Brett Kavanaugh, "I Am an Independent, Impartial Judge," *Wall Street Journal*, October 4, 2018.
97. Quoted in Adam Liptak, "Early Fan of Nominee Changes His Opinion," *New York Times*, October 4, 2018, A19.

98. H. J. Abraham, *Justices, Presidents and Senators*, 5th ed. (Lanham, Md.: Rowman & Littlefield, 2008).

99. M. Miller, *Plain Speaking: An Oral Biography of Harry S. Truman* (New York: Berkley, 1973), 225–26.

100. Letter, July 9, 1952, WHCF-PSF, Box 118, TPL.

101. Handwritten note by the President, PPF, Box 6, TPL.

102. *McGrath v. Kristensen,* 340 U.S. 162, 172 (1950) (Jackson, J., con. op., quoting Baron Bramwell).

103. Quoted in Abraham, supra note 100, at 72.

104. Clark Oral History Interview, at 212–13, TPL.

105. Kennedy Interview, KPL.

106. *National Federation of Independent Business v. Sebelius,* 132 S. Ct. 2566 (2012), and *King v. Burwell,* 135 S. Ct. 2480 (2015).

107. W. Rehnquist, "Presidential Appointments to the Supreme Court" (Lecture, University of Minnesota, October 8, 1984), appearing in 2 *Constitutional Commentary* 319 (1985).

108. See L. Tribe, *God Save This Honorable Court* (New York: Random House, 1985), chap. 2.

109. Jackson Interview, at 1104, CUOHP; "The Black Controversy," Jackson Papers, LC; and Sidney Fine Interview with William Douglas, at 8, BHLUM.

110. Letter, February 2, 1955, Frankfurter Papers, Box 1, HLS.

111. J. Lash, ed., *From the Diaries of Felix Frankfurter* (New York: W. W. Norton, 1974), 155.

112. This is based on the definitive study of extrajudicial activities by William Cibes, "Extra-Judicial Activities of Justices of the United States Supreme Court, 1790–1960" (Ph.D. diss., Princeton University, 1975) and the author's own study of papers of the justices and other presidential papers.

113. For a further discussion of off-the-bench commentaries, see A. Westin, "Out of Court Commentary by United States Supreme Court Justices, 1790–1962: Of Free Speech and Judicial Lockjaw," 62 *Columbia Law Review* 633 (1962); and "Introduction" in D. M. O'Brien, ed., *Judges on Judging* (Washington, D.C.: Congressional Quarterly*,* 5th ed., 2016).

114. Memorandum to Conference (June 12, 1991), in Blackmun Papers, Box 1407, LC.

115. Letter, August 8, 1793, reprinted in *The Correspondence and Public Papers of John Jay,* e.d. H. P. Johnston (New York: Putnam's, 1890), 488–89. For other correspondence see John Jay Papers, CU.

116. A. T. Mason, *William Howard Taft: Chief Justice* (New York: Simon & Schuster, 1965).

117. Cummings Diaries, UV; Memorandum, March 1, 1943, PSF, Box 76, RPL.

118. Newton Minow Oral History Interview, at 14, UK; Vinson Papers, Box 229, UK; Ayers Papers, Box 26, TPL.

119. Notes of telephone conversations, June 19, 1957, John Foster Dulles Papers, Box 12; and Papers as President-Ann Whitman Diary Series, EPL.

120. J. Ehrlichman, *Witness to Power: The Nixon Years* (New York: Simon & Schuster, 1982), 132–33.

121. See Nixon Presidential Materials, WHSF-PPF, Box 6; and WHCF-EXFG 51, Box 1, NACP.

122. E. Warren, *The Memoirs of Chief Justice Earl Warren* (New York: Doubleday, 1977), 339.

123. Warren, *Memoirs*, at 339; and Justice Brennan's memo on the Landau interview, Earl Warren Papers, Box 348, LC.

124. Senate Committee on the Judiciary, *Hearings on the Nomination of Abe Fortas of Tennessee to the Chief Justice of the United States*, 90th Cong., 2d sess., at 1303 (September 13, 1968) (Washington, D.C.: GPO, 1968).

125. A. Lief, *Brandeis: The Personal History of an American Ideal* (Harrisburg, Pa.: Telegraph Press, 1936), 409.

126. See B. Murphy, *The Brandeis/Frankfurter Connection* (New York: Oxford University Press, 1982).

127. Based on author's interviews with the former solicitor general and dean of Harvard Law School Erwin Griswold (November 15, 1983) and the Washington lawyer-lobbyist Thomas ("Tommy the Cork") Corcoran (November 20, 1982).

128. Note to President, October 26, 1938, PPF, Box 4877, RPL.

129. Justice Murphy's notes on his meetings with President Roosevelt during 1940–43 are in Eugene Gressman Papers, BHLUM; and Justice Byrnes's memoranda to the president and other White House advisers are in James F. Brynes Papers, Box 1229, CLE. See also Alpha Files, Boxes 607, 4877, and 6389, and PSF, Box 186, RPL.

130. WHCF-PSF, Boxes 118 and 284; PPF, Box 504, TPL. Robert Kennedy Interview and Robert Kennedy Papers, Box 16, KPL. WHCF-NS, Letter of March 22, 1966; White House-Famous Names, Letter of February 25, 1964; WHCF-FG, 535 and 505/9, JPL.

131. Goldberg attended fewer than half of the Cabinet meetings held during his first two-and-one-half years as ambassador to the United Nations. Memoranda and other materials in WHCF-Official Files of the President, Goldberg File, JPL.

132. Memo from Jim Jones to the President, November 2, 1967, White House Notes File; Meetings Notes File, November 2, 1967; March 20 and 27, 1968, Meetings Notes Files, JPL.

133. Diary Backup, Boxes 43, 60, 63, and 66, JPL.

134. Thruston Morton Oral History Interview, at 22, JPL.

135. WHCF, Fortas/Thornberry Series, Box 1, JPL; Diary Backup, Box 45, WHCF-Name File (Douglas); and Macy Papers (Fortas File), JPL.

136. Memorandum to Temple, WHCF, Fortas/Thornberry Series, Chron. File, JPL; and Letter, September 9, 1968, Warren Christopher Papers, Box 18, JPL.

137. Clark Clifford Oral History Interview, Tape 4, at 29; Paul Porter Interview, at 28–34; Macy Oral History Interview, at 726; and Larry Temple Oral History Interview, JPL.

138. Letter, July 25, 1968, Warren Papers, Box 352, LC.

139. Letter, July 24, 1968, John M. Harlan Papers, Box 531, MLPU.

140. Letter, May 14, 1969, Harlan Papers, Box 606, MLPU; and Warren Papers (Statement of Wolfson), Box 353, LC.

141. *Liljeberg v. Health Services Acquisition Corporation*, 486 U.S. 847 (1988). See also, generally, Robert Hume, *Ethics and Accountability on the U.S. Supreme Court: An Analysis of Recusal Practices* (Albany, N.Y.: SUNY Press, 2017).

142. See, generally, David M. O'Brien, ed., *Judges on Judging: Views from the Bench* 5th ed. (Washington, D.C.: C.Q. Press, 2016).

143. See Richard A. Posner, "The Supreme Court and Celebrity Culture," 88 *Chicago-Kent Law Review* 299 (2013); Christopher W. Schmidt, "Beyond the Opinion: Supreme Court Justices and Extrajudicial Speech," 88 *Chicago-Kent Law Review* 487 (2013); and Richard L. Hasen, "Celebrity Justice: Supreme Court Edition" (May 20, 2015), UC Irvine School of Law Research Paper No. 2015–61, available at SSRN http//ssrn.com/abstract=2611729.

144. See William H. Rehnquist, *Centennial Crisis* (New York: Knopf, 2004).
145. Letters in Willis Van Devanter Papers, Box 35, LC; and Stone Papers, LC.
146. Correspondence in PPF, File 1662, and PSF, Box 186, RPL; and Frankfurter Papers, Box 170, File 12, HLS.
147. Letter to Truman, February 13, 1946, Harold Burton Papers, Box 49, LC.
148. Address, Fordham-Stein Award Dinner (October 25, 1978).
149. Letters to and from the Justices, SC Papers, NARS.
150. Quoted in C. Fairman, *Mr. Justice Miller and the Supreme Court* (Cambridge, Mass.: Harvard University Press, 1939), 404.
151. Quoted in Mason, supra note 118, at 271.
152. See correspondence in William Day Papers, Box 29; Van Devanter Papers, Boxes 32, 33, 34, and 35, LC; and further discussion in Chapter 3.
153. Letters of April 8, 1937 (to and from Frankfurter and Stone), Frankfurter Papers, Box 171, HLS; and Letter, December 21, 1939, Stone Papers, Box 13, LC; and Charles Evans Hughes Papers, LC.
154. See, generally, P. Fish, *The Politics of Federal Judicial Administration* (Princeton, N.J.: Princeton University Press, 1973).
155. R. Hartmann, *Palace Politics* (New York: McGraw-Hill, 1980), 60. For a somewhat different view, see G. Ford, *A Time to Heal* (New York: Harper & Row, 1979), 90.
156. News Release, December 16, 1970, by Congressman Ford, Robert Hartmann Papers, Box 17, FPL. Also, Letter to Congressman Celler, Chairman of the Committee on the Judiciary, July 29, 1970, Hartmann Papers, Box 12, FPL.
157. Ford, in *Congressional Record*, 91st Cong., 2d sess. at 11912, 11913 (April 15, 1970).

THREE

Life in the Marble Temple

1. Undated letters to Elizabeth Woodbury, Levi Woodbury Papers, Box 7, LC.
2. B. Cardozo, *The Nature of the Judicial Process* (New Haven, Conn.: Yale University Press, 1921), 168.
3. Quoted by C. Warren, *The Supreme Court in United States History* (Boston: Little, Brown, 1922), 1:48.
4. C. Fairman, *Reconstruction and Reunion, 1864–1888* (New York: Macmillan, 1975), 69, no. 138.
5. *American State Papers, Misc.* I, no. 32.
6. Letter to Rufus King, December 19, 1793, in C. R. King, ed., *The Life and Correspondence of Rufus King* (New York: Putnam's, 1894), 126.
7. Quoted by G. Hazelton, *The National Capitol* (New York: Taylor, 1911), 141.
8. C. Swisher, *History of the Supreme Court of the United States: The Taney Period, 1836–64* (New York: Macmillan, 1974).
9. This was particularly true of Justice Joseph Story, who taught at Harvard and served as president of two banks and as a consultant to a number of firms and other organizations. See G. Dunne, *Justice Joseph Story and the Rise of the Supreme Court* (New York: Simon & Schuster, 1970), 121–23, 66–68 (on Justice John McKinley's frequent absence from Court sessions and his private legal practice).

10. The requirement of circuit riding was finally abolished by the Circuit Court of Appeals Act of March 3, 1891, Ch. 517, 26 Stat. 826. In 1793 Congress had provided a rotation system to cut back on the circuit riding of the justices, and in 1801 it eliminated the duties, only to reinstate the practice in 1802. Congress modified the requirements in 1803, 1837, and 1866. For discussions of the burdens of circuit riding, see S. J. Field, *Personal Reminiscences of Early Days in California* (New York: Da Capo, 1968); and J. Frank, *Justice Daniel Dissenting* (Cambridge, Mass.: Harvard University Press, 1964).

11. Quoted by Warren, supra note 3, 1:460–61.

12. See 5 Peters, preceding page 1, and 724 (Justice Baldwin dissenting) (1832); and 6 Wheaton v (1821), Henry Baldwin's papers, NARS. For a history of the rules governing briefs and records in the nineteenth century, see Morrison Waite Papers, Box 40 (Misc. File), LC.

13. See 44 Stat. 433 (1867), providing for the employment of messengers. The provision for hiring stenographic clerks for the justices is in 24 Stat. 254 (1886).

14. A. Beveridge, *The Life of John Marshall* (Boston: Houghton Mifflin, 1919), 4:90.

15. Letter from Marshall to Story, July 13, 1821, reprinted in 14 *Proceedings of the Massachusetts Historical Society,* 2d ser. 328 (1900–1901). See also Letter from Justice Story to Chief Justice Marshall, June 26, 1831, John Marshall Papers, CWM (original in Joseph Story Papers, Massachusetts Historical Society).

16. See Letters from Marshall to Story, May 3, July 26, October 12, and November 19, 1831, reprinted in J. Oster, *The Political and Economic Doctrines of John Marshall* 132–39 (New York: Neale, 1914). See also G. Haskins and H. Johnson, *Foundations of Power: John Marshall, 1801–1815* (New York: Macmillan, 1981), 382–89 and Table I at 652.

17. *Philadelphia Union,* April 24, 1819, quoted by D. Morgan, *Justice William Johnson: The First Dissenter* (Columbia: University of South Carolina Press, 1954), 173.

18. Letter to Jefferson, December 10, 1822, Thomas Jefferson Papers MS, LC, quoted by D. Morgan, "Mr. Justice William Johnson and the Constitution," 57 *Harvard Law Review* 328, 222–24 (1944).

19. Undated letter, John McLean Papers, Box 18, LC.

20. Justices Daniel, Campbell, and Curtis strongly objected to Chief Justice Taney's refusal to let the clerk give copies of his opinion in *Dred Scott* to other members of the Court. See Letters from Justices Daniel and Campbell, March 10 and 18, 1857, Office of the Clerk of the Supreme Court, NARS. Justice Curtis's lengthy correspondence on this matter is also reprinted in G. Curtis, ed., *Life and Writings of Benjamin Robbins Curtis,* 2 vols. (Boston: Little, Brown, 1879).

21. C. Fairman, *Mr. Justice Miller and the Supreme Court, 1862–1890* (New York: Russell & Russell, 1939), 279.

22. Fairman, *Mr. Justice Miller,* 121. See also Fairman, supra note 4, at 67–69; and Horace Gray Papers, Box 2; John M. Harlan (the first) Papers; and Rufus Peckham Papers, LC.

23. W. King, *Melville Weston Fuller: Chief Justice of the United States, 1888–1910* (New York: Macmillan, 1950), 191–92.

24. I am indebted to Erwin N. Griswold for this and other items of history of the Court.

25. "Recollections of Justice Holmes," Arthur Sutherland Papers, HLS.

26. D. Acheson, *Morning and Noon* (Boston: Houghton Mifflin, 1965), 41.

27. See, e.g., Memorandum by Howard Westwood, Harlan F. Stone Papers, Box 48, LC. For a fascinating account of Justice McReynolds, see J. Knox, "Experiences as Law Clerk to Mr. Justice James C. McReynolds of the Supreme Court of the United States"; James McReynolds Papers, UV; and D. Hutchinson and D. Garrow, eds., *The Forgotten Memoir of John Knox* (Chicago: University of Chicago Press, 2002).

28. F. Frankfurter, "Chief Justices I Have Known," reprinted in P. Kurland, ed., *Felix Frankfurter in the Supreme Court* (Chicago: Chicago University Press, 1970), 491.

29. Quoted by C. Wyzanski Jr., *Whereas—A Judge's Premises* (Boston: Little, Brown, 1944), 61.

30. See, e.g., Letters from Chief Justice Taft to Joseph Guerin, December 21, 1922, and to Justice Stone, May 28, 1925, William Howard Taft Papers, LC. See also H. F. Pringle, *The Life and Times of William Howard Taft*, vol. 2 at 1075–80 (New York: Farrar and Rinehart, 1939); and A. T. Mason, *William Howard Taft: Chief Justice* (New York: Simon & Schuster, 1965).

31. Letter from Chief Justice Fuller to Representative Joseph Cannon, December 21, 1896, Melville Fuller Papers, Box 4, LC. See also Letter of February 1, 1928, reprinted in *Congressional Record* 3285–86 (April 14, 1892). Several times around the turn of the century Congress had considered but failed to pass legislation for the construction of a building for the Court, Records of the Marshal's Office, NARS.

32. See Letter to Senator Reed Smoot, president of the Building Commission, June 8, 1926, signed by the chief justice and by Justices Van Devanter, Butler, Sanford, and Stone, Stone Papers, Box 81, LC.

33. Quoted in Drew Pearson, *The Nine Old Men* 15 (New York: Doubleday, 1936).

34. See Letter from Librarian, October 12, 1947, Stone Papers, Box 83, LC.

35. W. H. Taft, "The Jurisdiction of the Supreme Court under the Act of February 25, 1925," 35 *Yale Law Journal* 1, 2 (1925).

36. For a good discussion of nineteenth-century breaches of secrecy, see Fairman, supra note 4, at 121–37, 170–71, 231, and 268; Warren, supra note 3, II: 185–93 and 294–97.

37. See Memoranda to the Chief Justice, January 6, 1944, and May 21, 1945, William O. Douglas Papers, Box 228, LC; and Memorandum from Justice Douglas, January 5, 1944, Stone Papers, Box 74, LC. But see also A. Charns, *Cloak and Gavel: FBI Wiretaps, Bugs, Informers, and the Supreme Court* (Urbana: University of Illinois Press, 1992), which provides further evidence of Justice Fortas's indiscretions in discussing pending cases with members of the executive branch. See also William Domnarski, *The Great Justices, 1946–1954* (Ann Arbor: University of Michigan Press, 2009), 154–56; and David M. O'Brien, *Judges on Judging* 5th ed. (Washington, D.C.: CQ Press, 2017).

38. *Lindsley v. Natural Carbonic Gas Co.*, 220 U.S. 61 (1911); and *United States v. Southern Pacific Railroad*, 251 U.S. 1 (1919). See also John B. Owens, "The Clerk, The Thief, His Life as a Baker: Ashton Embry and the Supreme Court Leak Scandal of 1919," 95 *Northwestern University Law Review* 271 (2000).

39. Memo (December 7, 1955), Justice Frankfurter Papers, Box 177, File 1, HLS. Indeed, in the 1950s, following the school desegregation ruling in *Brown v. Board of Education* (1954), former clerks and the press created a controversy over the influence of law clerks in the Court's decision making. See "The Bright Young Men Behind the Bench," *U.S. News & World Report* 45 (July 17, 1957); William H. Rehnquist, "Who Writes Decisions of the Supreme Court," *U.S. News & World Report* 74 (December 13, 1957); William Rogers, "Clerks' Work Is 'Not Decisive of

Ultimate Result,'" *U.S. News & World Report* 114 (February 21, 1958); William H. Rehnquist, "Another View: Clerks Might 'Influence' Some Actions," *U.S. News & World Report* 116 (February 21, 1958); and Alexander Bickel, "The Supreme Court: An Indictment Analyzed," *New York Times Magazine* 16 (April 27, 1958).

40. Justice Blackmun's papers in the Library of Congress contain numerous email communications to and from clerks and the justice, for example. Justice Harry Blackmun Papers, LC. See also Aaron Nielson (a former law clerk), "D.C. Circuit Review: Breyer, Alito, and their Pals," *Notice & Comment* Blog (March 25, 2017).

41. See notes on proposed draft of "Code of Conduct for Supreme Court Law Clerks," Marshall Papers, Box 570, LC; see also Box 452, LC. See also, Byron White Papers, Memorandum for Conferences (November 16, 1988), Box 102, LC.

42. Justice Alito interview with Bill Kristol on SCOTUSBLOG.com/media/interview-with-justice-samuel-alito (accessed July 27, 2015).

43. Edward Lazarus, *Closed Chambers: The First Eyewitness Account of the Epic Struggles Inside the Supreme Court* (New York: Time Books, 1998).

44. See, e.g., Ted Cruz, *A Time for Truth: Reigniting the Promise of America* (New York: Broadside Books, 2015), at 68–96.

45. Bob Woodward and Scott Armstrong, *The Brethren: Inside the Supreme Court* (New York: Simon & Schuster, 1979).

46. See Scott Armstrong, "Supreme Court Clerks as Judicial Actors and as Sources," 98 *Marquette Law Review* 387 (2014).

47. See "Playboy Interview: Bob Woodward," 36 *Playboy* 51 (February, 1989); Stephen R. McAllister, "Justice Byron White and the Brethren," 15 *Green Bag* 2nd 159 (2012); and David J. Garrow, "The Supreme Court and The Brethren," 18 *Constitutional Commentary* 303 (2001).

48. *Bush v. Gore,* 531 U.S. 98 (2000); and see David Margolick, Evgenia Peretz, and Michael Shanyerson, "The Path to Florida," 530 *Vanity Fair* 310 (October 1, 2004).

49. See Jan Crawford, *Face the Nation* (CBS News television broadcast, July 1, 2012), available at http://www.cbsnews.com/8301-3460_162-57464549/robertsswitched-views-to-uphold-health-care-law/. See also Sam Baker, "Supreme Court Healthcare Ruling Leaks Have DC Buzzing: Who Is the Culprit?" *The Hill* (July 4, 2012), http://thehill.com/policy/healthcare/236197-supreme-court-talk-has-dc-buzzing-who-is-the-leaker; Todd C. Peppers, "Of Leakers and Legal Briefers: The Modern Supreme Court Law Clerk," 7 *Charleston Law Review* 95 (2012–2013); and Katharine Traylor Schaffzin, "The Great and Powerful Oz Revealed: The Ethics and Wisdom of the SCOTUS Leaks in *National Federation of Independent Business v. Sebelius*," 7 *Charlestown Law Review* 317 (2012–2013).

50. *National Association of Independent Business v. Sebelius,* 132 S. Ct. 2566 (2012).

51. Memorandum for Conference, December 9, 1990, Marshall Papers, Box 524, LC. See "History of Restrictions to Access to Supreme Court Audiotapes of Oral Arguments" in Oral Arguments Files, Harry Blackmun Papers, Box 1426, LC.

52. *New York Times Co. v. United States,* 403 U.S. 670 (1971).

53. See correspondence of the justices, Marshall Papers, Boxes 379 and 435, LC.

54. Letter from Chief Justice Rehnquist, October 27, 1989, Marshall Papers, LC.

55. See Jacob Gershman, "American Bar Association Wants Cameras Inside Supreme Court," *Wall Street Journal,* February 9, 2016.

56. Quoted in "Justice Breyer on the High Court's New Blood," *Washington Post,* March 9, 2006, A17.

57. *Citizens United v. Federal Election Commission,* 558 U.S. 310 (2010).

58. Mark Walsh, "In Wake of Secret Videos, Security Tweaks Evident as the Court," SCOTUSblog (March 3, 2014), http://www.scotusblog.com/2014/03/in-wake-of -secret-videos-security-tweaks-evident-at-the-court/.

59. See Ryan Black, Timothy Johnson, and Ryan Owen, "Chief Justice Burger and the Bench," 43 *Journal of Supreme Court History* 83–98 (2018).

60. See, e.g., Memorandum to Justice Douglas from the Marshal on his appointment to the Court, Douglas Papers, Box 229, LC. See also Thomas Snow, "Supreme Court Messenger, 1977 Term," 39 *Journal of Supreme Court History* 246 (2014); and Matthew Hofstedt, "Afterword: A Brief History of Supreme Court Messengers," 39 *Journal of Supreme Court History* 259 (2014).

61. Much of this and the subsequent discussion about the bureaucratization of the Court draws on conversations with Mark Cannon, Administrative Assistant to the Chief Justice (1972–1987).

62. Waite Papers, undated note and record of vote, Box 40, LC.

63. See, e.g., Douglas Papers, Box 218, LC. (Memo from Justice Rehnquist concerning the posting of opinions to be announced because "he goofed in failing to announce Bill Douglas' dissenting opinion.")

64. See Memoranda in Marshall Papers, Boxes 435, 452, and 493, LC.

65. Felix Frankfurter Papers, Box 108, File 2267, LC; Frankfurter's letter and Jackson's proposed dissent are also in Frankfurter Papers, Box 170, HLS.

66. E. Warren, "A Conversation with Earl Warren," WGBH-TV Educational Foundation, transcript (Boston: WGBH Educational Foundation, 1972).

67. Based on figures in House Committee on Appropriations, *The Judiciary Appropriations for 1952: Hearings before the Subcommittee,* 82d Cong., 1st sess., at 2 (Washington, D.C.: GPO, 1951); and House Committee on Appropriations, *Departments of Commerce, Justice, and State, the Judiciary, and Related Agencies Appropriations for 1984: Hearings before a Subcommittee,* 98th Cong., 1st sess., at 297 (Washington, D.C.: GPO, 1983).

68. Robert H. Jackson, *The Supreme Court in the American System of Government* (Cambridge: Harvard University Press, 1955; reprint New York: Harper Torchbooks, 1961), at 16.

69. J. M. Harlan , "A Glimpse of the Supreme Court at Work," 11 *University of Chicago Law School Record* 1, 1 (1963).

70. L. Powell, "What the Justices Are Saying . . . ," *American Bar Association Journal* 1454, 1454 (1976).

71. William J. Brennan Jr. Dean's Day Address, New York University Law School (1979), as quoted in Artemus Ward and David Weiden, *Sorcerers' Apprentices, 100 Years of Law Clerks at the United States Supreme Court* (New York: New York University Press, 2006), at 202.

72. H. Blackmun, "A Justice Speaks Out: A Conversation with Harry Blackmun," Cable News Network, transcript, at 4 (December 4, 1982).

73. See prepared statements of Justices White and Blackmun, in House Committee on Appropriations, *Departments . . . : Hearings before a Subcommittee,* 94th Cong., 2d sess., at 26 (Washington, D.C.: GPO, 1976); and Statement of Justice Powell, in House Committee on Appropriations, *Departments . . . : Hearings before a Subcommittee,* 95th Cong., 2d sess., at 181 (Washington, D.C.: GPO, 1978).

74. See, e.g., William J. Brennan Papers, Box 336, LC. In 1972, Justice Rehnquist requested, and the other justices agreed, to send all draft opinions and "join letters" in duplicate. See Brennan Papers, Box 279, LC.

75. Memorandum from Clerk, September 26, 1990, Marshall Papers, Box 523, LC.

76. Quotations from Michelle R. Smith, "Kagan: Justices Not Tech Savvy, Send Paper Memos," *Associated Press* (August 20, 2013); Nicole Mulvaney, "Justice Kagan Talks Equality, Justice with Princeton President," *Times of Trenton* (November 20, 2014); and Adam Laptak, "Justices Return to School and Speak of Lessons Learned," *New York Times* A17 (October 26, 2014).

77. W. Rehnquist, "Are the Old Times Dead?" (Mac Swinford Lecture, University of Kentucky, September 23, 1983) (copy on file with the author).

78. For two excellent studies of law clerks, see Todd Peppers, *Courtiers of the Marble Palace: The Rise and Influence of the Supreme Court Law Clerk* (Stanford, Calif.: Stanford University Press, 2006); and Ward and Weiden, *Sorcerers' Apprentices*.

79. See Artemus Ward, Christina Dwyer, and Kiranjit Gill, "Bonus Babies Escape Golden Handcuffs: How Money and Politics Has Transformed the Career Paths of Supreme Court Law Clerks," 98 *Marquette Law Review* 227 (2014).

80. See, e.g., Todd Peppers, "The Birth of an Institution: Horace Gray and the Lost Law Clerks," 32 *Journal of Supreme Court History* 229–48 (2007).

81. See Lawrence Baum, "Hiring Supreme Court Law Clerks: Probing the Ideological Linkage Between Judges and Justices," 98 *Marquette Law Review* 333 (2014).

82. See Tony Mauro, "SCOTUS Law Clerks: The Diversity Picture," *National Law Journal* (Dec. 11, 2017); Aaron Nielson, "D.C. Circuit Review—Reviewed: 'All-Purpose' Feeder Judges," *Notice and Comment* Blog (August 31, 2018); and Lawrence Baum and Corey Ditslear, "Supreme Court Clerkships and 'Feeder' Judges," 31 *The Justice System Journal* 26 (2010).

83. Letter of January 21, 1974, Stone Papers, Box 48, LC.

84. Memo to Clerks from Justice Burton, Harlan Papers, Box 561, MLPU.

85. Benno Schmidt Interview, at 8, CUOHP.

86. D. Acheson, "Recollections of Service with the Federal Supreme Court," 18 *Alabama Lawyer* 335, 364 (1957).

87. Acheson, supra note 26, at 80.

88. Quoted by Jennifer Senior, "In Conversation: Antonin Scalia," *New York Magazine* (October 6, 2013), available at http://nymag.com/news/features/antonin-scalia-2013 -10 (accessed July 28, 2015).

89. See Roger Newman, *Hugo Black* (New York: Pantheon, 1994), 325–26; and John Frank, *Marble Palace* (New York: Knopf, 1958), 116–17.

90. See Todd Peppers and Christopher Zorn, "Law Clerk Influence on Supreme Court Decision Making: An Empirical Assessment," 58 *De Paul Law Review* 51 (2008).

91. See William Nelson, "Supreme Court Clerkships Polarization," 13 *Greenbag 2D* 59 (2009).

92. *United States v. Carolene Products Co.*, 304 U.S. 144, 152 n. 4 (1938). See Stone Papers, Box 67, LC. The note was initially drafted by Louis Lusky, who went on to be a Columbia law professor.

93. Stone Papers, Box 48, LC.

94. See Hugo Black Papers, Box 60, LC. *Baker v. Carr*, 369 U.S. 186 (1962).

95. William O. Douglas, *The Court Years* (New York: Random House, 1980), 173. See also John Sapieza Oral History Interview, UK; and William Oliver Oral History Interview, BLUC.

96. Christopher Eisgruber, *The Next Justice: Repairing the Supreme Court Appointments Process* (Princeton, N.J.: Princeton University Press, 2009), 59.

97. Quoted in Letter from Frankfurter to Reed, December 3, 1941, Stanley Reed Papers, Box 171, UK.

98. Arthur Rosett Oral History Interview, UK.

99. On Warren's practice, see Schmidt Interview, at 256, CUOHP; and Martin Richman Oral History Interview, at 4–5, BLUC. The discussion of Rehnquist's practice is based on his remarks at the Jefferson Literary Society and Debating Meeting, Charlottesville, Va., September 20, 1985, and interviews in *This Honorable Court* (PBS, 1988) and *Book Notes* (C-SPAN, October 25, 1998).

100. Chief Justice Roberts, Fourth Judicial Conference Talk (aired on C-SPAN, June 25, 2011); Justice Thomas, Wake Forest School of Law Conversation (on YouTube, March 9, 2012); and Alito Interview in Brian Lamb et al., eds., *The Supreme Court: A C-SPAN Book* (New York Public Affairs, 2010).

101. Quoted by Jennifer Senior, "In Conversation: Antonin Scalia," supra note 88; and Scalia Interview, in B. Lamb, *The Supreme Court*, supra note 100, at 57.

102. Arthur Rosett Interview, UK. See also Gordon Davidson Interview, UK.

103. Recalled in F. Alley Allen Interview, UK.

104. Quoted in B. Schwartz and S. Lesher, *Inside the Warren Court* (New York: Doubleday, 1983), 39. Chief Justice Warren's instructions to his clerks on the preparation of *cert.* memos in Ifp cases are outlined in Memorandums for the Law Clerks, at 5–7, Earl Warren Papers, Box 398, LC. See also Suggestions in the Matter of Being a Law Clerk, Robert Garner Papers, Box 1, TPL.

105. See Ward and Weiden, *Sorcerers' Apprentices*, supra note 71, at 142.

106. W. J. Brennan Jr., "The National Court of Appeals: Another Dissent," 40 *University of Chicago Law Review* 473 (1973).

107. J. P. Stevens, "Some Thoughts on Judicial Restraint," 66 *Judicature* 177, 179 (1982).

108. Memorandum for Conference, September 24, 1986, Marshall Papers, Box 379, LC.

109. Bench memos, it bears emphasizing, serve two purposes: first, preparing justices for oral argument; and, second, providing a preliminary outline of a justice's possible opinion, particularly when a justice plans to write an opinion in the case, because of either the subject matter or the anticipated vote on the merits at conference. Warren Papers, Box 398, LC. See also Timothy R. Johnson, David Stras, and Ryan Black, "Advice from the Bench (Memo): Clerk Influence on Supreme Court Oral Arguments," 98 *Marquette Law Review* 25 (2014).

110. Like other justices, Frankfurter normally worked from a memorandum written by one of his law clerks, whether drafting an opinion for the Court or a concurring or dissenting opinion. See Frankfurter Papers, Box 177, Law Clerks File, HLS. See also "Notes to Law Clerks," Tom C. Clark Papers, UT; Burton's instructions to his clerks and those of Harlan in the Harlan Papers, Boxes 561 and 583, MLPU; Vinson Papers, UK; and Warren Papers, Box 398, LC.

111. Douglas, supra note 95, at 175.

112. W. Rehnquist, "Remarks," Ninth Circuit Conference, Coronado, Calif., July 17, 1982, printed draft delivery copy, at 24 (copy on file with the author).

113. W. Rehnquist, "Who Writes Decisions of the Supreme Court?" *U.S. News & World Report*, December 13, 1957, 74.

114. Vinson Papers, Box 217, UK. Justice Rehnquist recalled that when he clerked, that was true for Justice Jackson as well; William Rehnquist Interview, November 16, 1984, SC.

115. Alexander Bickel, "Supreme Court Law Clerks" (draft of manuscript in response to Rehnquist's article), Frankfurter Papers, Box 215 (Bickel File), LC. For a different view of the practices of law clerks, see "Views of a Leading Lawyer who in his day was one of the most esteemed of Mr. Justice Brandeis' law clerks," Frankfurter Papers, Box 177, File 1, HLS.

116. Memo, Robert Jackson Papers, LC. For a further discussion, see R. Kluger, *Simple Justice* 606–9 (New York: Vintage, 1977).
117. See Ryan Black, Christina Boyd, and Amanda Bryan, "Revisiting the Influence of Law Clerks on the U.S. Supreme Court's Agenda-Setting Process," 98 *Marquette Law Review* 75 (2014); and David Stras, "The Supreme Court's Gatekeepers: The Role of Law Clerks in the *Certiorari* Process," 85 *Texas Law Review* 947 (2007).
118. See Ryan C. Black and Christina L. Boyd, "Selecting the Select Few: The Discuss List and the U.S. Supreme Court's Agenda Setting Process," 94 *Social Sciences Quarterly* 1124 (2013).
119. Timothy R. Johnson, David R. Stas, and Ryan C. Black, "Advice from the Bench (Memo): Clerk Influence on Supreme Court Oral Arguments," 98 *Marquette Law Review* 25 (2014).
120. Justice Blackmun's case files contain numerous memos from law clerks in the 1980s and 1990s reporting conversations with law clerks in other chambers. See Blackmun Papers, LC.
121. See, e.g., Edward Lazarus, *Closed Chambers* (New York: Times Books, 1998), written by a former Supreme Court clerk; and Kenneth Starr, "The Supreme Court and Its Shrinking Docket: The Ghost of William Howard Taft," 90 *Minnesota Law Review* 1363 (2006).
122. See, e.g., Memorandum to Conference on *United States v. Nixon*, Brennan Papers, Box 329, LC.
123. See, e.g., The Legal Office End-of-Term Report, Blackmun Papers, Box 1423, LC.
124. Memorandum, February 27, 1975, Brennan Papers, Box 336, LC.
125. Memorandum to Justice Marshall, August 9, 1990, Marshall Papers, Box 494, LC. See also Memorandum to Justice Marshall, July 22, 1987, Marshall Papers, Box 406, LC.
126. Letter to author from Mary Ann Willis, Counsel of Legal Office (October, 9, 1998).
127. See Memorandum to the Court from Chief Justice Taft, February 12, 1928, Willis Van Devanter Papers, Box 35, LC; Memorandum Respecting the Compensation of the Clerk, Douglas Papers, Box 229, LC; and "Historical Note to the Clerk's Office Personnel," Frankfurter Papers, Box 182, File 11, HLS.
128. Jay to Fisher Ames, November 27, 1789, reprinted in *The Correspondence and Public Papers of John Jay*, ed. H. Johnston (New York: Franklin, 1970), 3: 379. For similar incidents, see correspondence—especially from Justices Duval, Taney, and Wayne—in Records of the Clerk of the Supreme Court, NARS.
129. Justice Grier's correspondence, as well as that of Justice Curtis, may be found in the Records of the Clerk of the Supreme Court, Letters to and from the Justices, NARS. See also Benjamin Curtis Papers, LC.
130. For further discussion of this history of the Office of the Reporter, see Letter from John Marshall to Dudley Chase, February 7, 1817, reprinted in Oster, supra note 16, at 80–83; and, generally, Sharon Hamby O'Connor and Morris L. Cohen, *A Guide to the Early Reporters of the Supreme Court of the United States* (New York: Fred B. Rodham & Co., 1995).
131. See, e.g., Harold Burton Papers, Box 96, LC.
132. *Wheaton v. Peters*, 8 Pet. (33 U.S.) 591 (1834).
133. Quoted in Swisher, supra note 8, at 50.
134. This story is detailed in Frank, supra note 10, at 170–72.
135. Because of controversies surrounding the writing of headnotes, the justices voted on what the reporter should and should not include in his headnotes. See Memo-

randum as to Reports, February 28, 1856, Records of the Office of the Marshal, NARS. The Court formally recognized that headnotes are not part of an opinion in *United States v. Detroit Lumber Co.*, 200 U.S. 321, 337 (1906). Note, however, that in this case the reporter thought it sufficiently important to note in a headnote that headnotes are prepared by the reporter and not considered binding by the Court. See also C. Butler, *A Century at the Bar of the Supreme Court of the United States* 80 (New York: Putnam's, 1942).

136. The first syllabus including a "lineup" was *North Carolina v. Alford*, 400 U.S. 25 (1970).

137. *Santa Clara County v. Southern Pacific Railroad Company*, 118 U.S. 398 (1886).

138. For a wonderful discussion of this event and its significance, see C. P. McGrath, *Morrison R. Waite: The Triumph of Character* (New York: Macmillan, 1963), at 224–25.

139. Quoted by C. Fairman, "What Makes a Great Justice? Mr. Justice Bradley and the Supreme Court," *Boston University Law Review* 49, 100 (1949/1950). For other illustrations of the problems of editing justices' opinions, see the interview with Henry Putzel, former reporter for the Court: "Double Revolving Peripatetic Nitpicker," *Supreme Court Historical Society Yearbook* 10 (1980).

140. See F. Barbash, "That Opinion Was Here Somewhere . . ." *Washington Post*, June 10, 1983, A5.

141. See Frank Wagner, "The Role of the Supreme Court Reporter in History," 26 *Journal of Supreme Court History* 9 (2001).

142. See Memorandum to the Conference, Re: *Jimenez v. Weinberger* (July 5, 1975), Brennan Papers, Box 363, LC. Occasionally, other close Court watchers, such as the solicitor general, will find errors in preliminary prints of opinions and suggest modifications before an opinion is published in the official *United States Reports*. See Sherman Minton Papers, Box 6, TPL.

143. See, e.g., *Barclay's Bank, Ltd. v. Franchise Tax Board of California*, 512 U.S. 298 (1994), where Justice Ginsburg inserted a bracketed statement clarifying the decision.

144. See Ryan Gabrielson, "It's A Fact: Supreme Court Errors Aren't Hard to Find," *ProPublica* (Oct. 17, 2017), at www.propublica.org/article/supreme-court-errors -are-not-hard-to-find.

145. Memorandum for Conference, April 22, 1986, Marshall Papers, Box 378, LC.

146. See Richard Lazarus, "The (Non)Finality of Supreme Court Opinions," 128 *Harvard Law Review* 1 (2015).

147. *Horne v. Department of Agriculture*, 135 S. Ct. 2419 (2015). SCOTUS Servo follows such corrections at https://twitter.com/scotus_servo.

148. Memorandum for Conference from Chief Justice Burger, in Brennan Papers, Box 640, LC.

149. Memorandum, November 3, 1983, in Brennan Papers, Box 640, LC. *Keeton v. Hustler Magazine, Inc.*, 465 U.S. 770 (1984).

150. *Citizens United v. Federal Election Commission*, 558 U.S. 310 (2010).

151. Letter to author from Shelley Dowling, Librarian of the Court (July 22, 1998) and Memorandum to the Conference, April 4, 1995, in Blackmun Papers, Box 1424, LC. See Ms. Dowling's essay on the library in L. Gasaway and M. Chiorazzi, eds., *Law Librarianship: Historical Perspectives* (Littleton: Rothman, 1996). The early history of the Supreme Court's library is set forth in a Memorandum by the Law Librarian of the Library of Congress, November 1, 1940, Frankfurter Papers, Box 182, File 19, HLS.

152. A partial listing of these responsibilities can be found as Appendix A in D. Meador, "The Federal Judiciary and Its Future Administration," 65 *Virginia Law Review* 1055–59 (1979). See also Warren Papers, Box 658, LC.
153. Quoted by A. Mason, *Harlan Fiske Stone: Pillar of the Law* (New York: Viking, 1956), 719. In the Stone Papers, LC, there are numerous other letters expressing his astonishment at the time-consuming administrative responsibilities of the chief justiceship.
154. Chief Justice Rehnquist Interview (November 13, 1998). For an overview of Chief Justice Rehnquist's administrative duties, see Russell R. Wheeler, "Chief Justice Rehnquist as Third Branch Leader," 89 *Judicature* 116 (November/December 2005).
155. Public Law 101–402, 110th Congress (October 13, 2008).
156. Toni House to the author (May 1998).
157. Data on filings and total docket for 1800–1913 were gathered by examining the Docket Books of the Supreme Court of the United States, NARS. Figures for the number of filings and docket for 1913–2001 are taken from *Annual Reports of the Office of the Clerk*, Supreme Court of the United States. Cases disposed of each term include both cases given plenary consideration and those summarily decided or otherwise disposed of. Figures for cases disposed of and carried over for the years 1800–1810, 1820, 1822–1846, 1850, 1860, 1870, 1880, and 1890 are based on the author's tabulation of cases contained in the Docket Books of the Supreme Court of the United States. Figures for 1890–1910 were taken from *Annual Reports of the Attorney General of the United States* (Washington, D.C.: GPO, 1891, 1901, 1911), David Brewer Papers, Box 13, YA. Data for 1913–2009 were taken from Statistical Sheet, Office of the Clerk, Supreme Court, and thereafter from the annual *Journal of the Supreme Court*. This section draws on the author's article, "The Supreme Court: A Co-equal Branch of Government," *Supreme Court Historical Society Yearbook* 90 (1984) and updates.
158. See F. Frankfurter and J. Landis, *The Business of the Supreme Court* (Cambridge, Mass.: Harvard University Press, 1927), 105–10.
159. See Letter of Chief Justice Taft to Justice Van Devanter, Van Devanter Papers, Box 34, LC.
160. See W. Taft, "The Jurisdiction of the Supreme Court under the Act of February 13, 1925," 35 *Yale Law Journal* (1925); letter to Senator Copeland, December 9, 1925, reprinted in *Congressional Record*, 68th Cong., 2d sess., 2916, 2920 (1925); and testimony of Chief Justice Taft and Justices Van Devanter, McReynolds, and Sutherland on the bill, in House Committee on the Judiciary, *Jurisdiction of Circuit Courts of Appeals and of the Supreme Court of the United States*, 68th Cong., 2d sess. House Report 8206, at 6–30 (Washington, D.C.: GPO, 1925). In a letter of March 9, 1925, to Mr. George Rose, Justice Van Devanter discusses the drafting of the bill by a committee of justices of the Supreme Court, Van Devanter Papers, Box 29, LC. Committees of justices drafted legislation altering the Court's jurisdiction earlier as well. See correspondence among Chief Justice White and Justices Van Devanter and Day in 1911 and 1914, William Day Papers, Boxes 27 and 29, LC.
161. Testimony of Justice White, in House Committee on Appropriations, *Departments . . . : Hearings before a Subcommittee*, 95th Cong., 1st sess., at 55 (Washington, D.C.: GPO, 1977).
162. Letter to Congressman Robert Kastenmeier, June 17, 1982, signed by all nine justices supporting the passage of H.R. 2406. Congress finally enacted legislation

eliminating most of the Court's remaining mandatory appellate jurisdiction in 1988. See Public Law 100–352.

163. See "Report of the Study Group on the Caseload of the Supreme Court," 57 *Federal Rules and Decisions* 573–650 (1973); and Commission on Revision of the Federal Court Appellate System, *Structure and Internal Procedures: Recommendations for Change* (Washington, D.C.: CRFCAS, 1975). See also D. M. O'Brien, "Managing the Business of the Supreme Court," 45 *Public Administration Review* 667–78 (1985).

164. John G. Roberts Jr., Memorandum for Fred F. Fielding on Creation of an Intercircuit Tribunal (April 19, 1983), WHORM, File FG 51, Box 10 (038900–379566), 13100–14999 Folder, RRPL. See also Roberts's letters to Judge Henry Friendly, in F05–139101, Box 29, Folder JGR/Intercircuit Tribunal, RRPL.

FOUR
Deciding What to Decide

1. *Gideon v. Wainwright*, 372 U.S. 335 (1963). See Anthony Lewis, *Gideon's Trumpet* (New York: Random House, 1964).
2. J. M. Harlan Jr., "A Glimpse of the Supreme Court at Work," 11 *University of Chicago Law School Record* 1, 4 (1963).
3. *Powell v. Alabama*, 287 U.S. 45 (1932).
4. *Johnson v. Zerbst*, 304 U.S. 458 (1938).
5. *Betts v. Brady*, 316 U.S. 455 (1942).
6. See also, e.g., *Holt v. Hobbs*, 135 S. Ct. 853 (2015) and *Hudson v. McMillian*, 503 U.S. 1 (1992). For an interesting story of one recent indigent's petition that was granted, see Shon Hopwood, *Law Man: My Story of Robbing Banks, Winning Supreme Court Cases, and Finding Redemption* (New York: Crown Books, 2012).
7. *Elk Grove Unified School District v. Newdow*, 542 U.S. 1 (2004).
8. *Snyder v. Phelps*, 443 U.S. (2011).
9. *Frank v. Gaos*, 586 U.S.__ (2019).
10. Testimony of Justice Rehnquist at appropriations hearings for the Supreme Court. House Committee on Appropriations, *Departments . . . : Hearings before a Subcommittee*, 96th Cong., 1st sess., at 21 (Washington, D.C.: GPO, 1980).
11. C. E. Hughes, *Addresses of Charles Evans Hughes* 185–86 (New York: Putnam's, 1916).
12. *United States v. Butler*, 297 U.S. 1 (1936).
13. *Flast v. Cohen*, 392 U.S. 83, 94–95 (1968).
14. See *Muskrat v. United States*, 219 U.S. 346, 362 (1911).
15. *Duke Power Co. v. Carolina Environmental Study Group*, 438 U.S. 59, 103 (1978) (con. op.). See also *Bellotti v. Baird*, 443 U.S. 622 (1979).
16. *Aetna Life Insurance Co. v. Haworth*, 300 U.S. 277 (1937).
17. *Immigration and Naturalization Service v. Chadha*, 462 U.S. 919 (1983).
18. *Data Processing Service v. Camp*, 397 U.S. 150, 151 (1970).
19. *Braxton County Court v. West Virginia*, 208 U.S. 192, 197 (1908); and *Coleman v. Miller*, 307 U.S. 433, 464 (1931) (Frankfurter, J., dis. op.).
20. *Frothingham v. Mellon*, 262 U.S. 447, 487–88 (1923).
21. *Flast v. Cohen*, 392 U.S. 83 (1968).
22. See *Laird v. Tatum*, 408 U.S. 1 (1972); and *Sierra Club v. Morton*, 405 U.S. 727 (1972).
23. *Sierra Club v. Morton*, 405 U.S. 727 (1972).

24. *United States v. SCRAP*, 412 U.S. 669 (1973).
25. *Paul v. Davis*, 424 U.S. 693 (1976).
26. *Valley Forge Christian College v. Americans United for Separation of Church and State*, 454 U.S. 464 (1982).
27. *Hein v. Freedom for Religion Foundation Inc.*, 551 U.S. 587 (2007).
28. *Lujan v. Defenders of Wildlife*, 504 U.S. 555 (1992).
29. *Elk Grove Unified School District v. Newdow*, 542 U.S. 1 (2004).
30. *Gill v. Whitford*, 585 U.S.__ (2018).
31. *Ex parte Baez*, 177 U.S. 378 (1900).
32. *Tileston v. Ullman*, 318 U.S. 44 (1943).
33. *Poe v. Ullman*, 367 U.S. 497 (1961).
34. *Griswold v. Connecticut*, 381 U.S. 479 (1965).
35. *Eisenstadt v. Balrd*, 405 U.S. 438 (1972).
36. *Defunis v. Odegarrd*, 416 U.S. 312 (1974).
37. *Regents of the University of California v. Bakke*, 438 U.S. 265 (1978).
38. *United States v. Microsoft*, 584 U.S.__ (2018).
39. *Luther v. Borden*, 7 How. [48 U.S.] 1 (1849).
40. See *Colegrove v. Green*, 328 U.S. 549 (1946).
41. *Baker v. Carr*, 369 U.S. 186 (1962).
42. J. Roche, "Judicial Self-Restraint," 49 *American Political Science Review* 762, 768 (1955).
43. L. Henkin, "Is There a 'Political Question' Doctrine?" 85 *Yale Law Journal* 597, 606 (1976).
44. *Burnet v. Coronado Oil*, 285 U.S. 393 (1932) (Brandeis, J., dis. op.).
45. W. O. Douglas, Interview, "CBS Reports," transcript, at 13 (New York: CBS News, September 6, 1972).
46. *Payne v. Tennessee*, 501 U.S. 808 (1991).
47. *Booth v. Maryland*, 482 U. S. 496 (1987); and *South Carolina v. Gathers*, 490 U.S. 805 (1989).
48. *CBOCS West, Inc. v. Humphries*, 128 S. Ct. 1951 (2008).
49. *Hein v. Freedom from Religion Foundation Inc.*, 551 U.S. 587 (2007).
50. Quoted in Ken Foskett, *Judging Thomas* (New York: Morrow, 2004), 281.
51. *Halliburton Co. v. Erica P. John Fund*, 134 S. Ct. 2398 (2014), quoting *John R. Sand & Gravel Co. v. United States*, 552 U.S. 130, 139 (2008).
52. *Kimble v. Marvel Entertainment, LLC,* 135 S. Ct. 2401 (2015).
53. See Michael H. LeRoy, "Death of a Precedent: Should Justices Rethink Their Consensus Norms?" 43 *Hofstra Law Review* 377 (2014).
54. See LeRoy, "Death of a Precedent"; Amy Coney Barrett, "Precedent and Jurisprudential Disagreement," 91 *Texas Law Review* 1711 (2013); and Christopher Banks, "The Supreme Court and Precedent: An Analysis of Natural Courts and Reversal Trends," 75 *Judicature* 262 (1992).
55. R. Jackson, "The Task of Maintaining Our Liberties: The Role of the Judiciary," 39 *American Bar Association Journal* 962, 962 (1953).
56. Justice Alito, Speech at the Federalist Society's Texas Chapter's Conference (September 21, 2015), as reported by Josh Blackman, "Justice Alito Reflects on his Tenth Anniversary on SCOTUS," available at joshblackman.com/blog/2015/09/21/justice-alito-reflects-on-his-tenth-anniversary-on-scotus (accessed on September 22, 2015).
57. Memoranda, March 21, 1989, and March 17, 1988, Thurgood Marshall Papers, Boxes 452 and 435, LC.
58. Letter to Chief Justice Burger, September 28, 1982, Marshall Papers, Box 307, LC.

59. Byron White Papers, Recusals, Box 100, LC. See, generally, Louis Virelli III, *Disqualifying the High Court: Supreme Court Recusal and the Constitution* (Lawrence: University Press of Kansas, 2017).
60. Letter to Frankfurter, March 30, 1937, Harlan F. Stone Papers, Box 13, LC. See also Letter from Clerk to Chief Justice Taft, March 27, 1928, Willis Van Devanter Papers, Box 34, LC.
61. F. Vinson, Address before the American Bar Association, September 7, 1949, reprinted in 69 S. Ct. v, vi (1949).
62. See Commission on Revision of the Federal Court Appellate System, *Structure and Internal Procedures; Recommendations for Change* (Washington, D.C.: CRFCAS, 1975), 11–19, 76–79, 91–111. The commission's estimate was criticized as too high by G. Casper and R. Posner, *The Workload of the Supreme Court* (Chicago: American Bar Foundation, 1976).
63. *United States v. Windsor,* 133 S. Ct. 2695 (2013).
64. *Obergefell v. Hodges,* 135 S. Ct. 2584 (2015).
65. *In re Jesse McDonald,* 489 U.S. 180 (1989).
66. See *In re Amendment Rule* 39, 500 U.S. 13 (1991). See also Memoranda from Chief Justice Rehnquist and Justice Kennedy, Marshall Papers, Box 524, LC.
67. Memorandum to the Conference by Frankfurter, 1951, 1953–1961, SC. These items are also in the John M. Harlan Papers, Boxes 499 and 587, MLPU; in the Felix Frankfurter Papers at HLS; as well as in the Tom C. Clark Papers, UT. For an excellent discussion of Frankfurter's efforts, see D. Hutchinson, "Felix Frankfurter and the Business of the Supreme Court, O.T. 1946–O.T. 1961," in P. Kurland and G. Casper, eds., *The Supreme Court Review* 143 (Chicago: University of Chicago Press, 1980).
68. Brandeis-Frankfurter Conversations, at 17 and 30, Frankfurter Papers, Box 224, LC.
69. See, e.g., Memorandum for the Conference by Chief Justice Warren, October 7, 1957, Frankfurter Papers, Box 220, File 4051, LC.
70. Letter from Justice Douglas to Justice Frankfurter, October 13, 1960, Frankfurter Papers, Box 152, Folder 9, HLS. The letter is also in the Harlan Papers, Box 49, MLPU.
71. Letter from Justice Black to Justice Frankfurter, October 13, 1960, Frankfurter Papers, Box 152, Folder 9, HLS. See also Memorandum to Conference by Justice Clark, October 7, 1957, Clark Papers, UT.
72. Based on statistics compiled by the Office of the Administrative Assistant to the Chief Justice.
73. "Memorandum of Mr. Justice Frankfurter on *In Forma Pauperis* Petitions," (November 1, 1954), Justice Harold Burton Papers, Box 314, LC.
74. Memorandum of Justice Frankfurter on *In forma pauperis* Petitions, November 1, 1954, Frankfurter Papers, Box 205, Folder 5, HLS. See also Stanley Reed Papers, Memo, November 1, 1944, Box 172, UK.
75. Memorandum from Chief Justice Burger, Hugo Black Papers, Box 58, LC.
76. Memorandum from the Chief Justice and NARS Report, Black Papers, Boxes 58 and 426, LC. See also Letter to Harlan, July 15, 1970, and Memoranda to the Conference, July 16 and 30, 1970, Harlan Papers, Box 490, MLPU. At other times, justices share the law clerks assigned to retired justices. See Memorandum from Chief Justice Burger, 1974, Clark Papers, UT.
77. Paul Freund telephone interview with author (October 15, 1984), quoted in D. M. O'Brien, "Managing the Business of the Supreme Court," 45 *Public Administration Review* 667, 670 (1985).

78. See memoranda to *cert.* pool clerks, Harry Blackmun Papers, Box 1374, LC.
79. Quoted by T. Clark, "Internal Operations of the United States Supreme Court," 43 *Judicature* 45, 48 (1959).
80. Robert H. Jackson, *The Supreme Court in the American System of Government* (Cambridge: Harvard University Press, 1955); and reprint (New York: Harper Torchback, 1961), at 20–21.
81. K. W. Starr, "Supreme Court Needs a Management Revolt," *Wall Street Journal,* October 13, 1993, A23.
82. Memos in Marshall Papers, LC, quoted by Tony Mauro, "Ginsburg Jumps In: Last One into the Cert. Pool Is a Rotten Egg," *Connecticut Law Tribune,* September 27, 1993, 1.
83. Quoted in Tony Mauro, "Justices Give Pivotal Role to Novice Lawyers," *USA Today,* March 13, 1998, A1, A2.
84. Quoted in Tony Mauro, "Alito Recaps First Year on the Court," *Legal Times* 1 (February 7, 2007).
85. David Stras, "The Supreme Court's Gatekeepers: The Role of Law Clerks in the Certiorari Process," 85 *Texas Law Review* 947 (2007).
86. See, e.g., Letter from Hughes to Stone, October 1, 1931, Stone Papers, Box 75, LC.
87. John Paul Stevens, *Five Chiefs: A Supreme Court Memoir,* (Boston: Little, Brown, 2011), 122–23.
88. Quoted in "The Supreme Court: How It Operates in Private Chambers outside Courtroom," *Smithsonian* magazine, special report, 1976.
89. Memorandum, Marshall Papers, Boxes 427 and 492, LC.
90. Memorandum, Marshall Papers, Box 452, LC.
91. See W. J. Brennan Jr., "The National Court of Appeals: Another Dissent," 40 *University of Chicago Law Review* 473, 478–79 (1973).
92. J. F. Byrnes, *All in One Lifetime* 154 (New York: Harper, 1958).
93. Interview with Chief Justice Rehnquist, *This Honorable Court,* PBS (outtake).
94. See, e.g., Memorandum to Justice Brennan, June 27, 1984, William J. Brennan Jr. Papers, LC.
95. Rehnquist Interview, PBS (outtake).
96. W. O. Douglas, *The Court Years* (New York: Random House, 1980), 223, 226, 227.
97. O. Roberts, Address, Meeting of the Association of the Bar of the City of New York and the New York County Lawyers' Association, December 12, 1946; and Robert Jackson Papers, LC.
98. Memorandum of Howard Westwood, Stone Papers, Box 48, LC. See also Memorandum of Talk with HFS, March 2, 1965, Frankfurter Papers, Box 171, File 14, HLS.
99. Author's interview with Justice Powell (February 16, 1987), SC.
100. Stevens, *Five Chiefs,* at 154.
101. Powell, quoted in "The Reasonable Man," *ABA Journal* 69 (October 1990), at 72; and Chief Justice Rehnquist Interview, *Booknotes,* aired on C-SPAN (July 5, 1992).
102. Memo to Chief Justice, June 20, 1975, Brennan Papers, Box 336, LC. For a similar incident, see Frankfurter's lengthy memo to Stone, December 12, 1939, Reed Papers, Box 171, UK.
103. See, e.g., memos between the chief justice and Blackmun, October 3, 1975, Brennan Papers, Box 363, LC.
104. Justice Blackmun, Speech at Eighth Circuit Judicial Conference, St. Louis, Mo., July 15, 1988.
105. Justice Thomas, Talk to Students and Leaders, May 20, 2003, aired on C-SPAN (May 24, 2003). See also Stevens, *Five Chiefs,* at 171.

106. Memorandum, May 8, 1990, Marshall Papers, Box 493, LC.
107. Memorandum, November 24, 1989, Marshall Papers, Box 492, LC.
108. Letter from Justice Stevens, December 19, 1989, Marshall Papers, Box 492, LC.
109. Justice Breyer quoted in "Justice Breyer on the High Court's New Blood," *Washington Post*, March 9, 2006, A17.
110. Stevens, *Five Chiefs*, at 210.
111. Chief Justice Roberts, May 21, 2006, Commencement Address, Georgetown Law School (aired on C-SPAN, May 27, 2006), available at http://www.law.georgetown .edu/webcast/assets/GL_2006523112710.mp3.
112. Quoted in Jeffrey Rosen, "Roberts' Rules," *Atlantic Monthly* (January/February, 2007).
113. Robert Jackson, Oral History, Jackson Papers, Box 259, LC, at 1108–9.
114. Comments at George Washington National Law Center, February 16, 1988, quoted in "Ruling Fixed Opinions," *New York Times*, February 22, 1988, A16.
115. Rehnquist Interview, PBS (outtake).
116. Quoted in Hugh Hewitt, "A High Court Too Far Above the Fray?" *San Francisco Examiner*, September 20, 2011.
117. B. White, "The Work of the Supreme Court: A Nuts and Bolts Description," 54 *New York State Bar Journal* 346, 383 (1982).
118. Clark, supra note 79, at 50.
119. See J. Palmer, *The Vinson Court Era: The Supreme Court's Conference Votes* (New York: AMS Press, 1990), 29.
120. H. Black, *Justice Black and the Bill of Rights*, CBS Special, transcript, at 5 (New York: CBS News, December 3, 1968).
121. H. Blackmun, *A Justice Speaks Out: A Conversation with Harry A. Blackmun*, Cable News Network, transcript, at 4 (December 4, 1982). See also Letters to Conference, discussing the voting procedure, from Justices Blackmun (September 23, 1980), Stewart (September 18, 1980), and Stevens (September 16, 1980), Marshall Papers, Box 263, LC.
122. Memorandum to Conference, October 1, 1986, Marshall Papers, Box 427, LC.
123. Oral History, April 24, 1995, Blackmun Papers, Box 1428, LC.
124. Quoted in Robert Barnes, "Justices Discuss a Changing Supreme Court," *Washington Post*, September 4, 2009, A27 (quoting a C-SPAN interview).
125. Quoted in the Notre Dame and Saint Mary's student newspaper, *The Observer*, September 3, 2015, 1.
126. Stevens, *Five Chiefs*, at 142.
127. Quoted by Kate Coscarelli, "Alito and Wife Look Back on Confirmation Ordeal," *Newhouse News Service* (August 25, 2006).
128. D. M. Provine, *Case Selection in the United States Supreme Court* (Chicago: University of Chicago Press, 1980), 32.
129. Data gathered from Memorandum to Conference, September 30, 1986, from Justice White, Marshall Papers, Box 427, LC.
130. Based on Justice Thurgood Marshall's Docket Books for the 1990 term, Marshall Papers, Boxes 561–566, LC.
131. W. H. Taft, testimony, *Hearings before the House Committee on the Judiciary*, 67th Cong., 2d sess., at 2 (Washington, D.C.: GPO, 1922).
132. P. Linzer, "The Meaning of *Certiorari* Denials," 79 *Columbia Law Review* 1227, 1302 (1979). See also Gregory A. Calderia, John R. Wright, and Christopher Zorn, "Sophisticated Voting and Gate-keeping in the Supreme Court," 15 *Journal of Law, Economics, & Organization* 549 (2001).

133. See, e.g., Joan Maisel Leiman, "The Rule of Four," 57 *Columbia Law Review* 975 (1957).

134. Testimony of McReynolds, *Hearings on H.R. 8206 before the Committee on the Judiciary*, 68th Cong., 2d sess., 1924.

135. C. E. Hughes, "Reason as Opposed to the Tyranny of Force" (speech delivered to the American Law Institute, May 6, 1937), reprinted in *Vital Speeches of the Day* 458, 459 (1937).

136. See Memorandum to Conference from Stevens, May 14, 1976, Brennan Papers, Box 363, LC. Conversely, the crucial fourth vote may be lost if a justice decided to deny rather than grant a case after the conference vote. See letter from Harlan, December 13, 1965, Clark Papers, UT. See also letter from Frankfurter to Burton, February 1, 1965, Frankfurter Papers, Box 169, File 6, HLS.

137. See, e.g., *Maryland v. Baltimore Radio Show, Inc.*, 338 U.S. 912 (1950); *Brown v. Allen*, 344 U.S 443 (1953); and *Daniels v. Allen*, 344 U.S. 443 (1953).

138. Memorandum from Justice Frankfurter on the Integrity of the *Certiorari* Process to Justice Harlan, February 21, 1957, Harlan Papers, Box 532, MLPU.

139. This discussion draws on D. M. O'Brien, "A Diminishing Plenary Docket: A Legacy of the Rehnquist Court," 89 *Judicature* 134 (2005).

140. Memos and correspondence in Justice Byron White's Papers, Box 50, LC; Justice Thurgood Marshall's Papers, LC; and Justice Lewis F. Powell Jr. Papers, WLLS.

141. *Jackson v. City and County of San Francisco*, 135 S. Ct. 2799 (2015).

142. *District of Columbia v. Heller*, 554 U.S. 570 (2008).

143. *McDonald v. Chicago*, 561 U.S. 767 (2010).

144. *Silvester v. Becerra*, 583 U.S.__ (2018).

145. Data for 1941–1971 are taken from the "Report of the Study Group on the Caseload of the Supreme Court," 57 *Federal Rules and Decisions* 573, 615 (1973). Data for 1981, and 1990–1991 are based on the author's analysis of Marshall's Docket Book, Marshall Papers, Boxes 561–566, LC.

146. Based on Bench Memoranda, Marshall Papers, Boxes 375–376 and 513–514, LC. Excluded here are three cases granted by an equally divided Court and one case in which five justices voted to grant but that was ultimately denied at the request of the solicitor general.

147. J. P. Stevens, "The Life Span of a Judge-Made Rule" (Lecture delivered at New York University School of Law, October 27, 1982), excerpt reprinted in D. M. O'Brien, ed., *Judges on Judging*, 4th ed. (Washington, D.C.: CQ Press, 2013).

148. Memorandum for Conference from Justice Marshall, September 21, 1983, in Brennan Papers, Box 640, LC.

149. Letter from Justice Stevens to Chief Justice Burger, August 31, 1983, in Brennan Papers, Box 540, LC.

150. Interview with Justice Stevens (October 16, 1988), SC.

151. Letters to author from Chief Justice Rehnquist (October 21, 1996) and Justice Blackmun (October 10, 1996), and telephone interview with Justice Stevens (October 8, 1996).

152. *Singleton v. Commissioner of Internal Revenue*, 439 U.S. 940, 942 (1978) (Stevens, J., op. respecting denial of *certiorari*).

153. *United States v. Carver*, 260 U.S. 482, 490 (1922).

154. *Brown v. Allen*, 344 U.S. 443, 542 (1953).

155. *Maryland v. Baltimore Radio Show*, 338 U.S. 912, 917–19 (1950).

156. *Brown v. Allen*, 344 U.S. 443, 542 (1953).

157. *Rogers v. Missouri Pacific Railroad Co.*, 352 U.S. 500, 528 (1957).

158. See *Rogers,* and *McBride v. Toledo Terminal Co.,* 354 U.S. 517, 519–20 (1957).
159. *United States v. Shannon,* 342 U.S. 288, 298 (1952).
160. *Darr v. Burford,* 339 U.S. 200, 226 (1950) (Frankfurter, J., dis. op.).
161. *Daniels v. Allen,* 344 U.S. 443, 491 (1953).
162. Letter to Frankfurter, March 30, 1937, Stone Papers, Box 13.
163. *Drake v. Zant,* and *Westbrook v. Balkcom,* 449 U.S. 999 (1980) (dissenting opinions by Justices Brennan, joined by Marshall, Stewart, and White). See also *Triangle Improvement Council v. Ritchie,* 402 U.S. 497 (1970) (where the four justices who voted to grant review joined in a dissent from the majority's decision to override the rule of four and dismiss the case as improvidently granted).
164. *Hirsh v. City of Atlanta,* 495 U.S. 927 (1990).
165. *McCleary v. Navarro,* 504 U.S. 966 (1992).
166. *Hunter v. Bryant,* 502 U.S. 224 (1991).
167. See *Garcia v. Texas,* 131 S. Ct. 866 (2011). See also statement issued by Justices Sotomayor, Breyer, Ginsburg, and Kagan on denial of review in *Gamache v. California,* 131 S. Ct. 591 (2010).
168. *Baze v. Rees,* 553 U.S. 35 (2008).
169. *Glossip v. Gross,* 135 S. Ct. 2726 (2015).
170. For further discussion, see Michael Solimine and Rafael Gely, "The Supreme Court and the DIG: An Empirical and Institutional Analysis," *Wisconsin Law Review* 1421 (2005); and Michael Solimine and Rafael Gely, "The Supreme Court and the Sophisticated Use of DIGS," 18 *Supreme Court Economic Review* 155 (2010).
171. Memorandum to Conference, June 25, 1984, Marshall Papers, Box 331, LC.
172. *In re Kevin Nigel Stanford,* 537 U.S. 968 (2002).
173. *Stanford v. Kentucky,* 492 U.S. 361 (1989).
174. *Roper v. Simmons,* 543 U.S. 551 (2005).
175. See *Lawrence v. Chater,* 516 U.S. 163 (1996), and *Stutson v. United States,* 516 U.S. 193 (1996). See also Erwin Chemerinsky and Ned Miltenberg, "The Need to Clarify the Meaning of Supreme Court Remands," 36 *Arizona State Law Journal* 513 (2003).
176. J. Goebel Jr., *Antecedents and Beginnings to 1801* (New York: Macmillan, 1971), Appendix, at 804.
177. This table incorporates data from and updates the statistics compiled in F. Frankfurter and J. Landis, *The Business of the Supreme Court* (New York: Macmillan, 1927), 302, Table 1 (data for 1825, 1875, and 1925); F. Frankfurter and J. Landis, "The Business of the Supreme Court in the October Term 1930," 45 *Harvard Law Review* 271, Table 9, at 9 (1930) (data for 1930); and E. Gressman, "Much Ado about Certiorari," 52 *Georgetown Law Journal* 742, 756–57 (1964) (data for 1935, 1945, and 1955). Data for 1960, 1965, 1970, 1975, 1985, 1995, 2005, and 2015 were compiled by the author. The table aims only to illustrate trends. The classification in this and other tables necessarily invites differences of opinion as to the dominant issue in a case.
178. See, e.g., Vanessa Baird, *Answering the Call of the Court: How Justices and Litigants Set the Supreme Court Agenda* (Charlottesville: University of Virginia Press, 2007).
179. Vinson, supra note 61, at vi.
180. *NAACP v. Button,* 371 U.S. 415, 429–30 (1963).
181. L. Powell, *The Powell Memorandum: Attack on American Free Enterprise System* 7 (August 24, 1971) (Chamber of Commerce of the United States, Washington, D.C.).
182. R. Jackson, *The Struggle for Judicial Supremacy* (New York: Knopf, 1951), 287.

183. For a study of interest-group litigation in the lower federal courts, see L. Epstein and C. K. Rowland, "Debunking the Myth of Interest Group Invincibility in the Courts," 85 *American Political Science Review* 205 (1991).

184. See Paul Collins, *Friends of the Supreme Court: Interest Groups and Judicial Decision Makers* (New York: Oxford University Press, 2008).

185. See S. Behuniak-Long, "Friendly Fire: *Amici Curiae* and *Webster v. Reproductive Health Services*," 74 *Judicature* 261 (1991), and Ryan J. Owens and Lee Epstein, "*Amici Curiae* during the Rehnquist Years," 89 *Judicature* 127 (November/December 2005).

186. Tony Mauro, "Court Affirms Continued Need for Preferences," *New York Law Journal* 1 (June 24, 2003); *Grutter v. Bollinger*, 539 U.S. 306 (2003); and *Gratz v. Bollinger*, 539 U.S. 244 (2003).

187. *National Federation of Independent Business v. Sebelius*, 131 S. Ct. 2566 (2012).

188. See *Green v. Biddle*, 21 U.S. 1 (1823).

189. See Collins, supra note 184.

190. Of the "Merits Cases" listed by SCOTUSblog only one case granted oral arguments in the 2014–2015 term did not have at least one *amicus* brief filed (http://scotusblog.com/case-files/terms/ot2014). See also R. Reeves Anderson and Anthony J. Franze, "Commentary: The Court's Increasing Reliance on Amicus Curiae in the Past Term," *National Law Journal* (August 24, 2011); and Joseph D. Kearney and Thomas W. Merrill, "The Influence of Amicus Curiae Briefs on the Supreme Court," 148 *University of Pennsylvania Law Review* 743 (2000).

191. Justice Ginsburg, Address to the American Association of Law Schools (aired on C-SPAN, January 8, 2000).

192. *Citizens United v. Federal Election Commission*, 558 U.S. 310 (2010).

193. See Kelly Lynch, "Best Friends? Supreme Court Law Clerks on Effective *Amicus Curiae* Briefs," 20 *Journal of Law & Politics* 33 (2004).

194. See Allison Orr Larsen, "Confronting Supreme Court Fact Finding," 98 *Virginia Law Review* 1255 (2012).

195. See Owens and Epstein, supra note 185.

196. See J. Tanenhaus, M. Schick, M. Muraskin, and D. Rosen, "The Supreme Court's *Certiorari* Jurisdiction: Cue Theory," in G. Schubert, ed., *Judicial Decisionmaking*, 111–32 (New York: Free Press, 1963); V. Armstrong and C. Johnson, "*Certiorari* Decisions by the Warren & Burger Courts: Is Cue Theory Time Bound?" *Polity* 141 (1983).

197. See S. S. Ulmer, "Selecting Cases for Supreme Court Review: An Underdog Model," 72 *American Political Science Review* 902 (1978); G. Caldeira and J. Wright, "Organized Interests and Agenda-Setting in the U.S. Supreme Court," 82 *American Political Science Review* 1111 (1988).

198. See, e.g., Margaret Meriwether Cordray and Richard Cordray, "The Solicitor General's Changing Role in Supreme Court Litigation," 51 *Boston College Law Review* 1323 (2010).

199. See Margaret Meriweather Cordray and Richard Cordray, "The Solicitor General's Changing Role in Supreme Court Litigation," 51 *Boston College Law Review* 1323 (2010), and Margaret Meriweather Cordray and Richard Cordray, "The Supreme Court's Plenary Docket," 58 *Washington & Lee Law Review* 737 (2001).

200. Data taken from Jonathan Rose, assistant attorney general, Department of Justice, "The Workload of the Supreme Court," *Testimony before the House*

Committee on the Judiciary, Subcommittee on Courts, Civil Liberties, and the Administration of Justice, at 5–6 (November 10, 1983). During 1928–1936, the government's success rate averaged 67 percent each term; between 1937 and 1944, it averaged 74 percent. See Memorandum for the Attorney General by Solicitor General Stanley Reed, June 1, 1937, Frankfurter Papers, Box 170, File 16, HLS; and Report to the Attorney General, June 20, 1945, Francis Biddle Papers, Box 2, RPL. See also Richard Pacelle, *Between Law & Politics: The Solicitor General and the Structuring of Race, Gender, and Reproductive Rights Litigation* (College Station: Texas A & M University Press, 2003); and Ryan Black and Ryan Owens, *The Solicitor General and the United States Supreme Court* (New York: Cambridge University Press, 2012).

201. See conference notes on *Melkonyan v. Sullivan,* Marshall Papers, Box 563, LC.
202. See, generally, R. Deen, J. Ignagni, and J. Meernik, "The Solicitor General as Amicus, 1953–2000: How Influential?" 87 *Judicature* 60 (September–October 2003); R. Deen, J. Ignagni, and J. Meernik, "Individual Justices and the Solicitor General," 89 *Judicature* 68 (September/October 2005); and Richard Pacelle Jr., *"Amicus Curiae* or *Amicus Praesidentis?* Reexamining the Role of the Solicitor General in Filing Amici," 89 *Judicature* 317 (May/June 2006).
203. John G. Roberts Jr., "Oral Advocacy and the Re-emergence of a Supreme Court," 30 *Journal of Supreme Court History* 68 (2005). See also Richard Lazarus, "Advocacy Matters Before and Within the Supreme Court: Transforming the Court by Transforming the Bar," 96 *Georgetown Law Journal* 1487 (2008).
204. Quoted by Joan Biskupic, Janet Roberts, and John Shiffman, *The Echo Chamber: A Reuters Special Report* (Washington, D.C.: Reuters, December 8, 2014).
205. See R. Pacelle Jr., *The Transformation of the Supreme Court's Agenda: From the New Deal to the Reagan Administration* (Boulder, Colo.: Westview Press, 1991).
206. Quoted by S. Duffy, "Inside the Highest Court," *Pennsylvania Law Weekly* 11 (April 17, 1995).
207. Interview with Tony Mauro, "Justices Give Pivotal Role to Novice Lawyers," *USA Today,* March 13–15, 1998, A2. See also David Stras, "The Supreme Court Gatekeepers: The Role of Law Clerks in the *Certiorari* Process," *Texas Law Review* (2007); David Stras, "The Supreme Court's Declining Plenary Docket," 27 *Constitutional Commentary* 151 (2010).
208. Black, supra note 120, at 5.
209. Letter to Senator Burton Wheeler, reprinted in Senate Committee on the Judiciary, *Hearings on the Reorganization of the Federal Judiciary,* 75th Cong., 1st sess., 1937, Senate Report 711, at 40.
210. J. Harlan, "Manning the Dikes," 13 *Record of the New York City Bar Association* 541, 547 (1958); W. O. Douglas, Interview, *CBS Reports,* transcript (New York: CBS News, September 6, 1972); Rehnquist, Remarks at the Jefferson Literary and Debating Society, Charlottesville, Va., September 20, 1985.
211. *Ex parte Brummett,* 295 U.S. 719 (1935); 299 U.S. 514 (1936); 302 U.S. 644 (1937); 303 U.S. 570 (1938); 306 U.S. 615 (1939); 309 U.S. 625 (1940); *Ex parte Brummitt,* 304 U.S. 545 (1938); 311 U.S. 614 (1940); 313 U.S. 548 (1941); and 314 U.S. 585 (1941).
212. Brennan, supra note 91.
213. See *In re Reverend Clovis Carl Green,* 669 F.2d 779, 781 (1981).
214. Memorandum to Conference, May 25, 1971, Harlan Papers, Box 434, MLPU.
215. W. O. Douglas, "The Supreme Court and Its Caseload," 45 *Cornell Law Quarterly* 401, 413–14 (1960).

FIVE

Deciding Cases and Writing Opinions

1. Interview with Potter Stewart (February 28, 1985), SC.
2. For an interesting study of the uses of *per curiam* opinions, see Laura Krugman Ray, "The Road to *Bush v. Gore*: The History of the Supreme Court's Use of *Per Curiam* Opinion," 79 *Nebraska Law Review* 517 (2000); and Ira Robbins, "Hiding Behind the Cloak of Invisibility: The Supreme Court and Per Curiam Opinions," 86 *Tulane Law Review* 1197 (2012).
3. Author interview with Justice Brennan (October 21, 1987), SC. The cases were *Cooper v. Aaron*, 358 U.S. 1 (1958), and *United States v. Nixon*, 418 U.S. 683 (1974).
4. C. E. Hughes, *The Supreme Court of the United States* (New York: Columbia University Press, 1928), 61.
5. W. J. Brennan, quoted in "Report of the Commission on Revision of the Federal Court Appellate System," *Structure and Internal Procedures: Recommendation for Change*, 67 *Federal Rules and Decisions* 195, 254 (1975).
6. See David C. Frederick, "Supreme Court Advocacy in the Early Nineteenth Century," 30 *Journal of Supreme Court History* 1 (2005).
7. *Gibbons v. Ogden*, 9 Wheat. 1 (1824).
8. *New York Times Co. v. United States*, 403 U.S. 670 (1971).
9. *Trustees of Dartmouth College v. Woodward*, 4 Wheat. 518 (1819).
10. Quoted by A. Beveridge, *The Life of John Marshall* (Boston: Houghton Mifflin, 1919) 4:249–50.
11. Quoted by C. Warren, *The Supreme Court in United States History* (Boston: Little, Brown, 1922) 1:603.
12. J. Clarke, "Reminiscences of the Court and the Law," 5 *Proceedings of the Fifth Annual Meeting of the California State Bar* 20 (1932).
13. Letter to Pollock, March 17, 1898, reprinted in *Holmes-Pollock Letters*, ed. M. Howe (Cambridge, Mass.: Harvard University Press, 1946), 81.
14. Undated note, Hugo Black Papers, Frankfurter File, Box 60, LC.
15. Speech before ABA Tenth Annual Appellant Advocate Institute Luncheon (May 13, 1996).
16. F. Frankfurter, *Proceedings in Honor of Mr. Justice Frankfurter and Distinguished Alumni* (Occasional Paper No. 3 of the Harvard Law School, 1960), 18.
17. W. Rutledge, "The Appellate Brief," 28 *American Bar Association Journal* 251, 254 (1942).
18. See C. H. Butler, *A Century at the Bar of the Supreme Court of the United States* (New York: Putnam's, 1942), 88.
19. Quoted in "Holding Court," *Washington Post,* March 6, 2008, A20.
20. See Barry Sullivan and Megan Canty, "Interruptions in Search of a Purpose: Oral Argument in the Supreme Court, October Terms 1958–1960 and 2010–2012," 2015 *Utah Law Review* 1005 (2015).
21. Rehnquist, "Oral Advocacy: A Disappearing Art" (Brainerd Currie Lecture, Mercer University School of Law, October 20, 1983; on file with the author).
22. Quoted in Robert Barnes, "Chief Justice Counsels Humility," *Washington Post,* February 6, 2007, A5.
23. Quoted by Tony Mauro, "Alito Recaps First Year on High Court," *Legal Times,* February 6, 2007, 1.
24. Justice Alito, Address to the Bar Association of Metropolitan St. Louis, May 16, 2011.

25. Justice Alito interview with Bill Kristol on SCOTUSBLOG.com/media/interview -with-justice-samuel-alito (accessed on July 27, 2015).

26. See "Guide for Counsel in Cases to Be Argued before the Supreme Court of the United States" (available at www.supremecourt.gov).

27. Antonin Scalia and Bryan Garner, *Making Your Case: The Art of Persuading Judges* (St. Paul, Minn.: Thomson/West, 2008).

28. The case was *Marvin Brandt Revocable Trust v. United States,* 134 S. Ct. 1257 (2014).

29. Quoted in the *Philadelphia Inquirer* (April 9, 1963), cited by H. Abraham, *The Judicial Process,* 4th ed. (New York: Oxford University Press, 1980), 203; and "Seminar with Mr. Chief Justice Warren," University of Virginia Legal Forum, at 9 (April 25, 1973).

30. Reported by J. Frank, *The Marble Palace* (New York: Knopf, 1958), 105.

31. Interview with Justice Kennedy in the film, *The Supreme Court of the United States* (York Associates, 1997).

32. Quoted by Adam Liptak, "Sotomayor Reflects on First Years on Court," *New York Times,* January 31, 2011.

33. Interview with Susan Swain with Chief Justice Roberts, C-SPAN (June 19, 2009), available at http://supremecourt.c-span.org/Video/JusticeOwnWords.aspx.

34. Quoted in the Notre Dame student newspaper, *The Observer,* September 3, 2015, 1.

35. Quoted in *Wisconsin State Journal* 1 (September 9, 2017).

36. See Lee Epstein, W. Landes, and R. Posner, "Inferring the Winning Party in the Supreme Court from the Pattern of Questioning at Oral Argument," 39 *Journal of Legal Studies* 433 (2010).

37. Quoted in Lawrence Wrightsman, *Oral Arguments before the Supreme Court: An Empirical Analysis* (New York: Oxford University Press, 2008); and see also Adam Liptak, "Clarence Thomas Breaks Ten Years of Silence at the Supreme Court," *New York Times,* available at http://www.nytimes.com/2016/03/01/us/politics /supreme-court-clarence-thomas.hmtl?_r=0.

38. Joan Biskupic, "Masters of the Hypothetical," *Washington Post,* January 3, 2000, A17.

39. Blackmun Speech before Eighth Circuit Judicial Conference (July 15, 1988); Antonin Scalia Interview, *This Honorable Court,* PBS; and Rehnquist, as quoted by Mary Stallcup, "Questions from the Bench," *Manhattan Lawyer* (May 24, 1988).

40. Kennedy Interview, supra note 31. Justice Breyer quoted in Hugh Hewitt, "A High Court Too Far Above the Fray?" *San Francisco Examiner,* September 20, 2011. See also Timothy Johnson, *Oral Arguments and Decision Making on the U.S. Supreme Court* (Albany, N.Y.: SUNY Press, 2004); Timothy Johnson, P. Wahlbeck, and J. Spriggs III, "The Influence of Oral Arguments on the U.S. Supreme Court," 100 *American Political Science Review* 99 (2006); and Timothy Johnson, Ryan Black, and Justin Wedcking, "Pardon the Interruption: An Empirical Analysis of Supreme Court Justices' Behavior During Oral Arguments," 55 *Loyola Law Review* 331 (2009).

41. L. F. Powell, "What Really Goes on at the Court," in *Judges on Judging,* 5th ed., ed. D. O'Brien (Washington, D.C.: CQ Press, 2017).

42. Memo from Justice Douglas to Conference, October 23, 1961, Black Papers, Box 60, LC.

43. Justice Alito interview with Bill Kristol on SCOTUSBLOG.com/media/interview -with-justice-samuel-alito (accessed July 27, 2015).

44. W. O. Douglas, *The Court Years* (New York: Random House, 1980), 34.

45. H. Hart Jr., "Foreword: The Time Chart of the Justices," 73 *Harvard Law Review* 84 (1959). See also Henry M. Hart Papers, HLS. Hart's estimate of the number of hours devoted to conference was slightly high. During the 1949–52 terms, the justices in fact met an average 119 hours per term. Earl Warren Papers, Box 660, LC.

46. Robert H. Jackson, *The Supreme Court in the American System of Government* 15 (New York: Oxford University Press, 1955).

47. Justice Scalia interview in Brian Lamb et al., eds., *The Supreme Court: A C-SPAN Book* 63 (New York: Public Affairs, 2010).

48. Letter from Frankfurter to Burton, Harold Burton Papers, Box 101, LC.

49. C. Thomas, Address to the National Center for Policy Analysis, Dallas, Texas, aired on C-SPAN (October 13, 1996).

50. Scalia Interview, York Associates (outtake).

51. D. Danelski, "The Influence of the Chief Justice in the Decisional Process," in *Courts, Judges, and Politics*, 4th ed., eds. W. Murphy and C. H. Pritchett (New York: Random House, 1986), 568.

52. A. T. Mason, *William Howard Taft: Chief Justice* (New York: Simon & Schuster, 1965), 220–21.

53. Letter to the author from Justice Blackmun (November 8, 1984).

54. Felix Frankfurter letter to Charles Fairman (December 27, 1945), Frankfurter Papers, Box 184, HLS.

55. E. Warren, "A Conversation with Earl Warren," WGBH-TV Educational Foundation, transcript, at 12 (Boston: WGBH Educational Foundation, 1972). Warren Papers, Box 571 and Docket Book, Box 367, LC; Robert Jackson Papers, LC; and Diary, Burton Papers, Box 3, LC.

56. See E. Warren, *The Memoirs of Chief Justice Earl Warren* (New York: Doubleday, 1977), 3–4; and D. M. O'Brien, *Justice Robert H. Jackson's Unpublished Opinion in* Brown v. Board (Lawrence: University Press of Kansas, 2017), 26–53.

57. Warren to Conference, October 7, 1957, Black Papers, Box 320, LC. See also Tom Clark Memo to Conference, October 7, 1957, Tom C. Clark Papers, UT.

58. Vinson to Frankfurter, October 11, 1951, William O. Douglas Papers, Box 224, LC.

59. Burger, *Supreme Court* film, transcript, at 12 (film shown to visitors to the Supreme Court until 1987).

60. *Miller v. California*, 413 U.S. 15 (1973).

61. Brennan Papers, Box 283, LC. See also letter from Chief Justice Taft, April 22, 1927, Willis Van Devanter Papers, Box 34, LC.

62. Douglas Memorandum to Conference, Black Papers, Box 60, LC. See also Justice Frankfurter's Memorandum on *Baker v. Carr*, Clark Papers, UT.

63. Quoted by D. Dorin, "Social Leadership, Humor, and Supreme Court Decision-making," 66 *Judicature* 462 (1983). See also Tom C. Clark Oral History Interview, at 50, UK.

64. Memorandum for Frankfurter, Clark Papers, UT.

65. W. J. Brennan Jr., "A Remembrance of William O. Douglas," 1990 *Journal of Supreme Court History* 104 (1991), at 105.

66. Quoted by W. Burger, "In Memoriam: John M. Harlan," 92A S. Ct. 5, 44 (1972).

67. Quoted by E. Gerhart, *America's Advocate: Robert H. Jackson* (New York: Bobbs-Merrill, 1958), 274.

68. Note to Clark, May 3, 1968, Clark Papers, UT. Justice Douglas later told the story in his autobiography, *The Court Years,* supra note 44, at 226.

69. The story is told in W. King, *Melville Weston Fuller: Chief Justice of the United States* (New York: Macmillan, 1950), 290.

70. Conference Notes, Frank Murphy Papers, Box 69, File 32, BHLUM.
71. Undated note, Black Papers, Box 61, LC.
72. Undated note, Felix Frankfurter Papers, Box 170, File 9, HLS.
73. Letter, Black Papers, Box 60, LC.
74. Unsigned note, January 4, 1941, Black Papers, Box 261, LC.
75. J. Harlan, "A Glimpse of the Supreme Court at Work," 11 *University of Chicago Law School Record* 1, 7 (1963).
76. *Heller v. Doe*, 509 U.S. 312 (1993).
77. Memo from Justice White to Justice Blackmun, June 15, 1999, Harry Blackmun Papers, Box 624, LC. See also Byron White Papers, Box 202, LC.
78. Quoted by A. T. Mason, review of *The Holmes-Einstein Letters*, in *New York Review of Books* 60 (November 22, 1964).
79. Oliver W. Holmes Papers, Box 42, File 35, HLS.
80. Interview with Justice Blackmun, *All Things Considered*, National Public Radio (December 28, 1993). See also Pamela Corley, "Bargaining and Accommodation on the United States Supreme Court," 90 *Judicature* 157 (2007).
81. Clark Oral History Interview, at 5, UK.
82. See John P. Lelsh, "The Opinion Delivery Practices of the United States Supreme Court, 1790–1945," 77 *Washington University Law Quarterly* 137 (1999); and William D. Popkin, *Evolution of the Judicial Opinion* (New York: New York University Press, 2007).
83. See G. Edward White, "Toward a Historical University of Supreme Court Decision-Making," 91 *Denver University Law Review Online* 201 (2014), at 207.
84. Quoted by J. McLean, *William Rufus Day* (Baltimore: Johns Hopkins Press, 1946).
85. See King, supra note 69, at 332–35.
86. See Danelski, supra note 51. Obviously, what "important constitutional cases" are is a matter of debate, and so the figures are only rough approximations of each chief justice's practice.
87. Memorandum of Howard Westwood, Harlan Stone Papers, Box 48, LC.
88. "Chief Justice Vinson and His Law Clerks," 49 *Northwestern University Law Review* 26, 31 (1954). The charts are in Fred Vinson Papers, Box 217, UK. See also S. Brenner and J. Palmer, "The Time Taken to Write Opinions as a Determinant of Opinion Assignments," 72 *Judicature* 179 (1988).
89. See, e.g., Assignment Books, Earl Warren Papers, Box 126, LC.
90. Based on data collected each term by the Clerk of the Supreme Court, "Sheet: Number of Printed Opinions and Memorandum," SC; and the author's own tabulations.
91. For further discussion see S. Davis, "Power on the Court: Chief Justice Rehnquist's Opinion Assignments," 74 *Judicature* 66 (1990); F. Maltzman and P. Wahlbeck, "Opinion Assignment on the Rehnquist Court," 89 *Judicature* 121 (2005); and T. Johnson, J. Spriggs, and F. Maltzman, "Passing and Strategic Voting on the U.S. Supreme Court," 39 *Law & Society Review* 349 (2005).
92. Memorandum to the Conference, November 24, 1989, Thurgood Marshall Papers, Box 492, LC.
93. Quoted by Robert Barnes, "For High School Students, Some Justice," *Washington Post*, March 6, 2008, A20; and talk at the Rehnquist Center at the University of Arizona College of Law (February 4, 2009), as reported by Tony Mauro.
94. Richard J. Lazarus, "Back to 'Business' at the Supreme Court: The 'Administrative Side' of Chief Justice Roberts," 129 *Harvard Law Review Forum* 33 (online) (November 9, 2015).
95. See Memorandum, May 27, 1948, Douglas Papers, Box 217, LC.

96. Quoted by A. McCormack, "A Law Clerk's Recollections," 46 *Columbia Law Review* 710, 712 (1946). For another, though less successful, switch of position when writing the Court's opinion, see Memo on *Bryan v. United States* (1950), Sherman Minton Papers, Box 1, TPL.

97. *Garcia v. San Antonio Metropolitan Transit Authority*, 469 U.S. 528 (1985).

98. *National League of Cities v. Usery*, 426 U.S. 833 (1976).

99. See *Hodel v. Virginia Surface Mining*, 452 U.S. 264 (1981); *FERC v. Mississippi*, 456 U.S. 742 (1982); *United Transportation Union v. Long Island Railroad Company*, 455 U.S. 678 (1982); and *EEOC v. Wyoming*, 460 U.S. 222 (1983).

100. Memo to Justice Powell, July 3, 1984, Blackmun Papers, Box 412, LC.

101. *Lee v. Weisman*, 505 U.S. 577 (1992).

102. Letter from Justice Kennedy to Justice Blackmun, March 30, 1992, Blackmun Papers, Box 586, LC.

103. See S. Brenner, "Fluidity on the United States Supreme Court: A Reexamination," 24 *American Journal of Political Science* 526 (1980); and S. Brenner, "Fluidity on the Supreme Court: 1956–1967," 26 *American Journal of Political Science* 388 (1982).

104. In another seven cases, Harlan circulated opinions as to why they should be granted or otherwise disposed of than as voted at the initial conference. After a subsequent change in the conference vote, these opinions were not filed. John M. Harlan Papers, Boxes 4, 18, 37, 55, 76, 101, 131, 154, 185, 214, 272, 295, 326, 369, and 407, MLPU. For a further discussion, see D. O'Brien, "John Marshall Harlan's Unpublished Opinions: Reflections of a Supreme Court at Work," *Journal of Supreme Court History* (1991), at 27.

105. Danelski, supra note 51, at 503. See also W. Murphy, *Elements of Judicial Strategy* (Chicago: University of Chicago Press, 1964).

106. *National Federation of Independent Business v. Sebelius*, 132 S. Ct. 2566 (2012). See also Jan Crawford, *Face the Nation* (CBS News television broadcast, July 1, 2012), available at http://www.cbsnews.com/8301-3460_162-57464549/roberts switched-views-to-uphold-health-care-law/.

107. Studies of the opinion assignment practices of chief justices vary in their database and, to some extent, in their conclusions. See Danelski, supra note 51, and S. Ulmer, "The Use of Power in the Supreme Court: The Opinion Assignments of Earl Warren, 1953–1960," 19 *Journal of Public Law* 49 (1970).

108. *Minersville School District v. Gobitis*, 310 U.S. 586 (1940).

109. *West Virginia Board of Education v. Barnette*, 319 U.S. 624 (1943).

110. *Smith v. Allwright*, 321 U.S. 649 (1944).

111. The story is ably told by Mason, *Harlan Fiske Stone* (New York: Viking, 1956), 614–15.

112. *Korematsu v. United States*, 323 U.S. 214 (1944).

113. *Mapp v. Ohio*, 367 U.S. 643 (1961).

114. See J. Frank, *Justice Daniel Dissenting* (Cambridge, Mass.: Harvard University Press, 1964), 181–83.

115. See Mason, supra note 52, at 206–8. On occasion, however, Taft did make assignments for expressly political reasons. He explained his assignment of one First Amendment case to Justice Pierce Butler as follows: "He is the only one to whom I can properly give it. He was appointed by Harding and not by Wilson, and I rather think we ought to have somebody other than an appointee of Wilson to consider and decide the case." Letter to Justice Van Devanter, July 9, 1926, Van Devanter Papers, Box 35, LC.

116. See D. Atkinson, "Opinion Writing on the Supreme Court, 1949–1956: The Views of Justice Sherman Minton," 49 *Temple Law Quarterly* 105 (1975).
117. *Romer v. Evans*, 517 U.S. 620 (1996).
118. *Lawrence v. Texas*, 539 U.S. 558 (2003).
119. *Bowers v. Hardwick*, 478 U.S. 186 (1986).
120. *United States v. Windsor*, 133 S. Ct. 2675 (2013).
121. *Obergefell v. Hodges*, 135 S. Ct. 2584 (2015).
122. See J. Howard, *Mr. Justice Murphy* (Princeton, N.J.: Princeton University Press, 1968), 237.
123. *Henson v. Santander*, 582 U.S.__ (2017).
124. See T. Bowen and J. Scheb, "Freshman Opinion Writing on the U.S. Supreme Court, 1921–1991," 76 *Judicature* 239 (1993); and E. Slotnick, "Who Speaks for the Court? Majority Opinion Assignments from Taft to Burger," 23 *American Journal of Political Science* 60 (1979); and C. Smith, J. Baugh, T. Hensley, and S. Johnson, "The First-Term Performance of Justice Ruth Bader Ginsburg," 78 *Judicature* 74 (1994).
125. Quoted by A. Lewis in "A Talk with Warren on Crime, the Court, the Country," *New York Times Magazine*, October 19, 1969, 130.
126. See also S. Brenner, "Issue Specialization as a Variable in Opinion Assignment on the U.S. Supreme Court," 46 *Journal of Politics* 1217 (1984); and S. Brenner and H. S. Spaeth, "Issue Specialization in Majority Opinion Assignment on the Burger Court," 39 *Western Political Quarterly* 520 (1986).
127. Walter Murphy Interview with Douglas, at 148, MLPU.
128. Waite's papers contain numerous examples of justices complaining about opinion assignments, as do other papers of the justices in regard to Vinson and Burger. See, e.g., Morrison Waite Papers, Box 40, Files for the 1878, 1879, and 1883 Terms, LC; Melville Fuller Papers, Boxes 4 and 6, LC; Frankfurter Papers, Box 108, File 2268, LC; Vinson Papers, Box 215, UK; and Douglas Papers and Brennan Papers, LC.
129. Letter to Brennan, RE: No. 30, Frankfurter Papers, Box 169, File 5, HLS.
130. Justice Thomas interview with Bryan Garner, 13 *The Scribes Journal of Legal Writing* 100 (2010).
131. Justice Scalia interview with Bryan Garner, Id., at 52.
132. See Letters from Gray to Fuller on the problems of reading opinions aloud at conference. Fuller Papers, Box 5, LC.
133. Quoted in A. Westin, *The Anatomy of a Constitutional Law Case* (New York: Macmillan, 1958), 123–24.
134. W. J. Brennan Jr., "State Court Decisions and the Supreme Court," 31 *Pennsylvania Bar Association Quarterly* 393, 405 (1960).
135. T. Clark, "Internal Operation of the United States Supreme Court," 43 *Judicature* 45, 51 (1959).
136. Conversation with Paul Freund (1984). And see Douglas, "Mr. Justice Cardozo," 588 *Michigan Law Review* 549 (1960).
137. Memo, Douglas Papers, Box 228, LC.
138. See J. Palmer and S. Brenner, "The Amount of Time Taken by the Vinson Court to Process Its Full-Opinion Cases," 1990 *Journal of Supreme Court History* 142 (1991).
139. See, e.g., Letter to Justice Byrnes, November 1, 1941, Stone Papers, Box 79, LC.
140. Clark Papers, UT. See also Clark Oral History Interview.
141. Undated note, Black Papers, Box 58, LC.

142. Marshall Papers, various case boxes, LC.
143. Memos to Byrnes and Reed, 1941, Douglas Papers, Box 228, LC.
144. Quoted by M. Pusey, *Charles Evans Hughes* (New York: Macmillan, 1951), 2:671.
145. Stone Papers, Box 75, LC.
146. Letter, December 20, 1940, Black Papers, Box 261, LC.
147. Quoted by A. T. Mason, *The Supreme Court from Taft to Burger*, 3rd ed. (Baton Rouge: Louisiana University Press, 1979), 65.
148. Quoted by Mason, supra note 52, at 501.
149. Letter to Reed, December 2, 1941, Douglas Papers, Box 128, LC.
150. Note, May 20, 1963, Harlan Papers, Box 538, MLPU.
151. *Tinker v. Des Moines School District*, 393 U.S. 503 (1969). See also Potter Stewart Papers, Series I, Box 57, YA.
152. Note, January 2, 1969, Harlan Papers, Box 338, MLPU; Abe Fortas Papers, YA.
153. *Shaw v. Reno*, 509 U.S. 630 (1993); for further discussion, see David M. O'Brien, *Constitutional Law and Politics*, 10th ed. (New York: W. W. Norton, 2017), vol. 1, chap. 8.
154. Letter from Chief Justice Rehnquist, June 7, 1993, Blackmun Papers, Box 624, LC.
155. Letter from Justice Scalia, June 17, 1993, Blackmun Papers, Box 624, LC.
156. *Miranda v. Arizona*, 384 U.S. 436 (1966).
157. Letter to Warren, May 11, 1966, Brennan Papers, Box 145, LC. See also memo, September 13, 1966, Warren Papers, Box 348; and Warren Papers, Boxes 616 and 617, LC.
158. *Griswold v. Connecticut*, 381 U.S. 479 (1965).
159. This and following extracts from letter of April 24, 1965, Brennan Papers, Box 130, LC. For the conference discussion, see Brennan Papers, Box 411; and Warren Papers, Box 267, LC. Douglas's first draft is in Brennan Papers, Box 130, LC.
160. Brennan Papers, Box 130, LC.
161. Letter of May 19, 1926, Van Devanter Papers, LC; reprinted in *Letters of Justice Louis D. Brandeis*, eds. M. Urofsky and D. Levy (New York: SUNY, 1978), 5:128.
162. Quoted by Murphy, supra note 105, at 53. Likewise, Sutherland wrote Holmes, "I voted 'yes' and would prefer that result. I am inclined to acquiesce and will." Holmes Papers, Opinion Book 1926, HLS. For other instances, see Louis Brandeis Papers, HLS.
163. Quoted by Murphy, supra note 105, at 52. On another occasion, Justice Butler indicated his preference for the opposite result but decided to acquiesce "unless someone initiates opposition." Note to Justice Holmes, Holmes Papers, Opinion Book 1926, HLS.
164. Memo, January 25, 1945, Stone Papers, Box 75, LC.
165. Note on draft opinion, Holmes Papers, Opinion Book 1919, HLS.
166. Response on draft of *Beaumont v. Prieto*, Holmes Papers, Opinion Book 1918, HLS.
167. *Colegrove v. Green*, 328 U.S. 549 (1946).
168. Letter to Black, January 31, 1962, Brennan Papers, Box 68, LC. See also Potter Stewart Papers, Series I, Box 14, YA.
169. Letter to Frankfurter, February 3, 1962, Clark Papers, UT.
170. Memorandum, March 10, 1962, Brennan Papers, Box 68, LC.
171. This discussion draws on the author's more extensive analysis, "Institutional Norms and Supreme Court Opinions: On Reconsidering the Rise of Individual Opinions," in *Supreme Court Decision-Making: Institutional Approaches to the Supreme Court*, eds. C. Clayton and H. Gillman (Chicago: University of Chicago Press, 1999), 91–113.

172. See Robert Post, "The Supreme Court Opinion as Institutional Practice: Dissent, Legal Scholarship, and Decisionmaking in the Taft Court," 85 *Minnesota Law Review* 1267 (2001).

173. See G. Edward White, "The Internal Powers of the Chief Justice: The Nineteenth Century Legacy," 154 *University of Pennsylvania Law Review* 1463 (2006).

174. William A. Bowen, "Dissenting Opinions," 17 *Green Bag* 690, 693 (1905).

175. Justice Holmes, dissenting opinion in *Northern Securities Co. v. United States,* 193 U.S. 197 (1904).

176. Quoted and discussed in Post, supra note 172; see also Barry Cushman, "The Hughes Court Docket Books: The Late Terms, 1937–1940," 55 *American Journal of Legal History* 103 (2015); and Madelyn Fife et al., "Concurring and Dissenting Without Opinion," 42 *Journal of Supreme Court History* 171 (2017).

177. Opinions refer to the number of opinions for the Court disposing of one or more cases on merits. Before 1801, the Supreme Court maintained the practice of issuing its opinions *seriatim.* Here each case disposed of in such a manner is counted as only one opinion. This practice was largely abandoned shortly before John Marshall became chief justice. The figures for the number of opinions for the terms 1791–1800 are taken from J. Goebel Jr., *History of the Supreme Court of the United States (1790–1800)* (New York: Macmillan, 1971), 811, Table XII. The numbers for those terms between 1800 and 1815 are taken from G. Haskins and H. A. Johnson, *Foundations of Power: John Marshall (1801–1815)* (New York: Macmillan, 1981), 653, Table 2. The numbers for the 1810, 1820, 1830, 1840, 1850, 1860, 1870, 1890, 1900, and 1910 terms are based on an analysis of decisions in *United States Reports* for those years. Excluded from those figures are short *per curiam* or memorandum orders denying review or not reaching the merits of a case or otherwise disposing of a case. Data for the October terms after 1913 are taken from "Statistical Sheet," Office of the Clerk, SC, and *Journal of the Supreme Court.*

Total number of opinions refers to both signed and *per curiam* opinions for the Court and dissenting, concurring, or separate opinions in cases given plenary consideration. Excluded, for example, are dissenting opinions from the denial of a petition for *certiorari.* Data for 1801–1814 are taken from Haskins and Johnson, *Foundations.* Figures for the 1800, 1810, 1820, 1830, 1840, 1850, 1860, 1870, 1880, 1890, 1900, and 1910 terms are based on an examination and tabulation by the author of opinions in *United States Reports* for those years. Figures for the October terms after 1913 are taken from the "Annual Statement of Number of Printed Opinions," Office of the Clerk, Supreme Court, with the exception of the 1924–1936 terms, for which the number of total opinions was taken from the *Harvard Law Review's Annual Survey* of those terms; since 2008 they are based on the author's tabulations.

Cases disposed of during term include both those given plenary consideration and those summarily decided or otherwise disposed of. Figures for cases disposed of and carried over for the years 1791–1810, 1820, 1822–1846, 1850, 1860, 1870, 1880, and 1890 are based on the author's tabulation of cases contained in the Docket Books of the Supreme Court of the United States (NARS). Figures for the terms between 1890 and 1910 are taken from the *Annual Reports of the Attorney General of the United States* (Washington, D.C.: GPO, 1891, 1901, 1911). Figures for October terms after 1913 are taken from "Statistical Sheet," Office of the Clerk, Supreme Court; and since 2008 they are based on the author's tabulations and data from the annual *Journal of the Supreme Court.*

178. Justice Stewart Interview with author (February 26, 1985), SC.

179. C. Herman Pritchett, *The Roosevelt Court: A Study in Judicial Politics and Values* (New York: Macmillan, 1948).

180. See Thomas Walker, Lee Epstein, and William Dixon, "On the Mysterious Demise of Consensual Norms in the United States Supreme Court," 50 *The Journal of Politics* 361 (1988). But for criticisms see David M. O'Brien, "Institutional Norms and Supreme Court Opinions: On Reconsidering the Rise of Individual Opinions," in *Supreme Court Decision-Making*, eds. Cornell W. Clayton and Howard Gillman (Chicago: University of Chicago Press, 1999), 91.

181. See Stacia Haynie, "Leadership and Consensus on the U.S. Supreme Court," 54 *The Journal of Politics* 1158 (1992).

182. See Lee Epstein, Jeffrey Segal, Harold Spaeth, and Thomas Walker, *The Supreme Court Compendium*, 2nd ed. (Washington, D.C.: CQ Press, 2001), 147–48, Table 3-1.

183. David J. Danelski and Joseph S. Tulchin, eds., *The Autobiographical Notes of Charles Evans Hughes* xxvi (Cambridge: Harvard University Press, 1973).

184. Charles Evans Hughes, *The Supreme Court of the United States* (New York: Columbia University Press, 1928), at 67.

185. See *Rodgers v. United States*, 332 U.S. 371 (1947).

186. Morton J. Horwitz, *The Transformation of American Law, 1870–1960* (New York: Oxford University Press, 1992), at 169.

187. See, e.g., Bradley J. Best, *Law Clerks, Support Personnel, and the Decline of Consensual Norms of the United States Supreme Court* (El Paso, Tex.: LFB Scholarly Publishers, 2002).

188. Walker, Epstein, and Dixon, supra note 180, at 386.

189. For plurality decisions before the 1969 term, see J. F. Davis and W. Reynolds, "Juridicial Cripples: Plurality Opinions in the Supreme Court," 1974 *Duke Law Journal* 59. For the 1969–1979 terms, see Note, "Plurality Decisions and Judicial Decisionmaking," 94 *Harvard Law Review* 1127, Appendix, at 1147 (1981). Plurality decisions in subsequent terms were tabulated by the author.

190. *Arizona v. Fulminante*, 499 U.S. 279 (1991).

191. See, e.g., *Chavez v. Martinez*, 538 U.S. 760 (2003), in which Justices Souter and Thomas delivered opinions for the Court. See also *United States v. Booker*, 543 U.S. 220 (2005), in which two opinions for the Court were delivered in a ruling that federal sentencing guidelines violate the Sixth Amendment because judges may impose enhanced sentences based on facts that a jury did not consider. Justice Stevens, joined by Justices Scalia, Souter, Thomas, and Ginsburg, ruled that the guidelines are not binding. Justice Breyer, joined by Chief Justice Rehnquist and Justices O'Connor, Kennedy, and Ginsburg, held that the guidelines should still be consulted and sentences reversed if appellate courts find them unreasonable.

192. *McConnell v. Federal Election Commission*, 540 U.S. 93 (2003).

193. Memorandum to Conference, October 28, 1961, Black Papers, Box 60, LC.

194. Letter to Charles Fairman (December 27, 1945), Frankfurter Papers, Box 184, File 16, HLS.

195. John Paul Stevens interview with the author (April 5, 1985), SC.

196. Quoted by McLean, supra note 84, at 60.

197. Hughes, supra note 4, at 68. See, more generally, Melvin Urofsky, *Dissent and the Supreme Court: Its Role in the Court's History and the Nation's Constitutional Dialogue* (New York: Pantheon, 2015).

198. *Chisholm v. Georgia*, 2 Dall. (2 U.S.) 419 (1793).

199. *Dred Scott v. Sanford*, 19 How. (60 U.S.) 393 (1857).

200. *Posadas de Puerto Rico v. Tourism Company of Puerto Rico*, 479 U.S. 328 (1986).

201. *44 Liquormart, Inc. v. Rhode Island*, 517 U.S. 484 (1996).

202. Frankfurter-Brandeis Conversations, Frankfurter Papers, Box 224, File 4101, LC. The original transcript of these conversations is in Brandeis Papers, Box 114, HLS.

203. Quoted in A. Bickel, *The Unpublished Opinions of Mr. Justice Brandeis* 18 (Chicago: University of Chicago Press, 1967).

204. Letter, December 8, 1915, William Day Papers, Box 30, LC.

205. *Bank of the United States v. Dandridge*, 25 U.S. 64, 90 (1827). See also letters from Justice Story by the reporter in 1818, telling of his agreement with the Court's opinion and providing a copy of a dissenting opinion that he suppressed; W. W. Story, *Life and Letters of Joseph Story* (Boston: Little, Brown, 1851), 1:303–8.

206. John Niven, ed., *The Salmon P. Chase Papers: Journals, 1829–1872* (Kent, Ohio: Kent State University Press, 1993), 1:517.

207. Quoted in Adam Liptak, "On Summer Docket, Blunt Talk on Big Cases," *New York Times* A13 (July 31, 2017).

208. Holmes's Opinion Books contain numerous examples of justices acquiescing in a unanimous decision even though as many as three or more disagreed with the ruling. See, e.g., Letter from Justice Brown to Holmes, April 25, 1899, in which he says, "The opinion was not quite so unanimous as it appears to be. There were three members of the Court who . . . threatened to dissent, but they finally acquiesced in the result." Holmes Papers, Box 45, File 24, HLS.

209. Quoted by Mason, supra note 52, at 61 and 223.

210. J. Campbell III, "The Spirit of Dissent," 66 *Judicature* 305 (1983); Jill Duffy and Elizabeth Lambert, "Dissents from the Bench: A Compilation of Oral Dissents by U.S. Supreme Court Justices," 102 *Law Library Journal* 7 (Winter 2010).

211. L. Brandeis, quoted in Alexander Bickel, *The Unpublished Opinions of Mr. Justice Brandeis* (Chicago: University of Chicago Press, 1967), 18.

212. See D. Dorin, "'Seize the Time': Justice Tom Clark's Role in *Mapp v. Ohio*," in V. Swigert, ed., *Law and the Legal Process* 21 (Beverly Hills, Calif.: Sage, 1982).

213. Quoted by Burger, "In Memoriam: Hugo L. Black," 92 S. Ct. 5, 79 (1972).

214. Reported in Paul Campos, "Roberts Writes Both Obamacare Opinions," *Salon* (July 13, 2012), http://www.salon.com/2012/07/03/roberts.

215. See, e.g., memoranda in Boxes 492, 523, and Memoranda for Conference from Justice Marshall on *Rust v. Sullivan*, Box 530, Marshall Papers, LC. See also B. Blair Cook, "Justice Brennan and the Institutionalization of Dissent Assignment," 79 *Judicature* 17 (1995); and Nancy Maveety, "The Era of the Choral Court," 89 *Judicature* 138 (November/December 2005).

216. *Cruzan by Cruzan v. Director, Missouri Department of Health*, 497 U.S. 261 (1990).

217. Memoranda from Justice Brennan, December 11, 1989, Marshall Papers, Box 502, LC.

218. Justice O'Connor, Lecture at the Marshall-Wythe School of Law, Williamsburg, Virginia, November 14, 1994, reported in *Amicus Curiae* (November 21, 1994). For other examples of justices assigning dissents or requesting such assignments, see memos in Marshall Papers, Boxes 423, 454, 470, 473, 511, and 602, LC.

219. See Richard L. Hasen, "The Most Sarcastic Justice," 18 *Green Bag* 2d 215 (2015).

220. *Lee v. Weisman,* 505 U.S. 577, 636, and 638 (1992) (Scalia, J., dis. op.).

221. *Austin v. Michigan Chamber of Commerce,* 494 U.S. 652, 685 (1990) (Scalia, J., dis. op.).

222. *Romer v. Evans,* 517 U.S. 620, 652–653 (1996) (Scalia, J., dis. op.).

223. *Obergefell v. Hodges*, 135 S. Ct. 2584 (2015) (Scalia, J., dis. op.).

224. Ruth Bader Ginsburg, "The Role of Dissenting Opinions," Leo and Berry Memorial Lecture (October 21, 2007).

225. A. Scalia, "Dissenting Opinions," *Journal of Supreme Court History 1994*, at 33–44.

226. See, e.g., Christopher W. Schmidt and Carolyn Shapiro, "Oral Dissenting in the Supreme Court," 19 *William & Mary Bill of Rights Journal* 75 (2010).

227. Undated Conference Note, Clark Papers, UT.

228. Memorandum for Conference, November 5, 1959, Harlan Papers, Box 486, MLPU.

229. F. Frankfurter, "The Zeitgeist and the Judiciary," in *Law and Politics*, eds. A. MacLeish and E. Prichard Jr. (New York: Harcourt, Brace, 1939).

230. Burger, Annual Judicial Conference, Second Judicial Circuit, Buck Hill Falls, Pa. (May 10, 1980) (unpublished manuscript on file with the author).

231. C. Thomas, Speech at Trinity United Methodist Church, aired on C-SPAN (April 12, 1997).

232. Chief Justice Burger Interview with author, January 15, 1985.

233. Memorandum to Conference, October 28, 1961, Black Papers, Box 60, LC.

234. Included in the number of opinion pages are those for signed majority, concurring, dissenting, and *per curiam* opinions. For the 1960, 1965, 1970, 1975, and 1979 terms, see House Committee on Appropriations, *Departments . . . : Hearings before a Subcommittee*, 97th Cong., 2d sess., pt. 4, at 380 (Washington, D.C.: GPO, 1982). Figures for the 1938 term and tabulations for the average length of opinions are the author's.

235. See David Stewart, "Quiet Times," *ABA Journal* 40 (October, 1994).

236. See Adam Liptak, "Justices Are Long on Words but Short on Guidance," *New York Times*, November 17, 2010.

237. Interview with Garner, *The Scribes Journal*, supra note 130, at 134.

238. See Antonin Scalia and Bryan A. Garner, *Reading Law: The Interpretation of Legal Texts* (St. Paul, Minn.: Thomson/West, 2012).

239. For a further discussion of the sources of interpretivist versus noninterpretivist approaches to constitutional interpretation, see D. M. O'Brien, *Constitutional Law and Politics*, 10th ed. (New York: W. W. Norton, 2017), chap. 1 of either vol. 1 or vol. 2.

240. G. Phelps and J. Gates, "The Myth of Jurisprudence," 31 *Santa Clara Law Review* 567 (1991), at 589. Their content analysis is further developed in J. Gates and G. Phelps, "Intentionalism in Constitutional Opinions," 49 *Political Research Quarterly* 245 (1996).

241. *Metromedia v. City of San Diego*, 453 U.S. 490 (1981).

242. *Utility Air Regulatory Group v. Environmental Protection Agency*, 134 S. Ct. 2427 (2014).

SIX

The Court and American Life

1. Newton Minow Oral History Interview, at 27–28, UK. See also Conference Lists, Hugo Black Papers, Box 310, LC.

2. Tom Clark Oral History Interview, at 10, UK. *Brown v. Board of Education*, 344 U.S. 1 (1952) (*per curiam* decision on postponement of oral arguments).

3. Letter to Charles Warren, July 19, 1923, Charles Warren Papers, Box 2, LC.

4. *Powell v. Alabama*, 287 U.S. 45 (1932).

5. Story related in a letter from Herbert Wechsler to Frankfurter, July 22, 1946, Felix Frankfurter Papers, Box 172, HLS.

6. *Cooper v. Aaron*, 358 U.S. 1 (1958).

7. Letter to Harlan, September 2, 1958, Frankfurter Papers, Box 169, HLS.

8. See letter from Stone to Frankfurter, March 17, 1943, Harlan F. Stone Papers, Box 13, LC; Earl Warren Papers, Box 125, LC; and *Supreme Court Journal* for June 21, 1969.

9. Memorandum for Conference, June 27, 1984, in William J. Brennan Papers, Box 670, LC.

10. W. O. Douglas, *The Court Years* (New York: Random House, 1980), 40.

11. "Frankfurter Dissent Provokes Warren to Rebuttal on Bench," *New York Times*, March 21, 1961, A1, col. 4. For another such story, see W. J. Brennan Jr., "Chief Justice Warren," 88 *Harvard Law Review* 1, 2 (1974).

12. See Jill Duffy and Elizabeth Lambert, "Dissents from the Bench: A Compilation of Oral Dissents Issued by U.S. Supreme Court Justices" (June 15, 2009), at SSRN:http://SSRN.com/abstract-1418218 (accessed August 29, 2009).

13. W. Brennan Jr., Remarks at Student Legal Forum, Charlottesville, Virginia, at 1 (February 17, 1959), SC.

14. Quoted in Robert Barnes, "Kagan Made Her Mark in a Bold Rookie Term," *Washington Post*, September 27, 2011, A1.

15. *Perry v. United States*, 294 U.S. 330 (1935).

16. Letter to Frankfurter from Reed, February 10, 1936, Frankfurter Papers, Box 170, HLS.

17. Memorandum to Members of the Court, May 7, 1954, Tom C. Clark Papers, UT; and Warren Papers, Box 574, LC.

18. See Memorandum to the Chief Justice from the Press Office, September 1, 1948, Stanley Reed Papers, Box 174, UK; and John M. Harlan Papers, Box 498, MLPU.

19. See Letter to the Chief Justice and "Background Paper for the Chief Justice," September 22, 1969, Harlan Papers, Box 606, MLPU.

20. Note, October 12, 1970, Brennan Papers, Box 487, LC.

21. W. E. Burger, foreword to *Views from the Bench: The Judiciary and Constitutional Politics*, eds. M. Cannon and D. M. O'Brien (Chatham, N.J.: Chatham House, 1985).

22. Lyle Denniston, "Reporter, SCOTUS Blog," in Brian Lamb et al., eds., *The Supreme Court: A C-SPAN Book* 273 (New York: Public Affairs, 2010). For recent reporters' experiences when covering the Court, see Timothy R. Johnson and Jerry Goldman, eds., *A Good Quarrel: America's Top Legal Reporters Share Stories from Inside the Supreme Court* (Ann Arbor: University of Michigan Press, 2009).

23. *National Federation of Independent Business v. Sebelius*, 132 S. Ct. 2566 (2012).

24. See E. Katsh, "The Supreme Court Beat: How Television Covers the U.S. Supreme Court," 67 *Judicature* 6 (1983); and E. Slotnick and J. Segal, *Television News and the Supreme Court: All the News That's Fit to Air?* (New York: Cambridge University Press, 1998).

25. Letter to Reed about *Cox v. New Hampshire*, March 28, 1941, Reed Papers, Box 171, UK.

26. E. Warren, *The Memoirs of Earl Warren* 285 (New York: Doubleday, 1977). See also Gordon Davidson Interview, UK; and Reed Papers, Boxes 41, 43, 50, and 331, UK.

27. See the discussion in Chapter 3 of the justices' disclosures leading to *The Brethren* and other more recent decisions, as well as Richard Davis, "The Symbiotic Relationship Between the U.S. Supreme Court and the Press," in Richard Davis, ed., *Covering the Supreme Court in the Digital Age* (New York: Cambridge University Press, 2014).

28. *Brown v. Board of Education*, 347 U.S. 483 (1954).

29. *Brown v. Board of Education*, 349 U.S. 294 (1955).
30. Transcript of Oral Argument, Reed Papers, Box 43, UK.
31. Memo summarizing conversation with the chief justice by John Fassett for Justice Reed, Reed Papers, Box 331, UK. See also Harold Burton Papers, Box 263, LC; and Clark Papers, UK.
32. Reed Papers, Box 331, UK.
33. Law Clerks' Recommendations for Segregation Decree, Clark Papers, UT; and Warren Papers, Box 574, LC.
34. Reed's notes of conference discussion, Reed Papers, Box 43, UK; "Diaries," Burton Papers, Box 3, LC; Frankfurter Papers, HLS; and Warren Papers, Boxes 571 and 574, LC.
35. *Virginia v. West Virginia*, 200 U.S. 1 (1911).
36. Memorandum to the Brethren, January 15, 1954, Burton Papers, Box 263, LC (quoting *Virginia v. West Virginia*, 200 U.S. 1 (1911)).
37. *Griffin v. Prince Edward County School Board*, 377 U.S. 218, 219, 234 (1964).
38. Dennis Hutchinson, "*Brown v. Board of Education*," in *The Oxford Companion to the Supreme Court of the United States* (2 ed.), Kermit Hall, ed. (New York: Oxford University Press, 2005), at 112.
39. Memorandum, School Openings and Desegregation, Lee White Papers, Box 5, JPL.
40. Ruby Martin Oral History Interview, at 12, JPL.
41. V. Navasky, *Kennedy Justice* (New York: Atheneum, 1971), 97–98. For a good survey of the activities and accomplishments of the Eisenhower administration in the area of civil rights, see Memorandum to the Attorney General, January 18, 1961, William Rogers Papers, Box 47; and Dwight David Eisenhower (DDE) Diaries, Box 33, EPL.
42. Memorandum on Civil Rights Legislation, WHCF—Executive Legislative Series, Hu, Box 65, JPL. See also Stephen Pollack Interview III, at 19, JPL; and WHCF-CF, Boxes 102 and 127, JPL.
43. See, generally, White Papers, Box 2; and WHCF-CF, Box 102, JPL.
44. *Alexander v. Holmes County Board of Education*, 396 U.S. 1218, 1220 (1969).
45. *Alexander v. Holmes County Board of Education*, 396 U.S. 19 (1969) (*per curiam*). The Court had previously held, in *Green v. County School Board of New Kent County*, 391 U.S. 430 (1968), that "freedom of choice" in achieving school desegregation was ineffective.
46. All quotations are from justices' memos; Harlan Papers, Boxes 487, 565, and 606, MLPU; and Brennan Papers, Box 218, LC.
47. *Carter v. West Feliciana Parish School Board*, 396 U.S. 290 (1970).
48. Based on figures in Appendix to Memorandum for the President, Gerald Ford Papers, WHCF—Special Files, Box 4, FPL. (The report considered districts with an "appreciable percentage" of minority students to have at least 5 percent minority students and segregated districts to have more than 50 percent nonminority students.)
49. Handwritten note of President Eisenhower, Papers as President—Administrative Series, Box 23, EPL.
50. Pollack Interview III, supra note 42, at 19.
51. See A. Hacker, *Two Nations: Black and White, Separate, Hostile, Unequal* (New York: Scribner's, 1992); G. Orfield, S. Eaton, and the Harvard Project on School Desegregation, *Dismantling Desegregation* (New York: New Press, 1996); and E. Frankenberg, C. Lee, and G. Orfield, *A Multiracial Society with Segregated Schools* (Cambridge, Mass.: Civil Rights Project, Harvard College, 2003).

52. *Missouri v. Jenkins*, 495 U.S. 33 (1990).
53. *Board of Education of Oklahoma City Public Schools v. Dowell*, 498 U.S. 237 (1991).
54. *Green v. County School Board of New Kent County*, 391 U.S. 430 (1968).
55. *Freeman v. Pitts*, 503 U.S. 467 (1992).
56. *Missouri v. Jenkins*, 515 U.S. 70 (1995).
57. Gary Orfield and Chungmei Lee, Brown *at 50: King's Dream or* Plessy's *Nightmare?* (Cambridge, Mass.: Civil Rights Project, Harvard University, 2004).
58. For further discussion, see Erica Frankenberg and Gary Orfield, eds., *Lessons in Integration: Realizing the Promise of Racial Diversity in American Schools* (Charlottesville: University of Virginia Press, 2007).
59. Gary Orfield and Jongyeon Ee, *Patterns of Resegregation in Florida's Schools* (LeRoy Collins, Florida State University, September 27, 2017).
60. *Gratz v. Bollinger,* 539 U.S. 244 (2003).
61. *Grutter v. Bollinger,* 539 U.S. 306 (2003).
62. *Parents Involved in Community Schools v. Seattle School District No. 1*, 1275 S. Ct. 2738 (2007).
63. *Schuette v. Coalition to Defend Affirmative Action, Integration and Immigrant Rights for Equality By Any Means Necessary,* 134 S. Ct. 1623 (2014).
64. *Gratz v. Bollinger,* 539 U.S. 306 (2003).
65. *Grutter v. Bollinger,* 539 U.S. 306 (2003).
66. See Emily Bazelon, "The Next Kind of Integration," *New York Times Magazine,* July 20, 2008.
67. See Leslie A. Maxwell, "60 Years After *Brown,* School Diversity More Complex Than Ever," *Education Week* 3 (May 14, 2014). See also Government Accounting Office, *K-12 Education: Better Use of Information Could Help Agencies Identify Disparities and Address Racial Discrimination* (Washington, D.C.: GPO, April 2016).
68. R. Dahl, "Decision-making in a Democracy: The Supreme Court as a National Policy-maker," 6 *Journal of Public Law* 279, 293 (1957).
69. G. Rosenberg, *The Hollow Hope: Can Courts Bring about Social Change?* (Chicago: University of Chicago Press, 1991).
70. Despite these risks, there are circumstances when only the Court is able to break through a political or institutional logjam. Though a solution arrived at through the political process of persuasion and bargaining might have been more effective, it was impossible at the time, since all of the key Senate committees were chaired by southerners unwilling to allow an emerging majority in favor of desegregation to pursue a political solution. Using the courts in such a situation makes sense, even if there are unintended consequences. See Gordon Silverstein, *Law's Allure: How Law Shapes, Constrains, Saves, and Kills Politics* (New York: Cambridge University Press, 2009).
71. R. Neustadt, *Presidential Power and the Modern Presidents* (New York: Free Press, 1990).
72. Matthew E. K. Hall, *The Nature of Supreme Court Power* (New York: Cambridge University Press, 2011).
73. Dahl, supra note 68.
74. F. P. Dunne, "The Supreme Court's Decisions," in *Mr. Dooley's Opinions* (New York: Harper, 1901).
75. Letter, October 15, 1937, Stone Papers, Box 13, LC.
76. See also Justice Frankfurter's correspondence with Paul Freund (October 18, 1953), Frankfurter Papers, Box 184, HLS, and David M. O'Brien, Box on "The 1937 'Con-

stitutional Crisis' and the Court's 'Switch-in-Time-that-Saved-Nine'" in *Constitutional Law and Politics* vol. I or II, chap. 1 (New York: W. W. Norton, 10th ed., 2017).

77. Gordon Silverstein and John Hanley, "The Supreme Court and Public Opinion in Times of War and Crisis," 61 *Hastings Law Journal* 1453 (2010).

78. Interview with Antonin Scalia, *This Honorable Court*, PBS, 1988.

79. Interview with Harry Blackmun, *Nightline*, ABC, November 18, 1993.

80. *Vacco v. Quill*, 521 U.S. 793 (1997); and *Washington v. Glucksberg*, 521 U.S. 702 (1997).

81. *Bowers v. Hardwick*, 478 U.S. 186 (1986).

82. *Lawrence v. Texas*, 539 U.S. 558 (2003).

83. See James Gibson and Gregory Caldeira, "Has Legal Realism Damaged the Legitimacy of the U.S. Supreme Court?" 45 *Law & Society Review* 195 (2011).

84. Letter, April 24, 1961, Frankfurter Papers, Box 171, HLS; and Memo to Conference, March 2, 1962, Clark Papers, UT. For another example of Frankfurter's appeal to the forces of public opinion, see his memorandum on *Reid v. Covert*, June 5, 1957, Warren Papers, Box 434, LC.

85. See Dahl, supra note 68. Barry Friedman, *The Will of the People: How Public Opinion Has Influenced the Supreme Court and Shaped the Meaning of the Constitution* (New York: Farrar, Straus and Giroux, 2009); and Thomas R. Marshall, *Public Opinion and the Rehnquist Court* (Albany, N.Y.: SUNY Press, 2008).

86. See D. Barnum, "The Supreme Court and Public Opinion: Judicial Decisionmaking in the Post–New Deal Period," 47 *Journal of Politics* 652 (1985); and James L. Gibson and Gregory A. Caldeira, "Knowing the Supreme Court? A Reconsideration of Public Ignorance of the High Court," 71 *Journal of Politics* 429 (2009).

87. See T. Marshall, *Public Opinion and the Supreme Court* (Boston: Unwin Hyman, 1989).

88. For an excellent overview and criticisms of research on courts and public opinion, see G. Caldeira, "Courts and Public Opinion," in *The American Courts: A Critical Assessment*, eds. J. Gates and C. Johnson (Washington, D.C.: CQ Press, 1991), 303.

89. See and compare J. H. Ely, *Democracy and Distrust: A Theory of Judicial Review* (Cambridge, Mass.: Harvard University Press, 1980); and W. Lasser, *The Limits of Judicial Power: The Supreme Court in American Politics* (Chapel Hill: University of North Carolina Press, 1988).

90. See V. O. Key, "A Theory of Critical Elections," 17 *Journal of Politics* 3 (1955).

91. See David Adamany, "The Supreme Court's Role in Critical Elections," in *Realignment in American Politics*, eds. B. Campbell and R. Trilling (Austin: University of Texas Press, 1980).

92. See J. Gates, *The Supreme Court and Partisan Realignment* (Boulder, Colo.: Westview Press, 1992); M. Graber, "The Nonmajoritarian Difficulty: Legislative Deference to the Judiciary" 7 *Studies in American Political Development* 35 (1993); and W. Lasser, "The Supreme Court in Periods of Critical Realignment," 47 *Journal of Politics* 1174 (1985).

93. See G. Casey, "Popular Perceptions of Supreme Court Rulings," 4 *American Politics Quarterly* 3 (1976); D. Jaros and R. Roper, "The Supreme Court, Myth, Diffuse Support, Specific Support, and Legitimacy," 8 *American Politics Quarterly* 85 (1980); P. Secret, J. Johnson, and S. Welch, "Racial Differences in Attitudes toward the Supreme Court's Decision on Prayer in Public Schools," 67 *Social Science Quarterly* 877 (1986); and Timothy R. Johnson and Andrew Martin, "The Public's Conditional Response to Supreme Court Decisions," 92 *American Political Science Review* 299 (1998).

94. Report, "Supreme Court Favorability Reaches New Low," The Pew Research Center for the People & the Press (May 1, 2012).

95. "Republicans' Approval of Supreme Court Sinks to 18%," *Gallup Poll* (July 16, 2015), available at http://www.gallup.com/poll/184160/republicans-approval -supreme-court-sinks.aspx (accessed July 19, 2015).

96. Pew Research Center, "Dim Public Awareness of Supreme Court as Major Rulings Loom" (May 14, 2015), available at http://www.pewresearch.org/fact-tank /2015/05/14/dim-public-awareness-of-supreme-court-as-major-rulings-loom/.

97. Caldeira, supra note 88, at 307.

98. Pew Research Center, "Growing Share of Americans Say Supreme Court Should Base Its Rulings on What Constitution Means Today" (May 11, 2018).

99. *Engel v. Vitale*, 370 U.S. 421 (1962).

100. *Abington School District v. Schempp*, 374 U.S. 203 (1963).

101. "Text of 96 Congressmen's Declaration on Integration," *New York Times*, March 12, 1956, 19. (Five congressmen later joined the manifesto.)

102. *Wallace v. Jaffree*, 472 U.S. 38 (1985).

103. *Lee v. Weisman*, 505 U.S. 577 (1992).

104. See *Zelman v. Simmons-Harris*, 536 U.S. 639 (2002).

105. *Van Orden v. Perry*, 542 U.S. 910 (2005); and *McCreary v. ACLU*, 545 U.S. 844 (2005).

106. *Town of Greece, New York v. Galloway*, 134 S. Ct. 1811 (2014).

107. *Marsh v. Chambers*, 463 U.S. 783 (1983).

108. *Miranda v. Arizona*, 384 U.S. 436 (1966).

109. Notes and Correspondence, *Miranda* File, Warren Papers, Box 617, LC; and Abe Fortas Papers, YA.

110. *Mapp v. Ohio*, 367 U.S. 643 (1961).

111. *Wolf v. Colorado*, 338 U.S. 25 (1949).

112. *Linkletter v. Walker*, 381 U.S. 618 (1965).

113. *Williams v. United States*, 401 U.S. 675, 677 (1971). See also *Gregg v. Georgia*, 428 U.S. 153, 180 (1976); and *Woodson v. North Carolina*, 428 U.S. 280, 299 (1976).

114. *Teague v. Lane*, 489 U.S. 288 (1989).

115. *Wharton v. Bockting*, 549 U.S. 406 (2007).

116. *Davis v. United States*, 131 S. Ct. 2419 (2011).

117. *Montgomery v. Louisiana*, 136 S. Ct. 718 (2016).

118. *Miller v. Alabama*, 132 S. Ct. 2455 (2012).

119. Frankfurter and Byrnes, both appointed by Roosevelt, had maintained a close relationship through the years; in 1953–1954, the latter, as governor, had made well known to Frankfurter his views that the Court would exceed its constitutional power in striking down segregation. See letters and memos, Warren Papers, Boxes 574 and 353, LC; discussion of *Cooper v. Aaron* in Chapter 5; J. Byrnes, "The Supreme Court Must Be Curbed," *U.S. News & World Report*, May 18, 1956, 50; and A. Bickel, "Frankfurter's Former Clerk Disputes Byrnes's Statement," *U.S. News & World Report*, June 15, 1956, 132. (A copy of Bickel's original and more extensive rebuttal of Byrnes's article may be found in Warren Papers, Box 353, LC.)

120. See Jeffrey Jones, "U.S. Abortion Attitudes Remain Closely Divided," *Gallup* (June 11, 2018).

121. "Showtime for Gay Marriage," *The Economist* 21 (May 2, 2015).

122. Memorandum on the Segregation Decree, Warren Papers, Box 574, LC.

123. J. Peltason, *Fifty-eight Lonely Men: Southern Federal Judges and School Deseg-regation* (New York: Harcourt, Brace and World, 1961) 9–10.

124. J. W. Howard, *Courts of Appeals in the Federal Judicial System* (Princeton, N.J.: Princeton University Press, 1981).

125. *Massachusetts v. Shepard*, 468 U.S. 981 (1984); and *United States v. Leon*, 468 U.S. 902 (1984).

126. *Arizona v. Evans*, 514 U.S. 1 (1995).

127. See *Herring v. United States*, 555 U.S. 135 (2009); and *Davis v. United States*, 131 S. Ct. 2419 (2011).

128. *Jaffree v. Board of School Commissioners*, 554 F. Supp. 1104 (1983).

129. *Wallace v. Jaffree*, 742 U.S. 38 (1985).

130. *Friedman v. City of Highland Park, Illinois*, 136 S. Ct. 447 (2015) (C. Thomas, and A. Scalia, dissenting).

131. See *District of Columbia v. Heller*, 554 U.S. 570 (2008); and *McDonald v. Chi-cago*, 561 U.S. 742 (2010).

132. *Brzonkala v. Virginia Polytechnic Institute and State University*, 169 F.3d 820 (1999).

133. *United States v. Morrison*, 529 U.S. 598 (2000).

134. *Report of the Committee on Federal-State Relationships as Affected by Judicial Decisions*, reprinted in *Congressional Record*, 73d Cong., 2d sess., Appendix, A7784, A7787 (daily ed., August 25, 1958).

135. *Katz v. United States*, 389 U.S. 347 (1967).

136. Letter, December 28, 1967, Harlan Papers, Box 301, MLPU.

137. Letter, January 29, 1968, Harlan Papers, Box 301, MLPU.

138. *Strange v. Searcy*, 135 S. Ct. 940 (2015).

139. *Pavan v. Smith*, 582 U.S.__ (2017).

140. *Masterpiece Cakeshop v. Colorado Civil Rights Commission*, 584 U.S.__ (2018).

141. Letter to Clark, January 25, 1962, Clark Papers, UT.

142. *Michigan v. Long*, 463 U.S. 1032 (1983).

143. Nicholas Kazenbach Oral History Interview, at 41, JPL.

144. *Stuart v. Laird*, 5 U.S. 299 (1803).

145. *Ex parte McCardle*, 74 U.S. 506 (1869).

146. See Linda Camp Keith, "The United States Supreme Court and Judicial Review of Congress, 1803–2001," 90 *Judicature* 166 (2007).

147. *Rasul v. Bush*, 542 U.S. 466 (2004); and *Hamdi v. Rumsfeld*, 542 U.S. 507 (2004).

148. *Hamdan v. Rumsfeld*, 542 U.S. 507 (2006).

149. *Boumediene v. Bush*, 553 U.S. 723 (2008).

150. In *Lauf v. E. G. Shinner*, 303 U.S. 323 (1938); however, the Court upheld the Norris-LaGuardia Act's removal of the power of lower federal courts to issue injunctions in labor disputes.

151. *United States v. Klein*, 80 U.S. 128 (1872).

152. C. H. Pritchett, *Congress versus the Supreme Court, 1957–1960* (Minneapolis: University of Minnesota Press, 1961), 122–23.

153. See Dion Farganis, "Court Curbing in the Modern Era: Should Supreme Court Justices Really Worry About Attacks from Congress?" (July 6, 2009) at SSRN: http://SSRN.com/abstract-1430723 (accessed September 9, 2009).

154. *Chisholm v. Georgia*, 2 Dall. (2 U.S.) 419 (1793).

155. *Pollock v. Farmers' Loan and Trust Co.*, 157 U.S. 429 (1895).

156. *Oregon v. Mitchell*, 400 U.S. 112 (1970).

157. *Minor v. Happersett*, 88 U.S. 162 (1875).

158. *Breedlove v. Suttles*, 302 U.S. 277 (1937).
159. *Barron v. Baltimore*, 7 Pet. (32 U.S.) 243 (1833).
160. *The Slaughterhouse Cases*, 16 Wall. (83 U.S.) 36 (1873).
161. *Pennsylvania v. Wheeling and Belmont Bridge Co.*, 13 How. (54 U.S.) 518 (1852).
162. These data are derived from William N. Eskridge Jr., "Overriding Supreme Court Statutory Interpretation Decisions," 101 *Yale Law Journal* 331, 338 (1991).
163. *Dickerson v. United States*, 530 U.S. 428 (2000).
164. *City of Boerne v. Flores*, 521 U.S. 49 (1995); and *Oregon v. Smith*, 494 U.S. 872 (1990).
165. *Sherbert v. Verner*, 374 U.S. 398 (1963).
166. See *Nevada Dept. of Human Resources v. Hibbs*, 538 U.S. 721 (2003) (upholding abrogation of states' Eleventh Amendment immunity from lawsuits under the Family and Medical Leave Act of 1993); and *Tennessee v. Lane*, 541 U.S. 509 (2004) (holding that states may be sued to enforce Title 2 of the Americans with Disabilities Act with respect to providing access to courts for the disabled).
167. *Holt v. Hobbs*, 135 S. Ct. 853 (2015). See also *Barwell v. Hobby Lobby Stores*, 134 S. Ct. 2751 (2014), and *Gonzales v. O Centro*, 546 U.S. 418 (2006).
168. *United States v. Morrison*, 529 U.S. 598 (2000).
169. *Kimel v. Florida Board of Regents*, 528 U.S. 62 (2000).
170. See L. Fisher, "Separation of Powers: Interpretation outside of Courts," 18 *Pepperdine Law Review* 57 (1990); J. Mitchell Pickerill, *Constitutional Deliberation in Congress* (Durham, N.C.: Duke University Press, 2004); and Jeb Barnes, *Overruled? Legislative Overrides, Pluralism, and Contemporary Court-Congress Relations* (Palo Alto, Calif.: Stanford University Press, 2004).
171. J. Califano, *Governing America* (New York: Simon & Schuster, 1981), 227.
172. Dahl, supra note 68.
173. *Worcester v. Georgia*, 31 U.S. 515 (1832).
174. Herbert Brownell Oral History Interview, at 33, EPL.
175. *Plessy v. Ferguson*, 163 U.S. 537 (1896).
176. Letter to Swede Hazlett, July 22, 1957, DDE Diaries, Box 25, EPL.
177. Quoted in R. Evans Jr. and R. Novak, *Nixon in the White House* (New York: Random House, 1971), 56.
178. *Alexander v. Holmes County School Board*, 396 U.S. 19 (1969).
179. *American Federation of Labor v. American Sash & Door Company*, 335 U.S. 538, 555–56 (1946).
180. See N. Glazer, "Toward an Imperial Judiciary," 40 *Public Interest* 104 (1975); D. Horowitz, *The Courts and Social Policy* (Washington, D.C.: Brookings Institution, 1977); and R. Berger, *Government by the Judiciary* (Cambridge, Mass.: Harvard University Press, 1977). But see Mark Kozlowski, *The Myth of the Imperial Judiciary* (New York: New York University Press, 2003). For a more extreme argument that courts cannot bring about social change see G. Rosenberg, *The Hollow Hope: Can Courts Bring about Social Change?* 2nd ed. (Chicago: University of Chicago Press, 2009); and M. J. Klarman, *From Jim Crow to Civil Rights: The Supreme Court and the Struggle for Racial Equality* (New York: Oxford University Press, 2004).
181. See Eugene Rostow, *Sovereign Prerogative: The Supreme Court and the Quest for Law* (New Haven, Conn.: Yale University Press, 1962); and Jeffrey Rosen, *The Most Democratic Branch: How the Courts Serve America* (New York: Oxford University Press, 2006).

Glossary

advisory opinion An opinion or interpretation of law that does not have binding effect. The Court does not give advisory opinions, for example, on hypothetical disputes; it decides only actual cases or controversies.

affirm In an appellate court, to reach a decision that agrees with the result reached in a case by the lower court.

amicus curiae A friend of the court, a person not a party to litigation, who volunteers or is invited by the court to give his or her views on a case.

appeal To take a case to a higher court for review. Generally, a party losing in a trial court may appeal once to an appellate court as a matter of right. If the party loses in the appellate court, appeal to a higher court is within the discretion of the higher court. Most appeals to the Supreme Court are within its discretion to deny or grant a hearing.

appellant The party that appeals a lower-court decision to a higher court.

appellee One who has an interest in upholding the decision of a lower court and is compelled to respond when the case is appealed to a higher court by the appellant.

brief A document prepared by counsel to serve as the basis for an argument in court, setting out the facts and legal arguments in support of his or her case.

case A general term for an action, cause, suit, or controversy, at law or equity; a question contested before a court.

case law   The law as defined by previously decided cases, distinct from statutes and other sources of law.

certification, writ of   A method of taking a case from appellate court to the Supreme Court in which the lower court asks that some question or interpretation of law be certified, clarified, and made more certain.

***certiorari*, writ of**   A writ issued from the Supreme Court, at its discretion and at the request of a petitioner, to order a lower court to send the record of a case to the Court for its review.

civil law   The body of law dealing with the private rights of individuals, as distinguished from criminal law.

class action   A lawsuit brought by one person or group on behalf of all persons similarly situated.

common law   The collection of principles and rules, particularly from unwritten English law, that derive their authority from long-standing usage and custom or from courts recognizing and enforcing those customs.

concurring opinion   An opinion by a justice that agrees with the result reached by the Court in a case but disagrees with the Court's rationale for its decision.

controversy   *See* justiciable controversy.

criminal law   The body of law that deals with the enforcement of laws and the punishment of persons who, by breaking laws, commit crimes against the state.

declaratory judgment   A court pronouncement declaring a legal right or interpretation but not ordering a special action.

de facto   In fact, in reality.

defendant   In a civil action, the party denying or defending itself against charges brought by a plaintiff. In a criminal action, the person indicted for the commission of an offense.

de jure   As a result of law, as a result of official action.

dicta   See *obiter dictum*.

discretionary jurisdiction   Jurisdiction that a court may accept or reject in particular cases. The Supreme Court has discretionary jurisdiction in over 90 percent of the cases that come to it.

dismissal   An order disposing of a case without a hearing or trial.

dissenting opinion   An opinion by a justice that disagrees with the result reached by the Court in a case.

docket   All cases filed in a court.

due process   Fair and regular procedure. The Fifth and Fourteenth Amendments guarantee persons that they will not be deprived of life, liberty, or property by the government until fair and usual procedures have been followed.

error, writ of   A writ issued from an appeals court to a lower court requiring that it send the record of a case so that it may review it for error.

ex parte   From, or on, only one side. Application to a court for some ruling or action on behalf of only one party.

exclusionary rule   An evidentiary rule requiring that evidence obtained in violation of an individual's constitutional rights under the Fourth Amendment must be excluded at trial.

habeas corpus   Literally, "you have the body"; a writ issued to inquire whether a person is lawfully imprisoned or detained. The writ demands that the persons holding the prisoner justify his or her detention or release him or her.

in forma pauperis   In the manner of a pauper, without liability for the costs of filing cases before a court.

injunction   A court order prohibiting a person from performing a particular act.

judgment   The official decision of a court.

judicial review   The power to review and strike down any legislation or other government action that is inconsistent with federal or state constitutions. The Supreme Court reviews government action only under the Constitution of the United States.

jurisdiction   The power of a court to hear a case or controversy, which exists when the proper parties are present and when the point to be decided is among the issues authorized to be handled by a particular court.

justiciable controversy   A controversy in which a claim of right is asserted against another who has an interest in contesting it. Courts will consider only justiciable controversies, as distinguished from hypothetical disputes.

majority opinion   An opinion in a case that is subscribed to by a majority of the justices who participated in the decision.

mandamus, **writ of**   "We command"; an order issued from a superior court directing a lower court or other government authority to perform a particular act.

mandatory jurisdiction Jurisdiction that a court must accept. The Supreme Court must decide cases coming under its appellate jurisdiction, though it may avoid giving them plenary consideration.

moot Unsettled, undecided. A moot question is also one that is no longer material, or that has already been resolved and has become hypothetical.

motion A written or oral application to a court or judge to obtain a rule or order.

obiter dictum A statement by a judge or justices expressing an opinion and included with, but not essential to, an opinion resolving a case before the court. *Dicta* are not necessarily binding in later cases.

opinion for the court The opinion announcing the decision of a court.

original jurisdiction The jurisdiction of a court of first instance, or trial court. The Supreme Court has original jurisdiction under Article III of the Constitution.

per curiam "By the court"; an unsigned opinion of the court.

petitioner One who files a petition with a court seeking action or relief, including the plaintiff or appellant. When a writ of *certiorari* is granted by the Supreme Court, the party seeking review is called the petitioner, and the party responding is called the respondent.

plenary consideration Full consideration. When the Supreme Court grants a case review, it may give it full consideration, permitting the parties to submit briefs on the merits of the case and to present oral arguments, before the Court reaches its decision.

plurality opinion An opinion announcing the decision of the Court but having the support of less than a majority of the Court.

political question Questions that courts refuse to decide because they are deemed to be essentially political in nature or because their determination would involve an intrusion on the powers of the executive or legislature.

remand To send back. After a decision in a case, the case is often sent back by a higher court to the court from which it came for further action in light of its decision.

respondent The party that is compelled to answer the claims or questions posed in a court by a petitioner.

reverse In an appellate court, to reach a decision that disagrees with the result reached in a case by a lower court.

ripeness   Situation when a case is ready for adjudication and decision; the issues presented must not be hypothetical, and the parties must have exhausted other avenues of appeal.

seriatim   Separately, individually, one by one. The Court's practice was once to have each justice give his opinion on a case separately.

standing   Having the appropriate characteristics to bring or participate in a case; in particular, having a personal interest and stake in the outcome.

stare decisis   "Let the decision stand." The principle of adherence to settled cases, the doctrine that principles of law established in earlier cases should be accepted as authoritative in similar subsequent cases.

statute   A written law enacted by a legislature.

subpoena   An order to present oneself before a grand jury, court, or legislative hearing.

subpoena duces tecum   An order to produce specified documents or papers.

summary decision   A decision in a case that does not give it full consideration; the Court decides a case without having the parties submit briefs on the merits of the case or present oral arguments before the Court.

tort   An injury or wrong to the person or property of another.

vacate   To make void, annul, or rescind the decision of a lower court.

writ   An order commanding someone to perform or not perform acts specified in the order.

Selected Further Readings

Bickel, Alexander, and Benno Schmidt. *The Judiciary and Responsible Government, 1910–21*. New York: Macmillan, 1984.

Dickson, Del. *The Supreme Court in Conference (1940–1985)*. New York: Oxford University Press, 2001.

Epstein, Lee, Jeffrey Segal et al., eds. *The Supreme Court Compendium*. 6th ed. Washington, D.C.: Congressional Quarterly Press, 2016.

Fairman, Charles. *Reconstruction and Reunion, 1864–1888*. New York: Macmillan, 1975.

Fiss, Owen. *Troubled Beginnings of the Modern State, 1888–1910*. New York: Macmillan, 1993.

Friedman, Leon, and Fred Israel, eds. *Justices of the United States Supreme Court*. 4th ed. 4 vols. New York: Facts on File, 2013.

Goebel, Julius. *Antecedents and Beginnings to 1801*. New York: Macmillan, 1971.

Hall, Kermit, ed. *The Oxford Companion to the Supreme Court of the United States*. 2nd ed. New York: Oxford University Press, 2005.

Hall, Matthew. *The Nature of Supreme Court Power*. New York: Cambridge University Press, 2011.

Haskins, George, and Herbert Johnson. *Foundations of Power: John Marshall, 1801–1815*. New York: Macmillan, 1981.

Irons, Peter. *A People's History of the Supreme Court*. New York: Viking Press, 1999.

McCloskey, Robert, revised by Sanford Levinson. *The American Supreme Court.* 6th ed. Chicago: University of Chicago Press, 2016.

Murphy, Walter. *Elements of Judicial Strategy.* Chicago: University of Chicago Press, 1964.

O'Brien, David. *Constitutional Law and Politics.* 11th ed. 2 vols. New York: Norton, 2017.

———, ed. *Judges on Judging: Views from the Bench.* 5th ed. Washington, D.C.: Congressional Quarterly Press, 2016.

Rosenberg, Gerald. *The Hollow Hope: Can Courts Bring about Social Change?* 2nd ed. Chicago: University of Chicago Press, 2009.

SCOTUSblog at www.scotusblog.com. Provides a great deal of information and analysis of pending cases and decisions each term, since 2007, as well as statistics on the Court's work and other commentary on the Court.

Shapiro, Stephen, Kenneth Geller, Timothy Bishop, Edward Hartnett, and Dan Himmelfarb. *Supreme Court Practice.* 10th ed. Washington, D.C.: Bureau of National Affairs, 2014.

Silverstein, Gordon. *Law's Allure: How Law Shapes, Constrains, Saves, and Kills Politics.* New York: Cambridge University Press, 2009.

Supreme Court Historical Society. *Journal of Supreme Court History.* Washington, D.C.: SCHS, 1976–.

Supreme Court of the United States at www.supremecourt.gov. Includes briefs, oral arguments (audio and transcripts), the Court's opinions and decisions, along with other information about the Court.

Urofsky, Melvin, ed. *100 Americans Making Constitutional History: A Biographical History.* Washington, D.C.: Congressional Quarterly Press, 2004.

———, ed. *The Public Debate over Controversial Supreme Court Decisions.* Washington, D.C.: CQ Press, 2006.

———. *Dissent and the Supreme Court: Its Role in the Court's History and the Nation's Constitutional Dialogue.* New York: Pantheon, 2015.

Warren, Charles. *The Supreme Court in United States History.* 3 vols. Boston: Little, Brown, 1922.

White, G. Edward. *The Marshall Court and Cultural Change, 1815–35.* New York: Macmillan, 1988.

Wiecek, William. *The Birth of the Modern Constitution: The United States Supreme Court, 1941–1953.* New York: Cambridge University Press, 2006.

Index